Mexican Migration to the United States

Mexican Migration to the United States

Perspectives from Both Sides of the Border

EDITED BY HARRIETT D. ROMO
AND OLIVIA MOGOLLON-LOPEZ

University of Texas Press ◆◆ *Austin*

First edition, 2016

Requests for permission to reproduce material from this work should be sent to:
  Permissions
  University of Texas Press
  P.O. Box 7819
  Austin, TX 78713-7819
  http://utpress.utexas.edu/index.php/rp-form

⊗ The paper used in this book meets the minimum requirements of ANSI/NISO
Z39.48-1992 (R1997) (Permanence of Paper).

Library of Congress Cataloging-in-Publication Data
Names: Romo, Harriett, editor. | Mogollon, O., editor.
Title: Mexican migration to the United States : perspectives from both sides of the
    border / edited by Harriett D. Romo and Olivia Mogollon-Lopez.
Description: First edition. | Austin : University of Texas Press, 2016. | Includes
    bibliographical references and index.
Identifiers: LCCN 2015037502 | ISBN 9781477308974 (cloth : alk. paper) |
    ISBN 9781477309025 (pbk. : alk. paper) | ISBN 9781477309667 (library e-book)
    | ISBN 9781477309674 (nonlibrary e-book)
Subjects: LCSH: Mexico—Emigration and immigration. | Mexicans—
    United States. | Immigrants—United States. | United States—Emigration
    and immigration—Government policy. | United States—Emigration
    and immigration—Economic aspects. | United States—Emigration and
    immigration—Social conditions. | Return migration—Mexico. | Emigrant
    remittances.
Classification: LCC E184.M5 M528 2016 | DDC 304.8/73072—dc23
LC record available at http://lccn.loc.gov/2015037502

doi:10.7560/308974

Contents

Acknowledgments

We are grateful to the University of Texas at San Antonio's Office of the Provost and UTSA's Vice President of Community Services, Dr. Jude Valdez, for funds that enabled the UTSA Mexico Center to organize a large conference on Mexico-US migration. This conference inspired the initiation of ongoing dialogue among scholars from Mexico and the United States whose work has focused on immigration, and these relationships led to this edited manuscript.

We would like especially to acknowledge Professor Katharine Donato for her careful reading of the manuscript and for her extremely helpful suggestions. We benefited greatly from the work of several graduate student researchers at the UTSA Mexico Center as we prepared this manuscript: Raquel Torres, Janeth Martinez, and Christina Lopez-Mobilia. We are also appreciative of the help of staff at the UTSA Mexico Center who pitched in when we needed extra assistance—thank you, Alexandra Romero, Sophia Ortiz, and David Rodriguez.

We recognize that collected editions take a long time in review and publication, so we also recognize the patience and cooperation of the authors, reviewers, and editors at University of Texas Press as we moved through the process of requests for manuscripts, reviews, edits, and revisions. We have enjoyed working with you, and we hope this volume leads to rigorous discussion of immigration policies in both the United States and Mexico.

Mexican Migration to the United States

INTRODUCTION

Policies, Dynamics, and Consequences
of Mexican Migration to the United States

HARRIETT D. ROMO

This volume presents the work of scholars from the United States and Mexico focusing on Mexican migration to the United States. The topic is one of long interest on both sides of the border and has been explored by many in academia. However, it is not often that we bring both Mexican and US scholars together to analyze these issues. Our aim is to present rational and empirically based discussions of key immigration policy issues from both a Mexican and US perspective. This volume incorporates empirical studies of labor markets, health, family adaptations, and educational processes related to incorporation of migrants in the United States and upon their return to Mexico. Such scholarship is needed to counter the many negative representations of immigrants and immigration that appear in the media.

The scholars included in this volume provide comprehensive research addressing the complex dynamics generating migration patterns and address human and political issues that both sending and receiving communities must accommodate. Theory and research have emphasized how economic and political forces shape the style, intensity, sanctions, and policies related to immigration. This volume includes policy essays, demographic assessments, analyses of immigration policy consequences, and ethnographic explorations of factors affecting migrants in the United States and the reincorporation of return migrants in Mexico. Several scholars included here are well known in the field of immigration studies and are presenting ideas drawn from their most recent work. Others are emerging scholars who bring fresh insights to the complexity of immigration processes and policies.

Mexico-US Migration: Legal Frameworks and Their Implications

In the months before the devastation by terrorists on September 11, 2001, Mexico's President Vicente Fox and US President George W. Bush had begun talks on migration. Expectations were high that long-term, mutually agreed-upon, bilateral strategies could be negotiated to regulate Mexico-US migration. In the following years, the United States experienced a deep economic recession, beginning during the Bush administration and continuing into the Obama administration, which caused high rates of unemployment in the United States and heightened US anti-immigration sentiment. US policy concerns turned to border security, the detention and deportation of undocumented immigrants, and prevention of additional terrorist attacks. Controlling undocumented immigration remained a deep concern.

According to Passel and Cohn (2011, 2014), just over half (51 percent) of all current Mexican immigrants in the United States are unauthorized, and some 52 percent of the estimated 11.2 million unauthorized immigrants are Mexican. Migration management is of primary importance for both countries, as is fair and credible enforcement of controls. Mexican and American government officials and scholars recognize that economic development in Mexico is a key component in reducing emigration and encouraging Mexicans to remain in Mexico. Passel, Cohn, and Gonzalez-Barrera (2012) have also stated that, along with decreasing birth rates, positive economic and social changes in Mexico are major factors in lessening the emigrant flows from Mexico.

Massey, Durand, and Pren (2014) confirm that economic conditions on both sides of the border have consistently fluctuated to increase or decrease undocumented migration over the past four decades, but economic incentives for unauthorized departure of Mexicans to the United States have not disappeared. Massey, Durand, and Pren (2014) claim that the sharp drop in Mexican childbearing and the rising age among household heads at risk of taking an undocumented trip to the United States have played a major role in the decline of Mexican migration. The magnitude of immigration from Mexico, the number of Mexican-origin persons living in the United States, and the long history of Mexico-US migration make it important to understand who comes, how, and why—and what impact US and Mexican policies have on those dynamics.

In addition to being the main country of origin for the majority of recent immigrants to the United States, Mexico experiences transit migration from Central America and other countries to the United States. Mexico is also a destination country for migrants from Central and South America, which means that Mexico must develop effective immigration controls and, in addition, must address the complexities of incorporating return migrants from the United States. Mainly because of wage disparities between the two countries and geographical location—Mexico shares with the United States one of the longest international borders in the world—Mexicans have been the key source of cheap labor for the US labor market. This long-standing tradition of supplying workers to the United States has shaped a network of complex social, cultural, and family ties between the two countries.

Historically, demographic changes in Mexico have played a key role in defining the dynamics of unregulated Mexican migration to the United States. In a context of explosive demographic growth in Mexico, internal and international migration served as escape valves for young people seeking work. At the same time, the United States demanded low-skilled workers for unfilled jobs in the agricultural, industrial, and service sectors. For a long time, a strong job market and the lack of clear and consistent immigration policies fueled the migration of population surpluses from Mexico to the United States, benefiting both countries.

Immigration has long been considered a vehicle for increasing the pool of workers during labor shortages in the United States (Clavita 1992), and immigrant remittances have been an important part of the Mexican economy. A good example of collaboration in the recruitment of Mexican workers to the United States was the Bracero Program (1942–1964), which allowed Mexican guest workers to mitigate the US wartime labor shortage. After the Bracero Program ended, many of the people who had worked legally in the United States under that program continued to cross the border, sometimes to work for the same employers but without official work-authorization documents.

Responding to pressures to control unauthorized immigration, in 1986 the US Congress passed the Immigration Reform and Control Act (IRCA), which regularized 3.2 million undocumented immigrants (2.3 million from Mexico). IRCA also implemented measures to strengthen border controls and increase sanctions on US employers hiring undocumented workers. Tightened border security transformed previous migratory patterns from circular migration to more permanent settlement (Passel et al. 2014). Furthermore, as a result of the terrorist attacks of September 11, 2001, migration became linked to US national security, and undocumented immigration was increasingly criminalized. A push by the United States to implement a mandatory Employment Eligibility Verification (E-Verify) program aimed at curtailing undocumented workers has made it even more difficult for unauthorized migrants to find employment in the United States.

Combinations of political, economic, and demographic factors have stemmed Mexican emigration. As a result, undocumented Mexican migration to the United States seems to have reached its peak in 2007. According to Passel, Cohn, and Gonzalez-Barrera (2013), Mexican unauthorized migration declined in 2008, 2009, and 2010 and leveled off in 2011. By 2012, the number of unauthorized Mexican immigrants in the United States was 5.9 million, 1 million fewer than in 2007 (Passel and Cohn 2014). In 2012 Castañeda and Massey in a *New York Times* editorial claimed those returning to Mexico equaled those migrating to the United States, bringing about "nearly everything immigration reform was supposed to achieve." A report from the Pew Research Center (Passel, Cohn, and Gonzalez-Barrera 2012) also confirmed that net Mexican migration to the United States was at a standstill. Passel, Cohn, and Gonzalez-Barrera (2012) drew from data that showed that after four decades of increasing Mexican migration to the United States that resulted in 12 million Mexican immigrants, most of whom came without official documents, migration from Mexico to the United States has slowed and may even have reached zero net migration.

Additionally, as immigration policies in the United States have become more restrictive and punitive, the risk and financial cost of crossing the border without authorization have increased substantially. The US financial crisis of 2008 severely impacted the flow of remittances back to Mexico, which provided a main source of financing for potential migrants. On the Mexican side, increased risk of violence from criminal organizations along the border has also served to dissuade potential migrants. Overall, the cost–benefit ratio for undocumented migrants has changed substantially, and migrating north is not clearly perceived as a safe investment anymore. Nonetheless, it is reasonable to assume that once migration flows dwindle, the United States may consider implementing policies to address the demand for labor required by the US economy and its aging population in an orderly and legal manner, but currently it is difficult to predict long-term trends.

Although economic downturn and high rates of unemployment in the United States are in large part responsible for the decrease in immigration from Mexico, insecurity caused by drug violence and threats of kidnapping are now a significant force pushing the movement of people from Mexico to the United States. This is particularly true in conflicted areas along the US-Mexico border, the northern Mexican industrial states, and Mexican interior states experiencing high levels of deaths related to organized crime. Passel, Cohn, and Gonzalez-Barrera (2012, 33) report that 37,100 homicides occurred in Mexico in 2011, an increase of 44 percent since 2005, largely sparked by the drug wars. The continuing high rate of crime and drug-related violence has made the issue of insecurity Mexicans' top national problem, according to the Pew Global Attitudes Project surveys (Passel, Cohn, and Gonzalez-Barrera 2012, 34).

Despite analyses that demonstrate a decline in overall migration, the lack of a comprehensive and sensible US immigration policy and the shrinking supply of low-educated US-born workers available to perform the low-skilled work needed in the United States continue to play a role in US-Mexican migration. US employers have argued that demand for low-skilled workers in US agriculture, manufacturing, service sectors, and construction cannot be filled by US citizens or legal residents, and this void has continued to encourage unauthorized entrants from Mexico. The failure of the US Congress to address comprehensive immigration reform has forced President Obama to use executive orders to try to resolve problems in immigration policy that have developed over several administrations (Hirschfeld Davis 2014). Mexicans are especially impacted by these policy changes, because they represent the largest number of unauthorized migrants currently residing in the United States. Many of these migrants have been working without documents, have resided in the United States for many years, and have established family and economic ties in their US communities. As undocumented families continue to live and work in the United States, many have US-born children. Researchers included in this book have documented how the incorporation experiences of those families and children are affected by the unauthorized status of immigrant parents.

Incorporation into Receiving Communities in the United States

Changes in US laws and policies have led to increased criminalization of undocumented immigrants and have had important impacts on immigrant incorporation (Menjívar and Kanstroom 2014). A study by King, Massoglia, and Uggen (2012) in the *American Journal of Sociology* documented historical variation in the number of US deportations and reported that removals increase during times of rising unemployment. Judges have substantial discretion in the implementation of deportation laws, and deportation decisions are often affected by elevated racialized discourse about immigration and labor.

President Obama's executive order allowing Deferred Action for Childhood Arrivals (DACA) grants protection from deportation and the possibility to apply for a work permit to certain people brought to the United States as children by undocumented parents. President Obama's deferred action initiative on June 15, 2012, gave approximately 1.7 million eligible undocumented young people between the ages of fifteen and thirty an opportunity to receive a two-year work authorization and protection from deportation. While this measure is not an amnesty and does not provide a pathway to residency or citizenship, it is a step forward in including undocumented youth as part of their communities and accepting them within the nation-state.

In addition, in November 2014 President Obama issued another executive order expanding eligibility for DACA and protecting the undocumented parents of children who are US citizens or legal permanent residents from deportation (Hirschfeld Davis 2014). It remains to be seen how this new policy will impact undocumented youth and their families. Numerous members of the Republican Party have threatened to pass legislation to overturn the president's executive orders, and twenty-six states led by Texas have contested in the courts President Obama's right to issue these policies. Furthermore, it is still uncertain what will happen to unauthorized youth who do not qualify for deferred action because of schooling requirements, criminal issues, or minor infractions.

First-generation migrants are a mobile population, often returning to their home country or moving back and forth, compared to their children, who often wish to stay in the United States and claim their rights as full members of US society (Passel et al. 2014). Contemporary migration is split between those who have high human capital (such as university-level professionals, technicians, and entrepreneurs) and those with low human capital, who are poorly educated workers. There are also differences in the contexts that receive them. The mode of incorporation in general is positive for high-human-capital immigrants, who have legal status and meet a more receptive stance by the US community where they reside (Portes and Rumbaut 2006). By contrast, manual-labor immigrants, who commonly arrive without legal documents, have a low level of education, and have predominantly nonwhite physical features, are subjected to negative reception by the authorities and the host population (Suarez-Orozco 1987; Rumbaut 2005). Divergent origins and diverse attributes of the immigrant first generation set the initial conditions for adaptation of the second generation (Haller, Portes, and Lynch 2011). Immigration status—whether one has appropriate legal documents to live and work in the United States—makes a significant difference in the experiences of migrants and their families.

With increased insecurity in Mexico and visa opportunities for professionals and entrepreneurs, a larger number of higher-educated Mexican immigrants are coming to the United States with their families. Mexican migrants help promote and sustain Spanish language use in US commercial establishments and work sites, respectful children's behavior, and Mexican cultural traditions. Mexican entrepreneurs often use Spanish in their work, maintain contact with friends and clients in Mexico in person or through the Internet, book frequent flights back to Mexico, and establish organizations to promote their business, social, and cultural interests and activities. Their strong cultural values and language skills replenish Mexican identity and ethnicity in US communities. Upper-income immigrants bring status to the Mexican ethnic group as they interact with other community members in elite social circles and business negotiations.

Return Migration and Reincorporation

According to US Homeland Security data, deportations from the United States reached a record high during fiscal year 2009, with nearly 390,000 noncitizens deported (Preston 2010). The Pew Research Center estimates that "of the 1.4 million Mexican immigrants and their children who returned to Mexico from the US between 2005 and 2010, anywhere from 5 percent to 35 percent were sent back by U.S. authorities" (Passel, Cohn, and Gonzalez-Barrera 2012, 22). Mexican returnees and deportees have received little attention even though this phenomenon has existed throughout the history of the US-Mexico border. Deportations affect many more than just the deported individual. Often the deported person is separated from a spouse or a child, or the return migrant can no longer send remittances to family members remaining in Mexico who are dependent upon that income. The numbers of return migrants in Mexico have increased due to reduced economic opportunities in the United States and enforcement of deportations by the US Office of Homeland Security. The Mexican government and local communities where these return migrants end up are struggling to reincorporate them into the Mexican education system and workforce and to provide the social services they need.

The Importance of This Volume

As a whole, the chapters included in this volume demonstrate the complexity of Mexican migration to the United States. The insights brought by the Mexican scholars enrich our understanding of the Mexican perspective of this migration and the diaspora's impacts in Mexico as well as in the United States. King, Massoglia, and Uggen (2012, 1793) argue that the media's reporting on immigration and its consequences for American workers becomes more heated as the economy worsens, and in these times academic discourse is increasingly needed to present factual data and rational arguments as a basis for policies and recommendations. The long history and legal, sociopolitical, and economic complexities of Mexican emigration and the dilemmas of incorporation or exclusion of Mexican immigrant workers and their children in the United States and of return migrants in Mexico are evident in these studies. There are many social and economic factors in play in Mexico today—insecurity, economic challenges, declining fertility rates, a culture of migration, and social network ties across the US-Mexico border—that influence emigration patterns. Understanding those factors as well as the political, economic, and social conditions in the United States shaping US immigration policies is essential.

The borderlands of the US Southwest, once the territory of Mexico, and the northern Mexican states share a regional economic and cultural environment and a long history of movement of people, goods, and services across the border. Many of the people of Mexican origin living in the United States continue to identify as Mexicans or Mexican Americans after many generations in the United States; others brought to the United States as children feel strongly that they are Americans, even if they lack official documents that support that identity. As the United States begins to acknowledge the importance of the growing Latino population in terms of political participation, economic resources, workforce contributions, and cultural influences, increasing attention will be drawn to US-Mexico relations. Mexico is one of the United States' largest trading partners, and as the Mexican economy prospers and Mexico's influence in Latin America increases, the economic and political importance of this relationship will also grow. Mexican migration to the United States is unique, and it is imperative that the United States and Mexico collaborate in developing immigration policies that serve the needs of people and promote economic prosperity in both countries. The chapters in this book help us understand the complexity of this collaboration.

References

Castañeda, Jorge G., and Douglas S. Massey. 2012. "Do-It-Yourself Immigration Reform." *New York Times*, June 1. Retrieved September 9, 2012, from http://www.nytimes.com/2012/06/02/opinion/do-it-yourself-immigration-reform.html?-r=1&pagewanted=print.

Clavita, Kitty. 1992. *Inside the State: The Bracero Program, Immigration and the I.N.S.* New York: Routledge, Chapman & Hall.

Haller, William, Alejandro Portes, and Scott M. Lynch. 2011. "Dreams Fulfilled,

Dreams Shattered: Determinants of Segmented Assimilation in the Second Generation." *Social Forces* 89(3):733–762.

Hirschfeld Davis, Julie. 2014. "Obama Takes an Action That Has Its Precedents But May Set a New One." *New York Times*, November 21, A19.

King, Rayan D., Michael Massoglia, and Christopher Uggen. 2012. "Employment and Exile: U.S. Criminal Deportations, 1908–2005." *American Journal of Sociology* 117(6):1786–1825.

Massey, Douglas S., Jorge Durand, and Karen A. Pren. 2014. "Explaining Undocumented Migration to the U.S." *International Migration Review*, 1–34. DOI: 10.1111/imre.12151.

Menjívar, Cecilia, and Daniel Kanstroom. 2014. *Constructing Immigrant "Illegality": Critiques, Experiences, and Responses*. New York: Cambridge University Press.

Passel, Jeffrey S., and D'Vera Cohn. 2011. *Unauthorized Immigrant Population: National and State Trends, 2010*. Washington, DC: Pew Research Hispanic Center. Retrieved December 18, 2014, from http://www.pewhispanic.org/2011/02/01/unauthorized-immigrant-population:binational-and-state-trends-2010/.

Passel, Jeffrey S., and D'Vera Cohn. 2014. *Unauthorized Immigrant Totals Rise in 7 States, Fall in 14: Decline in Those From Mexico Fuels Most State Decreases*. Washington, DC: Pew Research Center's Hispanic Trends Project. Retrieved July 17, 2015, from http://www.pewhispanic.org/2014/11/18/unauthorized-immigrant-totals-rise-in-7-states-fall-in-14/.

Passel, Jeffrey, D'Vera Cohn, and Ana Gonzalez-Barrera. 2012. *Net Migration from Mexico Falls to Zero—and Perhaps Less*. Washington, DC: Pew Research Hispanic Center. Retrieved December 18, 2014, from http://www.pewhispanic.org/2012/04/23/net-migration-from-mexico-falls-to-zero-and-perhaps-less/.

———. 2013. *Population Decline of Unauthorized Immigrants Stalls, May Have Reversed*. Washington, DC: Pew Research Center. Retrieved April 9, 2015, from http://www.pewhispanic.org/2013/09/23/population-decline-of-unauthorized-immigrants-stalls-may-have-reversed/.

Passel, Jeffrey S., D'Vera Cohn, Jens Manuel Krogstad, and Ana Gonzalez-Barrera. 2014. *As Growth Stalls, Unauthorized Immigrant Population Becomes More Settled*. Washington, DC: Pew Research Center's Hispanic Trends Project. Retrieved December 18, 2014, from http://www.pewhispanic.org/2014/09/03/as-growth-stalls-unauthorized-immigrant-population-becomes-more-settled/.

Portes, Alejandro, and Rubén G. Rumbaut. 2006. *Immigrant America: A Portrait*. 3rd ed. Berkeley: University of California Press.

Preston, Julia. 2010. "Deportations from the U.S. Hit a Record High." *New York Times*, October 6. Retrieved December 18, 2014, from http://www.nytimes.com/2010/10/07/us/07immig.html?_r=1&.

Rumbaut, Rubén G. 2005. "Turning Points in the Transition to Adulthood: Determinants of Educational Attainment, Incarceration, and Early Childbearing among Children of Immigrants." *Ethnic and Racial Studies* 28(6):1041–1086.

Suarez-Orozco, Marcelo. 1987. "Towards a Psychosocial Understanding of Hispanic Adaptation to American Schooling." In *Success or Failure? Learning and the Languages of Minority Students*, edited by H. T. Trueba, 156–168. New York: Newbury House.

PART 1

MEXICO-US MIGRATION: LEGAL FRAMEWORKS AND THEIR IMPLICATIONS

The first section of the book includes chapters by Francisco Alba, Jorge Durand, and Liliana Meza González and Michael Feil discussing Mexican perspectives on Mexico-US migration, while from the US side, Pia Orrenius, Jason Saving, and Madeline Zavodny suggest a labor-market approach to immigration policy, and Frank Bean, Susan Brown, and James Bachmeier explore how Mexican migration affects US workers. These chapters provide a basis for understanding the complexity of immigration policy-making and the manner in which policies implemented in one country affect both countries. What Mexico does as a nation-state regarding relations with the United States, whether Mexico decides to focus extensively on internal economic development to keep potential migrants at home, and how Mexico controls its own southern border have implications for the United States.

Francisco Alba, a researcher at El Colegio de México, provides a brief historical overview of approaches to handling migration from both the United States and Mexico and analyzes the diverging paths of Mexican and US migration policies, especially since the terrorist attacks of September 11, 2001, which caused the United States to heighten border security and tightly control immigration. Offering suggestions for pragmatic and accommodating migration reform in both countries, he calls for some processes of "earned regularization." Avenues for earned regularization seem to be absent from most efforts of US legislation to reform immigration, although such processes were included in early versions of the Bush immigration proposals and in some versions of the proposed Development, Relief, and Education for Alien Minors (DREAM) Act. Alba argues for temporary worker programs and measures to regularize a portion of the existing undocumented immigrant population currently residing in the United

States. Although Mexico has passed legislation to address Central American migrants and refugees, the Mexican southern border is still a policy issue. Alba suggests that the United States and Mexico are taking diverging paths to immigration, to the disadvantage of both nations. He cites the need for greater binational collaboration to address regional labor migrations that affect not only the United States, but also Mexico and the countries of Central America. Refuting racist and xenophobic rhetoric from both sides of the border, Alba criticizes nonconstructive approaches to unavoidable global processes and argues for more bilateral, informed, pragmatic, and gradual responses to migration.

Pia Orrenius and Jason Saving, researchers at the Federal Reserve Bank of Dallas, and their colleague Madeline Zavodny at Agnes Scott College explore United States visa policies and immigration priorities and how they have, in many cases, impeded the US economy. They present a detailed assessment of US immigration policy and critique US visa guidelines, which prioritize uniting families rather than focusing on labor needs. As these scholars demonstrate clearly, the type of migrants granted US visas and the US economic sectors with the greatest labor demands significantly affect which migrants may arrive in the United States with appropriate legal documents and which migrants have few or no options to cross the border legally.

Jorge Durand explores the history of Mexico-US migrations and argues that demographics, legislation, and political and economic factors influence migration patterns. Durand analyzes changes in migration dynamics as a result of the economic recession in the United States, efforts to grow the Mexican economy, and Mexico's emphasis on population control, all of which have resulted in a leveling off of Mexican migration to the United States (see Massey, Durand, and Pren 2014; Passel et al. 2014). At the present time, as Massey, Durand, and Pren (2014) note, it is difficult to determine whether this is a temporary decrease in migration or whether, as the United States economy becomes more robust, immigrants will again fill needed gaps in agricultural, service, construction, and caretaking sectors of the US labor market, with or without appropriate legal status.

These chapters provide historical context for current US-Mexico migration policies and make suggestions and speculations about future trends. Both Alba and Durand argue that despite the centrality of Mexico-US migration policies prior to and after the terrorist attacks on the United States on 9/11, other policies, such as those related to trade in the North American Free Trade Agreement (NAFTA), have been most dominant in negotiations between the two countries. NAFTA has affected the ability of many rural inhabitants of Mexico to make a living off their small farms or ranches, resulting in male heads of households migrating to the United States for economic reasons.

Increasing violence related to organized crime and drug trafficking in rural and border areas has also forced people to leave their homes. Liliana Meza González and Michael Feil, in the chapter "Public Insecurity and International Emigration in Northern Mexico," recognize the influence of social networks in migration patterns but argue that, increasingly, insecurity in Mexico drives people to the United States and deters them from returning to their communities of origin. The authors acknowledge the long history of Mexican migration to the United States, traditionally driven by economic and social factors such as social mobility and family reunification.

Meza González and Feil point out many areas throughout the world where violence and unrest are driving people from their home countries. Although the authors do not claim that conditions in Mexico have reached the extreme that causes people to become refugees, the chapter shows that a perception of insecurity may be promoting emigration from conflicted areas. Using data on homicide rates in Mexico, the researchers argue that these homicides are not randomly distributed throughout Mexico, but are mostly concentrated in a few Mexican states.

The authors concede that international migration is a complicated global phenomenon involving many different types of migrants with varied reasons for leaving their home communities. They argue that the concept of "environment of insecurity," first applied to the Kurdish conflict in Turkey and expanded to explain the international migration of Turkish Kurds, is related to sets of factors that may increase the chances of migration. Thus, an environment of insecurity may not necessarily influence those in greatest danger, but may trigger migration from relatively secure areas because people react to levels of direct and indirect violence.

Despite the limitations of linking an environment of insecurity to migration decisions, Meza González and Feil argue that it is worth analyzing data from Mexico and exploring correlations between violence and international migration. According to their analyses, migration and insecurity are positively correlated, and environments of insecurity are affecting migration patterns in Mexico. These findings suggest that effects on migration are factors that should be considered in Mexican policies in the war against drugs. Migration resulting from environments of insecurity will also have to be considered in US immigration policies and in future collaborations with Mexico.

Bean, Brown, and Bachmeier analyze data that show the extent of US economic expansion, the rapidity of US population growth, and the degree of educational upgrading in the US native-born population that, they argue, largely account for the demand for lesser-skilled Mexican labor. The children of unauthorized Mexican workers do obtain considerably more schooling than their parents because of the availability of public schooling in the United States, but the authors argue that this group of youth remain behind in educational attainment compared to their white US-born counterparts. As a result, they may count as a "drag" on socioeconomic incorporation for those of Mexican origin.

This chapter is an important addition to the discussion of upward mobility of the Mexican immigrant and Mexican American population, as the researchers discuss the advantages and disadvantages of using generational groups, cross-sectional analyses, or longitudinal studies to determine assimilation. The authors clearly show that educational gains are influenced by whether immigrants enter the country legally or are able to achieve legal status later. Their results emphasize the importance of opportunities for immigrants to legalize for maximizing the educational success of their children. They also discuss whether the availability of migrant workers willing to work for lower wages displaces US workers, especially African Americans and Mexican Americans.

These economic consequences of migration have been debated by other economists, some of whom demonstrate that certain sectors of the US workforce are affected by available immigrant workers. Others have shown that immigrants take jobs that US workers have left as they acquire higher levels of education. Immigrants also create new jobs that serve the immigrant community's needs (Griffith 2006). In fact, the Immigration Policy Center in Washington, DC, argues that high-skilled foreign workers do not harm native-born workers' job opportunities, are not poorly compensated, and are not "cheap foreign labor," and that their presence often leads to higher wages and more job opportunities for US citizens (Immigration Policy Center 2014). Lowell (2001) notes that unauthorized immigrants are typically low-skilled and are viewed as adversely affecting low-skilled US natives. His analysis of the literature suggests that if there is an effect of immigrants on natives in the labor market, it must be subtle, for it does not appear immediately in the data (Lowell 2001, 38). Harrison and Lloyd (2013) suggest that employers do engage in subtle practices that contribute to workplace inequalities, such as trying to maintain profits, managing their own concerns about immigration policing, asserting their own class identity, justifying the privileges that they and their US-born employees enjoy, and maintaining their own advantages. In their chapter, Bean, Brown, and Bachmeier expand this discussion about job displacement and assess the economic influence of unauthorized Mexican migration and the implications for the incorporation of later generations of Mexican Americans.

References

Griffith, David. 2006. *American Guestworkers: Jamaicans and Mexicans in the U.S. Labor Market.* University Park: Pennsylvania State University Press.

Harrison, Jill L., and Sarah E. Lloyd. 2013. "New Jobs, New Workers, and New Inequalities: Explaining Employers' Roles in Occupational Segregation by Nativity and Race." *Social Problems* 60(3):281–301.

Immigration Policy Center. 2014. "High-Skilled Workers and Twenty-First Century Innovation: The H-1B Program's Impact on Wages, Jobs, and the Economy." Washington, DC: American Immigration Council. Retrieved April 16, 2014, from http://www.americanimmigrationcouncil.org/just-facts/h-1b-pro gram%E2%80%99s-impact-wages-jobs-and-economy).

Lowell, B. Lindsay. 2001. "Skilled Temporary and Permanent Immigrants in the United States." *Population Research and Policy Review* 20(1–2):33–58.

Massey, Douglas S., Jorge Durand, and Karen A. Pren. 2014. "Explaining Undocumented Migration to the U.S." *International Migration Review*, 1–34. doi:10.1111/imre.12151.

Passel, Jeffrey S., D'Vera Cohn, Jens Manuel Krogstad, and Ana Gonzalez-Barrera. 2014. *As Growth Stalls, Unauthorized Immigrant Population Becomes More Settled.* Washington, DC: Pew Research Center's Hispanic Trends Project. Retrieved December 18, 2014, from http://www.pewhispanic.org/2014/09/03/as -growth-stalls-unauthorized-immigrant-population-becomes-more-settled/.

CHAPTER 1

Evolving Migration Responses in Mexico and the United States: Diverging Paths?

FRANCISCO ALBA

The US approach to managing Mexican migration changed radically after the attacks on US soil on September 11, 2001. Before the attacks, expectations were high, particularly among Mexican political leaders, that a long-term, mutually agreed-upon strategy could finally be implemented to manage the flows of Mexican migrants to the United States. Those expectations were based on multiple suppositions shared by policy makers and leaders of both the United States and Mexico. Assumptions included, among others, the advantages to key economic interests operating on both sides of the border of regularizing immigration flows; the important role played by Mexican migrants in the labor markets of both countries; the strategic and geopolitical conditions linking the two neighboring countries; and the existence of strong social networks supporting migration.

These ideas emerged from a realistic appraisal of the strong migratory pressures prevalent in the region. In such an environment, it appeared that the United States was willing to make significant concessions to Mexican migrants. That was the context in which, under the leadership of US president George Bush and Mexican president Vicente Fox, a high-level dialogue on migration between the United States and Mexico took place in early 2001 (Davidow 2004; Alba 2010a). Negotiations ended abruptly when the US World Trade Center Towers collapsed. After the September 11, 2001, terrorist attacks, the saliency of security concerns and the focus on border controls and antiterrorism measures emerged as main US policy priorities. In the United States after 9/11 the topic of migration became captive to a new reality and a new discourse. Immediately thereafter, "anti-immigration" forces toughened their actions and initiatives, precluding subsequent attempts to pass any broad immigration reform.

Meanwhile, Mexico tried to keep avenues open for its workers in the

United States in a new, less accommodating migration environment. In view of the rising pressures and difficulties faced by migrants in transit through Mexico, in 2011 the Mexican government passed a new Migration Law.[1] This new Migration Law, an amended General Population Law, and a new Refugees and Complementary Protection Law would constitute Mexico's migration policy for the twenty-first century (Gonzalez-Murphy and Koslowski 2011).

The great recession that began in the United States in late 2007, followed by a fragile and tepid recovery, brought about a significant reduction in migration flows. This situation resulted in a novel context in which the United States might deal differently with the issue of undocumented migration. The considerable downward trend in undocumented Mexican migration to the United States (Passel, Cohn, and Gonzalez-Barrera 2012) opened new opportunities for managing migration. Despite the new reality, developing constructive perspectives to deal with an issue that continues to be of importance to both countries remains a challenge for Mexico and the United States.

The current rift between US and Mexican migration policies is quite different from the context that prevailed in early 2001, before September 11. To gain insight into how things developed after September 11, 2001, it seems relevant to ponder, as a heuristic device, whether the two countries are following divergent paths regarding their responses to migration. This chapter is an exploratory inquiry into that question. In order to place current migration policies in a historical perspective and explore future possibilities, the first part of the chapter reviews previous major attempts to manage modern-era Mexico-US migration, which began after World War II and extended to September 11, 2001. The chapter then broadly discusses post-9/11 management of Mexico-US migration by both governments, strategies that could be perceived as diverging. As the two countries have moved apart, there have been fewer bridges and less common ground. Finally, the chapter explores the implications of this divergence and suggests possible avenues for managing regional migration flows differently in the near to long-term future.

A Review of Past Responses:
From the Bracero Program to the 2001 Negotiations

Any discussion regarding twenty-first-century management of Mexican migration must necessarily address the long-standing bilateral US-Mexico relationship. From a larger historical perspective, significant Mexican migration to the United States has been an almost uninterrupted phenomenon since the late nineteenth century. Current patterns of Mexican migration to the United States date back to World War II, when Mexico agreed to contribute to the United States' war effort by providing temporary agricultural labor. The Bracero Program provided the United States with short-term temporary migrant workers to offset labor shortages experienced during the war and its aftermath. Termination of the Bracero Program in 1964 did not imply the end of the migration stream, because Mexican migration to the United States has been primarily economically motivated. Wage differentials for manual and semiskilled jobs have hovered for years at a ratio of about ten to one in favor of the United States. Continued US economic growth led to a strong demand for Mexican workers, mostly at the lower end of the labor market, from seasonal agriculture to high-turnover manufacturing and service industries. Unequal economic, demographic, and social conditions have long fueled strong interconnections between US labor demands and Mexican labor supply.

Since the end of the Bracero Program, despite the absence of any formal agreement, Mexican migration to the United States has continued to be prevalent in the bilateral relationship (Tuirán and Ávila 2010). From the late 1960s to the mid-1980s, a tacit understanding between the two countries allowed an almost unimpeded, "unmanaged," circular flow of Mexicans as temporary migrant workers (Mexico-US Binational Study on Migration 1997). This arrangement seemed to be functional and convenient for the major actors involved, such as US agricultural businesses and entrepreneurs, rural Mexican workers, and the governments of both the United States and Mexico (Alba 2010b). In the 1970s the Mexican-born population in the United States had already begun to increase considerably. According to the Mexico-US Binational Study on Migration (1997), in the 1960s the growth of Mexican "permanent migrants" was a few thousand per year, but by the 1970s the number reached over one hundred thousand per year. This functional arrangement for both countries could be considered a converging path.

The 1980s marked a new era in migration policies, with a major push by the United States to control the flow of unauthorized Mexican migrant workers, referred to as the undocumented, or *indocumentados*, who constituted a large portion of the migration stream. The US Immigration Reform and Control Act (IRCA), enacted in 1986, was the first serious attempt to curtail Mexican migration to the United States. However, one of the most important long-term, unintended consequences of IRCA, in part due to its generous regularization component, was to foster the transformation of Mexican migration from a predominantly circular flow to a more permanent settlement. During the 1980s, on average, more than two hundred thousand Mexicans settled in the United States each year.

In 1990, the Mexican-born population in the United States reached 4.5 million (Passel, Cohn, and Gonzalez-Barrera 2012, 19). Although the break in circularity had begun earlier, it consolidated in the 1980s and early 1990s in part, according to most analysts, as a rational response to the perceived possibility that the border was not going to be as porous in the future as it had been in the past. Close to three hundred thousand migrants per year settled in the United States in the early 1990s. In response, major efforts to transform the patterns of Mexican migration occurred. Some efforts were unilaterally carried out by the United States, such as toughened enforcement at the US-Mexico border or enactment of restrictive legal measures. Other efforts were bilateral or trilateral, because Canada was also involved, as in the signing of the North American Free Trade Agreement (NAFTA). The NAFTA agreement was based on the presumption of a potential long-term reduction in migration because of increased trade. Indeed, it was expected that trade liberalization would discourage migration flows by increasing employment opportunities and wages in Mexico. Key policy makers in both Mexico and the United States broadly supported this converging strategy.

Although NAFTA's approach is correct—to promote better economic conditions in Mexico, to advance more rapidly toward economic convergence within North America, and to narrow the large socioeconomic gaps in the North American region—the boost in trade did not fully transform the Mexican economy, nor did it work as a substitute for labor mobility. Trade between the United States and Mexico certainly increased, but so did the number of migrants. By the late 1990s and early 2000s, net annual emigration from Mexico approached four hundred thousand migrants a year. Although NAFTA did not officially consider labor mobility as part of the agreement because of political opposition in the United States, the accord thus far has failed to deliver on its migration-related promises (Alba 2008).

The implementation of NAFTA, however, did not preclude the start of a process of border reinforcement in the 1990s, representing a "prevention through dissuasion" strategy. This strategy consisted of a series of "operations" along the US-Mexico border beginning in 1993. The purpose of these operations is evident in some of their names—for example, "Hold the Line" in El Paso, Texas, or "Gatekeeper" in Southern California (Nevins 2010). Nor did NAFTA prevent the enactment in 1996 of the restrictive Illegal Immigration Reform and Immigrant Responsibility Act (IIRIRA), which aimed to curb Mexican undocumented migration and included more stringent penalties for unauthorized immigration. IIRIRA's provisions included increased funding for resources and personnel assigned to immigration enforcement; important restrictions on the legal recourses available to challenge expulsion and deportation proceedings; and enactment of legal dispositions that barred, permanently or for several years, the readmission of persons found to reside in the United States without authorization.

These initiatives were ineffective, as the flows of undocumented Mexican migrants continued seemingly unabated. According to many scholars, more stringent border controls led to a greater tendency among migrants to settle permanently in the United States (Massey, Durand, and Malone 2002). Certainly, stagnant economic and social conditions in Mexico during the 1980s, 1990s, and early 2000s also worked as major determinants of the emerging new patterns of Mexican migration. Between 1982 and 2006, Mexico's gross domestic product (GDP) grew annually on average by a mere 2.3 percent, which translates barely into 1 percent in per capita terms, while the real minimum wage decreased by more than 4 percent annually during the same period. The fact that emigration became a nationwide phenomenon spreading into almost all of Mexico's regions could not be explained otherwise (Alba 2008).

Aggressive US border controls resulted in an escalating number of deaths along the border as migrants took greater risks in crossing into the United States through desolate and remote areas (Cornelius 2001). This development forced the Mexican government to actively engage with the United States regarding immigration. An unexpected implication of NAFTA, namely, a form of "legitimization" of Mexican demands for freer movement of Mexican workers to the United States, also prompted a more active engagement of the Mexican government in migration issues (Mexico-US Binational Study on Migration 1997). Indeed, NAFTA provided a suitable framework for bilateral dialogue on migration. The US effort to seal the border seemed, from the perspective of important Mexican actors and many other observers, inconsistent with NAFTA's objectives and the "NAFTA spirit." This trade agreement was seen as an initiative leading toward closer regional economic integration.

In the early 2000s an influential binational group of experts and analysts of US-Mexico relations estimated that strong incentives existed for the two countries to engage in migration negotiations (US-Mexico Migration Panel 2001). Indeed, the two new presidents, Vicente Fox of Mexico (inaugurated in December 2000) and George W. Bush of the United States (instated in

January 2001) took the bold determination in early 2001 to discuss migration, a decision with tremendous implications on both sides of the border (Joint Communiqué 2001).

In the United States, the decision to engage in serious high-level discussions with Mexico regarding migration changed the terms of the debate, even if for a very short time. First, migrants' economic contributions and their key role in the United States economy were recognized. Second, the geopolitical importance of Mexico and the value, for both countries, of economic integration and free trade and investment were acknowledged. Third, key US actors recognized the importance of moving toward regularization of undocumented migrants already in the United States and the need for comprehensive reform of US immigration laws. Finally, both countries considered the frequent occurrence of violence and death at the border an unacceptable development.

The decision to engage in negotiations with the United States had positive implications for the Mexican government's attitudes and responses to migration. The negotiations forced a shift from a migration policy based mostly on undisputed principles, such as the emphasis on the protection and defense of migrants, to a concrete and specific agenda. Mexico's policy makers and negotiators had to make potentially long-lasting choices in order to agree on the five major points that became the Mexican agenda in the negotiations: (1) regularization of undocumented workers already in the United States; (2) implementation of temporary-worker programs; (3) increased immigrant visas for Mexicans; (4) heightened security and safety at the US-Mexico border; and (5) cooperation and promotion of regional development (Alba 2003). The decision to engage in negotiations raised overall public awareness and recognition of the seriousness of the migration issue. It also generated awareness of the reality of Mexico as an out-migration country and compelled the Mexican government to come to terms with that reality and to shape its policies and agenda in accordance.

The high-level discussions and negotiations that took place in 2001 were an opportunity for a "great bargain" of the type that could have constructively helped to frame Mexico-US migration management. Such a bargain would have entailed major political moves on both sides of the border to deepen the ongoing integration process in North America by opening orderly and predictable channels for Mexican migration to the United States.

A great number of analysts and political actors believed that both governments would be able to find a mutually acceptable response to the vexing migration issue that had often placed the two countries at odds. Certainly, negotiations did not imply an agreement of any sort, but they signaled converging paths in regard to the approach to reach such an accord. In any event, expectations of arriving at a far-reaching agreement remained high, at least among the top echelons of Mexican political circles, until the full extent of the attacks on New York and Washington on September 11, 2001, became clear (Alba 2010a).

The Situation after 9/11: Divergent Paths?

The post 9/11 status quo stems from the reordering of US domestic and international priorities around the issues of national security, border control, and the fight against terrorism. As a result, the focus of many US actors shifted from migration negotiations to securing the US-Mexico border. Since 9/11, new and more aggressive efforts to stem the flow of unauthorized migrants have been enacted and are impacting the debate and policies regarding Mexican migration to the United States. In line with the US shift, Mexican attitudes moved toward a defensive and reactive mode. The following section presents a review of post-9/11 US migration policies and analyzes Mexican responses and positions.

Under the premise that the US immigration system was broken and needed fixing, in January 2004 President George W. Bush proposed the Fair and Secure Immigration Reform legislation, which attempted to address the new realities. This proposal de facto initiated the migration reform debate that has extended for an entire decade. One of the main objectives of the proposal was to secure and control the US borders without ignoring the factual realities of market forces. President Bush's proposal attempted to provide reliable channels, primarily through temporary-worker programs, to match willing foreign workers with willing American employers. The proposal offered avenues for unauthorized workers already in the United States to remain and work temporarily in the country, thus establishing mechanisms to keep track of undocumented migrants.

For a while, this proposal became the new frame for the migration debate in both countries. Although it made no reference to a special relationship with Mexico, or to any wide-ranging project for North American integration, the administration of Mexican president Vicente Fox considered the initiative a positive development. The Mexican government openly and pragmatically welcomed the proposal, viewing it as a continuation of previous political moves that acknowledged the US economy's demand for Mexican migrants and migrants' contributions to economic growth in the United States. The plan was viewed as a starting point for revamping the US migration system and was interpreted favorably within some Mexican governmental circles as an opening for more flexible positions in the future.

Since the Bush proposal, the immigration debate in the United States has coalesced around two main camps, comprehensive immigration reform supporters and enforcement-first or enforcement-only advocates. Although fluctuating over the years, the positions of the two opposing groups became more distant during the second Bush administration. There seemed to be a deadlock between the two immigration policy positions in the US Congress. In practice, however, the emphasis on strict enforcement and border control gained traction, as demonstrated by the increase in human and financial resources allocated for border control, the expansion of physical barriers along the border, and the deployment of several units of the National Guard along the southern US border.

In Mexico, discussions tended to revolve around the appropriate government response to new US policies and actions that attempted to severely curtail Mexican migration (Fernández de Castro and Clariond Rangel 2008). First, the Mexican government focused on the potentially adverse implications of the increasing criminalization of migrants. Prominent among Mexico's responses was the push to provide identification cards for the undocumented by offering the *matrícula consular*, a Mexican ID card for its migrant citizens abroad. Second, the Mexican government, aware of the direction in which the US immigration debate was heading, shifted Mexico's policy goals and migration objectives in order to prepare public opinion in Mexico for difficult and unpleasant trade-offs.

This strategy was unavoidable in the new context if Mexico hoped to be in a position to influence the US debate. The shift was not an easy one politically for Mexico. There were controversies and doubts in Mexico about the wisdom of engaging forcefully with the United States on immigration, given the latent and difficult trade-offs involved, such as demands from the United States for tighter control of Mexico's northern and southern borders. Mexico, for example, might be forced to implement measures to regulate and deter unauthorized migration in exchange for wide-ranging legalization of Mexicans in the United States, for major temporary-worker programs, or for limited, industry-specific temporary-worker programs.

In 2005, at the end of the Fox administration, the Mexican government and other nongovernmental actors involved in migration matters made an unprecedented effort to draft a Mexican migration policy. The result was a set of new policy directions, important new guiding principles, recommendations, and commitments to update Mexico's migration policy on topics such as undocumented migration, border and regional security, human smuggling and trafficking, and international cooperation. The principles of the Mexican response were delineated in a document titled "Mexico and the Migration Phenomenon." In it, the concept of *shared responsibility* was established as the guiding principle for Mexican governmental responses to migration. In 2006, both houses of the Mexican legislature, the Senate and the Chamber of Deputies, concurrently, and each house unanimously, passed a resolution (Punto de Acuerdo), adopting the document as their own.[2]

By embracing the concept of shared responsibility, Mexico signaled its willingness to do its part regarding migration management while at the same time insisting on the need to acknowledge the conditions fostering Mexican migration to the United States as bilateral. Under this guiding principle, Mexico assumed explicit responsibility for improving economic and social opportunities in Mexico and recognized the potentially beneficial implications of migration for Mexico's development. Components of this strategy to enhance the positive impacts of migration included a push to promote better use of remittances and to strengthen relations with Mexicans abroad (Délano 2011, 194). Mexico also committed to encouraging and assisting in the return and reincorporation of Mexicans into their communities of origin.

One of the goals of the Punto de Acuerdo was to influence legislative discussions in the United States regarding various immigration reform bills introduced in the US Congress since 2005. Based on this resolution, on March 20, 2006, the *New York Times, Wall Street Journal, Washington Post,* and several other US and Mexican newspapers published "A Message from Mexico about Migration," a full-page advertisement purchased by the Mexican government that emphasized Mexico's commitment and obligation to promote development, to reduce emigration, to secure the border, and to fight criminal organizations. Unfortunately, the effort did not have the intended effect on US immigration legislation. With this initiative, Mexico tried unsuccessfully to engage the United States in dialogue on migration issues (Alba 2010c). This episode illustrates a trend of diverging paths.

Perhaps as a reaction to previous developments, Mexican president Felipe Calderón (2006–2012) opted for a different strategy. He adopted a subtler, low-key approach to discussing migration matters with the United States. President Calderón proposed allowing greater mobility of Mexican labor within North America as a key element of a competitive regional economy. Calderón's administration also placed national security, the fight against organized crime, and drug trafficking at the top of its priorities. In support of those objectives, President Felipe Calderón and President George Bush signed the Merida Initiative in 2007. With the signing of this agreement Mexico probably expected to gain some dividends on the migration front, hoping that both countries' migration paths would converge again.

The context changed radically when the US recession began in late 2007. Although the Mexican economy was also experiencing a severe contraction (in 2009 Mexico's GDP fell by 6.6%), Mexican migration to the United States slowed dramatically given the severe reduction in demand for Mexican labor (Villarreal 2010). Additionally, pressure to return unauthorized migrants to their places of origin became strong.

Until the recession hit, it appeared that enhanced and new control measures did not considerably discourage poor, desperate, and ambitious Mexicans from crossing into the United States (Zúñiga and Molina 2008). Nor did it seem that the new security initiatives would, or could, alter the dependence of the US economy on Mexican migrant labor. Nevertheless, in an effort to return unauthorized migrants to their home countries, the Bush administration sent the "voluntary return" message by carrying out a number of quite visible raids to apprehend and deport undocumented migrants. In addition, several states introduced legal and administrative initiatives aimed at reducing the number of unauthorized migrants through attrition, by making their life in the United States difficult.

In 2009, with Barack Obama as the new president of the United States, guarded expectations rose in both countries regarding the possibility of a substantial change in the restrictive orientation of US immigration policies and the implementation of comprehensive immigration reform. However, the Obama administration kept the focus on enforcement—this time, not through highly publicized raids but through more systematic revisions of workplace labor records and the removal of unauthorized migrants with criminal records. During President Obama's first administration, deportations reached record numbers, to the dismay of many immigrant communities and the disbelief of Mexican society. In 2012, the US Department of Homeland Security removed close to 307,000 Mexican nationals (Simanski and Sapp 2013).

With deportations of Mexicans on the rise and transit migration from Central America to the United States becoming a sensitive social development and a significant public policy issue, Mexico slowly but surely started moving toward a new migration narrative (Alba 2013). On top of dealing with the complexity of Mexico-US migration, Mexico was also confronted with the task of reintegrating sizeable numbers of its long-term migrant citizens, at times with their US-born children, and of lawfully and humanely managing large Central American migration flows that mostly traverse

Mexico and continue on but that increasingly have remained in the country, whether temporarily or permanently.

Transit migration through Mexico declined with the onset of the great US economic recession. The number of deportable foreigners (*aseguramientos*) in Mexico hovered around two hundred thousand between 2003 and 2006 and leveled off below the one hundred thousand mark after 2008.[3] However, in recent years the number of unaccompanied Central American minors in transit through Mexico has increased considerably. In the summer of 2014, large numbers of child migrants, many of them traveling alone, placed pressure on Mexican policy makers to try to cope with the influx (Archibold 2014). On this front, Mexico chose to increase interior surveillance rather than concentrate on controlling its southern border. As a by-product of this strategy, detention facilities have sprawled throughout the Mexican territory. The number of immigrant detention centers in Mexico increased from twenty-two in 2000 to forty-eight in 2008.

At the same time, to counter numerous and highly visible complaints regarding the poor treatment given to detained migrants and the fact that many were victimized on their journey through Mexico to the United States, the Mexican government proposed a new narrative. Along this line, the country began by dismantling old legislation. Thus, in 2008 the Mexican Congress passed legislation that decriminalized irregular presence in the country. In 2011, Mexico enacted an unprecedented migration law (Ley de Migración) to ensure humane treatment of migrants in the country. The law intends to fully comply with international human rights stipulations ratified by Mexico, specifically with the International Convention on the Protection of the Rights of All Migrant Workers and Members of Their Families (ICMW). The new Migration Law also represents an attempt by the Mexican government to bring congruency to the way Mexico treats foreign migrants and the way it expects other countries to treat its migrant citizens abroad.

The Mexican Congress approved the new Migration Law in a rare unanimous vote. This display of consensus and the law's unambiguous protection of the rights of migrants, irrespective of their legal status, contrast with developments on the US side of the border. The US Congress has been highly divided, as have other levels of government and US society, regarding migration priorities and actions. Border security and immigration enforcement are the only two policy proposals that have been rather consensual (Meissner et al. 2013).

In early 2013, at the beginning of the second Obama administration, there were high expectations that comprehensive immigration reform legislation would take shape, given the growing pressures on both US political parties to deliver on this issue, particularly from Hispanic voters. Moreover, business demands for immigrant workers were rather vocal. Self-deportation proved not to be a viable strategy, and public support for some form of legalization for the estimated 11 to 12 million unauthorized immigrants, roughly half of those Mexican nationals, was also growing (Passel, Cohn, and Gonzalez-Barrera 2013). The approval by the US Senate, on June 27, 2013, of the Border Security, Economic Opportunity, and Immigration Modernization Act of 2013, or S744, made many believe that the US Congress would finally act. However, nothing has happened to further this bill at this point.

Mexico's President Enrique Peña Nieto seemed to consider the US debate on immigration reform a purely domestic matter. He believed negotiations regarding Mexico-US migration should be carried out through discreet diplomatic negotiations on regular administrative channels. On this position, there might be a point of convergence between the United States and Mexico. Migration continues to be an important topic within the complex Mexico-US relationship, and Mexico's management of this issue will be heavily influenced by any US legislative action on immigration reform.

At the same time, Mexican and Central American migration trends will certainly weigh on the US immigration debate and on Mexico's attitudes toward its southern border and its attempts to regulate transit migration. Although there have been no "massive voluntary returns" of Mexicans from abroad, fewer Mexicans have left Mexico since the US recession began. The rate of Mexican migrants departing for the United States in 2012 was roughly a third of the rate of those departing in 2006, while the rate of migrants returning to Mexico was almost unchanged between 2006 and 2010 (INEGI 2012). Indeed, Mexican migrants return home for reasons other than loss of jobs, such as family reunification and dislike of life in the United States, and they may remain in the United States because of established family and personal relationships and a greater sense of security.

After four decades of high migration rates that led to a population of around 6 million unauthorized Mexican immigrants residing in the United States (Passel, Cohn, and Gonzalez-Barrera 2013), the net migration flow from Mexico to the United States has declined and may have reversed, according to data from both countries (Passel, Cohn, and Gonzalez-Barrera 2012). Still, the flows in both directions are sizeable. Since 2006, the total number of unauthorized Mexicans apprehended crossing the border by US immigration authorities has fallen steadily to levels not seen since the early

1970s. Passel, Cohn, and Gonzalez-Barrera (2012) reported that apprehensions of unauthorized Mexicans dropped from more than 1 million in 2005 to 286,000 in 2011. Rates are at their lowest level since 1971. There is a real possibility that this decrease in migration will not be a temporary phenomenon. The US great recession, increased US border controls, lower fertility rates in Mexico, and increased work and educational opportunities for Mexican youth may be causing a longer-term shift in migration patterns.

This scenario of rapidly declining unauthorized Mexican migration to the United States constitutes an opportunity for both countries to explore avenues to manage migrations more constructively. However, recent developments have not altered the diverging paths that have characterized the two governments' responses to transborder movements.

Looking Ahead: Bringing In a Regional Perspective

There is no question that managing migration has become a defining issue for modern nation-states. Countries are confronted with a delicate balancing act in a quest to satisfy the imperatives of sovereignty, to respond to market forces—particularly strong in a globalized world—and to respect the fundamental human rights of individuals who seek better opportunities (Hollifield 2004). There are no easy policies, as evidenced by the notorious gaps over the last decades between migration outcomes and migration objectives in destination countries as well as in countries of origin (Cornelius, Martin, and Hollifield 1994).

This balancing act has to address contrasting conditions and interests of other nation-states. In a global system with no free labor mobility on the horizon, a regional perspective might be a viable and pragmatic strategy toward better migration management (Global Commission on International Migration 2005). The following considerations contribute to a needed exploration of what such a regional approach might look like in the context of the North American region, which includes Canada, the United States, Mexico, and Central America.

I begin by pointing out that securing the US-Mexico border is not sufficient to stem the influx of immigrants from Mexico and Central America. Many migration experts argue that increased enforcement cannot efficiently counterbalance human needs and desires to migrate that are relentlessly fueled by the increasing integration of economies and societies and by the multiple social and interpersonal networks that dominate the Mexico-to-US and Central America–to-US migration systems (Massey, Durand, and

Malone 2002). For Mexico to properly deal with transit migration, an interior enforcement strategy is insufficient and carries unbearable challenges, particularly when smuggling, human trafficking, and organized crime are involved. In Central America, violence, crime, and poverty are endemic, and those conditions continue to fuel large-scale emigration, especially in an institutional context of relatively unimpeded mobility. Since 2004, nationals of Guatemala, El Salvador, Honduras, and Nicaragua (known as the CA-4 countries) have had the right to move freely throughout the member countries without a passport (Alba and Castillo 2012).

Even if the United States adopted comprehensive immigration reform, it is doubtful that any reform would substantially modify the current restrictive immigration climate. Securing US borders, specifically the US-Mexico border, will foreseeably remain an essential component of any reform. In such a scenario, probably for the first time in decades, the persistence of Mexican migration cannot be taken for granted. A decrease in Mexico-US migration represents a serious challenge for the Mexican government and society and requires a thorough redefinition of Mexico's long-held positions on emigration policy (Alba 2011).

In this process of redefining policies, Mexico should take the opportunity to end unauthorized migration altogether by promoting among its population notions of orderly, safe, and legal emigration. To address the deeply engrained culture of unauthorized migration and to make migration a successful experience, there is a need for more active governmental involvement in preparing people who wish to emigrate. The government should allow, regulate, and supervise human resources companies to train and help place Mexican workers abroad. Additionally, the Mexican government should help migrants learn English and be involved in advising migrants in how to negotiate foreign work contracts to prevent exploitation.

In a context of restricted migration, the Mexican government must commit at the highest political level to improving economic and social opportunities for its population at home with the specific purpose of encouraging people to stay in Mexico. The Peña Nieto administration translated this need into the goal of growing the Mexican economy by at least 5 percent annually. To accelerate the pace of economic growth, President Peña Nieto was able to negotiate a common agenda with the three most important Mexican political parties to liberalize the energy and telecommunications sectors and to reform the Mexican educational system. The Constitution was modified in 2013 to accommodate these sought-after structural reforms. However, in that same year, the Mexican GDP grew by a scant 1.1 percent—or not at all in per capita terms.

Regardless of the level of dynamism and growth of the Mexican economy, given ingrained economic and social disparities, there will be strong migratory pressures either because labor demands in the US economy remain strong or because Mexicans will continue to want to migrate. Thus, one of the most pressing bilateral tasks facing the Mexican government continues to be reengaging the United States in serious discussions on migration. Moreover, Mexico has an obligation to employ all available legal options to support those migrants who want to regularize their immigration status in the United States or in any another country.

Finding acceptable solutions to the challenges posed by unauthorized Mexico-US migration continues to be a crucial issue in the bilateral agenda. In addition, transit migration and unauthorized crossings of Central Americans into US territory through Mexico have become critical regional foreign policy concerns. Slowly but consistently, Mexican and Central American migrant flows have generated a regional migration system that must be approached with a multilateral perspective. Mexico has already signed bilateral repatriation agreements with some Central American countries, including an accord with the CA-4 group, for the return of Central American nationals caught in unauthorized transit through Mexico. Certainly, national security concerns, the fight against drug trafficking and organized crime, and the rule of law have influenced Mexico's southern border policies. However, in order to organize this regional migration system, Canada, the United States, Mexico, and Central America should work together. In the longer term, the aim should be to establish a well-managed, safe, and thriving area of regional labor mobility.

The United States, as the main destination country and the dominant power in North America, should take responsible leadership in the effort to build an attractive regional vision. To encourage the institutionalization of this regional perspective, all countries involved should have a stake in the process.

The sharp slowdown in unauthorized Mexican migration presents the United States with a unique opportunity to rethink migration from a regional perspective. In a context of changing and increasingly interlocked demographic, economic, social, and political environments, the challenge is how to harness regional migration to make it play an acceptable role in the construction of stronger and sounder economies and societies. The nations involved must also take into consideration the geopolitical realities of border security concerns, institutional reforms, and respect for the rule of law. The ultimate goal of this regional perspective is to end "the culture of illegality that has defined immigration from the region in recent decades and create opportunities for the region to boost growth and competitiveness over the longer term" (Papademetriou, Meissner, and Sohnen 2013, 4).

According to experts, there will not be a sufficient supply of willing US native workers to meet future labor demands, particularly in the low-wage jobs likely to be generated by a dynamic US economy (Bean et al. 2013). Thus, there could be a politically feasible avenue for selective enactment of some components of a broader immigration reform agenda. Examples include some form of earned regularization, such as the one proposed in the Development, Relief, and Education for Alien Minors Act (DREAM Act),[4] which sought to provide a path to legalization for eligible unauthorized young adults, or some type of temporary migration program, such as the Agricultural Job Opportunities, Benefits and Security Act, known informally as the AgJOBS initiative.[5] Over the past few years, members of Congress have introduced several forms of these legislative proposals. The proposed DREAM Act legislation would provide conditional permanent residency to certain immigrants in good standing, such as graduates from US high schools who arrived in the United States as minors. The AgJOBS legislative proposals would provide agricultural employers with a stable, legal labor force, mostly under some form of temporary work programs. From a regional perspective, the inclusion of a regional preference for citizens of Canada, Mexico, and Central America in legislative proposals, such as the ones mentioned above, would be perceived as a pragmatic and cooperative response.

As for a longer-term vision, shared prosperity throughout the region is the only durable, long-term solution to mass emigration. From a regional perspective, notwithstanding the fact that NAFTA and the Central American Free Trade Agreement (CAFTA) have demonstrated that trade liberalization and freer capital movement by themselves will not lead to economic convergence, the logic behind NAFTA and CAFTA must be sustained. This requires putting in place mechanisms that facilitate economic convergence within the consolidating regional economy of North America. Thus far, this prosperity goal has been diluted by other pressing concerns. The biggest challenge to the consolidation of a shared regional vision is achieving prosperity for all.

In the short-to-medium term, a dynamic US economy would be able to incorporate an increased number of migrants from Mexico and Central America. That same dynamism would promote growth of other regional economies, enhancing their capacity to absorb their still rapidly expanding labor forces and diminishing migratory pressures within the region.

Rising aspirations of young people, families, and workers will certainly translate into additional migratory pressures, but this unavoidable development should be transitory. With the incorporation of workers into vibrant economies in the North American region, it is possible to foresee, in the long term, scenarios of more developed, less divergent, and more egalitarian economies and societies in Mexico and Central America. This could result in a region with increased labor mobility, less unorderly and massive migration, and more successful migrants. Bold leadership is essential if the governments of the region are to implement the multiple proposals associated with these scenarios.

It is only from a shared regional perspective that Mexico has any possibility of finding realistic and promising solutions to its migration dilemmas as a country of origin, return, transit, and destination. Any comprehensive strategy to manage migration in an orderly and humane manner must incorporate numerous elements. Among those, at least three components emerge as indispensable: the establishment of predictable rules of mobility within the region, the implementation of fair and credible controls and enforcement mechanisms for the agreed-upon rules of mobility and migration, and the promotion of shared prosperity. These elements should be viewed as parts of a whole. It would be very difficult to accept any one component in isolation from the others. It is also doubtful that any one component could be effective by itself, particularly in a context of strong migratory pressures.

The aim of this chapter has been to identify positive steps to manage migration flows. There has been and will continue to be progress and setbacks in regional, bilateral, and unilateral attempts to regulate migration. Managing migration in a globalized world implies devising rules for orderly movement of labor in a context in which the free movement of people across national borders is not the accepted norm, and where borders continue to delineate societies, economies, and states. The task is crucial given the growing interconnections of peoples, economies, and states.

Notes

1. The new Migration Law and amendments to the General Population Law were enacted May 25, 2011.

2. See *Gaceta del Senado*, LIX Legislatura, February 16, 2006; *Gaceta Parlamentaria*, year IX, num. 1949, February 17, 2006.

3. No numbers are available on deportable foreigners (*aseguramientos*) after 2011 from the Instituto Nacional de Migración (http://www.inm.gob.mx/).

4. The DREAM Act seeks to establish a path to legalization for eligible unau-

thorized youth and young adults. It does not provide permanent legal status outright to potential beneficiaries. Rather, it allows individuals to apply for legal permanent status on a conditional basis if, upon enactment of the law, they are under the age of thirty-five, arrived in the United States before the age of sixteen, have lived in the United States for at least the last five years, and have obtained a US high school diploma or equivalent. The conditional basis of their status would be removed in six years if they successfully complete at least two years of postsecondary education or military service and if they maintain good moral character during the time period (Batalova and McHugh 2001). A first version of the DREAM Act was introduced in the US Senate in 2001 by Senators Durbin (D-IL) and Hatch (R-UT). Although the act has been reintroduced several times, it has not been approved.

5. AgJOBS is a bipartisan bill that combines an earned legalization program for farmworkers with a reform of the H-2A temporary foreign agricultural worker program (American Immigration Council 2009).

References

Alba, Francisco. 2003. "Del diálogo de Zedillo y Clinton al entendimiento de Fox y Bush." In *México-Estados Unidos-Canadá 1999–2000*, edited by B. Mabire, 109–164. Mexico City: El Colegio de México.

———. 2008. "The Mexican Economy and Mexico-U.S. Migration: A Macro Perspective." In *Mexico-U.S. Migration Management*, edited by A. Escobar and S. F. Martin, 33–59. Lanham, MD: Lexington Books.

———. 2010a. "México: A Crucial Crossroads." *Migration Information Source.* Washington, DC: Migration Policy Institute. Retrieved February 25, 2013, from http://www.migrationinformation.org/feature/display.cfm?ID=772.

———. 2010b. "Respuestas mexicanas frente a la emigración a los Estados Unidos." In *Migraciones internacionales.* Vol. 3, *Los grandes problemas de México*, edited by F. Alba, M. Á. Castillo, and G. Verduzco, 515–546. Mexico City: El Colegio de México.

———. 2010c. "Rethinking Migration Responses in a Context of Restriction and Recession: Challenges and Opportunities for Mexico and the United States." *Law and Business Review of the Americas* 16(4):659–672.

———. 2011. "Hacer virtud de la necesidad. Hacia una nueva generación de políticas para la migración México-Estados Unidos." *Este País* 246:8–12.

———. 2013. "Mexico: The New Migration Narrative." *Migration Information Source.* Washington, DC: Migration Policy Institute. Retrieved April 23, 2014, from http://www.migrationpolicy.org/article/mexico-new-migration-narrative.

Alba, Francisco, and Manuel Angel Castillo. 2012. *New Approaches to Migration Management in Mexico and Central America.* Washington, DC: Migration Policy Institute.

American Immigration Council. 2009. "Facts about Farmworkers." Washington, DC: American Immigration Council. Retrieved August 12, 2014, from http://www.immigrationpolicy.org/just-facts/facts-about-farmworkers.

Archibold, Randal C. 2014. "On Southern Border, Mexico Faces Crisis of Its Own: Many Deported as Pressure Rises." *New York Times*, July 20, 5.

Batalova, Jeanne, and Margie McHugh. 2010. "DREAM vs. Reality: An Analysis of Potential DREAM Act Beneficiaries." Washington, DC: Migration Policy Institute. Retrieved August 12, 2014, from http://www.migrationpolicy.org/research/dream-vs-reality-analysis-potential-dream-act-beneficiaries.

Bean, Frank D., Susan K. Brown, Mark A. Leach, James Bachmeier, and Jennifer Van Hook. 2013. "Unauthorized Mexican Migration and the Socioeconomic Integration of Mexican Americans." *US 2010 Report*. New York: Russell Sage Foundation.

Cornelius, Wayne A. 2001. "Death at the Border: Unintended Consequences of U.S. Immigration Control Policy." *Population and Development Review* 27(4):661–685.

Cornelius, Wayne A., Philip L. Martin, and James F. Hollifield. 1994. "Introduction: The Ambivalent Quest for Immigration Control." In *Controlling Immigration: A Global Perspective*, edited by W. A. Cornelius, P. L. Martin, and J. F. Hollifield, 3–41. Stanford, CA: Stanford University Press.

Davidow, Jeffrey. 2004. *The U.S. and Mexico: The Bear and the Porcupine*. Princeton, NJ: Markus Wiener.

Délano, Alexandra. 2011. *Mexico and Its Diaspora in the United States: Policies of Emigration since 1848*. New York: Cambridge University Press.

Fernández de Castro, Rafael, and Roberta Clariond Rangel. 2008. "Immigration Reform in the United States." In *Mexico-U.S. Migration Management*, edited by A. Escobar and S. F. Martin, 145–177. Lanham, MD: Lexington Books.

Global Commission on International Migration. 2005. *Migration in an Interconnected World: New Directions for Action*. Switzerland: Global Commission on International Migration.

Gonzalez-Murphy, Laura V., and Rey Koslowski. 2011. "Understanding Mexico's Changing Immigration Laws." Washington, DC: Woodrow Wilson International Center for Scholars.

Hollifield, James F. 2004. "The Emerging Migration State." *International Migration Review* 38(3):885–912.

INEGI (Instituto Nacional de Estadística y Geografía). 2012. *Tasas brutas de migración internacional y saldo neto migratorio según periodo 2006–2012*. Aguascalientes, Ags., Mexico: Instituto Nacional de Estadística y Geografía. Retrieved September 29, 2014, from http://www.inegi.org.mx/inegi/contenidos/espanol/prensa/Boletines/Boletin/Comunicados/Especiales/2012/septiembre/comunica2.pdf.

Joint Communiqué, *Toward a Partnership for Prosperity: The Guanajuato Proposal*, February 16, 2001.

Massey, Douglas, Jorge Durand, and Nolan J. Malone. 2002. *Beyond Smoke and Mirrors: Mexican Immigration in an Era of Economic Integration*. New York: Russell Sage Foundation.

Meissner, Doris, Donald M. Kerwin, Muzaffar Chishty, and Claire Bergeron. 2013. *Immigration Enforcement in the United States: The Rise of a Formidable Machinery*. Washington, DC: Migration Policy Institute.

Mexico-US Binational Study on Migration. 1997. *Migration between Mexico and the United States*. Mexico: Ministry of Foreign Affairs and US Commission on Immigration Reform.

Nevins, Joseph. 2010. *Operation Gatekeeper and Beyond: The War on "Illegals" and the Remaking of the U.S.-Mexico Boundary.* New York: Routledge.

Papademetriou, Demetrios G., Doris Meissner, and Eleanor Sohnen. 2013. *Thinking Regionally to Compete Globally: Leveraging Migration & Human Capital in the U.S., Mexico, and Central America.* Washington, DC: Migration Policy Institute.

Passel, Jeffrey, D'Vera Cohn, and Ana Gonzalez-Barrera. 2012. *Net Migration from Mexico Falls to Zero—and Perhaps Less.* Washington, DC: Pew Hispanic Center.

———. 2013. *Population Decline of Unauthorized Immigrants Stalls, May Have Reversed.* Washington, DC: Pew Research Center. Retrieved October 29, 2014, from http://www.pewhispanic.org/2013/09/23/population-decline-of-unauthorized-immigrants-stalls-may-have-reversed/.

Simanski, John F., and Lesley M. Sapp. 2013. *Immigration Enforcement Actions: 2012.* Washington, DC: US Department of Homeland Security.

Tuirán, Rodolfo, and José Luís Ávila. 2010. "La migración México–Estados Unidos, 1940–2010." In *Migraciones internacionales.* Vol. 3, *Los grandes problemas de México,* edited by F. Alba, M. Á. Castillo, and G. Verduzco, 93–134. Mexico City: El Colegio de México.

US-Mexico Migration Panel. 2001. *Mexico-US Migration: A Shared Responsibility.* Washington, DC: Carnegie Endowment for International Peace/Instituto Tecnológico Autónomo de México.

Villarreal, M. Angeles. 2010. *The Mexican Economy after the Global Financial Crisis.* Washington, DC: Congressional Research Service. Retrieved October 15, 2014, from http://fas.org/sgp/crs/row/R41402.pdf.

Zúñiga, Elena and Miguel Molina. 2008. *Demographic Trends in Mexico: The Implications for Skilled Migration.* Washington, DC: Migration Policy Institute.

CHAPTER 2

An Economic Perspective on
US Immigration Policy vis-à-vis Mexico

PIA M. ORRENIUS, JASON SAVING,
AND MADELINE ZAVODNY

Migration defines US-Mexico relations more than any other issue. Since the turn of the last century, millions of Mexicans have migrated to the United States to work on US farms and construction sites, in factories and homes, behind stoves, and with shovels. Whereas most Mexican migrants used to return home, over time Mexican workers have increasingly settled permanently in the United States and been joined there by their families (Massey, Durand, and Malone 2002). As a result, over 10 percent of people born in Mexico currently live in the United States, and Mexicans make up 28 percent of US immigrants.[1]

Over the second half of this joint migration history, the United States has adopted fewer and fewer policies to accommodate the stream of Mexican migrants and focused increasingly on ways to impede it. Since the late 1970s, US immigration policy has severely restricted the number of Mexicans who can immigrate legally on a temporary or permanent basis. The United States has not had a large-scale labor migration program with Mexico since the Bracero Program, which ended in 1964. The great majority of Mexican migrants therefore enter the United States illegally. While some of these immigrants return to Mexico, many remain and try to find a way to legalize their status, but changes to US immigration policy have made it increasingly difficult to do so. In the past, many unauthorized immigrants pinned their hopes on a large-scale legalization program such as the Immigration Reform and Control Act (IRCA) of 1986, which legalized over 2 million Mexican immigrants. In recent years, immigrants have appeared more concerned about receiving deportation relief than US citizenship (Lopez et al. 2013). About 6 million unauthorized Mexican immigrants now live in the United States, alongside 5.5 million legal Mexican immigrants, some of whom have become naturalized US citizens (Passel, Cohn, and Gonzalez-Barrera 2013).

The magnitude of Mexico-US immigration makes it important to understand who comes, how, and why. Media reports can leave the impression that these flows occur independently of economic forces, but empirical evidence suggests otherwise. When US labor markets slumped during the 2007–2009 recession, for example, net Mexico-US migration fell to zero (Passel, Cohn, and Gonzalez-Barrera 2012). Noneconomic factors affect the migrant flow as well, such as desire to live near family members and friends in the United States and, in recent years, to escape drug-related violence in parts of Mexico. This chapter focuses on economic causes and effects, but policy also has to take noneconomic factors into account.[2]

US immigration policy plays a central role in the migrant flow as well, both in determining *how many* enter and *how* they enter: legally or illegally. The interplay between economic and regulatory forces also determines the volume and skill composition of Mexican immigration, which affects US labor markets and government budgets. After discussing these issues, this chapter explains why there is an imperative need for US immigration policy reform, what form it should take, and why policy makers should pay special attention to Mexico.

Who Comes and Why

Until the onset of the 2007–2009 recession, the number of unauthorized Mexican immigrants in the United States was rising by almost half a million each year. The US housing bust and ensuing financial crisis caused net migration from Mexico to fall to zero or less (Cave 2011; Passel, Cohn, and Gonzalez-Barrera 2012). Heightened border and interior enforcement likely also played a role in discouraging potential migrants, but the timing of this dramatic reversal points to the primary driver of Mexican immigration: economic forces.

Both push and pull forces underlie Mexico-US migration. Historically, poor economic conditions in Mexico have pushed migrants out while good economic conditions in the United States have pulled them in (Hanson and Spilimbergo 1999; Orrenius and Zavodny 2005). Higher wages have always been a draw for migrants, but in recent years safety and escape from violence have taken on a larger role (Escobar Latapí, Lowell, and Martin 2013). The household and community dynamics around migration continue to be important; empirical analysis suggests migrant networks exert a far more sizable impact on the probability of migration than does the international wage gap (Massey and Espinosa 1997). Networks and the deteriorating standing of nonmigrants (relative deprivation) form the basis for the cumulative causation of migration, where migration is sustained or accelerated even as economic drivers wane (Massey 1990). Migration has also been studied as a tool to mitigate the risks to household income, particularly in farming communities, where weather shocks can cut off agricultural production (Stark and Bloom 1985). The importance of the household and transnational relationships in migration decisions is reflected in remittance flows from the US to Mexico that have exceeded $22 billion annually for the last decade.

Labor supply matters too, especially in the long run. Large Mexican birth cohorts have traditionally meant more competition for limited economic opportunities at home and therefore more out-migration (Hanson and McIntosh 2010).[3] However, Mexican fertility rates have fallen from 6.8 children per woman in the 1970s to a historic low of 2.2 children per woman today, causing population growth to slow (Orrenius and Zavodny 2011). With shrinking cohorts of youth, the demographic impetus for Mexican migration to the United States is already weakening and will diminish further in coming decades.

Changes in the two countries' economic conditions affect not only how many Mexicans migrate but also who migrates. Improvements in US and Mexican economic conditions appear to lead to a decline in education levels among Mexican immigrants entering clandestinely (Orrenius and Zavodny 2005). Meanwhile, Mexican economic crises, such as the 1994–1995 "Tequila crisis," are correlated with a spike in migrants' education levels. Increased border enforcement also leads to higher education levels among unauthorized migrants, presumably because more-educated migrants are better able to afford the higher migration costs necessary to evade improved enforcement (Orrenius and Zavodny 2005).

The typical Mexican migrant has long been a relatively young man seeking better economic opportunities. Since the late 1980s, increasing numbers of women and children have migrated to the United States as well, although they are typically tied movers who accompany or rejoin family members (Donato 1993). Some enter legally, sponsored by relatives who were able to obtain legal status, while others enter clandestinely. The implementation of IRCA dramatically increased the number of Mexicans with legal permanent residence through both its direct impact and the concomitant increase in immigrants eligible to sponsor their family members.

Average education among Mexican immigrants to the United States has risen over time but remains far below that of US natives. Only about 5 percent of adult Mexican immigrants are college graduates, versus 30 percent of US natives and 38 percent of non-Mexican immigrants. Mexican immigrants constitute over one-fourth of all adults in the United States who do not have a high school diploma or equivalent (Pew Hispanic Center 2009).

Economic Effects of Immigration

Immigration boosts the labor force and benefits consumers by leading to lower prices for the goods and services that immigrant workers produce. It benefits employers, who face lower labor costs, and landowners, who receive a higher price (or rent) for their property. Low-education immigrant workers may complement more-educated workers by enabling them to spend more time on higher-value-added activities, boosting their productivity, employment, and earnings. For example, the influx of low-education immigrants has caused highly educated women to increase how much time they spend on paid work and decrease how much time they spend on household work (Cortés and Tessada 2011). Immigration can also help reduce slack in the economy and increase efficiency by alleviating labor shortages in certain sectors or regions. A compelling example is the massive migration of Hispanic immigrant workers to the Gulf Coast in the wake of Hurricane Katrina (Fussell 2009). Immigrants tend to move more readily than native workers to areas experiencing economic growth, which reduces regional bottlenecks and encourages regional wage convergence (Cadena and Kovak 2013).

While the influx of low-education immigrants from Mexico and other countries has broad economic benefits, it creates winners and losers in the labor market. Economic studies tend to find a small negative effect on the wages of competing native workers, for example. The magnitude of the effects depends on how substitutable immigrants are for native workers. Natives whose skills are complementary to those of immigrants are likely to gain from immigration, and natives with substitutable skills are likely to lose (Orrenius and Zavodny 2007; Ottaviano and Peri 2012). The brunt of the negative labor-market impact falls on earlier immigrants, not natives, because they are most similar to new immigrants and hence compete most closely with them.

The preponderance of empirical evidence indicates that the adverse impact of immigration on natives' wages is considerably smaller than might be expected given the magnitude of immigration to the United States, particularly of less-educated workers. For example, Card (2001) concludes that immigrant inflows reduced wages and employment rates of less-educated natives in traditional gateway cities like Miami and Los Angeles by 1–3 percentage points during the 1980s. Ottaviano and Peri (2012) find that immigration inflows during 1990–2006 reduced wages among natives without a high school diploma by about 1 percent in the short run and actually increased their wages slightly in the long run. Some other research indicates more negative effects, such as Borjas's (2003) conclusion that immigration inflows during 1980–2000 reduced wages among natives without a high school diploma by almost 9 percent. But research suggests that other factors, not immigration, played a dominant role in the long-term decline in wages for less-educated natives.[4]

In addition to economic effects, immigration has a fiscal impact. The fiscal impact is the difference between what families contribute in taxes and what they consume in publicly provided services. It is a net positive for high-education immigrants (and natives), who receive relatively high wages and qualify for relatively few transfer programs, but a net negative for low-education immigrants (and natives), whose wages tend to be lower and whose eligibility for transfer programs is therefore higher.

State and local governments end up bearing the majority of fiscal costs. Most of these costs occur in areas like education and health care, where the federal government has traditionally taken a backseat. And while welfare participation levels are higher among immigrants, this is not, contrary to what one might initially expect, because many low-education immigrants are unemployed in the United States. Instead, unlike the case in many other advanced economies, male low-education immigrants in the United States actually are much more likely to be employed than low-education natives. Rather, the difference is due to greater immigrant participation in public health insurance programs, such as Medicaid and the Children's Health Insurance Program. Immigrants also are more likely than US natives to have school-aged children.

It is important to note that, in the very long run, across generations, the negative fiscal impact of less-educated immigrants dissipates. This happens through the assimilation of their children, grandchildren, and later generations, who eventually reach average or above-average education and income levels and "pay back" the costs imposed by their ancestors. Rapid economic integration of the second and third generations, therefore, pays large economic dividends.

Because Mexican immigrants in particular have relatively low education levels, their fiscal impact is less positive (or more negative) than is the norm among immigrant groups. Estimates suggest that the average Mexican immigrant imposes a lifetime fiscal burden of $55,200 (Camarota

2001), which is roughly on par with estimates for low-education natives.[5] More broadly, estimates from 1997 indicate that low-education immigrants, those without a high school diploma or equivalent, impose a net fiscal cost of $89,000 over their lifetimes. As noted above, much of this is eventually offset by subsequent generations—their children and grandchildren—who assimilate toward natives' education levels (Smith and Edmonston 1997).[6]

With regard to unauthorized immigrants, most attempts to calculate their net fiscal impact conclude that they pay less in taxes than they receive in services, on average (Congressional Budget Office 2007). Like low-education legal immigrants or low-education natives, they receive more in government benefits than they pay in taxes, on average. However, since they are not eligible for most welfare programs, illegal immigrants have a smaller adverse fiscal impact than low-wage legal immigrants.

Current US Immigration Policy

The United States has more immigrants from Mexico than from any other country. This is not surprising given the two countries' two-thousand-mile shared border and the vast economic differences between them. Unlike Canada, with which the United States shares an even longer land border, Mexico is much poorer than the United States. Clemens, Montenegro, and Pritchett (2008) estimate that the average Mexican migrant can earn 2.5 times as much in the United States as in Mexico even after adjusting for cost of living differences. Given these potential wage gains, perhaps the question is not why so many Mexican workers migrate to the United States but rather why so few. One explanation is US immigration policy, which makes it extremely difficult for Mexican immigrants to enter the United States legally to work while making it expensive and dangerous to enter illegally.

There are three main ways workers migrate to the United States. First, they can receive a permanent resident visa ("green card"). These visas are obtained primarily through sponsorship by a close relative who is a US citizen or permanent resident or by a US employer (which almost always requires that the worker have a college degree). Second, they can come on a temporary-worker visa. Third, they can enter illegally or stay illegally by violating the terms of a visa. The first two ways are numerically limited in most cases, while US Border Patrol and Immigration and Customs Enforcement try to limit the third way.

The United States granted permanent resident status to over 158,000

Mexican-born individuals each year on average during fiscal years 2006–2012. Almost 60 percent of these green cards were issued to immediate relatives of US citizens and another third on the basis of other family ties. Only 6 percent were issued on the basis of employment.[7] This is not surprising since the United States limits the number of employment-based green cards for low-skilled workers to only five thousand annually, including accompanying dependents. Country quotas, a provision of US immigration law that caps yearly issuance of new green cards to people from any one country at 7 percent of total admissions across numerically restricted categories, also limit Mexican immigration. As a result, many potential Mexican immigrants must wait for years or even decades for a green card to become available.

The United States has a temporary foreign worker program specifically for Canada and Mexico called the Trade NAFTA (TN) program and three other programs that apply to all countries: the H-1B, H-2A, and H-2B programs. The TN program allows Canadian and Mexican professionals to enter the United States to work temporarily. The program requires that Mexicans (but not Canadians) have a TN visa, issued by the State Department. There is no numerical limit on the number of available TN visas.[8] Workers are typically required to have a bachelor's degree, work in a specialty occupation, and have a US offer of employment. The TN visa's duration was recently increased from one to three years. State Department data indicate that 9,548 TN visas were issued in fiscal year 2013. The TN visa was inspired by the H-1B program, which also admits skilled workers in certain occupations who hold at least a bachelor's degree. H-1B visas are capped at 65,000 visas a year plus 20,000 for holders of advanced degrees from US institutions. Few H-1B visas are issued to Mexicans—only about 2,800 per year during fiscal years 2006–2013, about 2.1 percent of all H-1B issuances.[9]

The H-2A and H-2B programs admit relatively low-skilled workers for agricultural and nonagricultural seasonal jobs, respectively. The number of H-2A visas is not numerically limited, but H-2B visas are limited to 66,000 per year. Mexicans dominate both programs, accounting for 94 percent of H-2A issuances and 73 percent of H-2B issuances and renewals during fiscal years 2012–2013. The H-2B program has been oversubscribed almost every year since its inception in 1990 and is nowhere near large enough to accommodate the number of Mexican workers who want to enter the United States in a typical year. The H-2A program, while numerically unlimited, has thus far not been as popular with farmers, perhaps due to the availability of a cheaper alternative: unauthorized workers.

Estimates suggest that a little over half of Mexican immigrants living in the United States are unauthorized immigrants. While most unauthorized immigrants cross the border illegally ("entry without inspection," in official parlance), others overstay or violate the terms of a visa, such as working while on a nonwork visa. Many unauthorized Mexican immigrants used to return home regularly to visit and eventually return permanently, but increased border enforcement has resulted in large numbers of unauthorized Mexican immigrants being "trapped inside the border" and bringing their families to join them in the United States. Increased border enforcement thus had the unintended effect of driving up the number of unauthorized immigrants as they opt to stay longer in the United States and even settle there permanently (Reyes 2004; Angelucci 2012).

It is currently very difficult for unauthorized immigrants to legalize their status. The 1996 Illegal Immigration Reform and Immigrant Responsibility Act requires people living illegally in the United States who are sponsored for a green card to leave the United States and wait for three or ten years in their home country before they are eligible to adjust status and re-enter the United States.[10] This three- or ten-year reentry bar has the unintentional consequence of making it more attractive for those workers to simply remain in the United States hoping that a broad-based amnesty will eventually be enacted. However, it has been over twenty-five years since the last legalization program. The US Congress appeared near enacting comprehensive immigration reform in 2006 and 2007, but disagreement over the terms of a legalization program derailed the bills. Another comprehensive immigration reform bill passed in the Senate in spring 2013 but was never brought up in the House. In January 2013, the Obama administration eased the three- and ten-year reentry bars for certain spouses and children of US citizens, but it is unclear how many additional unauthorized immigrants will be able to take advantage of the change since the policy still requires that US citizens demonstrate "extreme hardship" if separated from their immigrant family member.

Additional executive rule changes aimed at easing the burdens faced by undocumented immigrants have occurred in the last two years. Prosecutorial discretion of interior removal cases has reduced the number of deportations by focusing the government's efforts on deporting "criminal aliens" rather than those who are long-time residents with community ties who have not committed a serious crime. In addition, deferred deportation has been implemented for eligible unauthorized immigrant youth (so-called Dreamers), who as of fall 2012 could apply for temporary legal status and work permits. Deferred action was aimed at individuals under age thirty-one who had arrived in the United States before age sixteen, lived continuously in the United States for at least five years, had a high school diploma or equivalent or were enrolled in school, and did not have a criminal record.[11] As of January 2015, more than 638,000 immigrants had been granted deferred action, 88 percent of them from Mexico.[12] In November 2014, President Obama announced a similar deferred action program for the unauthorized parents of US citizen children and permanent residents. This executive action would temporarily legalize up to 3.7 million unauthorized immigrants, but the provision was blocked in federal court in February 2015.

The Need for Immigration Policy Reform

Although recent attempts were unsuccessful, there remains a critical economic need for comprehensive immigration reform, particularly vis-à-vis Mexico. Current US immigration policy reflects its historical emphasis on family reunification over employment-based admissions, making immigration less beneficial to the United States than it otherwise could be. The United States is an outlier among industrialized economies in admitting only 7 percent of permanent immigrants on the basis of work (Organization for Economic Cooperation and Development 2010), almost all of them highly skilled. Years of applying Band-Aid fixes to an immigration policy created in 1965 have resulted in convoluted policies that stymie potential immigrants and US employers alike. Potential immigrants wait for years or decades for green cards, while employers have difficulty bringing in both high- and low-skilled foreign workers.

The current environment also creates hardship among immigrants and slows assimilation, which some might argue lends further urgency to immigration reform. During the first decade of the 2000s, border and interior enforcement increased, avenues that allowed some illegal residents to adjust to legal status were eliminated, and a growing number of states adopted laws aimed at driving out unauthorized immigrants. Through programs such as Secure Communities, the US Department of Homeland Security (DHS) deported a near record 369,000 immigrants in fiscal year 2013, some 241,000 of whom were Mexican nationals.[13]

Increased enforcement both along the border and in the interior, combined with zero net growth in the undocumented population, may have finally set the stage for comprehensive immigration reform in the coming years. Reform would likely include a legalization program that would create a path to permanent residence and eventual US citizenship for unauthorized immigrants already present in the United States, though in late 2013 lawmakers began entertaining the idea of a type of permanent legal status that does not necessarily lead to citizenship (or rule it out). Reform to immigration policy going forward will likely emphasize employment-based migration, however, perhaps by low-skilled workers as well as by high-skilled workers. Mexicans would be the primary beneficiaries of a program for low-skilled foreign workers since the TN visa already serves as an avenue for high-skilled Mexican workers to come to the United States. How should such a program be designed to best accommodate employers' desire for low-skilled foreign workers while protecting the interests of both immigrants and natives?

Immigrant Policy Goals

As economists, we argue that the United States should design an immigration policy that is flexible and accommodates cyclical fluctuations in labor demand but also prioritizes long-run economic growth. Such a policy would focus on admitting workers whom employers want to hire; establishing a system of laws that are flexible, yet enforceable; allocating visas in a way that limits harm to US workers and taxpayers; and minimizing unauthorized immigration.[14] Such a policy would also take into consideration the special relationship, shared geography, and extensive migration history between the United States and Mexico.

Current policy reflects a number of priorities, including previous immigrants' desire to bring in their relatives, employers' desire to hire workers who are in short supply, and potential immigrants' desire to migrate to the United States. The first has won out. Under current policy, almost two-thirds of green cards are awarded on the basis of family ties without regard to the economic contribution they could make. The temporary foreign worker programs discussed earlier are a Band-Aid to try to accommodate employers. The diversity program, which awards fifty thousand green cards to immigrants from underrepresented countries, and the refugee and asylum programs are the main ways the system tries to accommodate other potential migrants.

The current program has several major inefficiencies, many of which are particularly problematic for Mexicans. Because of Mexico's large population and its proximity to the United States, it is natural that Mexican workers (and US employers) would need more visas than other countries. The one-size-fits-all category and country caps have disproportionately affected Mexicans, causing potential immigrants to languish in queues for years or even decades. Priority dates for Mexicans applying for family-sponsored categories stretch as far back as 1993, which means the DHS is currently processing individuals who applied for permanent residence over twenty years ago.[15] Mexicans sponsored by their employers under the third preference category for employment-based green cards have currently waited two years. Current law, by limiting immigration by country of origin through the country caps, essentially relegates citizens of high-immigration countries like Mexico, India, China, and the Philippines to the back of the line.

Visas are allocated either on a first-come, first-served basis or, for oversubscribed temporary-worker visas and the diversity-visa program, randomly via a lottery. Neither of these allocation methods addresses economic priorities. The same number of green cards and temporary-worker visas is available regardless of supply or demand. And since ways for low-skilled immigrant workers to enter the United States legally are limited, millions have entered illegally. Unauthorized immigrants live in the shadows, sometimes receiving lower wages or working in worse conditions than other similarly qualified workers because of their lack of legal status. Recent federal and state legislation targeting worksites through E-Verify mandates and other regulations have further marginalized unauthorized workers, pushing them off the books, out of the labor force, or into self-employment (Bohn and Lofstrom 2013). E-Verify mandates reduce the already-low wages of unauthorized Mexican men (Orrenius and Zavodny 2015).

Work-Based Immigration Reform for Mexico

The United States has inefficient immigration policies and practices that reduce the potential economic benefits immigration could create. Immigration reform that prioritizes employment-based migration, encourages short-term migration, and dismantles cumbersome regulations on employers would go a long way in resolving the current inefficiencies and inequities. A legalization program will likely be a part of any reform, but our focus here is on how a new immigration policy can best accommodate future flows of migrants, particularly from Mexico.

There is already a blueprint for Mexican migration in the TN visa. Canada, the United States, and Mexico essentially have free migration for highly skilled workers, at least as long as they work in specialty occupations and are sponsored by an employer. The TN visa does not stipulate prevailing wages or require labor certification or attestation, is not capped, is valid for three years, and is renewable. Despite its ease of use, relatively few Mexicans utilize the TN visa. This is a reflection not of a poorly designed visa but rather of the paucity of highly skilled Mexicans who want to work in the United States. Relatively few highly skilled Mexicans seek employment in the United States because Mexican professionals typically earn high wages in Mexico and enjoy lower costs of living, leaving little incentive to migrate.[16] TN visas are underutilized because they are not available to the workers who want them most—those with fewer skills.

The TN visa should be extended to low-skilled Mexican workers. This would create a practical alternative to unauthorized migration or the cumbersome H-2A and H-2B programs. In order to provide some disincentive for employers to hire foreign workers over natives, TN visas could carry an employer fee. If TN visas were numerically limited, they could be auctioned off. This would ensure two things: one, the employers have to pay a premium for foreign labor; and two, the most valuable candidates would get visas because the employers who bid the most for their workers would win the auction. Auctions would also allow the government to change the number of visas depending on labor demand, which would be readily observable in an auction setting.[17] Revenues from the auctions could be used to retrain any displaced US workers or to compensate states and localities for immigration-related fiscal costs.

TN visas do not allow migrants to remain permanently in the United States, but they do allow workers to bring their families. The family provision could be different for low-skilled workers to reduce the incentive to overstay, or conditions could be imposed, such as a requirement that they have health insurance coverage and a ban on participating in public-assistance programs. The intent of the visa would be to allow labor migration and ample circularity and flexibility while discouraging permanent settlement. This would limit the fiscal impact of low-skilled migration while still allowing migrant workers to take advantage of better economic opportunities and US employers (and consumers) to benefit from foreign workers.

One of the goals of a TN visa program aimed at low-skilled Mexican workers would be to discourage unauthorized immigration, but some unauthorized immigration would likely continue. Such a program therefore needs to be combined with fast and accurate verification of all applicants' right to work in the United States and penalties for employers who do not comply. This would aid interior enforcement efforts and also provide greater disincentive to migrate through extralegal channels.

Conclusion

At the turn of the last century, labor shortages in the US Southwest drove labor contractors deep into Mexico to implore Mexican laborers to come north to man farms and ranches and build railroads. Mexicans came sporadically and reluctantly for the first two decades of the twentieth century. It was not until political unrest in Mexico and the passage of restrictive US immigration laws in the early 1920s, which cut off labor migration from Europe, that Mexico-US migration got a real push. Since then, millions of Mexicans have benefited from employment opportunities in the United States, and the US economy has benefited from the efforts of Mexican immigrants. However, the benefits have come with fiscal costs, and some US native workers have been harmed by the low-skilled influx. The unauthorized nature of Mexican migration since the 1970s has further aggravated the situation, especially in the post-9/11 era.

The sensitivity of Mexican migration to the US business cycle and an extensive literature suggest that the availability of relatively high-paying jobs has been the main magnet for northward migration. While other factors have played an important role, such as migrant networks and family reunification, the main reason for US migration has been the promise of higher incomes and standards of living (Massey and Espinosa 1997).

Given that migration can benefit both migrants and natives, sensible immigration policy should provide a framework that takes advantage of the gains while controlling the costs. Current US policy, particularly vis-à-vis Mexico, falls short on both counts. It favors family reunification over employment-based immigration and also provides very limited opportunities for low-skilled Mexican workers to legally migrate to the United States on the basis of employment. A temporary-worker program similar to the TN visa for highly skilled workers but with eligibility extended to low-education workers would mark a substantial improvement over the status quo.

Notes

1. We use the terms "foreign born" and "immigrant" interchangeably to refer to individuals who are born abroad to non-US parents. Legal immigrants hold either a temporary or permanent visa, while unauthorized immigrants have illegally crossed the border or otherwise violated conditions of their visas, such as overstaying a tourist or student visa.

2. Humanitarian factors are playing an increasing role in migration from Central America, which is picking up pace as Mexico-US migration remains relatively subdued.

3. It bears noting that once mass emigration ensued, the Mexican government typically ignored or denounced the migrants. It was not until the Fox administration took power in 2000 that the Mexican government adopted a more positive stance toward the migrants.

4. The rising skill premium and changing labor-market institutions, particularly the fall in the real (inflation-adjusted) minimum wage, played a larger role than immigration (DiNardo, Fortin, and Lemieux 1996; Card and DiNardo 2002).

5. See, for example, the estimates in Khatiwada et al. (2007).

6. Poor and low-education immigrants show significantly more socioeconomic mobility across generations than do similarly educated natives.

7. Authors' calculations based on data on persons obtaining legal permanent resident status by broad class of admission and country of birth from the Department of Homeland Security. Retrieved from http://www.dhs.gov/files/statistics/publications/yearbook.shtm.

8. The quota of a maximum of 5,500 TN visas annually for Mexicans was lifted in 2004. Nevertheless, few Mexicans use the TN visa because it is limited to workers with a university-level education, which is not common in Mexico.

9. Authors' calculations based on data on nonimmigrant visa issuances from the US State Department, Bureau of Consular Affairs. Retrieved from http://travel.state.gov/visa/statistics/nivstats/nivstats_4582.html.

10. The 245(i) program allowed unauthorized immigrants to pay a fine and adjust to legal status without leaving the country and becoming subject to a reentry bar. It became crucial after IIRIRA went into effect. The 245(i) program ran from 1994 to 1998 and was reauthorized in late 2000 for a four-month period.

11. DACA guidelines also stated that honorably discharged veterans of the coast guard or armed forces of the United States were eligible for deferred action (Napolitano 2012). Under current law, immigrant noncitizens with legal permanent resident status are permitted to enlist in the US military (Office of the Under Secretary of Defense, Personnel, and Readiness 2010). DACA recipients may be eligible to serve in the military through the Military Accessions Vital to National Interest (MAVNI) program if considered "vital to the national interest and critical to the military service" (US Department of Defense 2014). Specific eligibility criteria apply to the MAVNI program.

12. See http://www.uscis.gov/sites/default/files/USCIS/Resources/Reports%20and%20Studies/Immigration%20Forms%20Data/All%20Form%20Types/DACA/I821d_performancedata_fy2015_qtr1.pdf.

13. See https://www.ice.gov/removal-statistics/.

14. See Orrenius and Zavodny (2010) for a proposal of comprehensive immigration reform.

15. The State Department Visa Bulletin publishes the availability of immigrant numbers by priority date and, if categories are oversubscribed for certain countries, by country of chargeability. See http://www.travel.state.gov/visa/bulletin/bulletin_5630.html.

16. Although Mexicans still use relatively few TN visas, their growth in the last

few years could be reflective of highly educated Mexicans fleeing the violence surrounding the government's war on drug cartels.

17. See Orrenius and Zavodny (2010) for a discussion of the benefits and costs of setting up an immigrant visa auction for employers.

References

Angelucci, Manuela. 2012. "US Border Enforcement and the Net Flow of Mexican Illegal Migration." *Economic Development and Cultural Change* 60(2):311–357.

Bohn, Sarah, and Magnus Lofstrom. 2013. "Employment Effects of State Legislation." In *Immigration, Poverty, and Socioeconomic Inequality*, edited by David Card and Stephen Raphael, 282–314. New York: Russell Sage Foundation.

Borjas, George J. 2003. "The Labor Demand Curve *Is* Downward Sloping: Reexamining the Impact of Immigration on the Labor Market." *Quarterly Journal of Economics* 118(4):1335–1374.

Cadena, Brian C., and Brian K. Kovak. 2013. "Immigrants Equilibrate Local Labor Markets: Evidence from the Great Recession." NBER Working Paper No. 19272.

Camarota, Steven. 2001. *Immigration from Mexico: Assessing the Impact on the United States*. Washington, DC: Center for Immigration Studies.

Card, David. 2001. "Immigrant Inflows, Native Outflows, and the Local Labor Market Impacts of Higher Immigration." *Journal of Labor Economics* 19(1): 22–64.

Card, David, and John E. DiNardo. 2002. "Skill-Biased Technological Change and Rising Wage Inequality: Some Problems and Puzzles." *Journal of Labor Economics* 20(4):733–783.

Cave, Damien. 2011. "Better Lives for Mexicans Cut Allure of Going North." *New York Times*, July 6.

Clemens, Michael, Claudio Montenegro, and Lant Pritchett. 2008. "The Place Premium: Wage Differences for Identical Workers across the US Border." Working Paper no. 148, Center for Global Development. Retrieved September 29, 2014, from www.cgdev.org/content/publications/detail/16352.

Congressional Budget Office. 2007. "The Impact of Unauthorized Immigrants on the Budgets of State and Local Governments." Washington, DC: Congressional Budget Office.

Cortés, Patricia, and José Tessada. 2011. "Low-Skilled Immigration and the Labor Supply of Highly Skilled Women." *American Economic Journal: Applied Economics* 3(3):88–123.

DiNardo, John, Nicole M. Fortin, and Thomas Lemieux. 1996. "Labor Market Institutions and the Distribution of Wages, 1973–1992: A Semiparametric Approach." *Econometrica* 64(5):1001–1044.

Donato, Katharine M. 1993. "Current Trends and Patterns of Female Migration: Evidence from Mexico." *International Migration Review* 27(4):748–771.

Escobar Latapí, Agustín, Lindsay Lowell, and Susan Martin. 2013. *Binational Dialogue on Mexican Migrants in the US and in Mexico*. Centro de Investigaciones y Estudios Superiores en Antropología Social. Retrieved March 23, 2015, from

http://www.ciesas.edu.mx/PDFS/Binational%20Dialogue%20Final%20Report
%20-%20April%2026.pdf.

Fussell, Elizabeth. 2009. "Hurricane Chasers in New Orleans: Latino Immigrants
as a Source of a Rapid Response Labor Force." *Hispanic Journal of Behavioral Science* 31(3):375–394.

Hanson, Gordon H., and Craig McIntosh. 2010. "The Great Mexican Emigration."
Review of Economics and Statistics 92(4):798–810.

Hanson, Gordon H., and Antonio Spilimbergo. 1999. "Illegal Immigration, Border Enforcement, and Relative Wages: Evidence from Apprehensions at the US-
Mexico Border." *American Economic Review* 89(5):1337–1357.

Khatiwada, Ishwar, Joseph McLaughlin, Andrew Sum, and Sheila Palma. 2007.
"The Fiscal Consequences of Adult Educational Attainment." Paper presented
at the National Commission on Adult Literacy.

Lopez, Mark Hugo, Paul Taylor, Cary Funk, and Ana Gonzalez-Barrera. 2013.
"On Immigration Policy, Deportation Relief Seen as More Important than Citizenship: A Survey of Hispanics and Asian Americans." Washington, DC: Pew
Hispanic Center.

Massey, Douglas S. 1990. "Social Structure, Household Strategies, and the Cumulative Causation of Migration." *Population Index* 56(1):3–26.

Massey, Douglas S., Jorge Durand, and Nolan Malone. 2002. *Beyond Smoke and
Mirrors: Mexican Immigration in an Era of Economic Integration.* Washington,
DC: Russell Sage Foundation.

Massey, Douglas S., and Kristin E. Espinosa. 1997. "What's Driving Mexico-US
Migration? A Theoretical, Empirical, and Policy Analysis." *American Journal of
Sociology* 102(4):939–999.

Napolitano, Janet. 2012. *Exercising Prosecutorial Discretion with Respect to Individuals Who Came to the United States as Children.* Memorandum. Washington, DC:
US Department of Homeland Security. Retrieved April 10, 2015, from http://
www.dhs.gov/xlibrary/assets/s1-exercising-prosecutorial-discretion-individuals
-who-came-to-us-as-children.pdf.

Office of the Under Secretary of Defense, Personnel, and Readiness. 2010. *Population Representation in the Military Services.* Washington, DC: US Department
of Defense. Retrieved April 6, 2015, from http://prhome.defense.gov/portals/52
/Documents/POPREP/poprep2010/index.html.

Organization for Economic Cooperation and Development. 2010. *International Migration Outlook.* Retrieved September 29, 2014, from www.oecd.org/
migration/imo.

Orrenius, Pia M., and Madeline Zavodny. 2005. "Self-Selection among Undocumented Immigrants from Mexico." *Journal of Development Economics* 78(1):
215–240.

———. 2007. "Does Immigration Affect Wages? A Look at Occupation-Level Evidence." *Labour Economics* 14(5):757–773.

———. 2010. *Beside the Golden Door: US Immigration Reform in a New Era of Globalization.* Washington, DC: American Enterprise Institute Press.

———. 2011. *From Brawn to Brains: How Immigration Works for America.* Federal Reserve Bank of Dallas 2010 Annual Report. Dallas, TX: Federal Reserve
Bank of Dallas.

————. 2015. "The Impact of E-Verify Mandates on Labor Market Outcomes." *Southern Economic Journal* 81(4):947–959.

Ottaviano, Gianmarco I. P., and Giovanni Peri. 2012. "Rethinking the Effects of Immigration on Wages." *Journal of the European Economic Association* 10(1): 152–197.

Passel, Jeffrey S., D'Vera Cohn, and Ana Gonzalez-Barrera. 2012. *Net Migration from Mexico Falls to Zero—and Perhaps Less.* Washington, DC: Pew Hispanic Center. Retrieved September 20, 2014, from http://www.pewhispanic.org/files /2012/04/Mexican-migrants-report_final.pdf.

————. 2013. *Population Decline of Unauthorized Immigrants Stalls, May Have Reversed.* Washington, DC: Pew Hispanic Center. Retrieved September 20, 2014, from http://www.pewhispanic.org/files/2013/09/Unauthorized-Sept-2013-FI NAL.pdf.

Pew Hispanic Center. 2009. "Mexican Immigrants in the United States, 2008." Washington, DC: Pew Hispanic Center. Retrieved September 20, 2014, from http://pewhispanic.org/files/factsheets/47.pdf.

Reyes, Belinda I. 2004. "US Immigration Policy and the Duration of Undocumented Trips." In *Crossing the Border: Research from the Mexican Migration Project*, edited by J. Durand and D. S. Massey, 299–320. New York: Russell Sage Foundation.

Smith, James P., and Barry Edmonston, eds. 1997. *The New Americans: Economic, Demographic, and Fiscal Effects of Immigration.* Washington, DC: National Academy Press.

Stark, Oded, and David E. Bloom. 1985. "The New Economics of Labor Migration." *American Economic Review* 75(2):173–178.

US Department of Defense. 2014. "Military Accessions Vital to National Interest (MAVNI) Program Eligibility." Washington, DC: US Department of Defense. Retrieved April, 6, 2015, from http://www.defense.gov/news/MAVNI -Fact-Sheet.pdf.

CHAPTER 3

Mexican Migration Dynamics: An Uncertain Future

JORGE DURAND

When we begin to think about Mexican migration dynamics, we see that Mexico is situated at a very unique geopolitical crossroad. Historically, Mexico is part of Mesoamerica and what used to be the Spanish colonial system and is thus linked with Latin America. At the same time, due to its geographic location and historic ties with the United States, Mexico is part of North America. In economic and commercial terms, Mexico is a partner with the United States and Canada in the North American Free Trade Agreement (NAFTA), which in 2015 constituted the largest trade bloc in the world (Office of the United States Trade Representative, n.d.). However, concerning labor mobility, relations become more complex. Mexicans are required to have a visa to enter the United States and Canada, despite Mexico's relationship as a major trading partner with these countries. In contrast, Mexicans do not need a visa to travel to Latin America. Yet Mexico requires visas for some Latin Americans entering Mexican territory, and Mexico struggles with large numbers of migrants from Central America crossing the Mexican southern border without authorization.

Mexico is a country of origin, transit, destination, and return of migrants. Due to its proximity to the United States and large wage differentials between the two countries, Mexico has become the main source of cheap labor for the North American labor market. Besides sharing a fluid border with the United States, Mexico has a young population that is not fully integrated into the Mexican labor market and logically opts to migrate. In addition, Mexico experiences a large influx of young migrants from Central America in transit to the United States.

Old patterns of migration from Mexico involved sojourns to work in US agricultural jobs, service areas, and construction industries and then return to communities of origin. These patterns have resulted, over a period of more than a century, in a very complex system of social, cultural, and family ties between both countries that interact with political and economic factors to generate migration flows. This migration tradition, which is common among large portions of the Mexican population, is complemented by an explicit US migration policy that uses Mexicans as the main reserve of available and disposable manpower.

Migratory flows are not endless, and Spain, Italy, and Ireland, among other countries, provide tangible proof of this fact. Even in the case of Mexico, one of the main migrant-sending countries in the world, declining emigration is a growing possibility. At least two structural factors are required for migratory flows to decrease or end: a marked decline in birthrates and several decades of sustained economic growth. The first condition already exists in Mexico, and the second is in process despite moderate rates of economic growth in the last two decades and recurring financial instability.

Mexican emigration to the United States has decreased every year since 2004 (Passel, Cohn, and Gonzalez-Barrera 2012), which is without doubt a reality that must be analyzed and explained. It is necessary to determine if the decline in the number of immigrants from Mexico is the result of a normal pattern in migratory flows, which usually reach a peak and start falling—a phenomenon sometimes referred to as a "migration hump"—or is a temporary consequence of the US financial crisis.

Migration Dynamics

The number of undocumented Mexicans in the United States reached its highest point in 2007, when the Pew Hispanic Center estimated that 6.9 million unauthorized Mexican immigrants resided in the United States (Passel and Cohn 2011, 2014; Warren and Warren 2013). Passel and Cohn (2014) noted a decline in the number of unauthorized Mexican migrants from 2007 to 2012, with 6.9 million undocumented migrants in the United States in 2007 and 5.9 million in 2012, a decrease of around 1 million irregular Mexican migrants in five years.

Several factors have contributed to the decline in the number of unauthorized Mexican migrants residing in the United States (figure 3.1). First, outgoing flows from Mexico have diminished dramatically. Second, systematic deportations at the border and in the interior of the United States have continued. Finally, the increase in recent years in the availability of

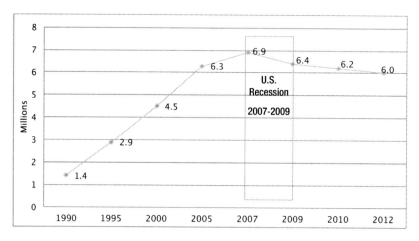

Figure 3.1. Estimates of unauthorized immigrant population from Mexico in the United States, 1990–2012. *Source*: Derived from Pew Research Center estimates based on residual methodology applied to March Supplements to the Current Population Survey for 1995–2004 and 2012 and to the American Community Survey for 2005–2011. Estimates for 1990 from Warren and Warren (2013) (Passel et al. 2013, 15).

different types of visas for Mexicans has contributed to the decrease in the number of undocumented Mexican immigrants. The previously prevailing guideline of automatically denying US visas based on economic criteria has been modified, thus dramatically impacting the likelihood of being granted a visa. According to a Mexican Migration Project model developed to estimate the rate of access to visas, in 1999 the rate of access for Mexicans was 0.024, while ten years later, during a full-blown economic crisis, it was 0.173.[1] H-2A and H-2B visas for agriculture and service workers, respectively, saw the greatest increases. In 2000, the United States recorded a total number of 84,754 nonimmigrant admissions with H-2A and H-2B visas. In 2012 the number of nonimmigrant admissions under these categories increased to 183,860 with H-2A and 82,921 with H-2B visas, and in 2013 to 204,577 admissions with H-2A and 104,993 with H-2B visas (US Department of Homeland Security 2010, 2013a; Foreman and Monger 2014).[2]

Visa policies implemented to manage migratory flows reflect the position of the US government on opening or closing the door to migrants at certain points in time. These visa-granting guidelines interact with structural factors, such as demographic and economic trends, and complementary factors, such as migratory, labor, and political issues, to determine migration patterns and intensity.

Structural Factors: Economic and Demographic Trends

Demographic trends are key in determining the volume of migration flows. In Thomas Robert Malthus's terms, Mexico experienced geometric population growth for over a quarter of a century (Malthus [1798] 1998). From 1950 to 1975 the population of Mexico grew from 27.7 to 60.7 million (United Nations 2007). This population boom is still impacting Mexico's demographic structure and generated what has been described as a "demographic bonus,"[3] that is, a population distribution in which the proportion of people of working age is larger than that of individuals of nonworking age (children and the elderly).

During the period of explosive population growth, various types of migration helped relieve the social and economic pressures generated by the rapid increase in the number of Mexican citizens. Paradoxically, this era coincided with a phase of high economic growth, known as the Mexican Miracle (1940–1970), during which Mexico consolidated both an agrarian reform in the rural sector and the government's resolution to use agricultural technology to improve and modernize the use of land, referred to as the "green revolution" (Hewitt de Alcántara 1976). Simultaneously, an economic model of import substitution[4] was successfully implemented (Alba 1978) in a context of big government, one-party rule, and state ownership of the main industries: electricity, oil, and communications, among others (Arias 1990).

Job availability in Mexican urban areas as a result of economic expansion, combined with domestic and international migration, relieved social pressures generated by the steep increase in population. Population growth in Mexico reached its highest point in 1965, with an average fertility rate of 6.9 children per woman. As a point of comparison, in the United States during the peak of the baby boom, in 1955, the US fertility rate was 3.7 children per woman, while in Mexico in that same year it was 6.8 children per woman (United Nations 2007).

Mexico's economic growth helped mitigate the challenges posed by the rapid increase in population. However, economic growth also generated population redistribution from rural areas toward the cities, which in many cases occurred in a chaotic and disorderly manner. By the late eighties, Mexico City had become a megalopolis and the most populated city in the world. The Mexican capital functioned as a magnet for rural-urban migration from the adjacent states in the central and southern regions of the country, areas with a significant indigenous population (Bataillon 1986; Bataillon and Panabiére 1988). The city of Guadalajara, a regional commercial and service center of attraction for neighboring states in the west, reached one million inhabitants at the end of the 1960s. The rate of urban growth was so high during the 1960s that the population in Guadalajara doubled (Rivière d'Arc 1973; Arias 1985). Monterrey served as a third population magnet. The city grew at a fast pace and became industrialized, attracting people from the northeastern region of Mexico (Balan, Browning, and Jelin 1973). Finally, the cancelation of the Bracero Program[5] in the mid-sixties unleashed the growth of border cities, especially Tijuana, Ciudad Juárez, and Nuevo Laredo. In addition, the traditionally uninhabited border region received migrants from all over the country who chaotically thronged to those areas to satisfy the demand for manual labor required by the *maquiladoras*, the new economic model of export assembly plants located on the Mexican side of the US-Mexico border (Travis 1985).

One last external factor that interacted with the internal restructuring of settlement patterns in Mexico to determine Mexico-US migration flows was the demand in the United States for workers from Mexico: first, for the war economy; later, for agricultural development; and finally, for the industry and service sectors. The US Bracero Program absorbed the surplus of rural population in the western region of Mexico, particularly in the states of Jalisco, Michoacán, Guanajuato, Zacatecas, San Luis Potosí, and Durango, which have historically been migration-sending regions (Durand and Massey 2003). This migration generated by the relentless demand for labor in the United States continued until recently.

Four Challenges

From the late 1970s to the present, Mexico has had to deal with four major challenges: recurring economic crises, a population explosion, internal migration, and irregular international migration. Regarding the first challenge, Mexico has not been able to resume the pattern of sustained growth the country experienced during the 1950s and 1960s. Since the devaluation crisis of 1976, when the value of the Mexican peso against the US dollar dropped by 60 percent, financial instability has been recurring.[6] In general, the Mexican economy has grown at an average rate of 2.3 percent in the last two decades (1993–2014) and has shown marked ups and downs as a result of external debt; instances of internal economic mismanagement, such as the so-called December mistake[7] of 1994; and a heavy dependence on the condition of the US economy. As long as there is no sustained economic growth in Mexico, expulsion factors will continue to operate and to apply pressure on migratory flows.

A second challenge for Mexico was to bring the untenable rate of population growth under control. The country has fully embraced the process of demographic transition and is very close to reaching the replacement point, where net population growth is at or very near zero. However, corrective actions were not implemented until the peak of the population boom, when the problem was already severe. The General Population Law of 1974 sought to limit population growth and regulate immigration and emigration. This was to be accomplished with the implementation of several initiatives outlined in the 1974 law: family planning programs through educational and public health services (Article 2); public policies to reduce mortality rates (Article 3); limiting immigration by foreigners to Mexico to those deemed essential to the country (Article 7); and restricting emigration of Mexican citizens if this benefited the national interest (Article 8).

Thirty-five years after the implementation of the General Population Law, Mexico succeeded in achieving its goals of reducing birth and mortality rates. The global fertility rate for Mexico dropped from 6.5 children per woman in 1975 to 2.2 in 2010. Along the same lines, infant mortality decreased from 69 per thousand in 1975 to 21 per thousand in 2005, and overall life expectancy improved from 62.1 years in 1975 to 75 in 2010 (United Nations 2007).

By and large, public policies enacted by the Mexican government have been effective in controlling birth rates and mortality factors but have been largely inefficient in regulating immigration and emigration. This, however, is common in democratic political settings. Only in dictatorial contexts has immigration or emigration been efficiently controlled through repressive methods.

In effect, while all efforts were directed toward reducing the rate of population growth, internal migration problems were completely neglected. The Mexican government responded to the demands for urban land and to the requests for public services (water, light, drainage, and pavement) through an exchange of services for political support (*clientelismo*), at a pace dictated by available resources and social pressure, or lack of them (Alonso 1980). In the end, it was the economic crisis that somehow slowed the rural-to-urban exodus.

Consistent with the goals of the General Population Law, Mexico closed its doors to legal migrants from Central America and other countries, limiting immigration, as the law expressly states, to categories of migrants deemed desirable. The Mexican government raised the level of difficulty in the immigration and naturalization processes for the few who wanted to stay and settle in the country. There was no reason to open the door to immigrants when Mexico's main problem was precisely excessive population growth. According to Pablo Yankelevich (2011), in postrevolutionary Mexico, migration policy was constructed in terms of "desirable and non-desirable" migrants, and Article 33 of the Mexican Constitution was implemented to exercise strict control over the foreign-born population. Article 33 states that the Mexican federal government has the exclusive power, without the need of preceding legal action, to force any foreigner to leave the country immediately if the government deems that person's presence in Mexico undesirable.

Although the Mexican government officially portrays the country as open to immigration and generous in granting refuge, the closed-door policy can easily be corroborated with data from the census. The 2010 Mexican census reports that only 961,121 foreigners, or 0.86 percent of the total population, lived permanently in Mexico. Furthermore, a portion of these foreigners, difficult to quantify statistically, comprises US-born children of Mexican nationals, who are counted in the Mexican census as citizens of the United States. Mexico's emigration-to-immigration ratio is 10 to 1.

Even though a strict policy of immigration control was implemented in Mexico, in regard to emigration the government followed the general principle stated in Article 8 of the General Population Law, which says that intervention is justified only "when the national interest requires it." This clause can be interpreted in several ways, but it mainly refers to a possible shortage of manpower in the country, something that has not happened so far.

Despite population relocation from rural to urban areas in Mexico, demographic pressure continued to build, especially after the 1970s, when the economic crisis reached the rural sector and land distribution (agrarian reform) ceased to be a solution for the new generations of small-scale farmers or campesinos (Arias 2009). With these developments, internal migration reached a limit and changed its orientation toward the United States. Mexican cities that had historically been recipients of domestic migrants became sending areas. International migration, which until the 1970s had been primarily a regional occurrence from western Mexico, became a national phenomenon encompassing all Mexican states and a vast majority of municipalities (Durand and Massey 2003; Alba 2010).

The number of undocumented migrants leaving Mexico for the United States increased every year, as an insatiable US labor market easily absorbed them. In this context, the Mexican government had no alternative proposals to regulate unauthorized international migration except renewing the Bracero Program. Consequently, during this period Mexico's de facto policy on migration can be regarded as "the policy of no-policy," where Mexico's sole position was to do nothing and wait for the United States to make a move (García and Verea 1988; Durand 2005; Alba 2010).

The inclusion of new contingents of international migrants from the emerging sending regions of central and southern Mexico, who no longer found work in Mexico City, notably increased the number of migrants to the United States. The requirements of the US labor market and the absence of migration policies in Mexico were the main engines behind the migratory flow that fed on Mexico's population boom.

Immigration Reforms

Until 1986 the United States regarded Mexican migrants as workers, not as immigrants, categorizing them as "undocumented migrant workers." The Immigration Reform and Control Act (IRCA), signed into US law in 1986, gave legal status and a path to citizenship to 3.2 million undocumented migrants living in the United States, 2.3 million of whom were Mexicans. The new law radically transformed previous migratory patterns, leaving behind a phase of undocumented circular migration (Durand 1996) and introducing a new stage of settlement and permanent relocation.

The enactment of IRCA in 1986 resulted in the implementation of four main programs: an amnesty for workers who could prove continuous residence in the United States for the previous five years and who had paid taxes; a Special Agricultural Worker program to provide work visas for more seasonal agricultural workers; and two additional complementary measures—stricter border controls and sanctions on employers who hired undocumented immigrants. The first two programs worked very efficiently. In contrast, border control was not fully accomplished, and sanctions on employers who hired undocumented workers were not consistently enforced and lacked an effective and compulsory system of administration.

IRCA had several significant consequences, some of which were unanticipated. Among them were the disruption of circularity in migration patterns, legal and irregular family reunification, lengthening of migrant stays in the United States, and an increase in the number of unauthorized migrants settling permanently in the United States. As border controls hardened, the cost and risks of undocumented migration escalated, leading to longer migrant stays in the United States, more permanent settlement in the United States, and increased migration to new-destination, nonborder states (Massey, Durand, and Malone 2009).

Since 1993, the Mexico-US border has undergone a radical transformation. Until 1965 the border was essentially open. Over time the border became porous, with only a wire mesh barrier in some urban areas. In 1993, with the implementation of operations in El Paso and the San Diego corridor, the border began to be monitored, and finally—after September 11, 2001—the US-Mexico border became a walled and militarized boundary, a virtually impenetrable barrier.

Until September 11, 2001, it was relatively easy, once across the border, to live and work in the United States undisturbed. After the terrorist attacks, however, an explicit official anti-immigrant campaign was unleashed. Immigration was directly linked with national security. Migrants were perceived as criminals and every path to legalization was closed for the 11.2 million undocumented immigrants living in the United States, 52 percent—or 5.9 million—of whom were Mexican (Passel and Cohn 2014).

A political campaign against undocumented migrants emerged parallel to the boost in border security. Right-wing US politicians used irregular immigrants as scapegoats. During Pete Wilson's campaign for governor of the state of California in 1994, for example, the SOS (Save Our State) initiative was launched. It later became Proposition 187, which sought to limit the access of "illegal" migrants in California to education, health, and social services. This proposal was approved by popular vote but was deemed unconstitutional after legislative review, given that migration matters fall under federal jurisdiction. Two years later, during President Bill Clinton's administration, the US Congress approved the 1996 Illegal Immigration Reform and Immigrant Responsibility Act (IIRIRA). This legislation enabled states to act on some issues related to the management of social services for the general population, including immigrants. The prevailing hostile environment triggered a series of state laws that found backing in antiterrorism policy and unleashed persecution of undocumented immigrants.

Arizona's SB 1070 and many other replicas, including the Alabama Act of 2011 (HB56), created a climate of terror and persecution for migrants and their families. Furthermore, provision 287(g), added to the Immigration and Nationality Act by IIRIRA in 1996, gave state and local law-enforcement agents the authority to perform the functions of federal immigration agents (Immigration Policy Center 2012). Provision 287(g) allows state and local agents to question individuals about their immigration status and enables them to detain anyone suspected of being an undocumented migrant until federal authorities arrive. This applies even to people who are stopped for misdemeanors or transit violations.

In 2012, the Department of Homeland Security had 287(g) agreements with fifty-seven local and state governments (Immigration Policy Center 2012). Revisions to the 287(g) Memorandum of Agreement (MOA) in 2009 and in 2013 resulted in increased supervision and training of local agents designated as immigration officers (US Immigration and Customs Enforcement 2013). Under 287(g) state and local law-enforcement entities may enter into an MOA with DHS "in order to receive delegated authority for immigration enforcement within their jurisdiction" (US Immigration and Customs Enforcement 2014, 1). As of October 2015 there were a total of thirty-two law-enforcement agencies in sixteen states with signed MOAs with Immigration and Customs Enforcement (US Immigration and Customs Enforcement 2015).

The electronic verification of employment eligibility (Employment Eligibility Verification Program or E-Verify) is one more component of the repressive US immigration policy. The purpose of this program is to make it practically impossible for undocumented migrants to work in the United States. The implementation of employment verification requirements has been a long and contradictory process. In 1952 the US government attempted to put into practice legal measures to punish employers who hired illegal immigrants. However, in response to this effort the so-called Texas Provision was issued, criminalizing migrants and exempting employers. In 1986, IRCA established penalties for employers who knowingly hired undocumented immigrants, but, in practice, it was hard to penalize employers given that companies had no way to verify the authenticity of the documents presented to them by those seeking work. Ten years later, in 1997, a pilot program was established for the verification of documents. In time it evolved into E-Verify, which encouraged employers, on a voluntary basis, to confirm the work eligibility of their potential employees. Recently, there has been a push to make the program mandatory in every state, even for workers in the agricultural sector, who had been previously excluded. The objective of E-Verify is not limited to sanctioning employers, but mainly aims at curtailing the likelihood of an undocumented migrant obtaining employment. Since 2011, various immigration reform proposals have included E-Verify. The Border Security, Economic Opportunity and Immigration Modernization Act, approved in the US Senate in 2013, proposed a gradual implementation of E-Verify.

Conclusion

US immigration policies aimed at curbing undocumented migration are starting to show results. It took twenty years, from 1987 to 2007, but finally irregular migratory flows have begun to diminish (Passel and Cohn 2011). The deterrence policy of increasing the cost and risk of crossing the border without legal documents has been effective. A smuggler's charge for helping an undocumented person cross the border has jumped to the equivalent of one thousand days of minimum wage in Mexico (around $5,000 US), which has severely constrained the prospect of emigrating for many Mexicans.

Although the number of Mexican workers in the United States sending money back to Mexico has fluctuated over time, the 2008 US economic crisis severely impacted the volume of remittances that established Mexican migrants were able to send home to finance new undocumented crossings. Migrants' working hours were significantly reduced, wages were lowered, and the threat of unemployment loomed constantly. Under these conditions, migrants were not in a position to help their relatives finance an adventure that, in addition to being expensive, could be fatal. Thus, the US economic crisis severely disturbed the flow of systemic remittances that had for a long time sustained migration from Mexico to the United States.

The increased risk of crossing the US-Mexico border through the desert has further complicated the journey north. In the early 1990s, 75 percent of migrants crossed the border through the Tijuana–San Diego corridor, but tighter border control diverted the routes to the dangerous Sonora and Altar Deserts. The risk of death has become an important deterrent for migrants and their families. Additionally, violence along the border and in the interior of Mexico has made the trip to the United States even more perilous. The mafia and other organized criminal groups have a reputation for blackmailing and murdering migrants from Mexico, Central America, and other countries.

But the risk extends far beyond the difficulties of crossing the border. Under present circumstances, the investment required to reach the United States is no longer as safe as it used to be. In the past, once across the border an undocumented migrant was almost certain of finding a job and working in the United States without serious risk of being deported. Since 2001, due to increased persecution and an anti-immigrant climate in the United States, the investment of a very considerable sum of money to finance unauthorized migration is risky. In sum, the cost-benefit ratio of undocumented migration has changed substantially.

Structural factors have also come into play. Smaller families in Mexico, with an average of two children, are no longer in imperative need of sending family members to the United States to diversify and increase their income, as was the case with large families in the past. In spite of Mexico's serious economic problems, including a high degree of inequality and rampant underemployment and unemployment, the gross domestic product per capita in 2010 was $13,900 (US dollars). This amount is similar to what a migrant working full-time in the United States at minimum wage ($7.50 per hour) could earn. For many Mexicans the wage differential between Mexico and the United States has decreased in the last decade. This can be explained in part as a result of the erosion of the purchasing power of the minimum wage in the United States and the great difference in the cost of living in the two countries.

Although all previously mentioned variables, in particular the downturn in the US economy, have come into play in determining the volume of Mexico-US migration, the factor that has contributed the most to the short- and long-term reduction in the flow of undocumented migrants is the persecutory immigration climate in the United States. The border has been virtually sealed. Net migration from Mexico is almost zero as those who are deported offset the few migrants who succeed in crossing the US-Mexico border. Nonetheless, if the US economy continues to improve and the demand for labor picks up, the pressure to open the door to the migrant workers required by the economy will build.

The decline in Mexican migration from 2007 to 2014 is in part the result of normal patterns of migration, which reflect complex changing population, political, and economic conditions. Still, evidence clearly shows that the decline in the number of Mexican immigrants to the United States has also been impacted by repressive US immigration policies and militarization of the Mexico-US border.

This chapter has attempted to present the historical foundations and complexity of factors influencing migration from Mexico to the United States. It has illustrated how policies and economic conditions in both countries impact patterns of migration. It remains to be seen whether we are observing a temporary migration hump or whether the decline in Mexican migration is a long-term trend.

Notes

1. The Mexican Migration Project (http://mmp.opr.princeton.edu/), directed by Jorge Durand and Douglas Massey, calculates accessibility to US visas using the following expression: $TIA/(TIA + GIE)$, where TIA = total immigrants admitted and GIE = gross illegal entries.

Total immigrants admitted is the number of Mexicans granted lawful permanent resident status by broad class of admission and region and country of last residence per fiscal year. The number of gross illegal entries per year is calculated as follows: $A(1 - PA/PA)$, where A = apprehensions and PA = the probability of apprehension (see Massey and Singer 1995).

2. "Nonimmigrant admissions refer to the number of events (i.e., admissions to the United States) rather than to the number of individual nonimmigrants admitted" (Foreman and Monger 2014, 2). H-2A and H-2B visas are the class of admissions.

3. The term "demographic bonus" refers to a demographic and economic change as a result of the increase in the proportion of the working-age population in relation to the number of inactive or non-working-age population (infants and the elderly) (Hernández López, López Vega, and Velarde Villalobos 2013).

4. Import substitution industrialization is an economic policy implemented by underdeveloped countries aimed at generating economic growth and socioeconomic modernization. This method "consists of establishing domestic production facilities to manufacture goods which were formerly imported" (Baer 1972, 95).

5. The Bracero Program was an agreement between Mexico and the United States to allow Mexican laborers to work legally on a temporary basis in US agricultural jobs. The Bracero Program was enacted in 1942 and ended in 1964 (http://braceroarchive.org/about).

6. Percentage of devaluation found in tables and graphs by Aguirre Botello (2014).

7. The "December mistake" of 1994, otherwise known as the Mexican peso crisis, was a severe financial crisis resulting from the devaluing of the peso on December 20, 1994, in response to an impending liquidity crisis (Whitehead and Kravis 1997).

References

Aguirre Botello, Manuel. 2014. "Devaluación-inflación México-U.S.A. 1970–2014: Valuación mensual del peso mexicano." Retrieved October 22, 2014, from http://www.mexicomaxico.org/Voto/SobreVal02.htm.

Alba, Francisco. 1978. "Industrialización sustitutiva y migración internacional: El caso de México." *Foro Internacional* 18(3):464–479. Retrieved July 9, 2015, from http://www.jstor.org/stable/27754718.

———. 2010. "México: A Crucial Crossroads." *Migration Information Source.* Washington, DC: Migration Policy Institute. Retrieved November 20, 2014, from http://www.migrationpolicy.org/article/mexico-crucial-crossroads/.

Alonso, Jorge, ed. 1980. *Lucha urbana y acumulación de capital.* Mexico City: Ediciones de La Casa Chata.

Arias, Patricia. 1985. *Guadalajara la gran ciudad de la pequeña industria.* Zamora, Mexico: El Colegio de Michoacán.

———. 1990. *Industria y estado en la vida de México.* Zamora, Mexico: El Colegio de Michoacán.

———. 2009. *Del arraigo de la diáspora: Dilemas de la familia rural.* Mexico City: Estados Unidos Mexicanos, Cámara de Diputados, LX Legislatura, Consejo Editorial.

Baer, Werner. 1972. "Import Substitution and Industrialization in Latin America:

Experiences and Interpretations." *Latin American Research Review* 7(1):95–122. Retrieved October 22, 2014, from http://www.jstor.org/stable/2502457.

Balan, Jorge, Harley L. Browning, and Elizabeth Jelin. 1973. *Migración, estructura ocupacional y movilidad social: El caso Monterrey*. Mexico City: UNAM, Instituto de Investigaciones Sociales.

Bataillon, Claude. 1986. *Las regiones geográficas en México*. Mexico City: Siglo XXI Editores.

Bataillon, Claude, and Louis Panabiére. 1988. *México aujourd'hui: La plus grande ville du monde*. Paris: Publisud.

Border Security, Economic Opportunity, and Immigration Modernization Act, S.744, 113th Congress (2013).

Durand, Jorge. 1996. *Migrations mexicaines aux Etats-Unis*. Paris: CNRS Editions.

———. 2005. "Políticas emigratorias en un contexto de asimetría de poder: El caso mexicano, 1900–2003." In *Globalización, poderes y seguridad nacional*. Vol. 1, edited by A. Nassif and J. A. Sánchez, 105–131. Mexico City: H. Cámara de Diputados, LIX Legislatura, CIESAS, Miguel Ángel Porrúa.

Durand, Jorge, and Douglas S. Massey. 2003. *Clandestinos: Migración México Estados Unidos en los albores del siglo XXI*. Mexico City: Editorial Miguel Ángel Porrúa, Universidad de Zacatecas.

Foreman, Katie, and Randall Monger. 2014. *Nonimmigrant Admissions to the United States: 2013*. Washington, DC: US Department of Homeland Security. Retrieved November 17, 2014, from http://www.dhs.gov/sites/default/files /publications/ois_ni_fr_2013.pdf.

García, Manuel, and Mónica Verea. 1988. *México y Estados Unidos frente a la migración de indocumentados*. Mexico City: Miguel Ángel Porrúa.

Hernández López, María Felipa, Rafael López Vega, and Sergio I. Velarde Villalobos. 2013. "La situación demográfica en México: Panorama desde las proyecciones de población." Mexico City: Consejos Nacional de Población. Retrieved November 12, 2014, from http://www.conapo.gob.mx/en/CONAPO/La _situacion_demografica_en_Mexico_Panorama_desde_las_proyecciones_de _poblacion.

Hewitt de Alcántara, Cynthia. 1976. *La modernización de la agricultura mexicana 1940–1970*. Mexico City: Siglo XXI Editores.

Illegal Immigration Reform and Immigrant Responsibility Act of 1996, Public Law 104-208, 110 U.S. Statutes at Large 3009-546 (1996).

Immigration Policy Center. 2012. "The 287(g) Program: A Flawed and Obsolete Method of Immigration Enforcement." Washington, DC: American Immigration Council. Retrieved November 12, 2014, from http://www.immigration policy.org/just-facts/287g-program-flawed-and-obsolete-method-immigration -enforcement.

Malthus, Thomas. [1798] 1998. *An Essay on the Principle of Population, as it Affects the Future Improvements of Society with Remarks on the Speculations of Mr. Godwin, M. Condorcet, and Other Writers*. London: Electronic Scholarly Publishing Project. Retrieved October 22, 2014, from http://www.esp.org/books/malthus /population/malthus.pdf.

Massey, Douglas S., Jorge Durand, and Nolan J. Malone. 2009. *Detrás de la trama:*

Políticas migratorias entre México y Estados Unidos. Mexico City: H. Cámara de Diputados, LX Legislatura, Universidad de Zacatecas, Miguel Ángel Porrúa.

Massey, Douglas S., and Audrey Singer. 1995. "New Estimates of Undocumented Mexican Migration and the Probability of Apprehension." *Demography* 32(2): 203–213.

Office of the United States Trade Representative. n.d. "North American Trade Agreement (NAFTA)." Washington, DC: Office of the President Executive. Retrieved November 11, 2014, from http://www.ustr.gov/trade-agreements/free -trade-agreements/north-american-free-trade-agreement-nafta.

Passel, Jeffrey S., and D'Vera Cohn. 2011. *Unauthorized Immigrant Population: National and State Trends, 2010.* Washington, DC: Pew Hispanic Center. Retrieved February 1, 2011, from http://www.pewhispanic.org/2011/02/01 /unauthorized-immigrant-population-brnational-and-state-trends-2010/.

Passel, Jeffrey S., and D'Vera Cohn. 2014. *Unauthorized Immigrant Totals Rise in 7 States, Fall in 14: Decline in Those From Mexico Fuels Most State Decreases.* Washington, DC: Pew Research Center's Hispanic Trends Project. Retrieved July 17, 2015, from http://www.pewhispanic.org/2014/11/18/unauthorized -immigrant-totals-rise-in-7-states-fall-in-14/.

Passel, Jeffrey S., D'Vera Cohn, and Ana Gonzalez-Barrera. 2012. *Net Migration from Mexico Falls to Zero—and Perhaps Less.* Washington, DC: Pew Research Center. Retrieved October 19, 2014, from http://www.pewhispanic.org /2012/04/23/net-migration-from-mexico-falls-to-zero-and-perhaps-less/.

———. 2013. *Population Decline of Unauthorized Immigrants Stalls, May Have Reversed.* Washington, DC: Pew Hispanic Center. Retrieved October 19, 2014, from http://www.pewhispanic.org/files/2013/09/Unauthorized-Sept-2013-FI NAL.pdf.

Rivière d'Arc, Hèléne. 1973. *Guadalajara y su región.* Mexico City: SepSetentas.

Travis, Roland. 1985. *Industrie et politique à la frontière Mexique-U.S.A.: Le cas de Nuevo Laredo, 1966–1984.* Paris: Editions du CNRS.

United Nations. Department of Economic and Social Affairs. 2007. *World Population Prospects: The 2006 Revision Highlights.* Retrieved September 20, 2014, from http://www.un.org/esa/population/publications/wpp2006/WPP2006_High lights_rev.pdf.

US Department of Homeland Security. Office of Immigration Statistics. 2010. *Yearbook of Immigration Statistics: 2009.* Washington, DC: US Department of Homeland Security.

———. Office of Immigration Statistics. 2013a. *Yearbook of Immigration Statistics: 2012.* Washington, DC: US Department of Homeland Security.

US Immigration and Customs Enforcement. 2013. "Updated Facts on ICE's 287(g) Program." Washington, DC: US Department of Homeland Security. Retrieved November 11, 2014, from https://www.ice.gov/factsheets/287g-reform.

———. 2015. "Delegation of Immigration Authority Section 287(g) Immigration and Nationality Act." Washington, DC: US Department of Homeland Security. Retrieved October 19, 2015, from https://www.ice.gov/factsheets/287g.

Warren, Robert, and John Robert Warren. 2013. "Unauthorized Immigration to the United States: Annual Estimates and Components of Change, by State, 1990 to 2010." *International Migration Review* 47(2):296–329.

Whitehead, John C., and Marie-Josee Kravis. 1997. "Lessons of the Mexican Peso Crisis." Washington, DC: Council on Foreign Relations. Retrieved October 22, 2014, from http://www.cfr.org/financial-crises/lessons-mexican-peso-crisis /p132.

Yankelevich, Pablo. 2011. *Deseables o inconvenientes: Las fronteras de la extranjería en el México posrevolucionario.* Mexico City: Madrid, Bonilla Artigas Editores.

CHAPTER 4

Public Insecurity and International Emigration in Northern Mexico: Analysis at a Municipal Level

LILIANA MEZA GONZÁLEZ AND MICHAEL FEIL

The main reasons behind most Mexican migration to the United States are employment and family reunification. During the last six or seven years, however, the increase in public insecurity may have promoted flows of emigration from Mexico that differ greatly from migration flows in previous years and decades. This new kind of emigration may be taking place while total flows are decreasing, which may appear paradoxical. We argue that while the economic downturn in the United States is in large part responsible for the drop in total migration flows, insecurity is now an incipient but significant force behind the movement of people—especially in those areas experiencing conflict.

People fleeing Mexico for security reasons is a recent phenomenon that needs better understanding. Economics are probably still the main force behind population movements from Mexico to the United States, but this chapter identifies certain correlations between insecurity and emigration, at least in the northern states of Mexico, that merit further study.

In different countries, environments of insecurity have triggered large flows of people moving to safer places (e.g., Haiti 1960s, Chile 1973–1995, Uruguay 1973–1976, and Argentina 1976–1980). These movements for security reasons differ from economic migration. Migrations as a result of insecurity are more prevalent among people with higher socioeconomic status who have the resources to migrate internationally. In recent years, Mexican border states have been greatly impacted by organized crime. According to Mexican federal law, when three or more persons conspire to commit acts that are considered criminal on a permanent or a persistent basis, they are considered de facto members of organized crime.[1] The crimes listed include terrorism, drug trafficking, currency counterfeiting, commercial activity funded with illicit resources, trafficking in arms, trafficking undocumented migrants, trafficking organs, corruption of minors, kidnapping, and vehicle theft. Some of these crimes (e.g., terrorism and drug trafficking) are exclusively handled at the federal level, while others fall under both federal and state regulation, which frequently creates conflicts over jurisdiction.

The objective of this chapter is to show that public insecurity is influencing the international migration decisions of people in the northern states of Mexico. In particular, our purpose is to present evidence regarding the impact of public insecurity (represented by deaths related to organized crime) on migration intensity in northern Mexican municipalities. Our results confirm existing research that suggests that social networks within the United States are a main factor encouraging migration. This is supported in our results by the proportion of dwellings in border municipalities that send migrants to the United States. Nevertheless, our work finds that insecurity is a small, albeit significant, force promoting migration along the Mexico-US border. Our findings also indicate that public insecurity deters circular migration. Despite the economic crisis in the United States and the lack of available jobs, insecurity in communities of origin is discouraging Mexican return migration.

This chapter is organized as follows: The first section presents data that illustrate how population has been displaced in Mexico and how insecurity is affecting the northern region of the country. A theoretical framework and a literature review place the analysis in context in the second section. We then present the data we analyzed, statistical models, our conclusions, and policy recommendations.

Insecurity in Northern Mexico

Emigration from Mexico to the United States has been historically determined by economic and social factors (e.g., social mobility and family reunification) in the context of a relatively open and porous border. These factors continue to be relevant to the decision to emigrate. Along with economic and social forces, there is a perception that public insecurity may be encouraging emigration from areas of conflict. Studies of the Colombian conflict show that there is a segment of the population that, under certain conditions, makes a preventative decision to migrate in response to threats of violence (Pedersen 2002). In Mexico, it appears that the war against organized crime, which was openly recognized by the federal government in 2007, has fostered population displacements mainly in the northern part of the country. The displacements may include movements to other areas of Mexico or to the United States. Data from the Mexican National Survey of Occupa-

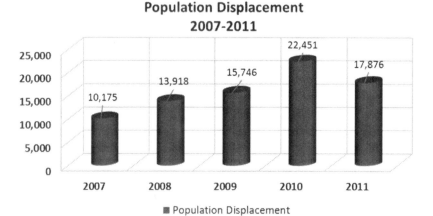

Figure 4.1. People who reported moving internally or outside the country due to public insecurity in Mexico (2007–2011). *Source*: Data from the National Institute of Statistics and Geography (INEGI), National Survey of Occupation and Employment (ENOE), 2007–2011.

tion and Employment (figure 4.1) indicate an increasing trend in internal and international movements of people due to insecurity.

Although the exact number of Mexicans fleeing their country for insecurity reasons is still unknown, data from the 2010 American Community Survey indicate that Mexican nationals who arrived in the US southern border states after 2005 are more affluent, more educated, younger, and more likely to be US citizens than Mexicans who arrived in the United States between 2000 and 2005.[2]

According to data from the Mexican Presidency, from December 1, 2006, to December 31, 2012, there were almost sixty thousand deaths related to organized crime in Mexico. It is generally accepted that most of these deaths were the result of confrontations among criminal organizations. However, the increase in homicides was not uniform across Mexico, and some states that were once considered the most insecure are now displaced by states in which rates of violent deaths are increasing. Data from the Mexican National Institute of Statistics and Geography (INEGI) show that nearly 84 percent of all homicides attributed to organized crime in 2010 occurred in just four of Mexico's thirty-two states (Chihuahua, Sinaloa, Guerrero, and Baja California), and that over 70 percent of such homicides occurred in 80 of the country's 2,455 municipalities (INEGI, n.d.).

Map 4.1 presents data on murders related to drug-trafficking organizations by state. The map shows that violence is highly concentrated along the

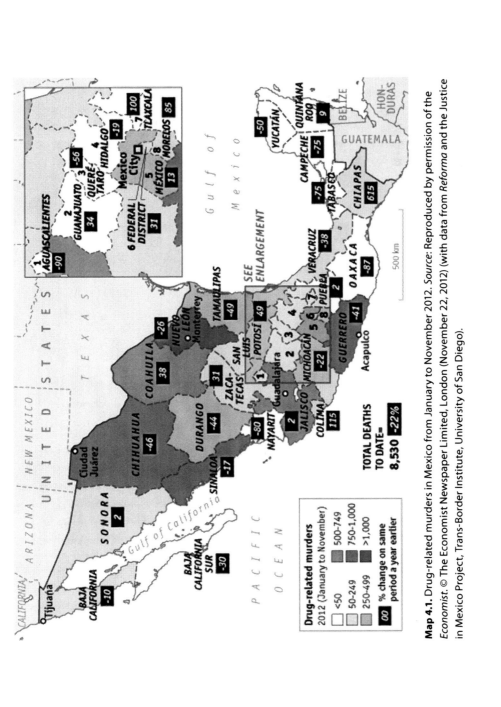

Map 4.1. Drug-related murders in Mexico from January to November 2012. *Source:* Reproduced by permission of the *Economist.* © The Economist Newspaper Limited, London (November 22, 2012) (with data from *Reforma* and the Justice in Mexico Project, Trans-Border Institute, University of San Diego).

Table 4.1. Homicides in Mexican border states, 2005–2010

Total homicides in border states, 2005–2010						
State	2005	2006	2007	2008	2009	2010
Baja California	441	465	369	1031	1530	1528
Coahuila	152	107	111	181	278	449
Chihuahua	570	648	518	2601	3671	6407
Nuevo León	150	168	279	241	343	951
Sonora	260	251	323	436	571	738
Tamaulipas	348	359	193	266	315	935

Border-state homicides as percentage of national total						
State	2005	2006	2007	2008	2009	2010
Baja California	4.44	4.45	4.16	7.36	7.73	5.93
Coahuila	1.53	1.02	1.25	1.29	1.4	1.74
Chihuahua	5.74	6.2	5.84	18.57	18.54	24.87
Nuevo León	1.51	1.61	3.15	1.72	1.73	3.69
Sonora	2.62	2.4	3.64	3.11	2.88	2.87
Tamaulipas	3.51	3.43	2.18	1.9	1.59	3.63

Source: Data from National Institute of Statistics and Geography (INEGI, n.d. Interactive Data Query [IDQ]).

northern border of the country, which is consistent with official information provided by the Mexican government. The four states with the most outstanding drug-related murders in 2011 were Chihuahua, Sinaloa, Guerrero, and Nuevo León, and the state with the largest increase in insecurity was, by far, Zacatecas. Table 4.1 shows the number of homicides in each of the six Mexican border states between 2005 and 2010 and the proportion of homicides that these numbers represent with respect to the total number of homicides in the country. Homicides in Chihuahua in 2010 represented roughly one-quarter of the total number of homicides in the country in that year.

According to Bailey (2010, 327), the actions of drug-trafficking organizations in Mexico are the most pressing symptom of a mix of forms of organized crime rooted in a robust informal economy and a culture marked by little confidence in the police-justice system. Assuming this is true, violence in Mexico cannot be considered a recent problem and will not be solved in the near future. In fact, elements of organized crime can be traced to at least the mid-1980s.

During the Calderón administration (2006–2012), the Mexican government developed a strategy to tackle organized crime in general and drug-trafficking organizations in particular. The strategy included multiple components and seemed to be internally coherent. Its main logic was to employ the armed forces, principally the army, to confront armed bands of criminals in selected areas to disrupt their activities and buy time to implement a long menu of institutional reforms. At some point, the armed forces were supposed to return to a secondary, backup role in police functions, and the reformed police-justice system would take the lead against organized criminal groups (Bailey 2010, 328).

Within this logic, the most important institutional reforms needed in Mexico to fight organized crime are reorganization of the Mexican police, reorientation of the justice system, and creation of an intelligence system—all with the backing of the three levels of government (municipal, state, and federal). These actions will certainly take time, which means that despite the judicial reform that was enacted in Mexico in 2008,[3] public insecurity may not decrease during President Peña Nieto's administration.

The position of the US government regarding public insecurity in Mexico has been to respond to the Mexican government's initiatives. For example, according to Bailey (2010, 328), in 2007 the executive branches in both countries followed Mexico's preferences in crafting the Mérida Initiative. It is generally assumed that as long as the Mexican government perseveres in the fight against organized crime, the US government will continue supporting federal and local punitive actions.

Theoretical Framework

Violence and socioeconomic deprivation can contribute to a general environment of insecurity, which in turn may foster emigration from conflict regions. However, it may also represent an opportunity for those who had existing migration "plans" (Icduygu, Romano, and Sirkeci 1999; Sirkeci 2006). During periods of war, migration networks are established as sizeable immigrant groups emerge in receiving communities. These networks (Massey 1990) may, indeed, serve as important facilitating factors for the potential emigration of more people from the conflict area. This is due, in part, to the perceptions of potential migrants that their family members and friends in the migration destination will be willing and able to assist them with challenges associated with immigration, such as finding housing, employment, and so on. As long as a conflict persists, there will be emigration of the most affected groups and of those with previous plans to emigrate, especially when migration networks exist.

Contemporary international migration is better understood as a complicated phenomenon involving different types of migrants, such as refugees, asylum seekers, family migrants, unauthorized migrants, migrant workers, and professionals. In most cases it is impossible to distinguish economic, political, or cultural reasons for migration, given that people often move with mixed and overlapping motivations. Environments of insecurity also interact with other factors to encourage international migration. Icduygu, Romano, and Sirkeci (1999) first formulated the concept of "environment of insecurity" to explain the Kurdish ethnic conflict in Turkey. Later, it was expanded to explain the interaction between international migration of Turkish Kurds and the ethnic conflict (Sirkeci 2006). The concept of environment of insecurity led to the formulation of "opportunity frameworks" of migration (Sirkeci 2006), another notion relevant for understanding international migration behavior.

An environment of insecurity has two primary components. The first relates to the material environment of insecurity, which is characterized by poverty, deprivation, and armed conflict. The second refers to the nonmaterial environment of insecurity, characterized by fear of persecution and discrimination (Sirkeci 2006). People exposed to an environment of insecurity have two options: experience the status quo or exit.

An environment of insecurity may improve the odds of migration for individuals already harboring migration plans who live in relatively secure areas near conflict zones. With the tightening of admission requirements in receiving countries, migration opportunities through legal or regular channels decrease. In contexts of restricted immigration, environments of insecurity may represent opportunity frameworks utilized by potential migrants, but not necessarily by those in greatest danger. For example, many Turks and Turkish Kurds claimed asylum in Germany despite coming from relatively secure areas of Turkey, such as the periphery of the major areas of conflict (Sirkeci 2006).

The case of Iraq is an example of international migration caused by an environment of insecurity. Colombia is another important example closer to the case analyzed here. The armed conflict over economic and political power in Colombia forced approximately 1.2 million people, the majority of them women and children, to leave their homes between 1985 and 1997 (Ibáñez and Vélez 2008).[4]

International human-rights law considers forced internal and international displacement a human-rights violation. Moreover, the consequences of displacement for the affected countries are severe. In receiving areas, it is common to experience increases in unemployment, a violent redistribution of land ownership, strong inefficiencies in resource allocation, and the effects of large and unplanned demographic inflows into cities and regions that receive the displaced. The Colombian government, the United Nations, the European Union, and many nongovernmental and religious organizations responded to this problem in Colombia by developing assistance programs. The majority of the programs focused on mitigating the consequences of displacement. However, the trend of displacement and the limited ability of receiving cities to absorb these immense masses of people made the implementation of prevention, assistance, and resettlement policies a priority. Understanding the decision-making processes underlying displacement is an essential condition for defining such policies.

Violence is the trigger of the kind of displacement considered here. People react differently to varying levels of direct and indirect violence. Frequently, a substantial portion of the population in areas of violence decides to stay despite the risk this implies for them. In a sense, deciding whether to move is a choice between two evils: staying and accepting the everyday risk of being a victim of violence, or leaving behind one's way of life and property and moving to an unfamiliar place.

Several scholars have studied the effect of violence on international migration (Kirchhoff and Ibáñez 2001). Bohra-Mishra and Massey (2011), using data at a household level, analyze how armed violence during a period of civil conflict in south-central Nepal influenced the likelihood of local, internal, and international migration. They found that violence has a non-linear effect on migration because low to moderate levels of violence reduce the odds of movement, while high levels of violence increase the odds of migrating. When Bohra-Mishra and Massey (2011) considered the influence of violence on micro-level decision making, they found that the effects of individual- and household-level determinants were consistent with the contemporary theories of voluntary migration and that no predictor of migration influenced the decision to migrate differently in the presence of violence. This means that at a micro level, Bohra-Mishra and Massey (2011) found no difference in the determinants of migration between violent and nonviolent areas.

Alvarado and Massey (2010) studied the effects of structural factors and violence on international migration from four countries in Latin America: Mexico, Costa Rica, Guatemala, and Nicaragua. They outlined a series of event-history models that predict the likelihood of initial migration to the

United States as a function of murder rates, economic openness, and selected controls in the country of origin. The researchers found that lethal violence was positively correlated to out-migration only in Nicaragua. In fact, the authors concluded that rising violence reduced the likelihood of emigration in Mexico, Costa Rica, and Guatemala. Therefore, they ascertain that violence does not appear to have uniform effects on patterns of international migration.

Shellman and Stewart (2007), on the other hand, sought to develop a general early-warning model for forced migration with data from Haiti for 1994–2004. They were especially interested in finding events that led to population displacement. Their study predicted forced international migration events related to civil violence, poor economic conditions, and foreign interventions. They restricted their model to forecast Haitian flight to the United States and succeeded in predicting weekly flows as opposed to annual flows. The authors concluded that it is possible to anticipate forced international migration events if economic instability, low-intensity civil conflict, state repression, rebel dissent, and foreign intervention are present.

In an older but seminal paper, Stanley (1987) analyzed the impact of political violence on international migration from El Salvador to the United States. The author used time-series analysis and found that political violence was an important motivation for Salvadorans who had migrated to the United States beginning in 1979. He explained that political-violence variables accounted for more than half of the migration variance and suggested that fear of political violence was probably the dominant motivation of these migrants. Stanley (1987) included economic variables in several of his formulations but eliminated them because they were not significant. This econometric strategy increases the degrees of freedom in the estimation but at a cost: the effect attributed to political factors may be exaggerated due to the absence of variables controlling for economic factors. The following section analyzes data from Mexico to sketch the correlation between violence and international migration.

Data and Methodology

To test the relationship between insecurity and international migration in the case of Mexico, we use data from INEGI (2010 and n.d.) and the National Population Council (CONAPO 2010). INEGI measures insecurity in different ways, but the indicator used in this work is the municipal rate of deaths related to organized crime. In this exercise, we use data from all

Table 4.2. Average homicide rate of border municipalities classified by migration intensity

	Migration intensity in groups of municipalities				
	Very high	High	Medium	Low	Very low
Average homicide rate (per 10,000 inhabitants)	27.5	14.2	15.2	20.5	12.2

Source: Data from National Institute of Statistics and Geography (INEGI 2010 and n.d. IDQ) and Consejo Nacional de Población (CONAPO 2010).

275 municipalities in the northern border states of Mexico: Baja California, Sonora, Chihuahua, Coahuila, Nuevo León, and Tamaulipas.

These municipalities display different levels of insecurity measured by the rate of deaths related to organized crime. They also present diverse levels of development and, therefore, different intensities of emigration. Emigration at a municipal level is calculated in three different ways based on data from the 2010 Mexican Population Census: the proportion of dwellings in the municipality that receive remittances from the United States; the proportion of dwellings with a family member living in the United States; and the proportion of dwellings in the municipality that have a circular migrant who moves back and forth from a community of origin in Mexico to a receiving community in the United States.

Table 4.2 includes homicide rates for five different groups of municipalities classified by their migration intensity—very low, low, medium, high, and very high migration intensity. No municipality presented null migration intensity in the northern border states. Migration intensity is measured by an index created by the Mexican National Population Council (CONAPO) using data from the 2010 Population Census.[5] The variables included in the index are the percentage of people living in the municipality in dwellings with at least one return migrant (someone who lived in the United States in 2005 and returned to Mexico between 2005 and 2010), the percentage of people living in the municipality in dwellings that receive remittances, the percentage of people living in the municipality in dwellings with a family member living in the United States, and the percentage of people living in the municipality in dwellings with a circular migrant.

Table 4.2 shows that the average homicide rate (calculated as the total number of homicides in the municipality per ten thousand inhabitants between 2007 and 2011) is higher in municipalities with very high migration intensity. The homicide rate in municipalities with very high migration intensity is more than double the rate in municipalities with very low migration intensity. This may indicate a certain correlation between insecurity and migration, but the evidence does not confirm causality between these two phenomena. Additionally, the homicide rate does not decrease as migration intensity decreases, questioning the validity of the hypothesized correlation between migration and insecurity.

Table 4.3 presents migration intensity of municipalities classified according to their degree of violence. We consider that municipalities with low homicide rates are those with fewer than five homicides per ten thousand inhabitants. Municipalities with medium homicide rates are those with rates between five and ten, and municipalities with high homicide rates are those with rates above ten. Homicide rates are calculated as total number of homicides in the municipality per ten thousand inhabitants for the period 2007–2011. Table 4.3 shows that migration intensity is higher in municipalities with high homicide rates. This fact, once again, suggests a certain correlation between these two phenomena, at least in the Mexican northern border states. To test this relationship we will use ordinary least squares regressions at a municipality level to control for other factors that may affect migration decisions.[6]

To better understand how insecurity and migration correlate, in table 4.4 we present municipalities classified by homicide rate and three indicators included in the calculation of the Migration Intensity Index. These indicators are percentage of population in dwellings receiving remittances, percentage of population in dwellings with emigrants in the United States, and percentage of population in dwellings with circular migrants. The Migra-

Table 4.3. Groups of border municipalities by degree of violence and migration intensity

	Homicide rate per 10,000 inhabitants		
	High (> 10)	Medium (5–10)	Low (< 5)
CONAPO Migration Intensity Index	0.544	0.508	0.504

Source: Data from National Institute of Statistics and Geography (INEGI 2010 and n.d. IDQ) and Consejo Nacional de Población (2010).

Table 4.4. Migration variables in border municipalities with high, medium, and low homicide rates

| | | Homicide rate | | |
		High	Medium	Low
Percentage of population in dwellings receiving remittances	Average	5.58%	4.11%	4.06%
	Standard deviation	4.87%	3.22%	3.73%
Percentage of population in dwellings with emigrants in the United States	Average	1.58%	1.43%	1.38%
	Standard deviation	1.24%	1.21%	1.31%
Percentage of population in dwellings with circular migrants	Average	0.54%	0.82%	0.76%
	Standard deviation	0.57%	0.75%	0.68%

Source: Authors' calculations based on data from the National Institute of Statistics and Geography (INEGI 2010 and n.d. IDQ) and Consejo Nacional de Población (CONAPO 2010).

tion Intensity Index is estimated with data from the 2010 Mexican Census of Population and Dwellings.

According to the data in table 4.4, the percentage of population in dwellings receiving remittances is higher in municipalities with higher homicide rates, and the variance of this indicator is also higher in municipalities with high homicide rates. Likewise, the percentage of population in dwellings with emigrants in the United States is higher in municipalities with high homicide rates. Regarding circular migrants, the percentage of population in dwellings with this kind of emigrants is higher in municipalities with medium homicide rates. Again, data suggests a positive correlation between insecurity and migration that needs to be tested with more sophisticated econometric tools.

Estimations at a Municipality Level

To better understand the correlation between insecurity and migration, we ran a series of ordinary least squares regressions and present them in tables 4.5, 4.6, and 4.7. We calculated estimations for three different dependent variables: percentage of population in each northern border municipality living in dwellings that receive remittances, percentage of population in the municipality in dwellings with an emigrant in the United States, and percentage of population in the municipality living in dwellings with circular migrants. The three dependent variables are indicators used by CONAPO to calculate the Migration Intensity Index. For each of the dependent variables we use three different models. In the first model, estimated to understand the determinants of the percentage of population receiving remittances in the municipality, we include an intercept and the rate of deaths related to organized crime as independent variables.[7] In the second model, we keep the first two explanatory variables and include a proxy for migration social networks in the municipality. In the third model, we add a variable that reflects the proportion of population in the municipality earning less than two minimum wages and a variable that shows a social lag in the municipality, defined as percentage of overcrowded dwellings, to account for the possible influence of the level of poverty on the decision to migrate.

Table 4.5 includes the three models estimated for the first of our dependent variables, the percentage of population in the municipality in dwellings receiving remittances. In the first model, we observe that the rate of deaths related to organized crime is positively correlated to the percentage of dwellings receiving remittances. The coefficient is statistically different from zero. Our model suggests that in municipalities experiencing more insecurity, families receive more transfers from members abroad. However, with cross-section information it is not possible to establish causality. Therefore, it could be the case that municipalities with migrants are more affected by insecurity and not necessarily that higher levels of insecurity result in more remittances, with remittances used as a proxy for migration.

In the second model, we include the percentage of population in the municipality living in dwellings with migrants in the United States between 1995 and 2000. This variable is used to represent migrant social networks in the municipality. As expected, this variable is positively correlated and explains remittances in a significant way. The size of the coefficient is forty-five times larger than the coefficient for the rate of deaths related to organized crime. This suggests that remittances in this model are mainly explained by social networks, but that insecurity contributes in part to the money transfers from the United States to Mexico.

In the third model two other explanatory variables are included: the percentage of population in the municipality earning less than two minimum wages and the percentage of population in the municipality in overcrowded dwellings. A dwelling is considered overcrowded if the ratio of people per

Table 4.5. Regression analysis predicting percentage of population in dwellings receiving remittances in border municipalities in Mexico

Independent variable	Dependent variable: Percentage of population in dwellings receiving remittances		
	Model 1	Model 2	Model 3
Intercept	4.324*	1.646*	5.327*
	(15.390)	(6.164)	(7.096)
Rate of deaths related to organized crime[a]	0.021*	0.016*	0.011*
	(2.837)	(2.949)	(2.205)
Social networks in the United States[b]	—	0.734*	0.569*
	—	(15.602)	(11.463)
Percentage of population earning up to two minimum wages	—	—	0.042*
	—	—	(3.889)
Percentage of overcrowded dwellings	—	—	−0.146*
	—	—	(−6.983)
R squared	0.029	0.486	0.567
F statistic	8.049	129.303	88.614
Sig. F	0.005	0.000	0.000
N	275	275	275

Source: Authors' calculations based on data from the National Institute of Statistics and Geography (INEGI 2010 and n.d. IDQ) and Consejo Nacional de Población (CONAPO 2010).
Note: t statistics are in parentheses.
[a]Defined as deaths in the 2007–2011 period due to aggressions or executions and in clashes per every 10,000 inhabitants.
[b]Percentage of dwellings with emigrants in the United States between 1995 and 2000.
*$p < .05$.

room is larger than 2.4. In this model all the explanatory variables are significant, and all, except the one that represents overcrowding, are positive. The largest coefficient in this regression corresponds to the variable that represents social networks, and the second-largest corresponds to overcrowding. This suggests that remittances are received mainly in municipalities with previous migration experience, and that the poorest municipalities are not as prone as relatively more affluent ones to receive them. The smallest coefficient corresponds to the variable that represents insecurity, but this coefficient is positive and significant. This suggests that relatives in the United States may be sending family members in Mexico remittances to help them cope with problems related to violence in their municipality.

In table 4.6, we present the three models estimated for the second dependent variable, the percentage of population in the municipality in dwellings with a migrant in the United States. In the first model, we observe that the rate of deaths related to organized crime is not correlated with the percentage of dwellings with emigrants in the United States. In the second model we include a proxy for migrant social networks in the municipality. In this case the effect of the insecurity variable becomes positive and significant, which suggests that insecurity is positively correlated with international migration at a municipality level. It is worth pointing out, however, that the size of the coefficient is small relative to the one corresponding to social networks, which in this case is represented by the percentage of population in dwellings with circular migrants between 2005 and 2010.

In the third model we include two other independent variables: the percentage of population in the municipality that earns less than two minimum wages and the percentage of population in the municipality self-identified as indigenous. As in the first estimation, all the explanatory variables are positive and significant except for the one that represents social lag (in this case, the proportion of indigenous population), which is significant but indicates a negative relationship. The largest coefficient corresponds to migrant social networks. The results of this model suggest that migration to the United States happens mainly in municipalities with migrant social networks and in municipalities with low proportions of indigenous population. The percentage of people earning up to two minimum wages in the municipality seems also to promote more migration, which suggests that income derived from labor is often used to finance the trip to the United States. In this regression, we also observe that insecurity is positively correlated with the proportion of migrants in the United States, which supports our hypothesis that insecurity encourages international emigration.

Finally, table 4.7 shows the results of the models for the third dependent variable, the percentage of population in dwellings in border municipalities with circular migrants. The first model includes an intercept and the insecurity variable, represented by the rate of deaths related to organized crime. The sign of the insecurity variable is negative, and the coefficient is significant, which suggests that circularity of migration tends to decrease in insecure municipalities.

In the second model we include a variable that represents migrant so-

Table 4.6. Regression analysis predicting percentage of population in dwellings with emigrants to the United States in border municipalities in Mexico

Independent variable	Dependent variable: Percentage of population in dwellings with emigrants to the United States		
	Model 1	Model 2	Model 3
Intercept	1.445**	0.660**	0.294*
	(16.922)	(6.516)	(1.674)
Rate of deaths related to organized crime[a]	0.001	0.004**	0.004**
	(0.485)	(2.212)	(2.059)
Social networks in the United States[b]	—	1.077**	1.003**
	—	(10.940)	(9.982)
Percentage of population earning up to two minimum wages	—	—	0.010**
	—	—	(2.689)
Percentage of indigenous population	—	—	−0.141**
	—	—	(−1.966)
R squared	0.001	0.305	0.327
F statistic	0.235	60.011	32.958
Sig. F	0.628	0.000	0.000
N	275	275	275

Source: Authors' calculations based on data from the National Institute of Statistics and Geography (INEGI 2010 and n.d. IDQ) and Consejo Nacional de Población (CONAPO 2010).
Note: t statistics are in parentheses.
[a]Defined as deaths in the 2007–2011 period due to aggressions or executions and in clashes per every 10,000 inhabitants.
[b]Percentage of dwellings with circular migrants between 2005 and 2010.
*$p < .01$.
**$p < .05$.

cial networks. The coefficient for the social networks variable is positive and significant. In this case, migration social networks are represented by the percentage of population in dwellings with circular migrants between 1995 and 2000. It is worth noting that the size of the coefficient of the social networks variable is much smaller in this case than in the scenarios presented in tables 4.5 and 4.6. This suggests that circularity of migration does not

Table 4.7. Regression analysis predicting percentage of population in dwellings with circular migrants in border municipalities in Mexico

Independent variable	Dependent variable: Percentage of population in dwellings with circular migrants		
	Model 1	Model 2	Model 3
Intercept	0.729*	0.671*	0.275*
	(16.663)	(14.639)	(2.690)
Rate of deaths related to organized crime[a]	−0.003*	−0.003*	−0.003*
	(−2.506)	(−2.838)	(−3.187)
Social networks in the United States[b]	—	0.048*	0.040*
	—	(3.571)	(3.034)
Percentage of population earning up to two minimum wages	—	—	0.011*
	—	—	(4.783)
Percentage of dwellings without piped water	—	—	−0.012*
	—	—	(−3.528)
R squared	.022	.066	0.145
F statistic	6.280	9.652	11.449
Sig. F	0.013	0.000	0.000
N	275	275	275

Source: Authors' calculations based on data from the National Institute of Statistics and Geography (INEGI 2010 and n.d. IDQ) and Consejo Nacional de Población (CONAPO 2010).
Note: t statistics are in parentheses.
[a]Defined as deaths from 2007 to 2011 due to aggressions or executions and in clashes per every 10,000 inhabitants.
[b]Percentage of dwellings with circular migrants in the United States between 1995 and 2000.
*$p < .05$.

depend much on social networks. As table 4.7 shows, the negative sign and significance of the insecurity variable represented by the rate of deaths related to organized crime do not change with the inclusion of more explanatory variables. This indicates robustness of the finding: public insecurity seems to deter circular migration. The negative sign of the coefficient for circular migration suggests that migrants already in the United States are less likely to return to communities of origin experiencing high levels of insecurity.

In the third model two other independent variables are included: the percentage of population in the municipality that earns up to two minimum wages and the proportion of population in the municipality in dwellings without piped water. As in the first two models, in this regression circularity decreases with insecurity and increases if the municipality has strong social networks in the United States. The negative relation between dwellings without piped water and dwellings with circular migration suggests that circularity is lower in poorer municipalities.

Conclusion

Mexico entered a period of increased insecurity due to government operations against organized crime during the Calderón administration (2006–2012). In this chapter, we found evidence at a municipality level of a positive relation between insecurity and migration in the northern border states of Mexico. This relationship suggests that the profile of Mexican migrants might be changing.

Theoretically, deciding to emigrate in an environment of insecurity represents a choice between two evils: staying and accepting the everyday risk of being a victim of violence or leaving behind one's way of life and property and moving to an unfamiliar place, having to find new employment and a new place to live.

Using data from 275 northern Mexican border municipalities, our analysis suggests that migration and insecurity are positively correlated when migration is measured either as the percentage of dwellings receiving remittances or the percentage of homes with migrants in the United States. When we analyze circular migration, the result changes: insecurity seems to promote less circularity. Our findings confirm the correlations between migration and insecurity even when we control for level of poverty and social networks. The results suggest that insecurity is higher in municipalities with migration experience or that people are emigrating from municipalities that are highly insecure. We consider that the second explanation is more plausible.

The hypothesis of a changing profile of Mexican migrants to the United States needs further analysis, but this study suggests that insecurity is significantly influencing the decision to migrate and the decision to return to communities of origin. Our results show that the insecurity effect on migration is still small, but the evidence is quite robust throughout the different variations of the tested models.

We are aware that we are testing emerging ideas regarding the effect of insecurity on migration. We also recognize that the phenomenon is too recent to show strongly in the data. This work might, however, begin a discussion about very important questions. Is the war against drugs promoting a displacement process that involves migration to the United States? If so, what can the Mexican government do to decrease the impact of insecurity on families and municipalities in Mexico? What might this mean for US policy and collaboration with Mexico?

For policy considerations, we do not suggest that these emerging findings signal a significant change in the strategic position of either Mexico or the United States. Friedman (2011, 213) stated that "drugs will continue to flow into the United States, vast amounts of money will continue to flow into Mexico, and violence in Mexico will continue until the cartels achieve a stable peace, as has happened with organized crime in other countries, or until a single group wipes out all the others." However, the findings in this chapter indicate that consideration should be given to tactical policy options. For Mexico, increased emigration among wealthier and more educated individuals departing from relatively affluent municipalities implies that Mexico may be losing some of the country's most promising middle-class performers. Today more than in the past, Mexico's economic success depends heavily on its skilled workers. In order to safeguard the potential that this group of wealthier and highly educated citizens represents, Mexican leaders need to consider how to balance protecting them while at the same time not neglecting those people with fewer socioeconomic assets who have no option but to rely on the government for security and quality of life. This is no simple task given the scarce resources in terms of police, security, military, and intelligence.

In the United States, tactical decisions related to this group of wealthier, more highly educated immigrants are not any easier. In the 2011 US presidential primary debates, candidates espoused the merits of encouraging the world's brightest and most productive individuals to legally move to the United States and become part of the US economic engine. With respect to educated middle-class migration from Mexico, the challenge for the United States is to decide where it is best to have those individuals and families live, work, and contribute to society. In the short term, the United States might benefit from increased immigration of upwardly mobile small-business owners or investors who can contribute to the economy. But in the long run, it might be better to have a stronger, richer, and more resilient neighbor.

Does the United States encourage, or quietly accept, immigration of the more capable Mexican citizens fleeing insecurity? Or does the United States collaborate with Mexico to control insecurity? Safe communities might prevent future migration and assist Mexico in retaining a greater potential for future sustained development. Even if one accepts a future scenario of more of the same—drugs, money, and migration—there are tactical-level policy choices that impact the lives of citizens in both countries. As mentioned above, a more in-depth evaluation of the effect of insecurity on migrants' decisions would help refine policy options.

Notes

1. "Ley Federal contra la Delincuencia Organizada." Retrieved from http://leyco.org/mex/fed/101.html.

2. Information available from the authors upon request. Retrieved from http://www.census.gov/acs/www/data_documentation/2010_release/.

3. In June 2008, Mexico adopted a series of far-reaching constitutional reforms designed to transform its criminal justice system from one based primarily on written record to a more open adversarial system of justice where trials are oral and public and a presumption of innocence is clearly established.

4. See Ibáñez and Vélez (2008). Data from *El Tiempo*, December 31, 1997.

5. The index is calculated using a principal component technique.

6. Ordinary least squares (OLS) regression is a statistical method of analysis that estimates the relationship between one or more independent variables and a dependent variable. The method estimates the relationship by minimizing the sum of the squares in the difference between the observed and predicted values of the dependent variable configured as a straight line. See International Encyclopedia of the Social Sciences, http://www.encyclopedia.com/doc/1G2-3045301826.html.

7. In a regression model, the intercept represents the value at which the regression line intersects the Y-axis (vertical axis). It indicates the value of the dependent variable when the value of the independent variable(s) is zero. See International Encyclopedia of the Social Sciences, http://www.encyclopedia.com/doc/1G2-3045301826.html.

References

Alvarado, Steven E., and Douglas S. Massey. 2010. "In Search of Peace: Structural Adjustment, Violence and International Migration." *The Annals of the American Academy of Political and Social Science* 630(1):137–161.

Bailey, John. 2010. "Combating Organized Crime and Drug-Trafficking in Mexico: What are Mexican and U.S. Strategies? Are They Working?" In *Shared Responsibility: U.S.-Mexico Policy Options for Confronting Organized Crime*, edited by E. L. Olson, D. A. Shirk, and A. Selee, 327–350. San Diego, CA: Woodrow Wilson International Center for Scholars and Trans-Border Institute, University of San Diego.

Bohra-Mishra, Pratikshya, and Douglas S. Massey. 2011. "Individual Decisions to Migrate during Civil Conflict." *Demography* 48(2):401–424.

CONAPO (Consejo Nacional de Población). 2010. *Índices de intensidad migratoria México-Estados Unidos 2010*. Mexico City: Consejo Nacional de Población. Retrieved May 5, 2015, from http://www.omi.gob.mx/es/OMI/Indices_de _intensidad_migratoria_Mexico-Estados_Unidos_2010.

Friedman, George. 2011. *The Next Decade: Where We've Been . . . and Where We're Going*. New York: Doubleday.

Ibáñez, Ana María, and Carlos Eduardo Vélez. 2008. "Civil Conflict and Forced Migration: The Micro Determinants and Welfare Losses of Displacement in Colombia." *World Development* 36(4):659–676.

Icduygu, Ahmet, David Romano, and Ibrahim Sirkeci. 1999. "The Ethnic Question in an Environment of Insecurity: The Kurds in Turkey." *Ethnic and Racial Studies* 22(6):991–1010.

INEGI (Instituto Nacional de Estadística y Geografía). 2010. *Censo de Población y Vivienda 2010*. Mexico City: Instituto Nacional de Estadística y Geografía. Retrieved May 5, 2015, from http://www.inegi.org.mx/est/contenidos/proyectos /ccpv/cpv2010/.

———. n.d. "Mortalidad, Conjunto de datos: Defunciones por homicidio. Información de 1990 a 2013. [Interactive Data Query]." Mexico City: Instituto Nacional de Estadística y Geografía. Retrieved May 5, 2015, from http://www .inegi.org.mx/sistemas/olap/proyectos/bd/continuas/mortalidad/defunciones hom.asp?s=est.

Kirchhoff, Stefanie, and Ana María Ibáñez. 2001. "Displacement Due to Violence in Colombia: Determinants and Consequences at the Household Level." ZEF Discussion Papers on Development Policy 41, Center for Development Research (ZEF), University of Bonn.

Massey, Douglas S. 1990. "Social Structure, Household Strategy and the Cumulative Causation of Migration." Stanford, CA: Stanford Center for International Development, Working Paper No. 2587, 1–24.

Pedersen, Duncan. 2002. "Political Violence, Ethnic Conflict, and Contemporary Wars: Broad Implications for Health and Social Well-Being." *Social Science and Medicine* 55:175–190.

Shellman, Stephen M., and Brandon Stewart. 2007. "Political Persecution of Economic Deprivation? A Time-Series Analysis of Haitian Migration to the United States." *Conflict Management and Peace Science* 24(2):121–137.

Sirkeci, Ibrahim. 2006. *The Environment of Insecurity in Turkey and the Emigration of Turkish Kurds to Germany*. Lewiston, NY: The Edwin Mellen Press.

Stanley, William D. 1987. "Economic Migrants or Refugees from Violence? A Time-Series Analysis of Salvadoran Migration to the United States." *Latin American Research Review* 22(1):132–154.

CHAPTER 5

Explaining Unauthorized Mexican Migration and Assessing Its Implications for the Incorporation of Mexican Americans

FRANK D. BEAN, SUSAN K. BROWN,
AND JAMES D. BACHMEIER

Mexican migrants have been coming to the United States in notable numbers since the development of rail connections between northern Mexico and the US interior in the 1880s (Cardoso 1980; Spener 2009). Today such migrants who lack official permission to enter would be called "unauthorized," "undocumented," or "illegal" entrants (Bean and Lowell 2007). But those arriving before World War I (and even long afterward) were not particularly viewed as immigrants and would scarcely have entertained the idea they were "illegal" (Massey, Durand, and Malone 2002). If anything, they tended simply to see themselves as Mexicans. Indeed, there was no official government agency charged with the responsibility of interdicting border crossers until 1924, when the Border Patrol was established, and the idea of "illegality" was not something that became a part of anyone's lexicon until the agency began the practice of deportation in the 1920s (Ngai 2004). All of this notwithstanding, most entrants, then as now, came to the country because US employers needed and sought their labor. For example, consistent with the idea that the United States has often needed Mexican workers, and given additional impetus by anticipated wartime labor shortages, the United States in 1945 overlooked its own stated aversion to reliance on contract labor and allowed workers from Mexico to enter the country legally through the Bracero Program (Tichenor 2002; Zolberg 2006).

When the Bracero Program ended in 1964, the number of unauthorized migrants began to escalate (Calavita [1992] 2010), both because American employers (especially those in agriculture) still needed labor and because Mexicans had increasingly become familiar with making the journey to the United States to work (Portes and Bach 1985; Massey et al. 1987). Moreover, in Mexico rapid population expansion had outstripped growth in new employment opportunities, further fueling flows (Bean, Edmonston, and

Passel 1990). But beginning in the mid-1990s, many of the migrants arriving in the United States, especially those in new destinations, faced rising hostilities and difficulties (Chávez [1992] 1998; Gonzalez 2006; Massey
2008; Massey and Pren 2012). As the reach and severity of legal penalties for unauthorized residence began to increase with the passage of anti-
crime and welfare legislation in 1996 (National Research Council 2011),
the hardships in the lives of many unauthorized workers became even more
severe. Yet today the country relies more than ever on unauthorized, less-
skilled Mexican labor (Bean, Brown, and Bachmeier 2009), a contradiction
that highlights the growing relevance for public policy of understanding
the origins, persistence, and magnitude of unauthorized Mexican migration and what such migration means for the integration of Mexican Americans in the country.

   In 2012, 40 million foreign-born persons were living in the United
States, a number that increased from 9.6 million in 1970. The population
share of foreign-born persons rose from 4.7 percent then to 13.0 percent
in the 2010s (Gryn and Larsen 2010; Brown and Patten 2014). The number of foreign-born persons exceeded the country's 34 million native-born
African Americans (US Bureau of the Census 2010). More important here,
within the foreign-born population, Mexican immigrants and their descendants are by far the largest group, because of both high immigration and
relatively high fertility (Passel, Livingston, and Cohn 2012). In 2012 alone,
more than 145,000 persons from Mexico became "legal permanent residents" (14.1 percent of the total) (Office of Immigration Statistics 2012). In
2006, the last year before the first stirrings of the Great Recession, about a
quarter of a million unauthorized Mexicans established de facto residency,
bringing the total number of unauthorized Mexicans to more than 6 million (or 56 percent of all unauthorized persons) (Passel 2010). The predominance of Mexican legal flows is reflected in the fact that the second-largest
number of legal entrants in 2012, from China, numbered only 78,000 persons, or 7.6 percent of all legal permanent residents. The predominance of
unauthorized Mexicans is evident by the second-largest number of unauthorized persons living in the country coming from all other Latin American countries altogether, with this total consisting only of 2.5 million people, or about two-fifths of unauthorized Mexicans.

   How did Mexican immigrants come to dominate both US legal and unauthorized migration flows? What accounts for the persistence of these
flows, even in the presence of unauthorized Mexicans often being viewed
so negatively? And what are the implications of unauthorized Mexican migration for the incorporation of such migrants' children and grandchil-

dren and for the long-term well-being of the country? To help answer these questions, this chapter addresses three objectives. First, it examines the US immigration-policy context that over the past half century has contributed to growth in US Mexican migration and the Mexican unauthorized population. Second, it charts the changes in the country's demography that have sharply shrunk the supply of low-educated native-born workers available to fill the low-skilled work that needs doing in the United States. This has created a growing demand for less-skilled immigrant workers from Mexico, a need that increasingly, in the absence of ways for such workers to enter the country legally, has been met by unauthorized entrants. Third, it reports the results of recent research that assesses what unauthorized status means for the incorporation prospects of Mexican immigrants and their descendants and what the growing unauthorized workforce in the United States means for its overall social and economic well-being.

The 1965 Immigration-Policy Reforms and Their Consequences

Although immigration scholars have often discussed how legislative reform ended national-origins quotas in 1965, the effects of the legislation on Mexican migration are much less understood.[1] The McCarran-Walter Act of 1952 set the stage for the 1965 act in a number of ways. First, by reaffirming the 1924 quotas, Congress dramatized their discriminatory nature. After World War II, national-origins quotas created difficulties for the effective implementation of Cold War foreign policies emphasizing anti-Communist alliances, yet the congressional vote underscored commitment to these discriminatory practices and placed such alliances at risk. Second, at the height of the McCarthy era, support for continuing the quotas reflected both xenophobia and the isolationist views of many lawmakers who presumably believed that domestic security concerns ought to trump Cold War foreign-policy needs. In the words of one, "criminals, Communists, and subversives of all descriptions are even now gaining admission into this country like water through a sieve" (as quoted from special documents made available to Tichenor 2002, 192). After the McCarran-Walter Act was passed over President Truman's veto, and up until the Kennedy administration, major immigration reforms were thus thwarted by political deadlock over the issue (Reimers 1983; Tichenor 2002; Martin 2011).

After President Kennedy's assassination in November 1963, however, the reform process changed. When Lyndon Johnson became president, those hoping for a legislative breakthrough were at first dismayed. Not only had

Johnson supported McCarran-Walter, but as Senate majority leader, he had often opposed efforts by Kennedy and others to introduce modifications to immigration law. As president, however, Johnson's priorities were to pass Kennedy's New Frontier proposals, even in fact to exceed them with his own Great Society initiatives. But initially he worried that immigration reform might hurt the chances of civil rights reforms and that he would generally lose political clout by endorsing something that did not enjoy broad public support, which was why he had unhesitatingly voted for the McCarran-Walter Act in 1952. However, Kennedy advisors and Johnson's own close advisor, Bill Moyers, convinced him that the immigration reforms were important and indeed consistent with his own major civil rights efforts (Tichenor 2002). In his 1964 State of the Union address, when Johnson outlined his proposals for pathbreaking civil rights legislation, he noted, "We must also lift by legislation the bars of discrimination against those who seek entry into our country" (Johnson 2011). After Johnson persuaded Senator James Eastland, D-Mississippi, the chair of the jurisdictional Committee on the Judiciary, not to block consideration of the legislation, the Immigration Reform Act of 1965 soon passed both houses of Congress with strong bipartisan support (Caro 2012). When, in 1965, he signed the Hart-Celler Act, or more formally, the Amendments to the Immigration and Nationality Act, Johnson said: "This bill is not a revolutionary bill. It does not affect the lives of millions" (Johnson 2011).

Although the Hart-Celler Act abolished national-origins quotas, it retained many of the restrictions from the McCarran-Walter Act of 1952 (Martin 2011). In addition, Hart-Celler imposed overall hemispheric caps on immigrant visas, initially 170,000 for the Eastern and 120,000 for the Western Hemispheres, and a per-country limit of 20,000 immigrant visas for the Eastern Hemisphere. This was the first time that any caps had been placed on the Americas. Although the Johnson administration had opposed the Western Hemisphere cap, members of the House and Senate Judiciary Committees argued for it on the grounds of both fairness of the application of the laws and fear of unregulated spillover from rapid nonwhite population growth in Latin America (Bartlett 1965; United Press International 1965; Zolberg 2006). The Western Hemisphere cap of 120,000 was 10,000 below the average annual migration from the region. But that count excluded the West Indies, whose immigration had been heavily circumscribed while its countries were under colonial quotas but whose independence had lifted those restrictions (Martin 2011).

Most important, besides replacing national-origins quotas with hemispheric caps, the Hart-Celler Act also emphasized family reunification. In particular, it set up a series of preference categories for immigrants from the Eastern Hemisphere. While broad preferences had existed under the McCarran-Walter Act, they had privileged highly skilled immigrants. Under the Hart-Celler Act, four of the top five preference categories gave priority to the reunification of families and amounted to nearly three-fourths of the slots (Zolberg 2006). In addition, the law added parents of adult US citizens to the list of immigrants not subject to numerical limitations (Keely 1971). Beyond that, up to 10 percent of slots were allotted to professionals, scientists, and artists; another 10 percent would go to skilled or unskilled workers in occupations with short supply. Refugees and a "nonpreference" residual classification rounded out the preference categories. In all these categories, minimal provision existed for unskilled migrant labor, despite the termination during the previous year of the Bracero Program, the treaty-based contract labor agreement under which tens of thousands of agricultural and other manual Mexican workers were admitted to the United States starting in 1942 (Zolberg 2006; Calavita [1992] 2010).

The provisions of the Hart-Celler Act to limit or change legal admission to the country through the "front door" also strongly affected "back-door" migration, especially from Mexico. While the members of the restrictionist coalition that had held sway for four decades prior to 1965 were influenced by the need to do away with discriminatory immigration, particularly given the Cold War imperatives for doing so, the fears of Southern Democrats and Western Republicans about nonwhite immigration led them to insist on unprecedented limitations of Western Hemisphere entrants as their price for going along with the new reforms. Thus, for the first time, this resulted in a ceiling of 120,000 visas per year on the number of such legal immigration approvals, including those involving migrants from Mexico. Moreover, applicants without immediate relatives who were citizens or legal permanent residents now needed a job offer from an employer who had to obtain certification from the Department of Labor that native workers were not available to do the work and that local wages would not be affected. Further legislation passed in 1976 expressly limited the number of such legal entrants from Mexico to 20,000 per year (Fragomen and Del Rey Jr. 1979; Cerrutti and Massey 2004). In short, a political compromise between conservatives and liberals within both parties, one that would prove difficult to resurrect in subsequent years, was instrumental in the passage of the 1965 legislation. Restrictionists were willing to support front-door modifications in exchange for ostensibly tightening back-door migration (Zolberg 2006).

But the unanticipated consequence was to increase unauthorized Mexican migration, something the southern and western senators had not been much worried about because they believed such migration was mostly temporary. Particularly significant in the new legislation were the labor certification changes that required employment clearances for those seeking to fill jobs in short supply. According to Keely (1971), the McCarran-Walters Act barred such workers if the Secretary of Labor certified that the United States had enough qualified labor to do the work or that the immigrants would depress US wages. Since this certification had seldom occurred, applicants were mostly free to enter. Under Hart-Celler, the burden of proof shifted in an effort to protect US labor. Immigrant workers were barred *unless* the Secretary of Labor had certified that the United States lacked enough suitable workers. Now, absent Labor Department certification, the default condition was that the country *did* have enough suitable workers. In effect, the applicant now had to show this was false. This, of course, was virtually impossible to do. As the inevitable regulatory backlog grew, the change in certification requirements fell particularly hard on applicants from the Western Hemisphere, who were not part of the preference system. In particular, Canadians were crowded out (Zolberg 2006). For many Mexicans, not all of whom considered themselves circulatory migrants, the only viable option was to enter the country illegally rather than as contract laborers given that the Bracero Program had become defunct. As a result, unauthorized migration grew substantially (Zolberg 2006).

Other unintended consequences can be traced to the 1965 law, principally the growth in the influence of the Border Patrol, which bore responsibility for "controlling" the southwestern border with Mexico. Hart-Celler alone did not unleash the unauthorized migration that rose shortly after its passage, but its limitations on legal entry certainly indirectly contributed. As unauthorized migration grew and eventually spread beyond the border states (Leach and Bean 2008; Massey 2008), the size and power of the Border Patrol continued to increase, in part from self-interest (Bean, Vernez, and Keely 1989; Calavita [1992] 2010). Policymakers repeatedly turned to border enforcement as a first line of defense (Bean and Lowell 2004). The effects of the Hart-Celler Act on legal Mexican migrant streams were more direct. Immigration from Europe shifted to the southern countries such as Greece, Italy, and Portugal. Immigration from the West Indies and Asia rose dramatically. The family reunification procedures also allowed for gradual growth in Latin American legal migration that was mostly Mexican (Keely 1971; Ueda 1998). The latter had averaged only about 30,000 per year during the 1950s, but after the 1965 law, legal permanent residents could more easily bring in immediate family members.

The Persistence and Magnitude of Unauthorized Migration

The immigration reforms passed in 1965, together with other changes in immigration policy adopted since then, clearly created circumstances conducive to increases in both legal and unauthorized migration from Mexico. This can be seen in the change after 1965 in the countries from which immigrants came. About two-thirds of those arriving after 1965 were from Asian, African, or Latino countries (Office of Immigration Statistics 2011). If we include the children of the foreign-born in the total, the number of immigrants now surpasses 68 million, more than twice the number of native black persons. As noted above, more of these parents were from Mexico than any other country. Many of these parents and children record themselves as nonwhite in the US census. As a result, almost 45 million first- or second-generation nonwhite persons are now living in the country (i.e., nonwhite, nonblack foreign-born persons and their children) (US Bureau of the Census 2010). In short, immigration trends since the passage of the 1965 legislation have led to a recent *nonwhite* minority living in the United States that is larger than the native black minority.

An increasingly nonwhite minority is not the only consequence of the legislation. Also, as noted above, Mexicans make up the bulk of the unauthorized. While most children of unauthorized parents, about 80 percent as of 2009, are born in the United States and are thus US citizens (Passel and Cohn 2009), Mexican-origin children account for the large majority of children with an unauthorized immigrant parent. According to current estimates, 70 percent of the 5.5 million children of unauthorized immigrants in the United States have a Mexican-born parent (Passel and Cohn 2011). These figures imply that more than half of the 7.3 million children of Mexican immigrants residing in the United States in 2010 had an unauthorized parent (King et al. 2010; Passel and Cohn 2011).

While the 1965 reforms increased immigration and changed its texture, they do not fully explain the *volume* of increases in Mexican migration, both legal and unauthorized. While a variety of factors may have contributed to this growth, the fact that Mexican migrants overwhelmingly come to the United States to work suggests why the numbers have grown so much (Massey et al. 1993; Massey et al. 1998; Bean and Stevens 2003). The United States needs labor. And given that the vast majority of the Mexicans who have come over the past forty years have had very low levels of education, the United States needs *lesser-skilled* labor. As counterintuitive as this statement seems at first, we note three broad factors that have increased such demand: the extent of US economic growth relative to its population growth, the decline of fertility after the baby boom ended, and the degree of educational upgrading in the US native-born population.

Since 1980, annual US population growth, including both legal and unauthorized immigration, has only rarely edged past 1 percent. During the past decade, population growth has actually fallen noticeably below this level. Economic growth over the same period, however, has for the most part been robust. Until the recent recession, the annual percentage change in gross domestic product has averaged more than 3 percent per year (US Department of Commerce 2010a, 2010b). Annual increases in population growth require the economy to add 1.3 to 1.5 million new jobs each year to keep up with the demand for jobs (Bean and Stevens 2003). Even when periods of economic recession are included in statistics, each decade has averaged job growth at or well above the levels needed to absorb population growth. For example, during the 1970s, economic growth in the United States generated an average of over 1.9 million new jobs per year, or about 50 percent *more* than the number required to absorb the baby boomers then coming of age, as well as immigrants. During the 1980s, job growth was almost as high, about 1.8 million new jobs per year, and during the 1990s, considerably higher still, averaging over 2.1 million jobs per year (US Bureau of Labor Statistics 2011). The ability of the economy, starting in the 1970s, to absorb so many new workers is noteworthy. The cohort born in 1950 numbered half a million more than the cohorts of the late 1940s, and the baby boom did not peak until 1957 (Bean 1983; Myers 2007). As young adults, the baby boomers themselves undoubtedly generated some "extra" economic and job growth during this period. But afterward, even during the 2000s and the recession of 2001, job growth matched the levels needed to absorb new native and immigrant workers up through 2007.

Since the baby boom ended in the early 1960s, US fertility rates have sharply declined, as measured by the total fertility rate, or the average number of children a woman would be expected to have if her childbearing followed the fertility pattern shown during that year. By the mid-1970s, fertility rates had dropped by about half, reaching levels below 2.1, the point at which population replacement occurs. After that, they moved up slightly, hovering for years around 2.0 to 2.1 children per woman (Centers for Disease Control and Prevention 2010). Thus, for a quarter of a century, the "extra" increment of persons coming into the labor market from earlier boomers coming of age has been subsiding, and the oldest baby boomers have now begun to retire. In fact, today's labor market is experiencing a dynamic opposite to the one of the 1970s and 1980s. Even as the baby boomers leave the labor force, growth in the number of natives coming of age and entering the labor market is declining. The native-born labor force will continue to dwindle, because the birth rate in the native-born population had dropped to 1.7 births per woman by 2010, a level about 20 percent below replacement level (Bean et al. 2012).

What does such low fertility mean? Roughly, it implies that every one thousand native women of childbearing age would need to have about four hundred more births per year to reproduce the native population. Over a ten-year period, this additional fertility would have resulted in about six million more births than actually occurred. Absent such fertility, the number of natives available to staff the workforce has been in both relative and absolute decline.

The numbers of natives available to fill less-skilled jobs over the past thirty years have also been influenced by factors other than demographic shifts. One in particular bears special scrutiny—the educational upgrading that began early in the twentieth century with the spread of the "high school completion" movement. This upgrading continued in the post-WWII era with the expansion of public higher education. Despite current debates about reasons for the slowing in the rate of increase in college attendance (Goldin and Katz 2008), the fraction of the population with some exposure to postsecondary schooling has steeply risen during most of the past sixty years and, recently, more so for women than men. For example, the percentage of adults (persons age twenty-five and over) with more than a high school education has gone up from 5.3 percent in 1950 to nearly 60 percent today (Current Population Survey 2010; Minnesota Population Center 2011). In absolute terms, the number of adults with a college degree was nearly 160 million in 2010, or more than twenty-five times as large as the number in 1950.

In other words, growth in graduation from college has mushroomed. The flip side of this picture, of course, is that there are now relatively and absolutely fewer numbers of persons with high school degrees or less. Particularly striking is the decline in the percentage of the population with less than a high school education. In 1950, over 87 percent of US adults fell into this category. By 2010, only 12.9 percent did. And the concomitant decline in absolute numbers was from about 80 million to 25.7 million. In short, by 2010, there were 68 percent fewer low-skilled persons in the country than in 1950, if by low-skilled we mean persons without a high school diploma or its equivalent (Current Population Survey 2010; Minnesota Population Center 2011). The magnitude of this drop is all the more remarkable if we consider that this is a figure for the entire adult population. That is, it makes no allowance for the sizeable immigration of the past three decades that has brought substantial numbers of low-skilled migrants to the country. If these were removed from the trend—that is, if we calculated the trend only for the native born—the drop-off in the fraction of less-than-high-school-educated persons would be even more pronounced. Nonetheless, the enormous educational upgrading of the US population is clear from the steep downward trajectory in the number of natives with less than a high school education.

One question that naturally arises in thinking about such a trend is whether there has been a similar shrinkage in less-skilled work needing to be done. Certainly, if we consider only manufacturing, the answer to this query would be "yes." From 1970 until today, the share of manufacturing jobs in the economy more than halved, dropping from more than one in four to about one in eight. The drop-off in the share of manufacturing jobs held by persons with a high school diploma or less has been similarly precipitous (also falling from approximately one in four in 1970 to approximately one in eight today). Interestingly, during this same time, the overall number of manufacturing jobs remained approximately 21 million (authors' tabulations from census data [Minnesota Population Center 2011]). But because of overall job growth, a relatively smaller *share* of less-skilled persons can count on manufacturing employment today compared to the past. Also, many of today's manufacturing jobs require at least some college. Thus, the relative demand for less-skilled workers in manufacturing has declined. However, during this same period, the share of the less-skilled workforce in service jobs has grown considerably (Freeman 2007). As a result, from 1980 until today, the number of nonmanufacturing jobs held by less-skilled, younger males of any kind (i.e., of any nativity or ethnoracial status), the group one might expect to compete most directly with young, male labor migrants if such competition occurs, has held steady at roughly 3.7 to 3.8 million, or approximately 45 percent of the less-skilled, younger male workforce (authors' tabulations from US census data [Minnesota Population Center 2011]). Thus, despite a decline in the relative demand for less-skilled manufacturing workers, the demand for less-skilled workers in general is as large today as it was forty years ago because of growth in the demand for less-skilled service workers.

If the trend just examined in the share of younger males constituting the less-skilled workforce suggests that the demand for unskilled work is as strong as ever in the economy, what does employment data about the nativity of less-skilled workers show about how immigrants are contributing to filling this need? And do the numbers examined broadly suggest a strong likelihood that any immigrants filling such demand are doing so at the expense of natives? To shed light on such questions, we again focus on young, male, unskilled members of the workforce (meaning those possessing either less than a high school education or only a high school diploma). This is the group that one might think would find itself most in competition with immigrants, in part because so many immigrants are also young male labor migrants seeking unskilled jobs. When we look at changes in the numbers of native- and foreign-born members of this group since 1970, we see that the numbers of foreign-born males in the two low-education categories have increased from a very small presence in the workforce in 1970 to approximately 2.7 million such workers today (Ruggles et al. 2010). Since 1990, the increase for this age group was about 1.7 million. The comparable native workforce, however, *lost* 2.8 million workers. In other words, the native male workforce of this age shrank more than the immigrant workforce expanded. As we noted above, declining fertility and educational upgrading contributed much of the shrinkage in the number of native males available to take low-skilled employment.

This is further evident in the gains or losses by nativity in the total sizes of these groups. If we look only at the numbers of natives and immigrants with less than high school educations, a drop (often very large) in the number of native persons who might be candidates to hold low-skilled jobs occurs every decade. The cumulative decline across decades is more than 1.6 million males. By contrast, the increase in the number of comparable foreign-born males is not quite one million (Bean et al. 2012). In short, the drop in low-education native males far exceeds the increase in low-education immigrants. At the level of having a high school diploma (but no further education), this deficit does not emerge until 1990, primarily because of the large numbers of high school diplomas earned in the baby-boom years. But once that demographic tidal wave subsided, declines in the numbers of natives with only high school diplomas also occurred, with the data showing shrinkages that again substantially exceed the growth in the numbers of comparable foreign-born males.

We have illustrated the above workforce needs by using statistics for young (ages twenty-five to thirty-four) native and foreign-born males. Similar tendencies exist for other age groups and for females, although perhaps not quite so dramatic. In any case, the point is clear: lower fertility and educational upgrading in the native-born population have led to large declines in the numbers of lower-education natives available to do such work. This has generated a need for other workers, and Mexican immigrants have become the predominant source of this kind of labor supply. This helps to explain both the persistence of unauthorized Mexican migration and its growth since 1990. Most of the void in the US-born less-skilled working-age population has been filled by Mexican immigrant workers—increasingly by those who are unauthorized.

Mexican American Incorporation

Most of the unauthorized Mexicans coming to the United States to work are very poor (Martin 2009). What does this mean for the integration, or incorporation, of their children? Education is particularly critical for overall integration. What does having unauthorized parents mean for the educational prospects of their children? We know that second-generation Mexican Americans obtain considerably more schooling than their parents, but much of this derives from the greater availability of public schooling in the United States than in Mexico and mandatory US attendance requirements up through age sixteen (Bean, Brown, and Bachmeier 2009). Second-generational education attainment still falls decidedly short of native-born white levels of schooling (Duncan, Hotz, and Trejo 2006; Telles and Ortiz 2008). But what about the schooling levels of second-generation students whose Mexican-immigrant parents are unauthorized? Are their schooling levels responsible for "dragging down" the average levels of the second generation? This might seem likely, given that families with unauthorized parents often need their children, especially their sons, to work to contribute to family finances (Bachmeier and Bean 2011). In short, even though the work of Mexican immigrants is needed in the United States, unauthorized migration may reduce socioeconomic mobility, a possibility we now examine.

Socioeconomic mobility can be fruitfully assessed by comparing the educational attainment of Mexican immigrants with that of their children and grandchildren.[2] Here we examine the results of recent research that not only does this but also takes into account the dampening influence of unauthorized parental entry on the educational attainment of children and grandchildren. But first it is important to note that certain methodological problems involving multigenerational studies can influence research conclusions. One is that intergenerational comparisons are subject to generation or cohort problems. Thus, in going from the second to later generations, research on the educational trajectory of the descendants of Mexican immigrants often provides ambiguous results (Zsembik and Llanes 1996; McKeever and Klineberg 1999; Farley and Alba 2002; Grogger and Trejo 2002; Reed et al. 2005), sometimes suggesting even significantly *lower* educational attainment for third-plus generations compared with second-generation Mexican Americans (Bean et al. 1994; Wojtkiewicz and Donato 1995; Keller and Tillman 2007). However, research has also often found a similar generational pattern within non-Hispanic and white immigrant groups (Kao and Tienda 1995; Boyd 2002; Chiswick and DebBurman 2003; Glick and White 2004; Ramakrishnan 2004), suggesting that the Mexican American pattern is not unique and that research results based on third-and-later-generation categories in general may be problematic.

Among Mexican Americans in particular, birth cohort heterogeneity may occur within generational groups because Mexican immigration has been ongoing for well over a century in the United States. Thus, Jiménez and Fitzgerald (2007, 342) noted that "using only a generation as a temporal marker of assimilation is . . . not enough. Each generation of Mexican-origin individuals is made of people from a mix of birth cohorts, and each birth cohort contains individuals from many immigrant generations." Ways to deal with this include controlling for age, making generational comparisons within relatively narrow age ranges, or using information that closely approximates longitudinal data. Longitudinal studies comparing actual parents with their children thus show more consistent evidence of assimilation than do cross-sectional studies. Smith (2003, 2006), for example, finds rising levels of education across three generations of men of Mexican origin and a corresponding decrease in the gap between their educational levels and those of non-Hispanic whites; he concludes that Hispanic men have made sizeable strides in closing the socioeconomic gap with whites. In another example, Telles and Ortiz (2008), using longitudinal data measuring individual Mexican American families, find education rising across the first three generations, although more at the level of high school than college completion.

Why, then, are the results of cross-sectional comparisons so ambiguous? The answer lies at least in part in problems in the definition of the third generation. Most of the above-cited studies use data that aggregate the third and later generations. As a result, a "third-plus" generational measure, which is all that is usually available, actually includes respondents from the fourth, fifth, sixth, and even later generations. Few studies are able to distinguish a true third generation (consisting of those with at least one Mexican-born grandparent) from later generations (consisting of those whose grandparents were all born in the United States). However, we know three studies that have been able to make this distinction. One (Alba et al. 2011) directly examined the educational difference emerging from using a "third-only" generation measure compared with a "third-plus" measure and found that the third-only measure shows *higher* education than the third-plus measure. A second study, by Telles and Ortiz (2008), shows generational improvement in high school completion but not college completion. Frank D. Bean and Susan K. Brown and their collaborators (Smith, Brown, and Bean 2011; Bean et al. 2012) have also used a third-only measure and found a deficit of 0.3 years of school for third-plus–generation males compared with third-only males. As a percentage of the Mexican third-generation/non-Hispanic attainment gap, a deficit of nearly a third of a year constitutes a substantial component (almost half of 0.7). Similarly, calculations of educational gain from the second to the third-plus generation substantially *understate* advancements in schooling. For females, similar results emerge, although they are not so extreme in magnitude. In sum, when researchers have no alternative other than to rely on third-plus measures, as is necessarily the case when using Current Population Survey data (currently the only large-scale national data with information on birthplace of parents), then assessments of education gaps between second- and third-plus–generation Mexican Americans and between third-plus–generation Mexican Americans and non-Hispanic whites are substantially biased.

Here we report the research results of Bean and Brown and their colleagues involving educational comparisons across generations of Mexican Americans (Bean et al. 2013). We focus on comparisons of the Mexican American third-only generation with non-Hispanic whites, for young adults (ages twenty to forty) in Los Angeles, examining Mexican immigrants (the first generation) and two groups of Mexican Americans—the second generation, including some who migrated to the United States as young children, and the third-only generation. We also report findings about the degree to which unauthorized status dampens educational attainment among the children of immigrants. Other research shows that the main migration status factor affecting second-generation educational attainment involves the mother's legal status (Bean et al. 2011). Second-generation Mexican American respondents with mothers who entered legally or became legal attain about two more years of schooling than do those with unauthorized mothers. With statistical controls (for both respondent and parental characteristics), this gross difference shrinks to one-and-one-half years, a gap that is still sizeable (and highly statistically significant). After employing still further statistical procedures to adjust for the possibility that even more factors could affect this difference, this research finds that the education premium for legal status is reduced further, to about one-and-one-quarter years (Bean et al. 2011). However, a substantial education premium of nearly one-and-one-quarter years of schooling remains that is connected with immigrant parents either entering the country legally or being able to achieve legal status later.

Table 5.1. Years of schooling completed by generation among Mexican-origin respondents and their parents

	Males		Females	
Generation of respondent	Father's average education	Respondent's average education	Mother's average education	Respondent's average education
0	5.7	N/A	4.7	N/A
First	7.4	9.6	6.6	8.5
Second	11.7	12.9	11.2	12.8
Third-only	N/A	13.4	N/A	13.6
Approximate period of high school attendance	1950–1980	1980–2000	1950–1980	1980–2000
Third+ non-Hispanic whites	14.6	14.5	14.0	14.9

Source: Immigration and Intergenerational Mobility in Metropolitan Los Angeles (IIMMLA) data (Bean et al. 2011). Reproduced by permission from John Wiley and Sons © 2011.

Given this, let's now examine the three-generational schooling pattern among Mexican Americans, relying on a third-only measure rather than a third-plus measure of the third-generational education attainment. When we do this, we find a higher level of schooling for third-only compared to second-generation respondents (see table 5.1). For example, third-only–males exhibit 13.4 years of school, a level up from 12.9 years in the second generation. This in turn is 3.3 years higher than the first generation's level of 9.6 years. We can also compare sons' schooling levels directly with those of their fathers. As in the case of previous research, the gains when examined this way are even bigger. For example, third-only–generation men exceed their fathers' level of schooling on average by 1.7 years. Women show similar cross-generational and intergenerational mobility patterns.

Despite this evidence of educational incorporation using third-only–generation data, the schooling levels in table 5.1 nonetheless continue to be affected by the dampening effects of unauthorized migration status. To account for these, we ask: what would the schooling levels of the second-generation sons look like if all of their mothers had come to the country legally or if they had legalized instead of staying unauthorized? Making a statistical adjustment to account for this yields an average schooling level of 13.3 years for second-generation sons (table 5.2) (Bean et al. 2012). In

Table 5.2. Respondents' average schooling by generation, adjusted for effects of unauthorized parental status

Generation of respondent	Males	Females
First	9.6	8.5
Second	13.3	13.2
Third-only	13.8	14.0

Source: Immigration and Intergenerational Mobility in Metropolitan Los Angeles (IIMMLA) data (Bean et al. 2011). Reproduced by permission from John Wiley and Sons © 2011.

the case of the third generation, an adjustment for grandparents' unauthorized status would produce an attainment level of 13.8 years of schooling for third-generation sons.[3] This reflects the level of schooling that would be expected if there were no adverse legacy effects of grandparents' unauthorized status on third-generation attainment. The results of similar statistical adjustments for females are also shown in table 5.2.

But these data are only from the Los Angeles metropolitan area. The remaining gap could be due to differential selective net migration patterns for Mexican Americans and whites into and out of Los Angeles or to differential discrimination in Los Angeles (Bean et al. 2012). It is not possible given the data at hand to assess which of these might be greater. Nonetheless, by removing the legacy effects of grandparents' unauthorized status from the schooling levels of males in Los Angeles, Bean et al. (2012) find that almost half of the educational attainment difference between Mexican American and white males is eliminated by the third generation. For females, less of this same gap is closed by the third generation. In sum, comparing the educational attainment of similar third-only–generation Mexican Americans and whites—and removing the negative legacy effect of unauthorized migration—explain a large portion, but not all, of the difference in schooling remaining between third-generation Mexican Americans and non-Hispanic whites.

Conclusion

These findings indicate the crucial importance of generating opportunities for unauthorized Mexican immigrants to legalize in order to maximize the educational success of their children. Given that most children of unauthorized immigrants are born in the United States, our analysis suggests that legislation providing the possibility of entry into full societal membership creates benefits not only for the immigrants themselves but also for their children and their children's children. When those unauthorized entrants who have the opportunity to legalize do so, both they and their children are able to overcome many of the disadvantages confronting them. This resourcefulness constitutes strong evidence in support of public policies that allow full societal membership. Because parents' socioeconomic status has sizeable effects on children's education (Fischer and Hout 2006), the positive influence of such membership in the immigrant generation carries over to later generations, boosting their schooling as well, as our results extrapolated to the third generation show.

Also, while the pattern of findings presented above does not rule out the possibility that ethnic discrimination accounts for educational differences between higher-generation Mexican Americans and non-Hispanic whites, it does imply the importance of a different kind of discrimination—namely, discrimination against unauthorized immigrants and their children. Because of their growing importance for the nation's workforce, unauthorized migrants will probably continue to come to the United States. The implication of the above findings is that later-generation gaps in educational attainment may persist as a result of discrimination against unauthorized migrants and their children as much as being a result of ethnoracial discrimination against legal Mexican immigrants and Mexican Americans per se (including discrimination against the third and later generations). In other words, a serious problem Mexican Americans face in the process of educational incorporation may stem from the initial disadvantages of lack of full membership in US society (i.e., unauthorized status). While the political resistance to changing unauthorized status may be related to ethnoracial discrimination, the disadvantage of unauthorized status itself appears to be hard and lasting, affecting citizen children and perhaps even their citizen grandchildren.

Notes

1. Parts of this section are adapted from Bean, Brown, and Castillo (2015).
2. Parts of the remainder of this section are adapted from Bean et al. (2013).
3. This adjustment involved assuming that those second-generation persons with unauthorized parental background had the same schooling level as those without such background and that the differential resulting from this assumption was the same as in the observed data.

References

Alba, Richard, Dalia Abdel-Hady, Tariqul Islam, and Karen Marotz. 2011. "Downward Assimilation and Mexican Americans: An Examination of Intergenerational Advance and Stagnation in Educational Attainment." In *The Next Generation: Immigrant Youth in a Comparative Perspective*, edited by R. Alba and M. Waters, 95–109. New York: New York University Press.

Bachmeier, James, and Frank D. Bean. 2011. "Ethnoracial Patterns of Schooling and Work among Adolescents: Implications for Mexican Immigrant Incorporation." *Social Science Research* 40:1579–1595.

Bartlett, Charles. 1965. "House Balky on Immigration Issue." *Los Angeles Times*, August 24, A5.

Bean, Frank D. 1983. "The Baby Boom and Its Explanations." *The Sociological Quarterly* 24:353–365.

Bean, Frank D., Susan K. Brown, and James Bachmeier. 2009. "Trends in U.S. Immigration: A Shift toward Exclusion?" In *Nations of Immigrants: The United States and Australia*, edited by J. Nieuwenhuysen and J. Higley, 42–55. Camberley, UK: Edward Elgar Publishing.

Bean, Frank D, Susan K. Brown, James Bachmeier, Zoya Gubernskaya, and Christopher Smith. 2012. "Luxury, Necessity and Anachronistic Workers: Does the United States Need Unskilled Immigrant Labor?" *American Behavioral Scientist* 56(8):1008–1028.

Bean, Frank D., Susan K. Brown, and Esther Castillo. 2015. "An Unexpected Legacy: The Positive Consequences of LBJ's Immigration-Policy Reforms." In *LBJ's Neglected Legacy: How Lyndon Johnson Reshaped U.S. Government*, edited by N. J. Glickman, L. E. Lynn, and R. H. Wilson, 124–150. Austin: University of Texas Press.

Bean, Frank D., Susan K. Brown, Mark A. Leach, James D. Bachmeier, and Rosaura Tafoya-Estrada. 2013. "The Implications of Unauthorized Migration for the Educational Incorporation of Mexican-Americans." In *Regarding Educación: Mexican-American Schooling in the 21st Century*, edited by A. Sawyer and B. Jensen, 42–66. New York: The Teachers College Press.

Bean, Frank D., Jorge Chapa, Ruth R. Berg, and Kathryn A. Sowards. 1994. "Educational and Sociodemographic Incorporation among Hispanic Immigrants to the United States." In *Immigration and Ethnicity: The Integration of America's Newest Immigrants*, edited by B. Edmonston and J. S. Passel, 73–100. Washington, DC: The Urban Institute Press.

Bean, Frank D., Barry Edmonston, and Jeffrey S. Passel. 1990. *Undocumented Migration to the United States: IRCA and the Experience of the 1980s*. Santa Monica, CA, and Washington, DC: RAND Corporation and The Urban Institute Press.

Bean, Frank D., Mark A. Leach, Susan K. Brown, James D. Bachmeier, and John R. Hipp. 2011. "The Educational Legacy of Unauthorized Migration: Comparisons across U.S. Immigrant Groups in How Parents' Status Affects Their Offspring." *International Migration Review* 45(2):352–389.

Bean, Frank D., and B. Lindsay Lowell. 2004. "NAFTA and Mexican Migration to the United States." In *NAFTA'S Impact on North America: The First Decade*, edited by S. Weintraub, 263–284. Washington, DC: Center for Strategic and International Studies.

———. 2007. "Unauthorized Migration." In *The New Americans: A Guide to Immigration Since 1965*, edited by M. C. Waters and R. Ueda, with H. B. Marrow, 70–82. Cambridge, MA: Harvard University Press.

Bean, Frank D., and Gillian Stevens. 2003. *America's Newcomers and the Dynamics of Diversity*. New York: Russell Sage Foundation.

Bean, Frank D., Georges Vernez, and Charles B. Keely. 1989. *Opening and Closing the Doors: Evaluating Immigration Reform and Control*. Santa Monica, CA; Washington, DC; and Lanham, MD: RAND Corporation and Urban Institute Press.

Boyd, Monica. 2002. "Educational Attainments of Immigrant Offspring: Success or Segmented Assimilation?" *International Migration Review* 36(4):1037–1060.

Brown, Anna, and Eileen Patten. 2014. "Statistical Portrait of the Foreign-Born Population in the United States, 2012." Washington, DC: Pew Research Center Hispanic Trends Project. Retrieved May 27, 2014, from http://www.pewhispanic.org/2014/04/29/statistical-portrail-of-the-foreign-born-population-in-the-united-states-2012/.

Calavita, Kitty. [1992] 2010. *Inside the State: The Bracero Program, Immigration, and the I.N.S.* New Orleans, LA: Quid Pro Books.

Cardoso, Lawrence A. 1980. *Mexican Emigration to the United States, 1897–1931: Socio-Economic Patterns*. Tucson: University of Arizona Press.

Caro, Robert A. 2012. *The Passage of Power: The Years of Lyndon Johnson*, vol. IV. New York: Vintage.

Centers for Disease Control and Prevention. National Center for Health Statistics. 2010. Vital Stats. Retrieved January 26, 2012, from http://www.cdc.gov/nchs/vitalstats.htm and http://www.cdc.gov/nchs/data/statab/natfinal2003.annvol1_07.pdf.

Cerrutti, Marcela, and Douglas S. Massey. 2004. "Trends in Mexican Migration to the United States, 1965–1995." In *Crossing the Border: Research from the Mexican Migration Project*, edited by J. Durand and D. S. Massey, 17–44. New York: Russell Sage Foundation.

Chávez, Leo. [1992] 1998. *Shadowed Lives: Undocumented Immigrants in American Society*. San Diego, CA: Harcourt, Brace, and Jovanovich.

Chiswick, Barry R., and Noyna DebBurman. 2003. "Educational Attainment: Analyses by Immigrant Generation." IZA Discussion Paper 731. Bonn, Germany: Institute for the Study of Labor.

Current Population Survey. 2010. *Annual Social and Economic (ASEC) Supplement* [Machine-readable data file (MRDF)]. Conducted by the Bureau of the Census for the Bureau of Labor Statistics. Washington, DC: US Census Bureau.

Duncan, Brian V., Joseph Hotz, and Stephen J. Trejo. 2006. "Hispanics in the U.S. Labor Market." In *Hispanics and the Future of America*, edited by M. Tienda and F. Mitchell, 228–290. Washington, DC: The National Academies Press.

Farley, Reynolds, and Richard Alba. 2002. "The New Second Generation in the United States." *International Migration Review* 36:669–701.

Fischer, Claude S., and Michael Hout. 2006. *Century of Difference: How America Changed in the Last One Hundred Years*. New York: Russell Sage Foundation.

Fragomen, Austin T. Jr., and Alfred J. Del Rey Jr. 1979. "The Immigration Selection System: A Proposal for Reform." *San Diego Law Review* 17:1–36.

Freeman, Richard B. 2007. *America Works: Critical Thoughts on the Exceptional U.S. Labor Market*. New York: Russell Sage Foundation.

Glick, Jennifer E., and Michael J. White. 2004. "Post-secondary School Participation of Immigrant and Native Youth: The Role of Familial Resources and Educational Expectations." *Social Science Research* 33(2):272–299.

Goldin, Claudia, and Lawrence F. Katz. 2008. *The Race between Education and Technology*. Cambridge, MA, and London: The Belknap Press of Harvard University Press.

Gonzalez, Gilbert G. 2006. *Guest Workers or Colonized Labor? Mexican Labor Migration to the United States*. Boulder, CO: Paradigm Publishers.

Grogger, Jeffrey, and Stephen J. Trejo. 2002. *Falling Behind or Moving Up? The Intergenerational Progress of Mexican Americans*. San Francisco: Public Policy Institute of California.

Gryn, Thomas, and Luke J. Larsen. 2010. "Nativity Status and Citizenship in the United States: 2009." *American Community Survey Briefs*. Washington, DC: US Bureau of the Census.

Jiménez, Tomás R. and David Fitzgerald. 2007. "Mexican Assimilation: A Temporal and Spatial Reorientation." *Du Bois Review* 4(2):337–354.

Johnson, Lyndon B. 2011. "Remarks at the Signing of the Immigration Bill (October 3, 1965, Liberty Island, New York)." *International Migration Review* 45(1): 200–204.

Kao, Grace, and Marta Tienda. 1995. "Optimism and Achievement: The Educational Performance of Immigrant Youth." *Social Science Quarterly* 76(1):1–19.

Keely, Charles B. 1971. "Effects of the Immigration Act of 1965 on Selected Population Characteristics of Immigrants to the United States." *Demography* 8: 157–169.

Keller, Ursula, and Kathryn Harker Tillman. 2007. "Post-secondary Educational Attainment of Immigrant and Native Youth." *Social Forces* 87(1):121–152.

King, Miriam, Steven Ruggles, J. Trent Alexander, Sarah Flood, Katie Genadek, Matthew B. Schroeder, Brandon Trampe, and Rebecca Vick. 2010. *Integrated Public Use Microdata Series, Current Population Survey: Version 3.0*. [MRDF]. Minneapolis: University of Minnesota.

Leach, Mark A., and Frank D. Bean. 2008. "The Structure and Dynamics of Mexican Migration to New Destinations in the United States." In *New Faces in New Places: The Changing Geography of American Immigration*, edited by D. S. Massey, 51–74. New York: Russell Sage Foundation.

Martin, Philip. 2009. *Importing Poverty? Immigration and the Changing Face of Rural America*. New Haven, CT, and London: Yale University Press.

Martin, Susan F. 2011. *A Nation of Immigrants*. New York: Cambridge University Press.

Massey, Douglas S. 2008. *New Faces in New Places: The Changing Geography of American Immigration*. New York: Russell Sage Foundation.

Massey, Douglas S., Rafael Alarcón, Jorge Durand, and Humberto Gonzáles. 1987. *Return to Aztlan: The Social Process of International Migration from Western Mexico*. Berkeley: University of California Press.

Massey, Douglas S., Joaquin Arango, Graeme Hugo, Ali Kouaouci, Adela Pellegrino, and J. Edward Taylor. 1993. "Theories of International Migration: A Review and Appraisal." *Population and Development Review* 19:431–466.

———. 1998. *Worlds in Motion: Understanding International Migration at the End of the Millennium.* Oxford and New York: Clarendon Press and Oxford University Press.

Massey, Douglas S., Jorge Durand, and Nolan J. Malone. 2002. *Beyond Smoke and Mirrors: Mexican Immigration in an Era of Economic Integration.* New York: Russell Sage Foundation.

Massey, Douglas S., and Karen A. Pren. 2012. "Unintended Consequences of US Immigration Policy: Explaining the Post-1965 Surge from Latin America." *Population and Development Review* 38(1):1–29.

McKeever, Matthew, and Stephen L. Klineberg. 1999. "Generational Differences in Attitudes and Socioeconomic Status among Hispanics in Houston." *Sociological Inquiry* 69(1):33–50.

Minnesota Population Center. 2011. *Integrated Public Use Microdata Series, International: Version 6.1* [MRDF]. Minneapolis: University of Minnesota.

Myers, Dowell. 2007. *Immigrants and Boomers: Forging a New Social Contract for the Future of America.* New York: Russell Sage Foundation.

National Research Council. 2011. *Budgeting for Immigration Enforcement: A Path to Better Performance.* Committee on Estimating Costs of Immigration Enforcement in the Department of Justice. S. Redburn, P. Reuter, and M. Majmundar, eds. Committee on Law and Justice, Division of Behavioral and Social Sciences and Education. Washington, DC: The National Academies Press.

Ngai, Mae M. 2004. *Impossible Subjects: Illegal Aliens and the Making of Modern America.* Princeton, NJ: Princeton University Press.

Office of Immigration Statistics. 2011. *2010 Yearbook of Immigration Statistics.* Washington, DC: US Department of Homeland Security.

———. 2012. *2011 Yearbook of Immigration Statistics.* Washington, DC: US Department of Homeland Security.

Passel, Jeffrey S. 2010. *The Size and Characteristics of the Unauthorized Migrant Population in the U.S.* Washington, DC: Pew Hispanic Center.

Passel, Jeffrey S., and D'Vera Cohn. 2009. *A Portrait of Unauthorized Immigrants in the United States.* Washington, DC: Pew Research Center.

———. 2011. *Unauthorized Immigrant Population: National and State Trends, 2010.* Washington, DC: Pew Hispanic Center.

Passel, Jeffrey S., Gretchen Livingston, and D'Vera Cohn. 2012. "Explaining Why Minority Births Now Outnumber White Births." Pew Research Social and Demographic Trends. Retrieved May 27, 2014, from http://www.pewsocial trends.org/2012/05/17/explaining-why-minority-births-now-outnumber-white -births/.

Portes, Alejandro, and Robert L. Bach. 1985. *Latin Journey: Cuban and Mexican Immigrants in the United States.* Berkeley: University of California Press.

Ramakrishnan, S. Karthick. 2004. "Second-Generation Immigrants? The '2.5 Generation' in the United States." *Social Science Quarterly* 85(2):380–399.

Reed, Deborah, Laura E. Hill, Christopher Jepsen, and Hans P. Johnson. 2005. *Educational Progress across Immigrant Generations in California.* San Francisco: Public Policy Institute of California.

Reimers, David M. 1983. "An Unintended Reform: The 1965 Immigration Act and

Third World Migration to the United States." *Journal of American Ethnic History* 3(1):9–28.

Ruggles, Steven, J. Trent Alexander, Katie Genadek, Ronald Goeken, Matthew B. Schroeder, and Matthew Sobek. 2010. *Integrated Public Use Microdata Series: Version 5.0* [MRDF]. Minneapolis: University of Minnesota.

Smith, Christopher D., Susan K. Brown, and Frank D. Bean. 2011. "Not So Big After All, But Maybe Getting Bigger? Generational Differences in Fertility between Mexican-American and Anglo Women." Paper presented at annual meeting of the American Sociological Association, August 19–21, Las Vegas, NV.

Smith, James P. 2003. "Assimilation across Latino Generations." *American Economic Review* 93(2):315–319.

———. "Immigrants and Their Schooling." *Journal of Labor Economics* 24:203–233.

Spener, David. 2009. *Clandestine Crossings: Migrants and Coyotes on the Texas-Mexico Border.* Ithaca, NY: Cornell University Press.

Telles, Edward E., and Vilma Ortiz. 2008. *Generations of Exclusion: Racial Assimilation and Mexican Americans.* New York: Russell Sage Foundation.

Tichenor, Daniel J. 2002. *Dividing Lines: The Politics of Immigration Control in America.* Princeton, NJ: Princeton University Press.

Ueda, Reed. 1998. "The Changing Face of Post-1965 Immigration." In *The Immigration Reader,* edited by D. Jacobson, 72–91. Malden, MA: Blackwell Publishers.

United Press International. 1965. "Johnson Stays Silent on Hemisphere Immigrants." *Los Angeles Times,* September 13, 14.

US Bureau of Labor Statistics. 2011. *Current Population Survey.* Washington, DC: US Government Printing Office. Retrieved September 20, 2014, from http://www.bls.gov/cps/#data.

US Bureau of the Census. 2010. *Current Population Survey: Annual Demographic Files.* Washington, DC: US Government Printing Office.

US Department of Commerce. 2010a. *Population Estimates.* Retrieved September 20, 2014, from http://www.census.gov/popest/data/historical/index.html.

———. 2010b. *Gross Domestic Product.* Retrieved September 20, 2014. http://www.bea.gov/national/index.htm#gdp.

Wojtkiewicz, Roger A., and Katharine M. Donato. 1995. "Hispanic Educational Attainment: The Effects of Family Background and Nativity." *Social Forces* 74(2):559–574.

Zolberg, Aristide R. 2006. *A Nation by Design: Immigration Policy in the Fashioning of America.* New York: Russell Sage Foundation.

Zsembik, Barbara A., and Daniel Llanes. 1996. "Generational Differences in Educational Attainment among Mexican Americans." *Social Science Quarterly* 77(2): 363–374.

PART 2

INCORPORATION INTO RECEIVING COMMUNITIES IN THE UNITED STATES

The previous chapters show how policies in both Mexico and the United States affect who migrates to the United States and who can legally remain. The chapter by Bean, Brown, and Bachmeier demonstrates that legal status has important consequences for the migrant and for future generations. This second group of chapters by Gonzales, Perez, and Ruiz; Salas, Preciado, and Torres; Melo and Fleuriet; and Romo and Mogollon-Lopez look at other barriers and processes of incorporation of Mexican immigrants in their US communities. These chapters in part 2 illustrate the precarious nature of immigration policies that depend on how immigrants are perceived under the law, their ages and the conditions of their coming to the United States, the difficulties immigrants face without documents, and the complex identities and circumstances undocumented youth confront.

As the earlier chapters have noted, for many years the US-Mexico border was relatively open. Migrants came to work, visited family members, and returned home to Mexico. Increasingly in the United States unauthorized migration has been constructed as "illegal" and "criminal" despite the longtime "profiting and recruitment of undocumented workers by U.S. employers" (Menjívar and Kanstroom 2014). With enforcement of border security and changing legal definitions, those who had crossed the border as workers became criminals who have violated US law. The recent criminalization of immigration, the sequestering of immigration enforcement from court oversight, and the ability of local police officers to detain persons suspected of lacking immigration documents have made enforcement of immigration at state and local levels central to immigration politics (Coleman 2007).

Indeed, migrant "illegality" has been constituted as the premier object of US immigration lawmaking and law enforcement since the Hart-Celler Immigration Act of 1965 (Genova 2014). More recently, an incarceration-oriented approach to dealing with unauthorized migration has redefined what it means to be undocumented in the United States (Martinez and Slack 2013). Criminalization of immigration has had serious impacts on young people who have grown up in the United States feeling included in US schools as Americans as a result of the *Plyler v. Doe* decision that allowed undocumented children a free education from kindergarten through twelfth grade. As they become young adults, many of these youth discover with shock that they lack official immigration documents.

In the chapter "Ni de aquí, ni de allá: Undocumented Immigrant Youth and the Challenges of Identity Formation amid Conflicting Contexts," Roberto Gonzales, Joanna Perez, and Ariel Ruiz address the increasingly harsh anti-immigrant contexts that Mexican immigrants and their children face in the United States. Gonzales, Perez, and Ruiz discuss the legal barriers undocumented children and youth experience even though they have been living in the United States and attending US schools since early childhood. The authors build on previous research about the everyday lives of undocumented immigrant students in the United States. Using data from California, Illinois, and Washington, the researchers explore the influence that unauthorized status and negative societal and community contexts have on the adolescent and adult trajectories of undocumented youth, their identity development, and the unique contours that shape their character.

Gonzales, Perez, and Ruiz note that many Mexican youngsters' identity formation is entangled between their experiences as undocumented immigrants and as American-raised students. As college-going youth, they can claim "cultural citizenship" and a more neutral social status as students rather than the stigmatized status of unauthorized immigrants. The researchers use a "critical interpretive qualitative methodological framework" and in-depth interviews to contextualize identity formation processes among these students. Students' interviews emphasized the various life transitions and rites of passage with which the undocumented youth struggled as they tried to define themselves and balance identities as Mexican immigrants and de facto Americans and as they experienced different forms of legal and social incorporation. Gonzales, Perez, and Ruiz present examples of students who excelled in academics but still found themselves limited to the same choices as older siblings or parents with little education. Students became increasingly aware of anti-immigrant climates, often manifested in attitudes and interactions in their everyday lives. As a result, the students became active in public demonstrations and civic and political activity to improve their circumstances. The researchers conclude that the identities of these youth are shaped by "a constellation of positive and negative contexts." Although their legal circumstances may change—allowing them to work, apply for residency, and become vital, contributing members of US society—many must wait and hope for changes in immigration policies, legislation, or contexts.

Kandy Mink Salas, Henoc Preciado, and Raquel Torres write about President Obama's executive orders permitting Deferred Action for Childhood Arrivals (DACA) and how unauthorized status affects student success in higher education. In their chapter the authors discuss in detail the legislative history of DACA, eligibility criteria and benefits for individuals approved for the program, the renewal process, the 2014 proposed DACA expansion, and the general outcomes of the policy. Salas, Preciado, and Torres provide examples of barriers that undocumented students have encountered as they seek degrees in higher education and apply for jobs with DACA temporary work permits. Youth are often afraid to disclose their undocumented status to teachers or peers for fear of being reported to immigration authorities. Many have been afraid to apply for DACA because it requires providing documentation about where they have lived, how long they have been in the United States, and other identifying information that might endanger family members. The authors focus particularly on the experiences of undocumented students enrolled in postsecondary education, many of whom have applied for and qualified for DACA status. These students struggle to determine whom to trust as they pursue higher education, how to achieve their academic goals, and what lies ahead in their futures with only temporary work authorization.

Taking on the responsibility to address these issues, young activists have organized student groups on various college and high school campuses, speaking out about the needs and rights of unauthorized students. At the national level, United We Dream (UWD), the largest immigrant-youth-led organization in the nation, established a nonpartisan network of fifty-five affiliate organizations in twenty-six states to advocate for immigrant youth and families. DREAMers, as these young activists call themselves, developed "tool kits" of information and resources available to youth, families, educators, and institutions of higher education to improve access to education for undocumented students (Richards and Bohorquez 2015). DREAMers have also worked to change organizational structures and policies, initiate scholarships, identify available financial aid programs, and support broader campaigns aimed at undocumented students' success in higher education and future work opportunities. Through their activism and initiatives, youth involved in the UWD movement have transformed the immigrant rights debate (Nicholls 2013).

Milena Melo and K. Jill Fleuriet offer a unique exploration of how low-income undocumented immigrants from Mexico living in deep South Texas experience access to medical care in a dynamic period of culture change. Their work explores the impacts of citizenship on health outcomes by showing how undocumented pregnant women can access prenatal health care for their unborn fetus because the baby will be born in the United States and will automatically become a citizen. In contrast, undocumented adults in need of critical care for diabetes cannot access preventative care and have limited access to crucial life-maintenance care at emergency centers, which is not cost effective. Fleuriet is a medical anthropologist and has conducted extensive fieldwork exploring health outcomes and cultural change among Mexican immigrant populations. Melo incorporates her fieldwork with Mexican undocumented immigrants attending emergency clinics in the Rio Grande Valley of South Texas and conducts ethnographic interviews and focus groups with undocumented patients to explore the structural barriers they encounter when seeking health care. Melo and Fleuriet detail the serious consequences of being an undocumented immigrant in the United States and being denied access to needed health care. They explore the ethical consequences of denial of needed medical care to undocumented adults while at the same time granting access to medical care to unborn fetuses because they will be born as US citizens. Thus, one's citizenship status has life-and-death consequences.

These three chapters illustrate the many ways in which the public sphere of immigration policy affects the private lives of families and youth, including a culture of fear, detentions and separations of family members, friction among members of mixed-status families, stigma in relationships outside the home, and access to resources (Dreby 2015).

The fear of deportation, separations of family members, and blocked upward mobility have severe consequences for low-income, unauthorized migrants, but not all immigration experiences are the same. Harriett Romo and Olivia Mogollon-Lopez present a qualitative study of the incorporation processes of Mexican immigrant spouses, exploring the experiences of upper-income immigrants who come to the United States as a result of insecurity in Mexico or to seek entrepreneurial and investment opportunities. Insecurity created by organized crime and drug cartels—particularly in the northern Mexican industrial border states, as documented in earlier chapters—and changes in business opportunity structures have drawn a more highly educated, prosperous group of Mexican immigrants to the United States. There are few studies of this type of Mexican immigrant because their numbers are small and they are not representative of the majority of Mexican immigrants, who tend to be agricultural, service, or low-skilled workers. It is difficult to obtain an accurate count of elite immigrants because many live transnational lives, with businesses, homes, family members, and investments on both sides of the border. They have the financial resources and higher levels of education to obtain investment or professional visas, which allow the head of household and investor to bring his or her family to the United States. Romo and Mogollon-Lopez use in-depth interviews and participant observations with respondents identified through community-based settings, such as soccer teams, private Catholic schools, nonprofit organizations, work contacts, and snowball referrals. The families interviewed maintained Mexican cultural traditions, especially around attending Catholic religious schools and services, speaking only Spanish in the home, reinforcing the importance of Spanish, honoring women's traditional roles as homemaker and caretaker of the children, valuing family relationships, and socializing with other Mexican immigrants of similar socioeconomic status.

Immigration policies that allow spouses of immigrants with professional or investment visas to work give spouses the opportunity to pursue their careers but may also challenge highly valued gender roles within the immigrant family. These higher-income families who move to the United States on investment or professional visas are able to migrate as a family unit. Many of these heads of households are in the high-demand areas of science, technology, engineering, and mathematics, or they bring large amounts of money to the United States as entrepreneurs to begin businesses or invest in the United States (Ruiz, Wilson, and Choudhury 2012; Anderson 2014). Once in the United States, the families face power, gender, and acculturation adaptations as they incorporate into the workforce, schools, cultural norms, and social relationships in their US communities. The high-income, professional Mexican immigrant families studied in the Romo and Mogollon-Lopez chapter are attempting to maintain the values and family dynamics brought from Mexico as they acculturate to US society. The perceived roles of women as well as US immigration policies are important in determining how the family and children deal with the incorporation process.

References

Anderson, Stuart. 2014. *American Made 2.0: How Immigrant Entrepreneurs Continue to Contribute to the U.S. Economy.* National Venture Capital Association, National Foundation for American Policy. Retrieved November 27, 2014, from http://www.nvca.org/index.php?option=com_content&view=article&id=254&Itemid=103.

Coleman, Mathew. 2007. "Immigration Geopolitics beyond the Mexico-U.S. Border." *Antipode* 1:54–76. doi:10.1111/j1467-8330.2007.00506.x.

Dreby, Joanna. 2015. *Everyday Illegal: When Policies Undermine Immigrant Families.* Berkeley: University of California Press.

Genova, Nicholas. 2014. "Immigration 'Reform' and the Production of Migrant 'Illegality.'" In *Constructing Immigrant "Illegality": Critiques, Experiences, and Responses,* edited by Cecilia Menjívar and Daniel Kanstroom, 37–62. New York: Cambridge University Press.

Martinez, Daniel, and Jeremy Slack. 2013. "'What Part of 'Illegal' Don't You Understand? The Social Consequences of Criminalizing Unauthorized Mexican Migrants in the United States." *Social and Legal Studies* 22(4):535–551. doi:10.1177/0964663913484638.

Menjívar, Cecilia, and Daniel Kanstroom, eds. 2014. *Constructing Immigrant "Illegality": Critiques, Experiences, and Responses.* New York: Cambridge University Press.

Nicholls, Walter J. 2013. *The DREAMers: How the Undocumented Youth Movement Transformed the Immigrant Rights Debate.* Stanford, CA: Stanford University Press.

Richards, Jamie, and Laura M. Bohorquez. 2015. *National Institutions Coming Out Day Toolkit: Institutional Policies and Programs with and for Undocumented Students.* Retrieved April 9, 2015, from www.UnitedWeDream.org/DEEP.

Ruiz, Neil. G., Jill H. Wilson, and Shyamali Choudhury. 2012. "The Search for Skills: Demand for H-1B Immigrant Workers in US." Washington, DC: The Brookings Institution. Retrieved December 19, 2014, from http://www.brookings.edu/research/reports/2012/07/18-h1b-visas-labor-immigration#overview.

CHAPTER 6

"Ni de aquí, ni de allá": Undocumented Immigrant Youth and the Challenges of Identity Formation amid Conflicting Contexts

ROBERTO G. GONZALES, JOANNA B. PEREZ,
AND ARIEL G. RUIZ

While recent migration trends suggest that the net migration flow from Mexico to the United States has stopped and may have reversed, possible explanations derive in part from an increasingly hostile anti-immigrant climate (Chavez 2008; Massey and Sanchez 2010; Passel, Cohn, and Gonzalez-Barrera 2012, 6). Indeed, contemporary economic instability, heightened border enforcement, and growing levels of interior policing have conspired to produce a negative context of reception for Mexican immigrants and their children. These trends have been evidenced by the recent escalation in deportation rates, a significant increase in the Immigration Customs Enforcement budget, anti-immigrant state laws like Arizona's SB 1070, and negative media portrayals of immigrants (Rumbaut and Komaie 2010). In addition to contributing to the stemming of net migration from Mexico, these negative contexts have also ratcheted up levels of fear among immigrant communities and are shaping the ways in which the children of Mexican immigrants come of age (Gonzales and Chavez 2012; Menjívar and Abrego 2012).

Despite existing and recent policies intended to address increasingly harsh sociopolitical contexts, many Mexican youngsters living in the United States continue to face additional legal barriers due to their own immigration status constraints. There are an estimated 2.1 million undocumented children and young adults who have been living in the United States since childhood (Batalova and McHugh 2010). While the *Plyler v. Doe* Supreme Court decision guarantees these young people access to a primary and secondary education, upon graduation, their access to higher education is contingent upon varying state polices (Gonzales 2011). In fact, once out of school, they face increased levels of inequality, including social, political, and economic barriers that prevent them from reaching their full potential (Contreras 2002; Stevenson 2004; Frum 2007; Rincón 2008; Perez 2009). Nevertheless, growing numbers of undocumented immigrant students are enrolled in universities across the nation.[1]

Undocumented immigrant students are engaged nationwide in advocacy efforts to increase access to higher education through the passage of state and federal legislation. According to the National Conference of State Legislatures (2014), there are at least eighteen states that allow eligible undocumented immigrant students to pay in-state tuition despite their lack of legal status. Yet in-state tuition laws are limited and are not implemented nationwide (Nguyen and Martinez Hoy 2015). At the federal level, the Development, Relief, and Education for Alien Minors (DREAM) Act would provide eligible undocumented immigrants, often labeled DREAMers, with a pathway to legalization if they enroll in higher-education institutions or enlist in the military (Barron 2011). Despite several lobbying efforts, however, the DREAM Act has failed to garner sufficient congressional support to become legislation. As a result, undocumented immigrant students began to implement grassroots organizing to "push for various measures that would increase opportunities for DREAMers and reduce the constant threat of deportation," including state versions of the DREAM Act (Nichols 2013, 150). Furthermore, beginning in fall 2011, undocumented immigrant students participated in several acts of civil disobedience to pressure President Obama to grant DREAM-eligible undocumented immigrants administrative relief through an executive order (Nichols 2013, 153). During fall 2012, President Obama responded by implementing Deferred Action for Childhood Arrivals (DACA), which provides eligible undocumented immigrant students the opportunity to obtain work authorization and defer their deportation[2] (Batalova, Hooker, and Capps 2013; Gonzales and Terriquez 2013; Gonzales, Terriquez, and Ruszczyk 2014). Through DACA, undocumented immigrant students have greater access to resources and opportunities, allowing them to "become more integrated into the nation's economic and social institutions" (Gonzales and Bautista-Chavez 2014). Nevertheless, recent research finds that DACA beneficiaries continue to face anxiety and fear for their families who are not eligible for the program (Gonzales and Bautista-Chavez 2014; Dreby 2015). Indeed, recent action at the state and federal levels has expanded access for numerous undocumented immigrant students. However, the uncertainty of their legal limbo continues to deeply impact undocumented immigrant youth and young adults around the country.

Thanks to a burgeoning body of research, we know much more about the everyday lives of undocumented immigrant students than we did even five years ago (Abrego 2008; Rincón 2008; Perez et al. 2009; Abrego and Gonzales 2010; Gonzales 2010, 2011; Gonzales and Chavez 2012). However, this research has yet to take up the important link between undocumented status and identity formation. Given the influence that unauthorized status and negative societal and community contexts have on the adolescent and adult trajectories of undocumented youngsters, we argue that they also have a strong influence on identity development and formation. Drawing from an unmatched set of data from three different state contexts—California, Illinois, and Washington—this chapter aims to fill this gap in the research by exploring the unique contours that shape identity among undocumented Mexican immigrant youth and young adults.

Shifting Identities amid Hostile Contexts

As scholarship over the last two to three decades has demonstrated, the ways in which today's children of immigrants are choosing to ethnically identify are complex and shaped by a variety of factors. Identity is commonly understood as "that part of individuals' self-concept which derives from their knowledge of their membership in a social group (or groups) together with the value and emotional significance attached to that membership" (Tajfel 1982, 2). But, rather than being static, the process of constructing one's identity involves trying on multiple traits that will ultimately be adapted or discarded, depending on the group's social standing and individual appraisals of those traits. As such, one's identity is fluid and reflects the changes one experiences across life stages (De Fina 2003).

Identity is also shaped by competing and complementary personal characteristics, including one's immigrant generation, immigration status, and position within the US racial and ethnic hierarchy. Those experiencing favorable processes of incorporation into mainstream society are said to shift to US American identities with greater speed and more optimism, while direct experiences of stigmatization and discrimination propel attitudes away from identifying as American[3] (Rumbaut 1997; Portes and Rumbaut 2001). This reaction is manifested in what Portes and Rumbaut (2001) call a "reactive ethnicity" and the renouncement of a hyphenated or American identity in favor of an immigrant identity.

Demographic changes over the last two to three decades have been met with a strong current of anti-immigrant rhetoric regarding "identity under threat" (Jenkins 1996, 6). Accordingly, the presence of large numbers of nonwhite immigrants has generated heightened levels of insecurity among native populations and a concern with issues of criminality and invasion (Fraga and Segura 2006). Anthropologist Leo R. Chavez (2008) argues that this "Latino threat narrative" has drawn attention to the notion that American culture is under attack. The response by a sector of the US population has been manifested in heightened levels of anti-immigrant sentiment, negative media portrayals, and stronger enforcement measures along the border and within the interior of the United States.

Massey and Sanchez suggest that through their daily social interactions, "immigrants discover categorical boundaries that facilitate or constrain their interactions with others and then engage in boundary work that either brightens or blurs the divisions they encounter" (Massey and Sanchez 2010, 183). Assimilation into the host society is, in effect, a process of "boundary-brokering" that enables immigrants to be active agents in identity negotiation and formation. In this process, reactive ethnicity "sees identity as arising in opposition to rejection and exclusion by members of the host society" (Massey and Sanchez 2010, 13). Moreover, as immigrants become cognizant about exploitative conditions and experience discrimination in their daily interactions, they are more likely to identify with their national origin or panethnic group rather than as American (Massey and Sanchez 2010, 212). Therefore, when Latin American immigrants realize the inimical realities of a negative context of reception in the United States, they quickly embrace a sense of solidarity through a Latino identity.

For undocumented 1.5-generation Mexican youngsters, uniquely shaped experiences place them in proximity to and separate from both their immigrant parents and their American-born peers. As a result, their process of identity formation is entangled between their experiences as immigrants and those as American-raised students. Sociological literature has highlighted the role schools play in immigrant students' process of socialization (C. Suárez-Orozco, M. Suárez-Orozco, and Todorova 2008; Gonzales 2011). In contrast to their parents' involvement in the low-wage labor force, schooling is the nexus of undocumented students' legal interaction and social identity formation. Not only is school the first legal institution that undocumented students encounter, but it is also where they live out their social reality and learn to be "American." As such, school functions as the most tangible gateway to society—particularly through peer interaction, undocumented students frame how they perceive themselves in comparison to others (Gonzales 2011).

Many college-going undocumented youth, in particular, assert a "cultural citizenship"—a set of claims to belonging that span beyond legal or political citizenship (Rosaldo 1994). Thus, despite the absence of legal recognition, these youth display creativity and agency as they construct their own identities (Garcia 2003). For instance, the passage of in-state tuition bills in several states has "provided undocumented students with a new, neutral, and more socially acceptable label that subsequently changes their social identity" (Abrego 2008, 723). By identifying with the legislation, undocumented youth in these states reappropriate a sense of congruence with the law even as they lack formal legal citizenship. They foster, in effect, a shift in "legal consciousness from being against the law to being with the law" (Abrego 2008, 729). This shift provides undocumented students a more welcoming avenue through which to interact within mainstream society and simultaneously reject the stigma of their immigration status.

As this brief review underscores, social identity creates a conceptual bridge between individual and social levels of the analysis of social reality. In other words, identity exists only in relation to and interaction with the social world. For undocumented youth, this interaction is a complex weaving of belonging and rejection, inclusion and exclusion, de facto legal and "illegal." Certainly, this process is not without conflict. Like their friends, these young people must find ways to fit in, but in doing so, they must also find ways to establish their own identities amid contexts of exclusion and rejection. In what follows, we seek to explore identity formation among undocumented Mexican immigrant students in three different states with varying legal and social contexts. We simultaneously investigate how their experiences and identity formation shape their adult trajectories.

Assessing Identities across Three State Contexts

According to a Department of Homeland Security report, there were approximately 11.5 million undocumented immigrants residing in the United States in January 2011 (Hoefer, Rytina, and Baker 2012, 1). Although the undocumented immigrant population is dispersed across the United States, about 73 percent is concentrated within ten states. California, with an estimated 2.8 million undocumented immigrants, hosts the largest number of undocumented immigrants. Illinois ranks number five, with an estimated 550,000, and Washington, with 260,000 undocumented immigrants, is number ten (Hoefer, Rytina, and Baker 2012, 5). These three states are home to nearly one-third of the nation's undocumented immigrants. Additionally, although there has been a slight increase of undocumented immigrants from countries outside of Latin America, 52 percent of the undocumented population in the nation hails from Mexico (Passel, Cohn, and Gonzalez-Barrera 2013).

Despite the growing anti-immigrant sentiment throughout the United States, California, Illinois, and Washington have enacted state legislation to increase postsecondary educational access. These states are three of eighteen that allow qualifying undocumented students to pay in-state tuition at public institutions of higher education (National Conference of State Legislatures 2014). In addition, these states have also enacted legislation that provides undocumented students access to private state-level need-based grants or scholarships (United We Dream 2014). Educational and political processes have encouraged civic engagement among many of these immigrant students (Gonzales 2008). Nevertheless, students in these states continue to face several obstacles that prevent them from reaching their full potential.

Through a qualitative methodological framework (Denzin and Lincoln 2008), we contextualize the identity formation process of Mexican undocumented immigrant students through in-depth interviews conducted between 2003 and 2011. Although we draw primarily from the West Coast Undocumented Youth Research Project, a multiyear qualitative study based in California and Washington, data for this chapter derived from a total of three studies: a longitudinal study in Los Angeles, involving extensive fieldwork and 150 individual semistructured interviews with 1.5-generation Mexican-origin young adults (twenty to thirty-four years old) who migrated before the age of twelve; a two-year study in the state of Washington, carried out between 2009 and 2011, involving in-depth semi-structured interviews with forty-five undocumented 1.5-generation high school and college students between the ages of seventeen and twenty-four; and an ongoing study in the state of Illinois that, thus far, has generated life-history narratives of five undocumented female students.

All two hundred participants have spent much of their childhood, adolescence, and early adulthood as undocumented immigrants. There are equal numbers of males and females among the three studies. While the Washington and Illinois samples consist exclusively of college-going young adults, the California study includes seventy-three participants who finished their education at or before high school graduation. To protect confidentiality, all names of individuals have been replaced with pseudonyms. The pool from which respondents were recruited for the study is made up of various community-based settings, including continuation schools, community organizations, college campuses, and churches. Researchers in all three states accompanied respondents throughout their school and work days, volunteered at local schools and community organizations, and sat in on numerous community meetings. Through these efforts, we located an initial group of respondents and then utilized snowball sampling to identify subsequent respondents.

Lastly, interviews ranged from 1 hour and 40 minutes to 3 hours and 20 minutes. Transcripts of interviews were analyzed using open-coding techniques. Conceptual labels were placed on responses that described discrete events, experiences, and feelings reported in the interviews. Next, each individual interview was analyzed across all questions to identify metathemes that emerged within each interview.

Understanding Liminal Lives

The academic literature has embraced the concept of liminality as illuminating the various transitions people experience as they move from one life stage to another. Immigration scholars have employed the concept to understand the experience of immigration in general and the lives of migrants with uncertain or undocumented status in particular.

Anthropologist Arnold van Gennep ([1960] 2004) emphasizes the importance of transitions along the life course as individuals move from group to group and from one social status to another. In theorizing these rites of passage he identifies a liminal stage between statuses that is characterized by ambiguity. During the liminal stage, individuals no longer belong to the group they are leaving behind but do not yet fully belong to their new social sphere. They are, thus, betwixt and between two often conflicting worlds or roles.

Many undocumented Mexican immigrants inhabit a liminal space once they cross the border into the United States, not able to attain a new status (Chavez 2008). For undocumented immigrant youth, this process is complicated, as they are integrated into the country's legal framework through their legal participation in kindergarten-through-twelfth-grade schools. Thus, early childhood experiences are buffered. However, as US culture defines what it means to successfully pass from one phase of development to the next—applying for a driver's license, obtaining a work permit, getting a library card, renting a movie, moving on to college—undocumented immigrant youth find themselves unable to complete these rites of passage. From about the ages of fifteen or sixteen on, these young people must reconcile conflicting experiences and positioning vis-à-vis their friends and family. As they make various transitions, they are, in their own words, "ni de aquí, ni de allá" (neither here nor there).

Liminality is experienced by 1.5-generation undocumented immigrant youngsters in multiple forms throughout their childhood, adolescence, and young adulthood. As members of the 1.5 generation—born abroad, but raised in the United States—they straddle the worlds of their immigrant parents and their native-born peers from school. But during adolescence, as friends begin to take part in various rites of passage, many find themselves unable to move forward with their lives, instead having to take on adult responsibilities. They struggle to define themselves between their school identities and their immigrant ones. And as they cope with negative messages, anti-immigrant animosity, and the stigma that comes with it, they struggle to balance their identities as Mexican immigrants and de facto Americans.

In-between Friends and Family

Underscoring a point made earlier, we note that undocumented immigrant children and their parents experience different forms of legal and social incorporation. While undocumented adults are absorbed into low-wage jobs and on the margins of society, their children are immediately integrated into the public school system, where they enjoy the legal pursuit of school, the formation of friendships, and important opportunities to learn the language, customs, and culture of their new country. This access to American life affords them an early development with few restrictions, resembling the course taken by their American-born friends. They grow up with the same popular-culture influences, experience childhood alongside a diverse group of peers, and carry out everyday lives with few legal restrictions. During this buffer stage, many of these young people express positive aspirations about their futures and are more resilient. As their everyday lives more closely resemble those of their friends, a greater cultural distance grows between them and their parents.

But with each year lived in the United States, they grow closer to realizing their legal limitations. While undocumented immigrant youth can attend school, at the time of our interviews they *could not* legally work, vote, receive financial aid, or drive in most states. As their peers move forward—taking a first job, applying for a driver's license, receiving financial aid for college—undocumented youth are unable to join in. Once the legal buffer that K–12 schools provide is no longer available, these youth begin to encounter legal barriers that turn their lives upside down. "With the awakening reality of their abject status as socially constituted noncitizens, these young people [come] to realize they [are] not like their peers" (Gonzales and Chavez 2012, 266). Direct legal limitations on college access, driving, and international travel—as well as deportation concerns—widen the social gap, prohibiting them from joining their friends (Gonzales 2011). During this stage of their lives, they realize they are culturally and legally different from both their parents and their friends. Indeed, they share distinct commonalities with both but are uniquely in-between.

Their early socialization is facilitated largely through the family and school. Min Zhou (1997, 79) argues that "the family is the most important institutional environment outside of school for socialization, adaptation, and the future social mobility of children." Although some undocumented immigrant parents may not possess high levels of human capital, many encourage their children to succeed in school. Parental encouragement, though, is shaped by scarce material resources to provide their children. Often, migrant parents endure unimaginable working conditions for meager wages and few benefits, if any. While parents may be making such sacrifices so that their children can have better lives, spending long hours away from home undoubtedly takes its toll on their ability to spend time with their children (Yoshikawa 2011).

As a single parent, Pedro's mom struggled to meet the basic needs of her family. She worked long hours cleaning houses for wealthy families in the coastal region of Southern California and was hardly home. Her absence had far-reaching consequences, as she rarely had time for her family. This put strains on her relationship with her children, and Pedro grew up yearning to have quality time with his mom: "Back then I didn't, I couldn't, really understand. I mean, I blamed [my mom] for everything that was bad happening to me. I couldn't see that she was just trying to put food on the table for us."

For many young people, like Yolanda from Illinois, the lives of their parents become a strong motivator to do well in school. "My parents worked a lot . . . you know they always said this is the only way out [through education]. These are the sacrifices that we've made, so you have to do good in school. . . . Growing up and knowing that we didn't have the financial resources, it was always tough. And so for me and for all of my siblings, [we knew that life] need[ed] to be better than this, not only for ourselves but for them."

In stark contrast, their lives in school provide important opportunities to experience childhood alongside American-born friends and through the activities of their particular generation. Together, they grow up and move through childhood with similar experiences of teachers, significant events, and social and cultural influences. Because day-to-day life involves little need for legality, there are very few differences between them and their legal peers. Take Marisol, for example. She enjoyed school and loved the freedom it gave her. While in school, she did not have to worry about the problems at home or her family's financial woes. However, for Marisol and others, there comes a time when legal limitations begin to separate them from their peers. Undoubtedly, this affects what they can and cannot do, but it also affects their self-perception and their friendships. As Alicia from Illinois puts it, such restrictions dissolve existing friendships and longtime feelings of togetherness with friends: "I often feel like I am a hassle because I can't do certain things, like drive and things like that. I can't be a second driver on road trips, so in that sense, I do see myself backing off a bit from really being in any type of relationships because that way I don't have to deal with any of this stuff."

In-between Adults and Children

As Alicia's narrative illustrates, the sudden transition to lives of exclusion separates undocumented young people from peers and also serves to halt their adolescent and adult trajectories. As exclusions from working, driving, voting, and nightlife leave them without significant options to participate in adult society, their friends are making seamless transitions into new roles and responsibilities. Unable to participate in many of the activities that culturally define adolescence and young adulthood, they experience a developmental limbo and are confined to the activities and environments of early adolescents. As legal limitations draw a small circle around what is possible, adolescent and adult trajectories come to a halt.

Such an unfortunate and detrimental reality often leads undocumented students to feel as though they are eternal children. This is powerfully exemplified in the words of Diana from Illinois.

> I don't even feel like an adult because I can't really do anything . . . because you do feel like a child. I am a babysitter, and if I moved out of my house I would not be able to support myself. And so in that sense I still feel like a child because I still depend on my parents for a lot of things. And, like, I think if I could have my driver's license, I could get a better job and sustain myself, but I don't have the requirements to do that because I am undocumented. So you do feel like an eternal child, and you get constant reminders of the many things you can't do. You are always thinking, "if only this and if only that." It is easy to lose your motivation, and unless you have that support system, I do not know how you would get through it.

Cory vividly expressed the same kind of frustrations about being stuck: "I feel as though I've experienced this weird psychological and legal stunted growth. I'm stuck at sixteen, like a clock that has stopped ticking. My life has not changed at all since then. Although I'm twenty-two, I feel like a kid. I can't do anything adults do" (Gonzales 2011).

For Cory and others, legal vulnerability becomes detrimental to their autonomy. But as the experiences of other respondents demonstrate, legal obstacles, while daunting, can be overcome. Many participants found ways to negotiate adult identities in a manner that allowed them to experience important forms of adult life. However, to do so, they had to find alternative routes. For example, when seeking housing, Alicia looks for roommates who are not undocumented: "I live off-campus in an apartment because I can afford it more and because I live with a roommate who is not undocumented and she can be the main person on the contract since I do not have a Social Security number—like, everything is under her name, all of our bills and stuff, 'cause I cannot do any of that because I am undocumented, which is oftentimes really frustrating."

Indeed, legal exclusions narrowly shrink the worlds of our respondents. But coming of age also brings increased responsibilities. For many respondents in families with at least one undocumented parent, limited job options—and thus restricted social and economic mobility—constrain parents' earning power and available resources. These families often face the untenable mismatch between rising costs of living and meager earnings. In many such families, multiple members are needed to pitch in. For those in their teens, while they are legally prohibited from the activities that define their entry into adolescence and adulthood, their families see their age as increasing their potential earning power.

Nearly all Los Angeles respondents contributed money to their families. While some respondents provided more than $1,000 monthly, the mean was $300 per month. After high school, Oscar moved from job to job, not staying in any one very long. He was dissatisfied with the meager wages and did not like how employers treated him. However, each new job proved no better than the previous one. Over time, he realized he had few job choices: "I wasn't prepared to do that kind of work. . . . It's not like I can get an office job. I've tried to get something better, but I'm limited by my situation."

For Oscar and many others, the conflicting realities of severely narrowed options and increased responsibilities place them in an untenable limbo. They cannot legally work or drive, but their family's need compels them to do so. While many find ways to participate in adult life, these critical tensions play out in a variety of ways that do not allow them to settle into either role.

In-between Achievers and Undocumented Immigrants

Among high-achieving undocumented young people exists another level of in-betweenness. School provides them the opportunity to assert a positive identity that is constructed through their achievements and positive appraisals by teachers and counselors. Marisol, like many other respondents, held tightly to the label of student, for it provided her an identity that was based on her positive accomplishments (something she earned), rather than a negative label that did not seemingly reflect her life. Her love for school and quest for education was nurtured by her teachers and peer group. One particular teacher helped her through her difficulties at home and encouraged her to pursue college. Similarly, Marisol's peer group kept her motivated and focused: "We believed in education and pushed each other. We helped each other with homework and talked about college."

Many of the other high-achieving young adults we spoke to provided affirmative responses when asked about their school experiences. Irene, who received a bachelor's degree in a competitive film program, was part of a selective academy while in high school that accepted a small number of students who stayed together with the same teachers for their four years. Over that period, and as a result of numerous affirming experiences, Irene saw herself as a successful young woman: "My teacher mentored me to make sure I was college material."

However, as Marisol, Irene, and many others came to find out, their identities as students were often in tension with their legal limitations and the designation of undocumented immigrants. While they speak English with much greater fluency than their parents and achieve levels of education that surpass those of their parents and other family members, they are confined to the same narrowly circumscribed range of options.

Irene had lived in the United States for nearly twenty years when a troubling incident forced her to deal with this conflicting reality. She was returning from class at her university and was pulled over by a police officer less than six blocks from her house. She explained that the incident was quite an awakening for her. She had her radio on and was thinking about her class and her upcoming test. When the officer stopped her, she became angry and shouted at him, showing her university sweatshirt. He was ready to run a check on her driver's license when he received a call. Although

Irene was let off with a warning, she nearly escalated the situation to the point where she put herself in danger. However, she felt as though her high-achieving status would set her apart from other immigrants on the road. When she came home and told her father, he broke out in tears, instructing her to never again talk to a police officer in such a manner. Indeed, Irene's father knew very well the consequences her undocumented status carried for her safety and ability to move freely in the world.

Irene's experience also highlights the ways in which immigration status overwhelms other identities. As the onset of late adolescence halts and delays trajectories, undocumented youth confront a set of choices of considerably poorer quality compared to previously held expectations and aspirations. Their years in school and mastery of the English language engender feelings of entitlement to claims of better lives. Whether or not they envisioned attending college, most expected to do much better than their parents and had well-articulated conceptions of what constitutes an immigrant job as opposed to the range of jobs they desire. However, these students find themselves limited to the same choices as older siblings or parents who possess significantly lower levels of English and years of schooling. Coming to terms with this reality is not easy. Undocumented students often resent their circumstances, question ideals they previously held, and try to cope with the shame and embarrassment they feel in their jobs.

Margarita was popular in high school and carried a B average. She aspired to be a pharmacist. Many of her friends have graduated from college and have started careers. They make enough money to make car payments, go out on the weekends, and go shopping. Margarita works with her mom and older sister, cleaning houses in affluent neighborhoods. She has been doing so for almost four years. Her parents do not let her drive, so she rides with her mom to work or takes the bus when she does not have a ride. Her world has become very small, and she says that often makes her sad. When asked whether she felt as though she was more successful than her parents, she responded:

> Well, you know, it's a difficult one. That's hard to answer 'cause I graduated from high school and have taken some college credits. Neither of my parents made it past the fourth grade, and they don't speak any English. But, well, I'm, I'm right where they are. I mean, I work with my mom. I have the same job. I can't find anything else. It's kinda ridiculous, you know. Why did I even go to school? It should mean something. I mean, that should count, right? You would think. I thought. Well, here I am, cleaning houses. (Gonzales 2011)

Many other respondents had similar reactions, saying that they felt as though their levels of achievement had surpassed those of their parents, but that their circumstances were the same or worse. Many of them had difficulty reconciling the perceived mismatch between their education and employment options, and how they perceived themselves as students and undocumented immigrants.

In-between Mexicans and Americans

The terms "undocumented," "immigrants," and "Mexican" have increasingly become synonymous in sectors of the US population. As anti-immigrant rhetoric has taken on a decidedly racial tone, attacks on immigrants have been leveled against persons of Mexican origin. Often, individuals are targeted because of an assumed Mexican identity, as was the case of a young Ecuadorian man in New Jersey who was stabbed to death in Long Island, New York, by a group of teens who allegedly were "beaner bashing" (Buckley 2008).

As undocumented youngsters make critical transitions to adolescence and young adulthood, they also move into a highly stigmatized identity, that of the undocumented immigrant, or "illegal alien" in the pejorative. Attached to this stigma are negative images about their unlawful presence, but also about their community and culture. For these young people, core identity is tied to experiences as Mexicans *and* Americans. However, they are frequently made to feel as though they need to choose (or, in some cases, cannot choose). While, for some, their condition of illegality abates their ability to appropriate an American identity, it does not necessarily lead all to succumb to their abject status (Gonzales and Chavez 2012, 267). Indeed, while some become ensnarled in the stigma of the undocumented immigrant, others engage in civic and political activities in an attempt to feel part of the larger community around them.

Many of our respondents encountered negative experiences on the basis of their ethnic identity as well as their immigration status. Most of our rural Washington respondents, in particular, described school and community contexts as isolating and rife with anti-immigrant, anti-Mexican sentiment. For example, Tina recounted a friend's negative experience obtaining a transcript needed for a college application. When a staff member confronted her, it made the respondent's friend feel as though she should not be applying to college. "Why do *you* want a transcript?" she was asked. She also felt as though she received "weird looks" from others in the office, which she attributed to being Mexican. While she did not have any direct evidence, her impression was formed on the basis of several negative incidents. On a separate occasion, she recalled an incident involving students at her school. "Yesterday, someone tagged up a bathroom in Lobby H and I heard some white students talking. This one kid said that 'H' stands for the Hispanic lobby. They tried to blame the graffiti on us, the Latinos."

For many of our respondents, anti-immigrant climates are manifested in the attitudes of, and their interactions with, a variety of individuals in their everyday lives. For example, Alicia recounted occasions when she felt as though her achiever status was being contradicted by individuals on her college campus.

> I would say that the campus climate is really hostile sometimes . . . like, one time when I was boarding the bus and I forgot to show my student ID, the bus driver just looked at me and [asked] me, "Why don't you just go back to Mexico?" Or, like, for Halloween, when I saw so many people dressed as border patrol and some people dress up like "Mexicans" and they would go off in pairs and it's just, like, really demeaning and it just makes me feel awful and, like, makes me feel there is no hope for people to change their minds.

Other Washington respondents described similar interactions with peers and school personnel that involved what they perceived to be negative appraisals based on their ethnic background. Rocio's experiences in community and school compelled her to distrust people. "There are people that say that [undocumented students] don't have any rights and that we should go back. . . . I don't feel comfortable talking to my counselor about my status." Noemi and Enrique, in separate interviews, also expressed that they did not feel comfortable reaching out to their administrators or counselors due to similar negative encounters.

At the same time, most of our respondents articulated an identity that bridged their Mexican roots and their Americanizing experiences. Josue, a high-achieving high school student who has lived in the United States since the age of five, put it this way: "I am the same as [documented students] are. I live here, I go to school with them, and they are my friends. I don't think there is any difference. Everybody is a person." Manuel similarly explained: "They have more [financial] opportunities, but we are really the same."

Despite the negative messages many of our respondents have received about their identities, and the consequent dangers involved in speaking out publicly, many have become frustrated and want to do something to remedy their situation. As their recent growth and presence in activism have attested, undocumented immigrant students from all over the United States are finding strength and courage in numbers. Thousands of high school and college students have demonstrated to the country, as well as their families and peers, that they are willing to engage in the civic and political activity necessary for improving their circumstances.

The position of Andrea, from Anaheim, California, exemplifies the spirit of activism of many undocumented Mexican immigrant students. In a conversation, she expressed strong feelings that while she believes advocates and allies are important to the student movement, it is important for people to hear directly from undocumented students through their own narratives, circumstances, and struggles. She explained, "It's time for undocumented students to stand up for ourselves, and if we do not do it for ourselves, we will have lost everything we're fighting for" (Gonzales 2008).

Conclusion

The experiences of 1.5-generation undocumented Mexican youth and young adults paint a rich and textured portrait of identity formation under constrained circumstances. The young men and women we talked to inhabit a space between worlds—between the worlds of their parents and their friends, between static definitions of adults and children, between their identities as academic achievers and their legal designation as undocumented immigrants, and between their origins as Mexican immigrants and their destinies as Americans. These identities are shaped by a constellation of positive and negative contexts that uniquely shape everyday life. But, as we have shown, these identities are not static—over time individuals experience a great deal of change in their lives. For many of these young people, legal circumstances could change overnight, potentially shifting the balance of conflicting contexts and validating many of the positive aspects of their lives.

With President Obama's implementation of the DACA program on August 15, 2012, a substantial number of undocumented immigrant youth have taken significant steps toward bridging everyday experiences defined by illegality and experiences of belonging. DACA provides its beneficiaries with important opportunities to obtain work authorization and Social Security numbers, opening up avenues to enter the formal employment sector (Batalova, Hooker, and Capps 2013, 11), and to apply for drivers' licenses across the majority of states (National Immigration Law Center 2015). Recent research suggests that those who are granted DACA have access to better economic opportunities, can live without the fear of their own deportation, and are able to become more incorporated into society (Gonzales and Terriquez 2013, 1; Gonzales, Terriquez, and Ruszczyk 2014).

The extent to which DACA positively influences the transition to adulthood and processes of identity formation of undocumented youth and young adults is multifaceted. In addition to provisional relief from deportation, obtaining a newfound range of employment and career opportunities allows some DACA beneficiaries to overcome previous elements of exclusion in their everyday life. "Taken together, the relief from enforcement and the powerful symbolic function of DACA should mitigate some anxieties and fears about deportation, thus lessening negative aspects of the condition of illegality" (Gonzales, Terriquez, and Ruszczyk 2014, 1867). In other words, having DACA can contribute to positive emotional well-being, allowing individuals to form healthy identities. Considering the liminal identities that were important to our participants, obtaining DACA may provide undocumented youth the ability to more easily identify with their friends as adults, achievers, and Americans.

While several hundred thousand young people have benefited from DACA, many of their neighbors, friends, and family members have not. Immigrants who were over thirty as of June 15, 2012, or who have been convicted of a "significant misdemeanor," for example, do not meet the initial program requirements. In November 2014, President Obama issued a set of executive memoranda extending these benefits to a wider sector of students as well as to parents of US citizens or lawful permanent residents, but the implementation of those orders remains uncertain due to legal challenges. As a result, becoming "DACAmented" in a mixed-status family or community that continues to be inundated by hostile national and local contexts may do little to assuage the hardships and anxiety of family separation, thereby possibly stunting self-worth and exacerbating social withdrawal. In addition, many DACAmented young people may now be taking on additional obligations within the household—for example, driving undocumented family members to work or appointments—as well as added responsibility for working and helping to pay bills.

Therefore, although becoming DACAmented provides a substantial group of young undocumented immigrants access to important economic opportunities, it has not addressed the entirety of their problems; it may also have created new dilemmas. Future research will be needed both to better understand the impact of DACA over a longer period and to assess its effects on family members. What is certain is that DACA is temporary and partial, and, as an administrative policy, it does not provide a pathway to legalization. This is in the hands of the US Congress. But while lawmakers continue to debate immigration reform, undocumented young people must carry out their daily lives, navigating through multiple identities.

Notes

1. In 2003 the demographer Jeffrey Passel estimated that approximately seven thousand to thirteen thousand undocumented students were enrolled in two- or four-year colleges and universities across the United States. However, since then several states have passed tuition-equity bills that have likely increased the number of undocumented immigrant students in postsecondary institutions (Passel 2003).

2. In order to qualify for DACA, an undocumented immigrant had to meet the following requirements: be under the age of thirty-one as of June 15, 2012; have entered the United States before the age of sixteen; have continuously resided in the United States since June 15, 2007, and up to the present time; be physically present on June 15, 2012, and at the time of application; be currently in school, have graduated from high school or earned a GED, or be an honorably discharged veteran of the US armed forces; have not been convicted of a felony, significant misdemeanor, or three or more misdemeanors, or otherwise pose a threat to public safety or national security; and have entered the country illegally or overstayed his or her visa prior to June 15, 2012 (Batalova and Mittelstadt 2012, 1).

3. Subsequent references to US American identities will employ the term "American." While we acknowledge that the term applies broadly to the Americas, what we describe in this chapter refers specifically to the US context.

References

Abrego, Leisy J. 2008. "Legitimacy, Social Identity, and the Mobilization of Law: The Effects of Assembly Bill 540 on Undocumented Students in California." *Law & Social Inquiry* 33:709–34.

Abrego, Leisy J., and Roberto G. Gonzales. 2010. "Blocked Paths, Uncertain Futures: The Postsecondary Education and Labor Market Prospects of Undocumented Latino Youth." *Journal of Education for Students Placed at Risk* 15: 144–157.

Barron, Elisha. 2011. "Recent Development: The Development, Relief, and Education for Alien Minors (DREAM) Act." *Harvard Journal of Legislation* 48: 623–655.

Batalova, Jeanne, Sarah Hooker, and Randy Capps. 2013. "Deferred Action for Childhood Arrivals at the One-Year Mark: A Profile of Currently Eligible Youth and Applicants." Washington, DC: Migration Policy Institute.

Batalova, Jeanne, and Margie McHugh. 2010. "Dream vs. Reality: An Analysis of Potential DREAM Act Beneficiaries." Washington, DC: Migration Policy Institute.

Batalova, Jeanne, and Michelle Mittelstadt. 2012. "Relief from Deportation: Demographic Profile of the DREAMers Potentially Eligible under the Deferred Action Policy." Washington, DC: Migration Policy Institute.

Buckley, Cara. 2008. "Teenagers' Violent 'Sport' Led to Killing on Long Island, Officials Say." *The New York Times*, November 20. Retrieved November 25, 2014, from http://www.nytimes.com/2008/11/21/nyregion/21immigrant.html ?pagewanted=all&_r=0.

Chavez, Leo R. 2008. *The Latino Threat: Constructing Immigrants, Citizens, and the Nation*. Stanford, CA: Stanford University Press.

Contreras, Reynaldo A. 2002. "The Impact of Immigration Policy on Education Reform: Implications for the New Millennium." *Education and Urban Society* 34:134–155.

De Fina, Anna. 2003. *Identity in Narrative: A Study of Immigrant Discourse*. Philadelphia, PA: John Benjamin's Publishing North America Co.

Denzin, Norman K., and Yvonna S. Lincoln. 2008. "Introduction: Critical Methodologies and Indigenous Inquiry." In *Handbook of Critical and Indigenous Methodologies*, edited by N. K. Denzin, Y. S. Lincoln, and L. T. Smith, 1–20. Thousand Oaks, CA: SAGE Publications.

Dreby, Joanna. 2015. *Everyday Illegal: When Policies Undermine Immigrant Families*. Berkeley: University of California Press.

Fraga, Luis Ricardo, and Gary M. Segura. 2006. "Culture Clash? Contesting Notions of American Identity and the Effects of Latin American Immigration." *Perspectives on Politics* 4:279–287.

Frum, Jennifer L. 2007. "Postsecondary Educational Access for Undocumented Students: Opportunities and Constraints." *American Academic* 3(1):81–107.

Garcia, Ruben J. 2003. "Across the Borders: Immigrant Status and Identity in Law and LatCrit Theory." *Florida Law Review* 55:511–537.

Gonzales, Roberto G. 2008. "Left Out but Not Shut Down: Political Activism and the Undocumented Student Movement." *Northwestern Journal of Law and Social Policy* 3(2):1–22.

———. 2010. "On the Wrong Side of the Tracks: The Consequences of School Stratification Systems for Unauthorized Mexican Students." *Peabody Journal of Education* 85(4):469–485.

———. 2011. "Learning to be Illegal: Undocumented Youth and Shifting Legal Contexts in the Transition to Adulthood." *American Sociological Review* 76(4): 602–619.

Gonzales, Roberto G., and Angie M. Bautista-Chavez. 2014. "Two Years and Counting: Assessing the Growing Power of DACA." American Immigration Council Special Report.

Gonzales, Roberto G., and Leo R. Chavez. 2012. "'Awakening to a Nightmare:' Objectivity and Illegality in the Lives of Undocumented 1.5 Generation Latino Immigrants in the United States." *Current Anthropology* 53(3):255–281.

Gonzales, Roberto G., and Veronica Terriquez. 2013. "How DACA Is Impacting the Lives of Those Who Are Now DACAmented: Preliminary Findings from the National UnDACAmented Research Project." Washington, DC: Immigration Policy Center.

Gonzales, Roberto G., Veronica Terriquez, and Stephen P. Ruszczyk. 2014. "Becoming DACAmented: Assessing the Short-Term Benefits of Deferred Action for Childhood Arrivals (DACA)." *American Behavioral Scientist* 58(14):1852–1872.

Hoefer, Michael, Nancy Rytina, and Bryan C. Baker. 2012. "Estimates of the Unauthorized Immigrant Population Residing in the United States: January 2011." Office of Immigration Statistics. Washington, DC: Department of Homeland Security.

Jenkins, Richard. 1996. *Social Identity*. New York: Routledge Sage Foundation.

Massey, Douglas S., and Magaly Sanchez. 2010. *Brokered Boundaries: Creating Immigrant Identity in Anti-Immigrant Times*. New York: Routledge Sage Foundation.

Menjívar, Cecilia, and Leisy J. Abrego. 2012. "Legal Violence: Immigration Law and the Lives of Central American Immigrants." *American Journal of Sociology* 117(5):1380–1421.

National Conference of State Legislatures. 2014. "Allow In-State Tuition for Undocumented Students." Washington, DC: National Conference of State Legislatures.

National Immigration Law Center. 2015. "Access to Driver's Licenses for Immigrant Youth Granted DACA." Washington, DC: National Immigration Law Center.

Nguyen, David H. K., and Zaliden R. Martinez Hoy. 2015. "'Jim Crowing' Plyler v. Doe: The Resegregation of Undocumented Students in American Higher Education through Discriminatory Sate Tuition and Fee Legislation." *Cleveland State Law Review* 63:355–371.

Nichols, Walter J. 2013. *The DREAMers: How the Undocumented Youth Movement Transformed the Immigrant Rights Movement*. Stanford, CA: Stanford University Press.

Passel, Jeffrey S. 2003. "Further Demographic Information Relating to the DREAM Act." Washington, DC: The Urban Institute.

Passel, Jeffrey S., D'Vera Cohn, and Ana Gonzalez-Barrera. 2012. "Net Migration from Mexico Falls to Zero—and Perhaps Less." Washington, DC: Pew Hispanic Center.

———. 2013. "Population Decline of Unauthorized Immigrants Stalls, May Have Reversed." Washington, DC: Pew Hispanic Center.

Perez, William. 2009. *We are Americans: Undocumented Students Pursuing the American Dream*. Sterling, VA: Stylus Publishing.

Perez, William, Roberta Espinoza, Karina Ramos, Heidi M. Coronado, and Richard Cortes. 2009. "Academic Resilience among Undocumented Latino Students." *Hispanic Journal of Behavioral Sciences* 31(2):149–181.

Portes, Alejandro, and Rubén G. Rumbaut. 2001. *Legacies: The Study of the Second Immigrant Generation*. Los Angeles, CA: University of California Press.

Rincón, Alejandra. 2008. *Undocumented Immigrants and Higher Education: Sí Se Puede!* El Paso, TX: LFB Scholarly Publishing.

———. 2010. "Si Se Puede! Undocumented Immigrants' Struggle for Education and Their Right to Stay." *Journal of College Admission* 206:13–18.

Rosaldo, Renato. 1994. "Cultural Citizenship and Educational Democracy." *Cultural Anthropology* 9(3):402–411.

Rumbaut, Ruben G. 1997. "Assimilation and its Discontents: Between Rhetoric and Reality." *International Migration Review* 31:923–60.

Rumbaut, Ruben G., and Golnaz Komaie. 2010. "Immigration and Adult Transitions." *The Future of Children* 20:39–63.

Stevenson, Andrew. 2004. "Dreaming of an Equal Future for Immigrant Children: Federal and State Initiatives to Improve Undocumented Students' Access to Postsecondary Education." *Arizona Law Review* 46(3):551–580.

Suárez-Orozco, Carola, Marcelo M. Suárez-Orozco, and Irina Todorova. 2008. *Learning a New Land: Immigrant Students in American Society.* Cambridge, MA: Harvard University Press.

Tajfel, Henri, ed. 1982. *Social Identity and Intergroup Relations.* Cambridge: Cambridge University Press.

United We Dream. 2014. "Tuition Equity for Undocumented Students: Access by State." Washington, DC: United We Dream.

Van Gennep, Arnold. [1960] 2004. *The Rites of Passage.* London: Routledge and Kegan Paul.

Yoshikawa, Hirokazu. 2011. *Immigrants Raising Citizens: Undocumented Parents and Their Young Children.* New York: Russell Sage Foundation.

Zhou, Min. 1997. "Growing up American: The Challenge Confronting Immigrant Children and Children of Immigrants." *Annual Review of Sociology* 23:63–95.

CHAPTER 7

Deferred Action for Childhood Arrivals (DACA) and Student Success in Higher Education

KANDY MINK SALAS, HENOC PRECIADO,
AND RAQUEL TORRES

Undocumented youth in the United States have long hoped for federal legislation that would resolve their residency status and bring some stability and peace to families who have been living in uncertainty. In light of the deadlock in the US Congress, which has failed to pass immigration reform, in 2012 President Barack Obama took the affirmative step of implementing via executive action the Deferred Action for Childhood Arrivals (DACA) policy. Secretary of Homeland Security Janet Napolitano announced to the press the deferred action process for young people considered low enforcement priorities:

> Certain young people who were brought to the United States as young children, do not present a risk to national security or public safety, and meet several key criteria will be considered for relief from removal from the country or from entering into removal proceedings. Those who demonstrate that they meet the criteria will be eligible to receive deferred action for a period of two years, subject to renewal, and will be eligible to apply for work authorization. (USDHS 2012)

This policy was enacted after a long history of stops and starts in federal legislation reform efforts. The implementation of DACA has generated both opportunities and unique challenges for colleges and universities working to serve the undocumented student population and for "DACAmented" students themselves.[1] With a focus on the implications for undocumented college students, this chapter discusses the history, requirements, and results of President Obama's executive order. The authors make recommendations for higher-education professionals and institutions working with these students. The quotes from students included in this chapter are drawn from a research project at the University of Texas at San Antonio Mexico Center that included interviews with student activists who have organized to share their stories and demand immigration reform. Several students interviewed had recently received their DACA status.

Legislative History

In what is known as the 1982 *Plyler v. Doe* ruling, the US Supreme Court banned public schools from denying undocumented immigrant students access to public education. The Supreme Court ruling struck down a Texas state statute that denied educational funding for undocumented children. At the same time, the court blocked a school district's attempt to charge undocumented families an annual fee for each enrolled undocumented student in order to compensate for the state costs of educating those children (Soltero 2006; Olivas 2009). The judges argued that undocumented children have the same right to a free public education as US citizens or legal permanent residents. The *Plyler v. Doe* ruling has been limited to public kindergarten through twelfth grade and does not confer any rights to undocumented students to pursue public higher education (Soltero 2006; Olivas 2009).

Since 2001 the US Congress has repeatedly introduced and debated the Development, Relief, and Education for Alien Minors (DREAM) Act (American Immigration Council 2010). If approved, this legislation would grant undocumented young individuals who were brought to the United States as children a path to permanent residency and eventual citizenship. Under the DREAM Act, eligible young people would have to meet certain requirements, including enrolling in college or the military upon high school graduation. By the end of the 113th US Congress (2013–2015), the DREAM Act had not gained sufficient support in either the Senate or House of Representatives to become law.

During the summer of 2013, the Democrat-controlled Senate passed the Border Security, Economic Opportunity, and Immigration Modernization Act, a bipartisan bill aimed at implementing comprehensive immigration reform (American Immigration Council 2013). That proposed legislation incorporated portions of past versions of the DREAM Act and detailed a pathway to citizenship for undocumented individuals brought to the United States as children. Operating under what is referred to in politics as the Hastert Rule, the Speaker of the House did not introduce the bill in the House because the majority of Republicans did not support the Senate-passed proposal (Sherman 2013). In addition, while it was not formally introduced to the legislative body, a new bill known as the Kids Act was intended to provide legal status to undocumented young individuals who met certain requirements (Foley 2013). Still, lack of support for the Kids Act suggested that the House of Representatives remained unwilling to tackle comprehensive immigration reform.

DACA Origins, Implementation, and Outcomes

After many unsuccessful attempts to pass the federal DREAM Act, on June 15, 2012, President Obama announced the DACA program. Through a memorandum signed by Secretary of Homeland Security Napolitano, the Obama administration instructed US Immigration and Customs Enforcement (ICE), US Customs and Border Protection, and US Citizenship and Immigration Services (USCIS) to exercise prosecutorial discretion when enforcing immigration laws affecting certain young individuals who, through no fault of their own, were brought to the United States without proper documentation when they were children (Napolitano 2012). On August 15, USCIS started processing applications for deferred action under DACA (USCIS 2014a).

Nationally, many states welcomed the implementation of DACA. In April 2014, Virginia's attorney general announced that students lawfully present in the state under the DACA program would qualify for in-state college tuition. In the state of Washington, DACA recipients planning on enrolling in the state's public higher-education institutions became eligible for the State Need Grant program. California immediately began implementing policies and regulations that aligned with the mission of DACA (National Conference of State Legislatures 2014). In the states responding positively to DACA, government and private organizations began mobilizing to educate potential DACA-eligible individuals about the benefits of applying for and receiving DACA. These educational efforts were conducted in offices, churches, colleges and universities, community organizations, and other public venues.

In other states, such as Arizona, the reception of DACA was not positive (NCSL 2014). The Arizona Governor immediately took a public stance against DACA and banned DACAmented individuals from receiving state benefits (such as a driver's license). In July 2014 a federal appeals court based in San Francisco overruled the governor's order (Immigrant Law Group PC 2014). As of 2015, undocumented students were eligible for in-state tuition in eighteen states through state provisions or legislation (National Conference of State Legislatures 2015). Three states—Arizona, Georgia, and Indiana—prohibited in-state tuition for undocumented students, and Alabama and South Carolina banned the enrollment of undocumented students at any public institution of higher education (NCSL 2015). In addition, Texas legislators initiated efforts in 2015 to repeal in-state tuition for undocumented students (Ura and McCollough 2015).

Other challenges to DACA came from within the federal government itself. When first implemented, DACA was the subject of litigation initiated by ICE personnel (Foley 2012). In a case against Homeland Security Secretary Napolitano, immigration personnel argued that implementation of DACA prevented them from enforcing the US Constitution and claimed that they were being ordered to break federal law (Foley 2012). A federal court rejected their claims.

DACA Eligibility and the Application Process

In order to meet criteria outlined in the June 15, 2012, memo (USCIS 2014b), eligible youth had to be under the age of thirty-one as of June 15, 2012; must have come to the United States before reaching their sixteenth birthday; must have continuously resided in the United States since June 15, 2007; and must have been physically present in the country on June 15, 2012, and at the time of making the request for consideration of deferred action. Youth must have entered without inspection or have had their lawful immigration status expire as of June 15, 2012, and must be enrolled in school, have graduated or obtained a certificate of completion from high school or a general education development (GED) certificate, or have been honorably discharged from the US Coast Guard or armed forces. Eligible applicants cannot have been convicted of a felony, a significant misdemeanor, or three or more other misdemeanors, and not otherwise pose a threat to national security or public safety. In addition to providing supporting documentation proving that they met all the eligibility guidelines, applicants had to pay a $465 processing fee to cover the costs of implementing the program (USCIS 2014a).

DACA Benefits

Young people who became DACAmented under President Obama's 2012 executive order received a two-year temporary relief from deportation. According to USCIS, DACA can be renewed every two years as long the program is in place. In addition to protection from deportation, the 2012 executive order also grants DACAmented individuals work permits that authorize them to legally work in the United States for two years with a possibility of renewal. In most US states, deferred action and a work permit qualify individuals to obtain a Social Security number, a state-issued identification card, and a state-issued driver's license. DACA beneficiaries can also request advance parole to travel outside the United States for educational, employment, or humanitarian purposes (USCIS 2014b). This travel permission has allowed qualifying youth to reunite with relatives they had not seen for many years and has enabled students to participate in academic programs and work-related travel.

DACA Renewal and Expansion

On June 5, 2014, the new Secretary of Homeland Security, Jeh Johnson, announced the DACA renewal process (USDHS 2014) allowing eligible persons to apply for an additional two years of deferral. As outlined by USCIS, in order for individuals to renew their DACA status they had to meet the initial DACA requirements and, in addition, must not have traveled outside the United States without advance parole and must have continuously resided in the United States since their last DACA approval (USCIS 2014c). Applicants had to submit their renewal forms at least 120 days before their deferred action expired and were required to pay a renewal filing fee of $465 (USCIS 2014c).

On November 20, 2014, President Obama announced a new executive order that included an expansion of DACA and created a new program, the Deferred Action for Parents of Americans and Lawful Permanent Residents (DAPA) (Immigration Policy Center 2014).[2] The 2014 executive action eliminated the age ceiling and changed the cutoff date for DACA eligibility to January 1, 2010, instead of June 15, 2007. With these changes, an additional 330,000 undocumented immigrants became eligible for deportation relief through DACA (Krogstad and Gonzalez-Barrera 2014). In addition, deferred action and work authorization were extended to three years instead of two for those who had already applied and for those eligible under the 2014 expansions (Johnson 2014). However, legal action against President Obama's 2014 executive orders by Texas and twenty-five other states blocked the implementation of DACA expansions a day before the initiation of the new program (Preston 2015). In response, immigration advocacy organizations filed briefs with the US Fifth Circuit Court of Appeals defending the deferred action initiative and requesting the courts to lift the injunction to allow the implementation of the policy (American Immigration Council 2015). On May 26, 2015, the Fifth Circuit Court of Appeals denied the request to stay the injunction blocking the implementation of DAPA and the expanded DACA.

DACA Outcomes

From the program's implementation in 2012 to 2015, USCIS received a total of 794,501 requests for DACA. From these initial applications, 748,789 were accepted for review and 664,607 received approvals. Since 2014, when the DACA renewal process was announced, 381,188 youth have applied for renewal as their two-year DACA permission expired; 355,805 of these applications were accepted, and 243,872 were approved for extension (USCIS 2015). The difference between the number of DACA requests and the number of DACA approvals reflects the fact that many applicants lack adequate documentation to receive approval.

The top six countries of origin of youth requesting DACA were Mexico, El Salvador, Guatemala, Honduras, Peru, and South Korea; the six states with the highest number of DACA applications were California, Texas, Illinois, New York, Florida, and Arizona.[3]

Not all DACA-eligible individuals applied for deferred action.[4] When compared with DACA recipients, eligible youth who did not apply tended to have less schooling and to be less connected with schools and organizations in their neighborhoods. Undocumented youth who had legal infractions or lacked sufficient documentation to prove their age of arrival and time of residency in the United States potentially faced complicated legal cases in the DACA application process (Gonzales and Bautista-Chavez 2014).

It is important to remember that DACA does not provide a permanent solution to the immigration challenges of undocumented youth. As a presidential executive order, DACA can be rescinded by a future president or by an act of Congress. As individuals continue to apply and reapply for DACA, a major question remains: What will happen if DACA is terminated? The future of DACA remains uncertain, especially in light of evolving hostile sentiments toward undocumented individuals and continued challenges in the courts. In this context, youth and their families must weigh whether the immediate benefits of a temporary reprieve from deportation and authorization to work and drive legally outweigh the risks associated with providing the federal government the information required to process the DACA application. Some of these risks include having one's name in a database of known undocumented individuals residing in the United States and the uncertainty of knowing which legal services to trust in asking for help in preparing the documents necessary to apply for DACA.

Opportunities and Uncertainties for DACAmented College Students

The implementation of DACA has had important consequences for undocumented students enrolled or planning to enroll in higher education. One of the most significant new opportunities for DACAmented students is the possibility to work legally to help pay for college expenses, which relieves some of the financial pressures these students and their families face (Teranishi, C. Suárez-Orozco, and M. Suárez-Orozco 2011). This is particularly relevant because undocumented students, even those who are DACAmented, do not qualify for federal financial aid and are not eligible to receive federal work-study funds.

Prior to DACA, most undocumented college students were uncertain about their professional futures and worried about finding gainful and meaningful employment after having invested many years in their education. DACA has allowed these well-prepared students to enter the US workforce and to utilize their training and education to work legally and pursue postgraduate careers, even if on a temporary basis.

Another important benefit of DACA is the possibility of obtaining a driver's license. Before DACA, undocumented students had to address transportation issues in typically one of three ways: by using public transportation, often adding considerable travel time to an already busy day; by relying on other licensed drivers, including family and friends; or by risking driving themselves without a license. These options were not ideal and added to the stress of everyday life for undocumented youth dealing with the pressures of university studies.

According to the National Immigration Law Center (2015), as of May 2015, "all fifty states and the District of Columbia now issue driver's licenses to otherwise-eligible immigrant youth granted DACA." Only two states, Arizona and Nebraska, initially declared that DACA recipients were not eligible to apply for a driver's license. Arizona was ordered by a district court on January 22, 2015, to permanently end the policy of denying licenses to DACA recipients. In May 2015, the Nebraska legislature determined that DACA recipients can obtain driver's licenses (National Immigration Law Center 2015).

A driver's license is a government-issued document that also serves as an important form of identification. A state-issued ID is required to apply for many crucial services, such as opening a bank account and setting up basic services such as utilities or telephone. In addition, a driver's license is a valid form of identification that allows a person to pass through airport security.

The creation of DACA opened travel opportunities for undocumented students. Prior to DACA, many undocumented students were reluctant to leave the United States, not knowing if they would be allowed to return. Travel constraints prevented these students from attending professional conferences, conducting research, taking advantage of internships or fellowships in different parts of the country, and participating in class field trips. With DACA and the protection of federal- and state-issued documents deferring deportation, students now feel more comfortable with air travel, near-border travel, and international travel.

Daily life is fraught with concern and anxiety for undocumented individuals, who constantly worry about the possibility of deportation for themselves and their family members (Dreby 2015). Researchers such as Dozier (1995) and Pérez et al. (2010) have commented on the anxiety and fear experienced by undocumented college students. One young woman explained her struggles:

> I didn't qualify for federal financial aid, so it just made me more conscious of where I spent my money because I knew that I didn't have a work permit. I began to think about the future, like after I graduate, am I going to be able to get a job? Am I going to be able to pay all these loans off . . . because I didn't know if I was going to have money after I graduated. It made me want to focus on school more, but at the same time I think it gives you really high anxiety because of all those worries.[5]

For students who received DACA, becoming DACAmented lessened this daily fear, lowered stress, improved their positive self-image, and increased hope for the future. Roberto, a student from Texas, explained how he felt after receiving DACA status:

> I even made a joke about it to one of my friends, "Hey, I can finally be normal!" I can actually be normal in a sense that . . . I can do stuff that everyone else can do. I'm about to graduate in May, so when I applied and I was waiting for it [DACA], I was, like, I'm just hoping I can get something and

hoping to apply for a job, so that I can get a job. Like a driver's license. I can actually, I can drive! And not be scared.[6]

Although DACA has helped eliminate some of the fear experienced by undocumented youth, many worry about what will happen next with immigration reform in the United States. They remain concerned for family members who are not able to take advantage of DACA. Several scholars have written about the struggles of undocumented youth (DeGenova 2002; Abrego 2006; Gonzales 2007, 2011; Teranishi, C. Suárez-Orozco, and M. Suárez-Orozco 2011; Gonzales, Suárez-Orozco, and Dedios-Sanguineti 2013; Gonzales and Terriquez 2013). While certainly not perfect and not reaching all undocumented people in the United States, the DACA policy brought some psychological relief to the youth who qualified for the program. The legal challenges to DACA, however, continue to make the future of these young people extremely insecure.

Most participants and allies do not see DACA as a permanent solution and desire a more solid determination of the future via comprehensive immigration reform. There is heightened anxiety about being involved in a federal program where participants voluntarily register their undocumented status and place themselves in a national database of undocumented people. DACA applicants take a leap of faith that the US government will not later use this information to deport them. Some youth who are eligible for DACA have not applied because of this fear, even if doing so might provide relief from a very stressful situation.

Another source of anxiety for undocumented and DACAmented students revolves around the decision to disclose their immigration status and the determination of who is "safe" to tell. These students are continually assessing those they come into contact with—faculty, staff, fellow students—to decide whether, when, and how to share their status. With the ability to apply for employment, either while a student or post-graduation, DACA-mented individuals must decide how and when to share their immigration status with a potential employer. While this may be an easy process when discussing DACA status with an on-campus employer, particularly an ally, it may be more challenging with a potential off-campus employer. Youths fear that employers may be reluctant to hire them because of a lack of understanding of the executive order and concerns about the uncertainty of DACA.

With the creation of DACA, some families are experiencing less apprehension because they know that the young people they brought to the United States as children have some protection under the law. However, for many families the implementation of DACA has meant that, even more than before, the immigration status of the various family members is dissimilar: some may be US citizens or legal permanent residents, others may be DACAmented, and others may remain undocumented. Often college students feel guilty that they now have rights and privileges that their relatives and friends do not have.

Worries about deportation continue for family members. The fear of being separated as a family can make it difficult for students to concentrate on studies and other obligations. A student at a Texas university explained that she was appreciative of DACA, but she also worried about her family:

> It's not just students, but for the parents who are trying to provide for their families. That's the main thing I think . . . because that's urgent, you know, people are trying to provide for their families. People are trying not to get deported. I mean, people are fighting not to get separated from their families. That's just, it's basic. I feel like [you] start with DACA and then you can worry about a path to citizenship, to be fair, you know?[7]

The newly DACAmented student may also face new expectations at home. With access to a driver's license and the possibility to work legally, the student may be expected to financially contribute more in support of the family or to provide transportation for others. A young woman struggling to complete her degree told us:

> Your parents rely on you a lot. My mom needs paperwork signed for a loan and I have to be the one to take her because, you know, she can drive, but if she gets pulled over, then that would not be a good thing. So having a valid driver's license and getting deferred action means that you are in a position where you're taking care of other people . . . [Other students] are not spending money on anyone but themselves, right? But for me, I have to be really conscious of where my money goes, and I have to take care of other people at the same time.[8]

Another student who had received her DACA status explained how she had worked to pay the $465 for her own application fee and then $465 for someone else. She laughed, noting that "I think it just makes you go crazy with all the money that you spend . . . you just have to pay application, after application, after application fee." She acknowledged, however, that "being able to work and being able to contribute financially gives you a sense of inclusion that you don't have otherwise. That's why so many people come to the United States, for economic reasons, so I think not being able to partic-ipate in that definitely makes you feel a little less American than all those other people around you."[9]

Implications of DACA for Colleges and Universities

The implementation of DACA as a federal policy has transformed the lives of eligible undocumented college students and has brought about significant changes in how educators work with these students. It is important that campus personnel, especially in states with the highest numbers of DACA-mented individuals, are informed of the existence of DACA, understand how best to advise students, and have knowledge of referral resources both on and off campus. Faculty and student affairs professionals should be fa-miliar with policies and regulations regarding the rights now afforded to this population of students.

Providing training for university employees on DACA and other issues of importance for undocumented students is crucial so that students are not denied opportunities and benefits they are entitled to receive. College per-sonnel may regularly come into contact with DACAmented and undoc-umented students and may not be aware of their status. Helping college personnel understand the issues faced by DACAmented students and pro-viding them with resources to refer students to needed services, such as le-gal aid, scholarships, or counseling, will greatly improve the educational ex-perience of this group of students.

University faculty and staff need to be aware of the social, educational, political, and legal challenges undocumented students face and the high ed-ucational achievement and civic engagement that motivate undocumented students who complete higher education (Pérez 2009). Campuses should institutionalize training programs for faculty and staff on student life and policy matters related to DACAmented and undocumented students. Of-ten, universities will leave this work to students and student organizations. To emphasize the importance of this information, campuses should take steps to include this training in regular and ongoing offerings from human resources or other campus departments.

Any type of training for university employees and counselors should consider the psychological and psychosocial challenges DACAmented stu-dents face. Feelings of relief mixed with continued anxiety over the future are common, as are feelings of guilt associated with gaining a benefit that is not available to parents and other family members. If possible, especially in colleges with a large number of undocumented students, counseling centers should recruit professionals with particular expertise in this area. DACA-mented students should be made aware of the counseling services available. Mental-health strategies and stress management could be discussed at student organization meetings. Peer support is especially important for undocumented youth. Organizations such as United We Dream and local campus groups that have assisted the DREAM Act movement allow students to share their stories and support one another.

Colleges and universities should consider establishing centralized service locations for undocumented students, such as DREAM centers or offices of undocumented student services. In these centers, undocumented and DACAmented students could seek information about their rights and responsibilities and about DACA and how it impacts their lives as college students. Personnel in these offices should be made aware of the DACA program, be prepared to advise students on the basic tenets of the policy, and know when to refer students to off-campus services for specific legal advice.

With new opportunities to enter the US workforce, DACAmented students may need coaching on workplace organizational and cultural practices. Like many first-generation college students and low-income students, DACAmented individuals may need additional mentoring and instruction as they transition from their role as college students to new professionals. Academic departments and career centers should make concerted efforts to reach out to DACAmented student populations to conduct workshops and provide coaching opportunities focused on US workplace culture and successful job-seeking behaviors.

DACAmented students can also benefit from advice on when and how to disclose their DACA status during the hiring process. Dolores, who has a degree in computer technology, explained:

> So employers are looking for people who they can invest in for the long term, right? With DACA you only have a work permit for two years. That's not long term, right? In the eyes of corporations. I'm not going to tell you [employer] that I have a work permit, I mean you need to know that I have a work permit and that it's gonna be up for renewal soon, but you don't want to emphasize that your time is possibly limited because that puts you at another disadvantage compared to all the other applicants.

Dolores was conflicted about how much to explain to potential employers, many of whom, she said, "did not understand the difference between a green card and a work permit."[10]

In addition to new employment alternatives, DACA has opened up internship opportunities for undocumented students. This is especially relevant for college majors that require internship credits for graduation. Before DACA, few internships were available for undocumented students, and the process of applying for them was complicated. Some internships required a criminal background check prior to appointment, and with no driver's license or Social Security number, an undocumented student would often be uncertain how to proceed. In addition, background checks are typically processed at the university police department or college security office. Understandably, prior to DACA undocumented students were reluctant to voluntarily request a background check.

University faculty and staff can provide positive role models, encouragement, and guidance, not only in the students' academic pursuits but as they enter the job market as DACAmented workers (Pérez 2012). As one DACAmented student said: "DACA has opened so many doors. Thanks to the support of mentors, professors, and staff, I have been made aware of these doors and have walked into new opportunities confident and equipped with the skills necessary to be successful."[11]

Student Activism in Higher Education

Undocumented and DACAmented students themselves have taken a proactive stance in improving their academic opportunities and educational outcomes (Nicholls 2013). United We Dream, the largest immigrant-youth-led organization in the United States, for example, has developed and implemented resources and programs to support undocumented students, eligible DACA recipients, and families with information about immigrant rights, DACA application procedures, and access to higher education.

Founded by undocumented college students in 2008, United We Dream developed the Dream Educational Empowerment Program (DEEP) in an effort to advance educational justice and empowerment for undocumented students. DEEP offers an array of resources, including toolkits that provide educators, staff, and undocumented college students with information and guides to increase campus support systems and awareness at their institutions (United We Dream 2015a). These toolkits offer guidance for parents and students regarding financial aid, student rights, and access to higher education for undocumented youth. DEEP's most recent initiative is the "UndocuPeers: Liberating Campus Climate," a four-hour interactive ally certificate training program designed to increase participants' knowledge and understanding of undocumented students (United We Dream 2015b).

United We Dream also instituted a National Educators Coming Out Day and a National Institution Coming Out Day. These initiatives are aimed at increasing awareness about undocumented students on college campuses, building commitment, and promoting systematic policy changes "to begin or to help continue conversations on how to build institutional support with and for undocumented students" (United We Dream 2015a).

The Implications of DACA for Immigration Policy

Although DACA has provided relief from deportation to more than 664,000 youth from its implementation in 2012 to March 2015 (USCIS 2015), the policy should be seen as a partial and temporary solution to a broken immigration system. Studies by the Pew Research Center's Hispanic Trends Project reveal that of the 11.2 million undocumented individuals living in the United States in 2012 (Passel et al. 2014), 4.4 million were thirty years old or younger (Passel and Lopez 2012). Of these 4.4 million undocumented individuals, 1.7 million were eligible for DACA (Passel and Lopez 2012).

Data from the Hispanic Trends Project (Passel and Lopez 2012) also show that of the 1.7 million undocumented individuals eligible for DACA in 2012:

- 700,000 were between the ages of eighteen and thirty in high school or with a high school diploma
- 250,000 were between the ages of fifteen and seventeen and enrolled in high school
- 320,000 were ages sixteen to thirty with no high school diploma or GED (and not enrolled in school)
- 450,000 were between the ages of five and fourteen (and will become eligible to apply for DACA once they turn fifteen)

The data above show that large numbers of youth who have lived most of their lives in the United States and are currently enrolled in US schools may qualify if DACA continues. Thus, it is vital that teachers, counselors, and administrators understand the benefits and implications of DACA so that they can best advise undocumented students and their families. It is also important to note that many undocumented youth cannot qualify for DACA. Those youth and their undocumented family members remain at risk of family separations due to deportations. While research demonstrates that DACA has positively contributed to US society by increasing opportunities for youth and building human capital, improving access to post-secondary education, and providing a boost to the economy,[12] it does not provide a route to legal permanent residency or citizenship, and there is no guarantee that the policy will be allowed to continue.

Notes

1. *DACAmented* is an informal term used to identify youth who have received DACA status.

2. DAPA, generally speaking, follows the same eligibility guidelines as those established for DACA. One significant difference, though, is that individuals must have had, on or before November 14, 2014, a son or daughter who was a US citizen or lawful permanent resident (Johnson 2014).

3. See the following link for more data on the number of considerations for DACA by fiscal year: http://www.uscis.gov/sites/default/files/USCIS/Resources /Reports%20and%20Studies/Immigration%20Forms%20Data/Naturalization %20Data/I821d_performancedata_fy2015_qtr2.pdf.

4. An accurate estimate of the nonapplicant population is not feasible; however, it is estimated to be in the hundreds of thousands. Researchers with the National UnDACAmented Project interviewed 244 respondents who were DACA eligible but did not apply. These participants indicated that they were not able to afford the application fee (43%), did not know how to apply (10%), were missing paperwork (22%), had legal concerns (17%), had a fear of providing personal information to the government (15%), or were waiting for better options to arise (30%) (Gonzales and Bautista-Chavez 2014).

5. Interview conducted May 22, 2013.

6. Interview conducted March 11, 2013.

7. Interview conducted March 25, 2013.

8. Interview conducted May 22, 2013.

9. Interview conducted May 22, 2013.

10. Interview conducted May 22, 2013.

11. Interview conducted May 22, 2013.

12. According to the 2014 report *Two Years and Counting: Assessing the Growing Power of DACA*, by Roberto G. Gonzales and Angie M. Bautista-Chavez, based on a national survey of 2,684 DACA-eligible young adults between the ages of eighteen and thirty-one, 59 percent of the DACA beneficiaries surveyed had obtained new jobs, and 45 percent had increased job earnings since receiving DACA. New jobs and increased earnings have translated into a greater tax base and a boost to the US economy.

References

Abrego, Leisy J. 2006. "'I Can't Go to College Because I Don't Have Papers:' Incorporation Patterns of Latino Undocumented Youth." *Latino Studies* 4(3):212–231.

American Immigration Council. 2010. "The DREAM Act: Creating Economic Opportunities." Washington, DC: Immigration Policy Center.

———. 2013. "A Guide to H.R. 15: The Border Security, Economic Opportunity, and Immigration Modernization Act." Washington, DC: Immigration Policy Center.

———. 2015. "Unprecedented Coalition Ask Court to Reverse Texas Ruling Blocking Immigration Initiatives." Washington, DC: American Immigration Council. Retrieved April 7, 2015, from http://www.americanimmigration council.org/newsroom/release/unprecedented-coalition-ask-court-reverse-texas -ruling-blocking-immigration-initiate.

DeGenova, Nicholas P. 2002. "Migrant 'Illegality' and Deportability in Everyday Life." *Annual Review of Anthropology* 31:419–447.

Dozier, Sandra. B. 1995. "Undocumented Immigrant Students at an Urban College: A Demographic and Academic Profile." *Migration World* 23(1–2):20–22.

Dreby, Joanna. 2015. *Everyday Illegal: When Policies Undermine Immigrant Families.* Berkeley: University of California Press.

Foley, Elise. 2012. "Kris Kobach Represents Immigration Agents in Lawsuit Against Obama Administration." *Huffington Post*, August 23. Retrieved September 1, 2012, from http://www.huffingtonpost.com/2012/08/23/kris-kobach -immigration-lawsuit-obama_n_1825272.html.

———. 2013. "Eric Cantor, Bob Goodlatte on KIDS Act to Address Dreamers." *Huffington Post*, July 11. Retrieved August 1, 2013, from http://www.huffing tonpost.com/2013/07/11/eric-cantor-bob-goodlatte-kids-act_n_3581635.html.

Gonzales, Roberto G. 2007. "Wasted Talent and Broken Dreams: The Lost Potential of Undocumented Students." *Immigration Policy in Focus* 5(13):1–11.

———. 2011. "Learning to Be Illegal: Undocumented Youth and Shifting Legal Contexts in the Transition to Adulthood." *American Sociological Review* 76(4): 602–619.

Gonzales, Roberto G., and Angie M. Bautista-Chavez. 2014. *Two Years and Counting: Assessing the Growing Power of DACA.* Washington, DC: American Immigration Council.

Gonzales, Roberto G., Carola Suárez-Orozco, and Maria Celia Dedios-Sanguineti. 2013. "No Place to Belong: Contextualizing Concepts of Mental Health among Undocumented Immigrant Youth in the United States." *American Behavioral Scientist* 20(10):1–26. doi:10.1177/0002764213487349.

Gonzales, Roberto G., and Veronica Terriquez. 2013. "How DACA Is Impacting the Lives of Those Now DACAmented: Preliminary Findings from the National UnDACAmented Research Project." Washington, DC: Immigration Policy Center.

Immigrant Law Group PC. 2014. "Arizona Dreamers Get a Chance to Hit the Road." Portland, Oregon: Immigration Law Group. Retrieved August 1, 2014, from http://www.ilgrp.com/arizona-dreamers-get-a-chance-to-hit-the-road/.

Immigration Policy Center. 2014. "A Guide to the Immigration Accountability Executive Action." Washington DC: American Immigration Council. Retrieved December 1, 2014, from http://www.immigrationpolicy.org/special-reports /guide-immigration-accountability-executive-action.

Johnson, Jeh Charles. 2014. *Exercising Prosecutorial Discretion with Respect to Indi-*

viduals Who Came to the United States as Children and with Respect to Certain Individuals Who Are the Parents of US Citizens or Permanent Residents [Memorandum]. Washington, DC: US Department of Homeland Security.

Krogstad, Jens Manuel, and Ana Gonzalez-Barrera. 2014. "If Original DACA Program is a Guide, Many Eligible Immigrants Will Apply for Deportation Relief." Washington, DC: Pew Research Center. Retrieved December 15, 2014, from http://www.pewresearch.org/fact-tank/2014/12/05/if-original-daca-program-is-a-guide-many-eligible-immigrants-will-apply-for-deportation-relief/.

Napolitano, Janet. 2012. *Exercising Prosecutorial Discretion with Respect to Individuals Who Came to the United States as Children* [Memorandum]. Washington, DC: US Department of Homeland Security.

National Immigration Law Center. 2015. "Access to Driver's License for Immigrant Youth Granted DACA." Washington, DC: National Immigration Law Center. Retrieved July 3, 2015, from http://www.nilc.org/dacadriverslicenses2.html.

NCSL (National Conference of State Legislatures). 2014. "Undocumented Student Tuition: State Action." Washington, DC: National Conference of State Legislatures. Retrieved July 1, 2014, from http://www.ncsl.org/research/education/undocumented-student-tuition-state-action.aspx.

———. 2015. "Undocumented Student Tuition: Overview." Washington, DC: National Conference of State Legislatures. Retrieved April 21, 2015, from http://www.ncsl.org/research/education/undocumented-student-tuition-overview.aspx.

Nicholls, Walter J. 2013. *The DREAMers: How the Undocumented Youth Movement Transformed the Immigrant Rights Debate.* Stanford, CA: Stanford University Press.

Olivas, Michael A. 2009. "Plyler v. Doe: Still Guaranteeing Unauthorized Immigrant Children's Right to Attend US Public Schools." Washington, DC: Migration Policy Institute. Retrieved July 1, 2014, http://www.migrationpolicy.org/article/plyler-v-doe-still-guaranteeing-unauthorized-immigrant-childrens-right-attend-us-public.

Passel, Jeffrey S., and Mark Hugo Lopez. 2012. *Up to 1.7 Million Unauthorized Immigrant Youth May Benefit from New Deportation Rules.* Washington, DC: Pew Research Center. Retrieved July 1, 2014, from http://www.pewresearch.org/2013/08/14/pew-hispanic-center-renamed-pew-research-centers-hispanic-trends-project/.

Passel, Jeffrey S., D'Vera Cohn, Jens Manuel Krogstad, and Ana Gonzalez-Barrera. 2014. *As Growth Stalls, Unauthorized Immigrant Population Becomes More Settled.* Washington, DC: Pew Research Center. Retrieved July 16, 2015, from http://www.pewhispanic.org/2014/09/03/as-growth-stalls-unauthorized-immigrant-population-becomes-more-settled/.

Pérez, William. 2009. *We ARE Americans: Undocumented Students Pursuing the American Dream.* Sterling, VA: Stylus Publishing, LLC.

———. 2012. *Americans by Heart: Undocumented Latino Students and the Promise of Higher Education.* New York: Teachers College Press.

Pérez, William, Richard D. Cortés, Karina Ramos, and Heidi Coronado. 2010.

"'Cursed and Blessed': Examining the Socioemotional and Academic Experiences of Undocumented Latina and Latino College Students." *New Directions for Student Services* 131:35–51. doi:10.1002/ss.366.

Plyler v. Doe, 457 US 202 (1982).

Preston, Julia. 2015. "States Are Divided by the Lines They Draw on Immigration." *New York Times*, March 30, A10.

Sherman, Jake. 2013. "John Boehner: Hastert Rule Applies to Immigration Conference Report." *Politico*, June 27. Retrieved June 30, 2013, from http://www.politico.com/story/2013/06/john-boehner-hastert-rule-immigration-93511.html.

Soltero, Carlos R. 2006. *Latinos and American Law: Landmark Supreme Court Cases.* Austin: University of Texas Press.

Teranishi, Robert T., Carola Suárez-Orozco, and Marcelo Suárez-Orozco. 2011. "Immigrants in Community Colleges." *Future of Children* 21(1):153–169.

United We Dream. 2015a. "National Institutions Coming Out Day: Institutional Policies and Programs With and For Undocumented Students Toolkit." Washington, DC: United We Dream. Retrieved April 6, 2015, from http://unitedwedream.org/wp-content/uploads/2015/01/UWDN_InstitutionalToolKit_final-1.pdf.

———. 2015b. "Learn How You Can Use the UndocuPeers: Liberating Campus Climate Curriculum at your School." Washington, DC: United We Dream. Retrieved April 20, 2015, from http://unitedwedream.org/learn-can-use-undocu peers-liberating-campus-climate-curriculum-school/.

Ura, Alexa, and Jolie McCullough. 2015. "Interactive: Undocumented Students on In-State Tuition." *Texas Tribune*, June 16. Retrieved April 21, 2015, from http://www.texastribune.org/2015/04/16/colleges-undocumented-students-with-state -tuition/.

USCIS (US Citizenship and Immigration Services). 2014a. "Consideration of Deferred Action for Childhood Arrivals (DACA)." Washington, DC: Department of Homeland Security. Retrieved September 26, 2014, from http://www.uscis .gov/humanitarian/consideration-deferred-action-childhood-arrivals-daca.

———. 2014b. "Deferred Action for Action for Childhood Arrivals Process (Through Fiscal Year 2014, 3rd Qtr.)." Washington, DC: US Department of Homeland Security. Retrieved September 26, 2014, from http://www.uscis.gov /sites/default/files/USCIS/Resources/Reports%20and%20Studies/Immigration %20Forms%20Data/All%20Form%20Types/DACA/DACA_fy2014_qtr3.pdf.

———. 2014c. "Renew Your DACA." Retrieved September 26, 2014, from http://www.uscis.gov/humanitarian/consideration-deferred-action-childhood -arrivals-process/renew-your-daca.

———. 2015. "Number of 1-821D, Consideration of Deferred Action for Childhood Arrivals by Fiscal Year, Quarter, Intake, Biometric and Case Status: 2012–2015 (March31)." Washington, DC: US Department of Homeland Security. Retrieved June 26, 2015, from http://www.uscis.gov/sites/default/files/USCIS /Resources/Reports%20and%20Studies/Immigration%20Forms%20Data /Naturalization%20Data/I821d_performancedata_fy2015_qtr2.pdf.

USDHS (US Department of Homeland Security). 2012. "Secretary Napolitano Announces Deferred Action Process for Young People Who Are Low Enforcement Priorities." Washington, DC: US Department of Homeland Security. Office of the Press Secretary. Retrieved September 26, 2014, from https://www .dhs.gov/news/2012/06/15/secretary-napolitano-announces-deferred-action -process-young-people-who-are-low.

———. 2014. "Secretary Johnson Announces Process for DACA Renewal." Washington, DC: US Department of Homeland Security. DHS Press Office. Retrieved June 10, 2014, from https://www.dhs.gov/news/2014/06/05/secretary -johnson-announces-process-daca-renewal.

CHAPTER 8

Who Has the Right to Health Care and Why? Immigration, Health-Care Policy, and Incorporation

MILENA ANDREA MELO AND K. JILL FLEURIET

In this chapter, we highlight the ways in which constructions of person-hood and citizenship directly influence immigrant health and health-care eligibility. We use contrasting case studies of prenatal care for undocu-mented immigrant women and dialysis for undocumented immigrants with advanced diabetes and hypertension in communities in South Texas. In the case of prenatal care, undocumented immigrant women have access to pre-ferred medical care, which is correlated with improved birth and child and adult health. In the case of undocumented immigrants with advanced dia-betes, hypertension, and related conditions, care is irregular and fragmented at best, which increases morbidity and mortality. Both case studies are com-plicated by state definitions of deservingness-of-care criteria for publicly funded health care. State criteria for who receives health care, in turn, are shaped by understandings of what constitutes a person and a citizen. For analysis, we draw from our respective ethnographic work in Hidalgo and Cameron Counties in the lower Rio Grande Valley of Texas. We illustrate how access to health care fundamentally shapes the well-being of immi-grant communities. We conclude with a discussion as to how differential access to health care can shape immigrant experiences of incorporation, us-ing Portes and Böröcz's (1989) typology of modes of incorporation, and how these analyses could inform policy.

Who Is a Person? Which Persons Have Rights and Access to Health Care?

Low-income immigrants from Mexico often face a hostile policy environ-ment and negative civic opinion in the United States (Portes and Böröcz

1989; Chávez 2001, 2004). Sociologists and anthropologists have explored how these structural and social disadvantages limit the kinds of political citizenship available to undocumented immigrants, which, in turn, impacts experiences of incorporation (for reviews, see Portes and Böröcz 1989; Brettell and Hollifield 2007; Schmitter Heisler 2007). Anthropologists have also considered how public health and other health-care institutions engage in different practices of citizen-making that can reinforce public opinion and stereotypes about immigrants (Horton and Barker 2009, 2010; Galemba 2013).

These citizen-making processes are embedded within health institutions to which immigrants have unequal access. In turn, dominant ideas of deservingness of care and personhood influence what kind of health care is available. Notions of who deserves care emerge from historical influences of publicly funded health care for the poor and a unique employer-provided health-care model in the United States (Starr 1984; Dolgoff and Feldstein 2007). Common definitions of personhood derive from long-standing rights discourses and ongoing debates about birth control, abortion, and end-of-life decision making (Himma 2005; Will 2013; Radha Krishna 2014). Religious and medical authorities are polarized over questions of when a person begins and thus can be granted legal rights. Similarly, the debate over who, if anyone, can choose to end a life is mired in long-standing religious-medical debates. For immigrant health care, these notions of personhood become entangled with disputes over rights-based citizenship for immigrants and deservingness-of-care criteria.

Citizenship engages modes of belonging that emerge from distinct geopolitical, institutional, and occupational citizenship-making processes (Rosaldo 1994; Ong 1999; Horton 2004; Rose and Novas 2005; Wailoo, Livingston, and Guarnaccia 2006; Castle 2008). Several of these definitions inform the projects discussed in this chapter: cultural, flexible, and biological citizenship. Cultural citizenship (Rosaldo 1994) is granted by one's primary community through involvement in the surrounding society—for example, paying taxes, working in the community, or being a part of a school's parent organization. Flexible citizenship (Ong 1999) recognizes that an individual can select or have multiple kinds of citizenship at different points in time and geography, such as having the right to be informed on minimum wage yet being unable to demand such rights and information due to fear of deportation. Biological citizenship privileges the ways in which citizenship has been constructed in relation to the body and the kinds of claims citizens can make based upon their bodies. For example, citizenship and the rights it entails dictate the health-care access and treatment granted to immigrants (Rose and Novas 2005; Fassin 2009). Because the fetus can be defined by state law as a person-citizen, the fetus is therefore entitled to certain kinds of health care. In US states that do not recognize the fetus as a person-citizen, the fetus is not a body with rights (Fleuriet 2009b). Thus, the ways in which individuals are categorized by the state determine the boundaries of access to health resources (Castañeda and Melo 2014).

When examining citizenship as a category of exclusion in health care, "illegality" and "deservingness" have been key terms in sociological and anthropological research. "Illegality" is a category of exclusion that puts undocumented individuals at risk for increased poor health and suffering (De Genova 2005; Castañeda 2009; Gomberg-Muñoz 2011; Sargent 2012; Willen 2012a, 2012b). Becker (2004) connects deservingness with productivity and wealth, such as the ability to obtain financial resources to cover medical expenses. Lives in "illegality" are compounded by poverty. Without financial resources, exclusion for undocumented immigrants becomes all the more salient, because publicly funded welfare is inaccessible. Poverty raises the question of legality, shaping well-being so that it is largely determined by state exclusionary practices (Fassin 2001, 2011; Becker 2004; Castañeda 2009; Willen 2012a, 2012b). As part of the migration and assimilation process, immigrants develop strategies to circumvent these policies and receive health care, for example, seeking treatment at federally qualified health centers that utilize factors such as income and family size as the qualifying criteria for care instead of citizenship or immigration status.

Below, we document how different American cultural criteria for persons and citizens and notions of deservingness of care create very different health-care landscapes and experiences. We contrast the case studies of pregnancy and advanced diabetes among undocumented immigrants from Mexico living in the lower Rio Grande Valley of Texas. We draw from our ethnographic projects within these communities to demonstrate how larger cultural definitions of citizen, person, and deservingness of care can directly influence access to health care and health outcomes for low-income, undocumented immigrants. We conclude with a discussion of the direct health impacts of these definitions, potential influences on incorporation and assimilation experiences, and policy recommendations.

The Lower Rio Grande Valley of Texas

The lower Rio Grande Valley of Texas, our research site, is characterized by some of the highest poverty and uninsured rates in the country (US Census Bureau 2013c). This continued to be true with the advent of the Affordable Care Act (ACA) in 2014, because the ACA does not cover undocumented immigrants. We work in Hidalgo and Cameron Counties in South Texas. Hidalgo County is 91 percent Latino, and 85 percent of residents speak Spanish (US Census Bureau 2013a). Cameron County is 88.4 percent Latino, and 73.1 percent speak Spanish (US Census Bureau 2013b). Hidalgo is also one of the most medically underserved counties of the United States—characterized by gaps in public health services, poor access to care, significant environmental health concerns, elevated rates of chronic disease, an endemic poverty rate of 35 percent, the second-highest rate of obesity in the United States at 38.3 percent (McIntyre 2014), and the highest uninsured rate in the country at almost 40 percent (Hidalgo County Health and Human Services 2012). Both Cameron and Hidalgo Counties are federally classified as Medically Underserved Areas (HRSA 2013). In Cameron County, 36.6 percent of residents lacked health insurance in 2009 (Texas Health and Human Services Commission 2009), and 34.9 percent of residents lived below the poverty line in 2008–2012 (US Census Bureau 2013b). The majority of uninsured in both counties are undocumented, so these rates will remain largely unchanged even with the implementation of the ACA (Chu and Posner 2013).

The research site is rich in cultural citizenship. Prior to the increased border militarization and drug-related violence, the lower Rio Grande Valley was also characterized by regular and massive flows of people and ideas back and forth across the US-Mexico border (Martínez 1994, 1996; Vila 2000). Undocumented immigrants enter these spaces with less formal access to health care, which shapes their ability to maintain health, participate in social and economic networks, and, in effect, incorporate into the United States. At the same time, language is rarely a barrier to health care and social services in this area, because many on both sides of the border are bilingual. Although unable to access insurance, undocumented immigrants still access health-care services through charity and indigent programs, federally qualified health centers, community health fairs, and hospital emergency rooms. As part of their migration and assimilation process, undocumented immigrants become part of community and social networks that share information about locations and programs that offer health-care services regardless of citizenship and immigration status.

Since 91 percent of the population is Hispanic and shares a binational culture in this area, it is often difficult to distinguish undocumented immigrants from second-generation Mexican Americans, except for citizenship status. In many ways, undocumented immigrants are American in every aspect except on paper, as argued by Jose Antonio Vargas, a Pulitzer Prize winner who officially came out as undocumented in 2011 (Vargas 2011). Undocumented immigrant children and adults are educated in the United States in public and private grade schools, technical programs, colleges, universities, and continuing education programs. They are often highly involved in their local communities, participating in civic organizations and volunteering in parent-teacher associations. They are loyal members of various church congregations. They hold and create jobs and pay into the local and federal economy. Their daily interactions or involvement in American life could classify them as culturally American (Rosaldo 1994; Vila 2000; Chávez 2012). The only distinguishing factor is the lack of official papers, such as a Social Security number or birth certificate, which bars them from obtaining all of the resources open to American citizens. These identifying documents indicate citizenship and legality and determine access to health care.

Research Methods

Fleuriet's research sites included two community clinics that serve the majority of low-income women in two Cameron County cities and an alternative birthing center in Hidalgo County whose clientele is over 90 percent low-income Mexican immigrant women. Qualitative data included here are from the 2011–2012 and 2003–2005 stages of a multiyear project (Fleuriet 2009a, 2009b) examining cultures of pregnancy among low-income Mexican American women and undocumented immigrant women from Mexico. In 2003–2005, Fleuriet conducted interviews with twenty-eight Mexican women and six clinical staff, held two focus groups with women and their partners, and conducted participant observation with undocumented immigrant women at the birthing center. In 2011–2012, bilingual community health workers interviewed twenty Mexican American women and fifty-nine Mexican immigrant women. At both stages, the interview goal was to elicit narratives of the pregnancy experiences of the women, family members, or close friends in the United States and, if appropriate, in Mexico. Fleuriet inductively analyzed interview transcripts and field notes pertaining to health-care preferences, pregnancy experiences in Mexico and at other clinics in the United States, barriers to health care, and social support.

Melo's research site is Hidalgo County, where, according to the 2010 US Census, one-third of the population is foreign born (97% from Mexico) (US Census Bureau 2013a). Qualitative data included here are from two projects conducted in the summers of 2012 and 2013 examining the diabetes narratives and health-care concerns of uninsured and undocumented Mexican immigrants. In June and July 2012, Melo conducted fifty initial semi-structured interviews and thirty follow-up interviews with fifty uninsured, diabetic Mexican immigrants about their illness experiences with type 2 diabetes. All interviews were conducted in Spanish, and participants were recruited from local flea markets throughout Hidalgo County. Flea markets are a key source of under-the-table economic activity where undocumented immigrants can sell items to earn an income regardless of their immigration status.

In June and July 2013, Melo conducted a second project within the same community focused on identifying the top health-care barriers and most prevalent and serious illnesses for undocumented immigrants in the Rio Grande Valley. Melo interviewed seventy Mexican immigrants to formulate a community-guided approach to the top health concerns and illnesses for uninsured Mexican immigrants living in the Rio Grande Valley. Ten of these participants were Medicare/Medicaid dialysis patients. All interviews were conducted in Spanish, and participants were recruited from flea markets, community rights organizations, and federally qualified health centers in Hidalgo County. Nuestra Clínica del Valle, the federally qualified health center serving Starr and Hidalgo Counties, serves undocumented populations for primary health-care services. In 2012, 83 percent of the 31,887 patients at Nuestra Clínica had incomes below the federal poverty level, and 82 percent had no public or private health insurance (Lucy Ramirez, Nuestra Clínica del Valle executive director, personal communication, May 16, 2013). Melo analyzed interview transcripts using primary themes of diabetes experiences, access to care, immigration, social support, barriers, and comparisons between the United States' and Mexico's health care. Fleuriet's and Melo's projects were approved by the Institutional Review Board at the University of Texas at San Antonio.

Prenatal Care among Undocumented Immigrant Women from Mexico

In every culture, pregnancy is a primary symbol of social and biological reproduction (Jordan and Davos-Floyd [1993] 1978; Davis-Floyd and Sargent 1997; Rapp 2001; Unnithan-Kumar 2004). The symbolic value of pregnancy depends on the status of the sociocultural spaces that the pregnant woman occupies. Anthropologists have demonstrated the significant influence of class (Lazarus 1994; Inhorn 2003), religious affiliation (Gerber 2002), political affiliations (Ginsburg 1989; Sargent 2005), citizenship (Chávez 2001, 2004; Sargent 2006), and other local categories of social status on women's access to preferred social and clinical pregnancy resources as well as their individual and collective beliefs and behaviors surrounding pregnancy. In the United States, for example, age, socioeconomic status, sexual orientation, marital status, and citizenship are some of the variables used to understand and attach meanings to a given woman's pregnancy (Lazarus 1994; Ellison 2003; Chávez 2004; Fleuriet 2009b). Thus, to understand a woman's pregnancy experience in its larger sociocultural context, it is imperative to understand the hierarchies and systems of meaning that imbue pregnancy as well as those that define the individual woman, such as class and minority status.

Anthropological work among immigrant populations focuses on documenting and analyzing the multiple points where meanings about pregnancy and prenatal care are produced and interact, including the patient and her immediate sociocultural group; the professional medical or healing cultures of the health-care provider; and larger structures and discourses, such as the American health-care system and national opinions on immigration, citizenship, personhood, and deservingness-of-care, which shape access to and the content of prenatal care (Fleuriet 2009b).

Access to prenatal care for low-income pregnant undocumented immigrant women in Texas is shaped by a combination of assumed and contested notions of personhood, citizenship, and deservingness-of-care criteria for health care. Women's reproductive health care in the Texas borderlands is highly politicized due to the Texas legislature's 2013 rejection of Medicaid expansion and the Texas legislature's abortion restrictions. The restrictions demonstrate another facet of defining personhood at conception, which also legally entitles low-income pregnant undocumented immigrant women in Texas to formal prenatal care but little maternal health care. Socioeconomic status and patterns of poverty influence access to prenatal care. Access remains a practical issue for undocumented immigrant women in the borderlands because Cameron and Hidalgo Counties have insufficient health-care resources (HRSA 2013).

Low-income undocumented immigrant women have legal access to prenatal care in Texas through the Children's Health Insurance Program (CHIP) Perinatal. In 2002, the "unborn child" rule went into effect under the Separate Children's Health Insurance Program. This rule defined a "child" as starting from conception (Texas CHIP Coalition 2005). The "unborn child" rule stipulates the legal beginning of a person: "Child means an individual under the age of nineteen including the period from conception to birth" (US Department of Health and Human Services 2002, 61956). States had the option to include this definition in their child insurance programs. In 2005, Texas adopted the "unborn child" rule. Combined with *jus soli*, that is, birthright citizenship, this definition of personhood beginning at conception made prenatal care available to low-income undocumented immigrant women through Medicaid because their fetuses are de facto citizens. As a result of this definition, prenatal care became included in health care for children. The ninety-day waiting period for CHIP was waived, and prenatal care could begin immediately. Any pregnant woman in Texas, regardless of citizenship, who is at or below 200 percent of the federal poverty line and who is ineligible for Medicaid or another health plan qualifies for CHIP Perinatal. A woman who meets all other criteria but has a higher income may still qualify (TDHHS 2014). Any maternal care considered nonessential for prenatal care is not included in CHIP Perinatal because the pregnant woman is not a citizen. The undocumented pregnant woman is incorporated into the formal health-care system through Medicaid by virtue of her pregnancy status but is then ineligible for Medicaid for her own care after delivery. Thus, in Texas, citizenship, health insurance, and extreme poverty are not legal barriers to formal prenatal care, a fact that becomes crucial when considering access to prenatal care, birth outcomes, and future child and adult health.

In Cameron and Hidalgo Counties there are two major health plans that accept CHIP Perinatal. Between them, there are fifteen clinics in Cameron and twenty-three clinics in Hidalgo with obstetrics and gynecology providers. These include private clinics, community health centers, and qualifying birth centers. Once enrolled in CHIP Perinatal, a pregnant woman receives up to twenty prenatal visits, prescriptions and prenatal vitamins, hospital labor and delivery, two doctor visits for the postpartum mother, and regular doctor visits, immunizations, and prescriptions for the baby through the twelve-month coverage period. CHIP Perinatal coverage includes regular diagnostic and specialty tests for the fetus, inpatient and outpatient care for miscarriages, coverage for pregnancy complications, and emergency services relevant to the health of the pregnancy (Texas Children's Health Plan 2012). Any hospital visits unrelated to labor and delivery (including false labor) and specialty treatment for the mother (including mental health or chronic conditions such as asthma) are not covered (TDHHS 2014). Pregnant undocumented immigrant women who do not qualify for CHIP Perinatal because of income can self-pay for prenatal care at community health centers, county health clinics, and migrant health centers.

Often, community health centers and birth centers supplement CHIP

Perinatal and prenatal care for uninsured patients with additional outreach and care programs based on need and income, not citizenship. For example, one of the primary community health centers that accept CHIP Perinatal in Harlingen and Brownsville in Cameron County offers programs in personalized case management for diabetes and comprehensive education for the community, individual counseling for women with high-risk pregnancies, breast-cancer screening, and social service case management, funded by federal and private agencies. The other main community health center in Brownsville provides additional outreach services to low-income families in the areas of parenting education, housing, health, security, prevention of gestational diabetes, nutrition, diabetes prevention and management, mental health, patient empowerment, and community development. These programs are funded by private organizations, such as the Marguerite Casey Foundation, and federal agencies, such as the US Health and Human Services Administration's Maternal and Child Health Bureau. Potential patients are identified by social service case managers based on criteria of need and low income. Such outreach and additional care programs supplement prenatal care offered through CHIP Perinatal, but their funding and continuity are often uncertain.

Other examples of supplemented prenatal care include a migrant health center and birthing center in Hidalgo. At one large, multi-sited migrant health center, prenatal care for CHIP Perinatal women can be enhanced through complementary programs, such as parenting education, comprehensive nutrition education and counseling, mental health with short- and long-term individual and group treatment options, and social services that locate additional resources for specific patient needs. A free-standing birth center in Hidalgo similarly offers parenting, childbirth, and breastfeeding classes; additional prenatal visits; mother/infant nutrition; family nutrition; first aid; pregnancy counseling; women's annual exams; and social service case management to connect patients with other resources based on need. The birth center also provides material support, including food, clothing and toys, and in-kind payment options. Federal and private grants and donations through the Catholic Church, other community organizations, and individuals fund these programs.

What these clinics and centers recognize is that the CHIP Perinatal program does not provide comprehensive prenatal care because it excludes non-emergency mental health, chronic illness care, and comprehensive health care and social services for the pregnant woman. Pregnancy and birth outcomes are heavily influenced by the woman's social, emotional, and physical environments and health. The primary professional association of obstetricians (ACOG 2008) and cross-cultural grassroots organizations such as the International MotherBaby Childbirth Initiative (2008) agree that in addition to risk screening, optimal prenatal care includes ability to exercise prenatal care preferences, positive psychosocial health—such as low levels of stress and anxiety—and material security, such as adequate food and housing.

The narratives and prenatal care experiences of pregnant undocumented immigrant women from Mexico before and after the 2005 implementation of CHIP Perinatal provide experiential data to illustrate the impact of both the legal provision of prenatal care and the remaining barriers to care due to finances and immigration status. Prior to 2005, the primary structural barrier to accessing preferred prenatal care was cost, which was a significant barrier to incorporation vis-à-vis the formal health-care system, notably private care. Other barriers that persisted after CHIP Perinatal's implementation in 2005 included transportation, lack of child care, language differences, and fear of immigration authorities. Women also believed that some providers gave poorer care to low-income patients (Fleuriet 2009a, 2009b). Women explained that staff at county health clinics did not respect patients due to their poverty. They reported that staff often acted as if the women were unhygienic or uneducated about pregnancy. For example, Rosa, a twenty-eight-year-old woman from Veracruz, said:

> When I was going to [the county health clinic for my second pregnancy], they were really ugly. They were not nice, and maybe it's because it's free. . . . They were like, "Well, you couldn't wait to have another baby, huh?" They were really like that. And I don't know, I really didn't like it, and I told my husband, I don't want to go to that clinic anymore. I love my baby . . . but [according to the clinic staff] you were bad for getting pregnant. So I go [to the community health center], even if we have to pay.

Perceived staff attitudes and cost are common barriers for low-income and undocumented immigrants (Heyman, Núñez, and Talavera 2009), along with wait time, transportation, language differences, and negative perceptions of providers and staff (Fleuriet 2009b).

Not surprisingly, undocumented immigrant women desire affordable medical prenatal care that could ensure that the baby is healthy and delivered by female prenatal and obstetrical care providers (Fleuriet 2009b). We include the strong preference for female providers in this analysis to show that not all prenatal care preferences are rooted in structural influences of citizenship and class status in the United States. The individual and collective experiences of the mother, family, and friends also orient women in specific ways to pregnancy and prenatal care. For example, low-income undocumented immigrant women preferred doctors and certified nurse mid-wives, rather than lay midwives, and these women espoused a similar med-ical model of pregnancy as American women. Undocumented immigrant women from Mexico expected female prenatal care providers to have both clinical and practical knowledge about pregnancy.

Immigrant women also believed female prenatal care providers would be more emotionally supportive. For example, Marisa, a twenty-six-year-old woman from Matamoros, explained: "The male doctor is colder because he is a man. They can't feel what you're going through." Silvia, a twenty-nine-year-old woman, further elaborated, saying: "I feel more comfortable and trusting with a woman, a person of my same sex. I'll ask her questions when I wouldn't have if it had been a [male] doctor. I feel more secure that she'll have the answers to my questions." Veronica, in her early twenties and in her third pregnancy, said of Mexican women: "We relate more to [female doctors] . . . my family taught me that women are the ones that have ba-bies. Women are the ones that know what happens. Men don't know what it is to go through an experience like that, so women know best." The immi-grant women additionally wanted an emotionally supportive prenatal care provider who delivered timely clinical information (Fleuriet 2009a, 2009b). This is a common preference cross-culturally (Lazarus 1994; Davis-Floyd and Sargent 1997), along with open communication, respect, and informa-tional support. In sum, immigrant women had an easier time relating to a female prenatal care provider because the women expected such providers to share an intuitive understanding of what it meant to be pregnant. In ad-dition, they believed female providers could offer emotional and informa-tional support.

Thus, undocumented immigrant women want the formal prenatal care offered by the United States, although they have certain preferences within that prenatal care. In this case, these women are able to access their pre-ferred medical care because citizenship status is not a barrier to prenatal care. The pregnant undocumented immigrant woman has access to formal prenatal care because her fetus is legally defined as a person who will be born in the United States as a US citizen.

Advanced Diabetes and Dialysis among Undocumented Immigrants: A Contrasting Example

Except in prenatal care, undocumented immigrants in the United States do not have access to most publicly funded health care because of their unau-thorized status. As a result, undocumented immigrants with chronic, debil-

itating illness struggle to find adequate treatment for conditions that are often life-threatening. In the case of type 2 diabetes, the vast majority of the
uninsured Mexican immigrant participants have at least one complication as
a result of their diabetes, including high blood pressure, amputations, blind-
ness, strokes, and renal failure (known as end-stage renal disease, or ESRD).

The ability to manage diabetes care and resulting complications is very
different for undocumented immigrants when compared to their US citizen and legal immigrant counterparts. First and foremost, the costs associated with treating type 2 diabetes must often compete in undocumented households with family necessities such as buying food or paying
bills. Diabetic undocumented immigrants have less access to necessary diabetic care not only because of the associated costs, but also because of additional barriers, such as transportation, difficulty scheduling around other
obligations such as child care and employment, and fears and risks associated with immigration status. Diabetes that is treated only sporadically or
not at all often results in complications, of which the most serious is ESRD
(NIDDKD 2006).

ESRD is complete, permanent kidney failure that requires regular dialysis treatment three times a week for three to four hours per day, depending on severity. Upon diagnosis, US citizens and permanent residents receive the standard of ESRD care, consisting of thrice-weekly maintenance
dialysis through Medicare, Medicaid, or private insurance at outpatient facilities. However, since undocumented immigrants with ESRD are not
only noncitizens but also in the United States under an unauthorized immigration status, government policies make irregular treatment the only
option for them. In this case, their "illegality" immediately invokes a discourse about their "deservingness" of any treatment that goes beyond the
bare emergency minimum as dictated by government regulation. Undocumented dialysis patients cannot receive treatment in outpatient facilities because of their inability to pay the cost associated with dialysis, which is approximately $6,000 per treatment. They are also ineligible for maintenance
dialysis, which is covered by insurance available to US citizens and permanent residents. Therefore, they must rely on Emergency Medicaid to cover
unscheduled and irregular intermittent care in hospital emergency rooms
when available (Sheik-Hamad et al. 2007; Hurley et al. 2009; Campbell,
Sanoff, and Rosner 2010).

Emergency Medicaid is available to anyone, regardless of citizenship,
who has been residing in the United States for at least six months and whose
income falls under a given threshold, usually below 200 percent of the federal poverty level. In order to qualify, the emergency-room visit must be

deemed a "true emergency," defined by federal legislation as "a medical condition (including emergency labor and delivery) manifesting itself by acute symptoms of sufficient severity (including severe pain) such that the absence of immediate medical attention could reasonably be expected to result in (a) placing the patient's health in serious jeopardy, (b) serious impairment to bodily functions, or (c) serious dysfunction of any bodily organ or part" (Campbell et al. 2010, 185).

In 1972, US Public Law 92-603 granted access to dialysis for patients with ESRD with no requirement of citizenship for eligibility of treatment (Campbell et al. 2010). This, however, changed in 1986 when two revisions were passed as the Consolidated Omnibus Budget Reconciliation Act. The first revision prohibited federal Medicaid payments for undocumented immigrants, except in emergency situations in which the patient would have otherwise qualified for Medicaid based on income (known as Emergency Medicaid). The second revision was the inclusion of the Emergency Medical Treatment and Active Labor Act (EMTALA). EMTALA requires all hospitals receiving Medicare funds to triage, treat, and stabilize patients who request services at emergency departments regardless of their ability to pay or legal status. In 1996, the Personal Responsibility and Work Opportunity Reconciliation Act placed the responsibility on individual states to determine what coverage they would provide for their undocumented immigrant population. Texas provides no other coverage. This act, along with the Illegal Immigration Reform and Immigrant Responsibility Act passed in 1996, has generated serious barriers to accessing health care, since it requires patients to provide a Social Security number in order to qualify for publicly funded health care. Federal funding currently available to help with health-care costs of undocumented immigrants are Emergency Medicaid and Medicaid Disproportionate Share Hospital funds. Other sources of funds that fill the gaps of uncompensated care debts are not as easily documented but often consist of payments made by hospital systems, charities, private practitioners out of their own funds, and undocumented immigrants (Campbell et al. 2010).

Although it varies based on hospital and health conditions, most undocumented immigrants receive dialysis only once or twice a week when the emergency-room physician and lab results determine that they are "sick enough" to need dialysis. While US citizens and permanent residents on dialysis report to and are received by their outpatient facilities when scheduled for treatment, undocumented immigrants often spend several days in emergency-room lobbies, waiting for their chance to receive treatment. According to dialysis treatment policies, this is not the standard of care, and this practice places undocumented immigrants in a physical state where they are constantly close to death. While it is possible to live a long and normal life on dialysis when diagnosed with ESRD, the physicians I consulted stated that undocumented immigrants on irregular dialysis live much shorter lives than the national averages for dialysis patients. Lack of access to regular dialysis treatment dramatically decreases the quality and length of the lives of undocumented immigrants.

Undocumented ESRD immigrants must constantly expend energy and exercise agency to obtain treatment by navigating health-care institutions. Actors in these institutions are expected to serve as extensions of the state and its exclusionary health-care policy, but they also sometimes act to help undocumented patients (Gomberg-Muñoz 2011). Each interaction in health-care institutions creates spaces that either reinforce exclusion or include patients within the possibility of dialysis. In order to improve their chances of receiving treatment, undocumented dialysis patients may exercise their agency by, for example, not taking their blood pressure medications or drinking extra water. These strategies often produce symptoms and lab results that make doctors deem them "sick enough" for treatment and rush them into dialysis. Due to hospital costs and their unauthorized status, undocumented immigrants are often discouraged and indirectly urged by hospital employees not to return to that particular hospital again for treatment. However, because of ESRD, returning is unavoidable, and undocumented immigrants may try to rotate to different hospitals in the area until they find a location where they feel comfortable with the treatment provided. For undocumented immigrants, negotiating and obtaining dialysis treatment is a full-time job with calculated risks.

There are other challenges for undocumented immigrants with ESRD besides access to treatment. Dialysis often leaves patients weak, disoriented, and unable to perform daily tasks. This frequently means they can no longer work; therefore, family members must make up for lost income. This becomes more problematic when the responsibility of providing transportation to and from dialysis is factored into the equation. While Medicaid and most private insurance policies cover transportation for US citizens and permanent residents to their dialysis appointments, undocumented immigrants must rely on family members, friends, or public transportation, or risk driving themselves, in order to get to the hospital for dialysis treatment. Since their dialysis schedule and the intake time are so unpredictable, relying on others is difficult in light of family members' other obligations. Furthermore, undocumented immigrants in Texas are unable to obtain valid driver's licenses; thus, driving to and from dialysis puts them and their families at risk of being stopped by police officers or Border Patrol and being deported.

Undocumented dialysis patients in the US-Mexico borderlands of South Texas face barriers to accessible health care that are physical, such as police, ICE (Immigration and Customs Enforcement), and Border Patrol checkpoints, and institutional, such as access to treatment in dialysis centers. These immigrants find themselves in a paradoxical situation in which their suffering is identified but not adequately treated. The resulting limited access to treatment produces more human suffering, demonstrated by higher morbidity and mortality rates, and significantly increased economic costs (Hurley et al. 2009; Campbell et al. 2010). These immigrants are aware of an effective form of care that constantly eludes them because of lack of citizenship or authorized immigration status.

The Implications of Cultural Definitions of Personhood, Citizenship, and Deservingness-of-Care on Health and Well-Being

The differences in access to prenatal care and dialysis for low-income undocumented immigrants from Mexico living in the United Sates directly impact the health and well-being of immigrant communities. In the case of prenatal care, early onset of prenatal care and diagnosis of risk during pregnancy correlate with positive birth outcomes and child and adult health. Prenatal care can reduce the risk of low birth weight, which is a primary cause of infant mortality (Stein, Siegel, and Bauman 2006; Behrman and Butler 2007; Rosenberg et al. 2007; Dunkel Schetter and Tanner 2012). Low birth weight is also associated with impaired physical development and long-term disability (Stein et al. 2006; Dunkel Schetter and Tanner 2012).

The benefit of prenatal care depends on the timing of onset and duration of care. Early and adequate prenatal care, as determined by several standard adequacy indices (Krueger and Scholl 2000), is regularly associated with normal birth weight in women with a history of physical or mental health risk factors for low birth weight, such as infertility (Alibekova, Huang, and Chen 2013) and depression (Chen and Lin 2011). There is debate as to whether prenatal care improves other aspects of infant or child health (Cogan et al. 2012; Noonan et al. 2013), though it does correlate with significantly more well-child visits among Medicaid populations (Van Berckelaer, Mitra, and Pati 2011; Cogan et al. 2012). One factor that may impact the correlation between prenatal care and health outcomes is the duration and content of prenatal care, particularly care given to higher-risk populations, such as low-income immigrant women.

Since the 1980s, maternal and child health experts have argued for prenatal care that begins *before* conception, includes maternal and family health assessments and care, and extends through postpartum (Waggoner 2013). Since the early 2000s, the Centers for Disease Control, the American College of Obstetrics, and the American Academy of Pediatricians have agreed with international midwifery groups that optimal prenatal care includes preconception care (Centers for Disease Control 2006; Davis-Floyd et al. 2009; Waggoner 2013; for review, see M. C. Lu and J. S. Lu 2008; Fleuriet 2009b). Medicaid populations are less likely to have adequate and timely preconception or postpartum care (Weir et al. 2011). Finally, content and delivery matter when assessing the benefit of prenatal care, especially for vulnerable populations such as low-income undocumented women. Prenatal care models that include self-assessment, group education, and an emphasis on maternal psychosocial health, such as the CenteringPregnancy approach (Rising and Jolivet 2009), are associated with a reduction in preterm births and an increase in health-care utilization, particularly among low-income Latinas (Tandon et al. 2012; Tandon et al. 2013).

In contrast to the positive outcomes from access to prenatal care, the lack of regular dialysis for ESRD patients leads to significantly worse health outcomes and increased costs. Sheik-Hamad et al. (2007) conducted a study in Texas that compared two groups of dialysis patients: one group consisted of individuals who underwent standard maintenance dialysis therapy of three weekly treatments, and the other group received emergency dialysis during two to three unscheduled visits a week in the emergency department. The results showed that patients in the first group stayed in the hospital only an average of 10.1 days per year versus 162 for the second group. The first group also had fewer emergency-department visits, 1.4 versus 26.3 days. The emergency group had more blood transfusions (24.9 versus 2.2), underwent fewer dialysis treatments per year (98 versus 154), and suffered more physical pain and lower function levels. The emergency group received temporary venous catheters that were removed after each treatment.

The difference in cost between the two groups' treatments was considerable; care for the standard maintenance group was $76,906 per person annually compared to the emergency-care cost of $284,655. Although hospitals may be compensated for dialysis treatments of undocumented patients in their emergency departments through Emergency Medicaid, this is only recovered at taxpayers' expense. A more efficient alternative, which would include scheduled, standard maintenance dialysis treatments, would cost almost a fourth of what emergency treatments cost per year and result in higher-quality health outcomes. This inefficient use of taxpayer funds results in other health complications that lead to higher cost and increased morbidity and mortality rates (Campbell et al. 2010).

Incorporation Implications and Policy Recommendations

Access to formal prenatal care allows for both political and biological citizenship for the fetuses of pregnant undocumented immigrant women. Birthright or political citizenship is granted to the fetus at conception, with legal certification upon delivery and, as a result, the citizen child is eligible for publicly funded health care. Because the fetus is considered a citizen prior to birth, assumptions of fetal personhood also allow for publicly funded prenatal care. American constructions of biological and political citizenship thus inform deservingness-of-care criteria for pregnant undocumented immigrant women. This status remains tenuous as current political debates surrounding fetal personhood, reproductive rights, and public funding of health care have led to reduced access to prenatal care overall in the borderlands of South Texas. In the adult stages of life, neither birthright nor biological citizenship is granted to undocumented immigrants with diabetes and hypertension resulting in ESRD. Consigned to irregular, emergency dialysis, undocumented immigrants with advanced diabetes have negative health outcomes.

The health and financial consequences of these differences are clear. Prenatal care access correlates with improved birth outcomes, higher likelihood of well-child visits, and healthier maternal behaviors. Lack of dialysis for undocumented immigrants with advanced diabetes and hypertension leads to increased morbidity, mortality, and financial hardship. These results also have implications for incorporation experiences. Following Portes and Böröcz's (1989) framework for analyzing incorporation, low-income undocumented migrants from Mexico typically immigrate to a medium-to-low-receptivity environment, defined as a hostile policy context, prejudiced public opinion, and relatively strong immigrant communities (Chávez 2001, 2004; Fleuriet 2009b). Health-care policy, though, is different for the undocumented pregnant woman and the undocumented immigrant with advanced diabetes and hypertension. Different reception environments shape "more or less coherent patterns organizing the life changes of newcomers . . . alter[ing] their aspirations and plans and can channel individuals of similar backgrounds into widely different directions" (Portes and Böröcz 1989, 618). Policy and health-care disparities based on deservingness of care translate into significant differences for undocumented immigrants who are pregnant and immigrants with chronic illness. Definitions of citizenship and of who is deserving of care influence access to "linking social capital," or the "vertical relations that help individuals gain access to resources from formal institutions for social and economic development" (Cheong et al.

2007, 29). For example, once a patient has access to regular dialysis, he or she can develop professional and personal relationships with a variety of health-care and outreach staff and health-care providers who can link the patient with additional health care and social services within the hospital, clinic, and/or dialysis center.

The determination of deservingness-of-care and the ability to adequately assimilate into the formal health-care system differ for unauthorized pregnant immigrants and immigrants with ESRD. The capacity or incapacity to assimilate into the formal health-care system, in turn, impacts their health and ability to work. CHIP Perinatal facilitates enrollment of US-born children into Medicaid and provides additional clinical resources and social services outreach through prenatal visits. There are potential benefits to household economic health, as well. Since prenatal care helps identify and reduce pregnancy and birth risks, mothers with healthier babies are better able to enter the workforce earlier and have fewer child health-care costs. In contrast, immigrants with advanced diabetes, hypertension, and inadequate dialysis care are less able to participate in the labor force, and their financial needs have to be shouldered by the family.

If evidence-based research were the primary guide for health-care policy, the content and form of delivery of prenatal care and dialysis for undocumented immigrants would be quite different. CHIP Perinatal would extend to preconception education and health assessment among reproductive-age immigrant women. Once pregnant, the women would already be integrated into the health-care system and would be more likely to initiate early prenatal care. Prenatal care would include maternal and family health assessments and intervention, emphasizing well-being and directing the pregnant woman to social services that could help the family. While the primary health-care centers in the research site already do some of this, these services are funded largely by short-term, targeted initiatives, which leave gaps in comprehensive health care and make health care dependent on funding priorities and availability. Finally, CHIP Perinatal could provide more robust postpartum care that would extend past two visits and would include maternal and family physical and psychosocial health assessments and, if needed, interventions. Though initially costly, these early assessments and interventions could help improve child, adult, and family health and reduce costs in the long term.

A model exists to improve policy regarding delivery of dialysis to undocumented immigrants with advanced diabetes and hypertension. Undocumented immigrants living in the Rio Grande Valley and requiring dialysis care are shunted to hospital emergency rooms for treatment. However, this is not always the case for ESRD undocumented patients. In Houston, Texas, as part of the Harris Health System, the county opened an outpatient dialysis facility, Riverside Dialysis Center, which has served patients with little to no health insurance since 2008 (Johnson 2008). ESRD US citizens and permanent residents automatically qualify for Medicare or Medicaid, or have private insurance that covers treatment at private outpatient dialysis facilities. Thus, the grand majority of the uninsured patients that utilize this center are undocumented immigrants. County officials realized that they could not only lower hospital costs by providing these services but also reduce the morbidity and mortality rates of their dialysis patients. Harris County is one of the few health systems that have recognized the limitations and shortcomings of Emergency Medicaid and radically changed the provision of services to undocumented dialysis patients. This facility has allowed hundreds of undocumented dialysis patients to undergo maintenance dialysis treatment three times a week. Unfortunately, the facility has reached capacity. Even though the county added a fourth shift of service at the Riverside Dialysis Center, there is still an influx of patients in emergency rooms on a daily basis.

Although this model is not a permanent solution, it demonstrates the potential and positive impact of opening outpatient facilities to serve those who only qualify for Emergency Medicaid but require regular dialysis treatment. Hidalgo County, and more broadly the Rio Grande Valley, would especially benefit from an outpatient dialysis treatment facility due to the high rates of diabetes and obesity prevalent in the area, the lack of a county hospital to serve the indigent, and the large number of undocumented immigrants residing there.

Beginnings and Endings

Kaufman and Morgan (2005) reviewed the extensive literature and recent attention of anthropologists to "beginnings" and "endings" of life. This chapter illustrates the "dissimilar conditions that allow humans to come into and out of existence, and the range of analytic reflection on socially significant thresholds and borders" (Kaufman and Morgan 2005, 318). The beginnings, or validation and social recognition of unborn citizens, are marked by health-care access to CHIP Perinatal, enabling incorporation and assimilation into the US health-care system. The endings are marked by the lack of access to medical care that results in significant challenges to the incorporation and assimilation of undocumented immigrants. The contrasting cases presented here document a need for further research that ties personhood, citizenship, and deservingness into understanding immigrant health at beginnings and endings of life. Citizenship shapes those beginnings and endings. In sum, a complex understanding of immigrant health has to be mindful of the larger cultural definitions of citizen, person, and deservingness-of-care and the legal and policy implications of access to care. Access to health care has direct consequences for individual health outcomes and the effective incorporation of immigrants into the United States.

References

ACOG (American College of Obstetricians and Gynecologists). 2008. "Covering Specific Services in Women's Health." Washington, DC: Department of Government Affairs. Retrieved May 20, 2008, from http://www.acog.org/~/media/Departments/Government%20Relations%20and%20Outreach/hcfwhcfa-specificservices.pdf?dmc=1&ts=20140626T1157102222.

Alibekova, Raushan, Jian-Pei Huang, and Yi-Hua Chen. 2013. "Adequate Prenatal Care Reduces the Risk of Adverse Pregnancy Outcomes in Women with History of Infertility: A Nationwide Population-Based Study." *PLoS One* 8(12):e84237.

Becker, Gay. 2004. "Deadly Inequality in the Health Care 'Safety Net': Uninsured Ethnic Minorities' Struggle to Live with Life-Threatening Illnesses." *Medical Anthropology Quarterly* 18(2):258–275.

Behrman, Richard E., and Adrienne Stith Butler, eds. 2007. *Preterm Birth: Causes, Consequences, and Prevention*. Washington, DC: National Academies Press.

Brettell, Caroline B., and James F. Hollifield. 2007. "Introduction: Migration Theory: Talking Across Disciplines." In *Migration Theory: Talking Across Disciplines*. 2nd ed., edited by C. B. Brettell and J. F. Hollifield, 1–30. New York: Routledge.

Campbell, G. Adam, Scott Sanoff, and Mitchell H. Rosner. 2010. "Care of the Undocumented Immigrant in the United States with ESRD." *American Journal of Kidney Disease* 55(1):181–191.

Castañeda, Heide. 2009. "Illegality as Risk Factor: A Survey of Unauthorized Migrant Patients in a Berlin Clinic." *Social Science & Medicine* 68(8): 1–9.

Castañeda, Heide, and Melo, Milena. 2014. "Health Care Access for Latino Mixed-Status Families: Barriers, Strategies, and Implications for Reform." *American Behavioral Scientist*, 58(14):1891–1909.

Castle, Tomi. 2008. "Sexual Citizenship: Articulating Citizenship, Identity, and the Pursuit of the Good Life in Urban Brazil." *PoLAR: Political and Legal Anthropology Review* 31(1):118–133.

Centers for Disease Control. 2006. *Proceedings of the Preconception Health and Health Care Clinical, Public Health, and Consumer Workgroup Meetings*. Atlanta, GA: Centers for Disease Control.

Chávez, Leo R. 2001. *Covering Immigration: Popular Images and the Politics of the Nation*. Berkeley: University of California Press.

———. 2004. "A Glass Half Empty: Latina Reproduction and Public Discourse." *Human Organization* 63(2):173–188.

———. 2012. *Shadowed Lives: Undocumented Immigrants in American Society.* Boston, MA: Cengage Learning.

Chen, Chia-Hui, and Herng-Ching Lin. 2011. "Prenatal Care and Adverse Pregnancy Outcomes among Women with Depression: A Nationwide Population-Based Study." *Canadian Journal of Psychiatry* 56(5):273–280.

Cheong, Pauline Hope, Rosalind Edwards, Harry Goulbourne, and John Solomos. 2007. "Immigration, Social Cohesion and Social Capital: A Critical Review." *Critical Social Policy* 27(24):24–49.

Chu, Anna and Charles Posner. 2013. "The Counties that Need the Affordable Care Act the Most." Washington, DC: Center for American Progress Action Fund. Retrieved September 26, 2014, from http://www.americanprogressaction .org/wpcontent/uploads/2013/07/UninsuredCountries_ACA-5.pdf.

Cogan, Lindsay W., Raina E. Josberger, Foster C. Gesten, and Patrick J. Roohan. 2012. "Can Prenatal Care Impact Future Well-Child Visits? The Experience of a Low Income Population in New York State Medicaid Managed Care." *Maternal and Child Health Journal* 16(1):92–99.

Davis-Floyd, Robbie, Lesley Barclay, Betty-Anne Daviss, and Jan Tritten. 2009. "Introduction." In *Birth Models That Work*, edited by R. E. Davis-Floyd, L. Barclay, B. A. Daviss, and J. Tritten, 1–30. Berkeley: University of California Press.

Davis-Floyd, Robbie E., and Carolyn F. Sargent, eds. 1997. *Childbirth and Authoritative Knowledge: Cross-Cultural Perspectives.* Berkeley: University of California Press.

De Genova, Nicholas. 2005. *Working the Boundaries: Race, Space, and "Illegality" in Mexican Chicago.* Durham, NC: Duke University Press.

Dolgoff, Ralph, and Donald Feldstein. 2007. *Understanding Social Welfare: A Search for Social Justice.* Boston, MA: Pearson.

Dunkel Schetter, Christine, and Lynlee Tanner. 2012. "Anxiety, Depression and Stress in Pregnancy: Implications for Mothers, Children, Research, and Practice." *Current Opinion Psychiatry* 25(2):141–148.

Ellison, Marcia A. 2003. "Authoritative Knowledge and Single Women's Unintentional Pregnancies, Abortions, Adoption, and Single Motherhood: Social Stigma and Structural Violence." *Medical Anthropology Quarterly* 17(3):322–347.

Fassin, Didier. 2001. "The Biopolitics of Otherness: Undocumented Foreigners and Racial Discrimination in French Public Debate." *Anthropology Today* 17(1):3–7.

———. 2009. "Another Politics of Life is Possible." *Theory, Culture & Society* 26(5): 44–60.

———. 2011. "Policing Borders, Producing Boundaries: The Governmentality of Immigration in Dark Times." *Annual Review of Anthropology* 40:213–226.

Fleuriet, K. Jill. 2009a. "La Tecnología y Las Monjitas: Constellations of Authoritative Knowledge at a Religious Birthing Center in South Texas." *Medical Anthropology Quarterly* 23(3):212–234.

———. 2009b. "Pregnant, Uninsured, and Undocumented: Prenatal Care of Immigrant Women in South Texas." *The Applied Anthropologist* 29(1):4–21.

Galemba, Rebecca B. 2013. "Illegality and Invisibility at Margins and Borders." *PoLAR: Political and Legal Anthropology Review* 36(2):274–285.

Gerber, Elaine Gale. 2002. "Deconstructing Pregnancy: Seeing 'Eggs' and the Ambiguity of Very Early Conceptions." *Medical Anthropology Quarterly* 16(1): 92–108.

Ginsburg, Faye D. 1989. *Contested Lives: The Abortion Debate in an American Community*. Berkeley: University of California Press.

Gomberg-Muñoz, Ruth. 2011. *Labor and Legality: an Ethnography of a Mexican Immigrant Network*. New York: Oxford University Press.

Heyman, Josiah McC, Guillermina Gina Núñez, and Victor Talavera. 2009. "Healthcare Access and Barriers for Unauthorized Immigrants in El Paso County, Texas." *Family and Community Health* 32(1):4–21.

Hidalgo County Health and Human Services. 2012. "Diabetes Awareness: November is Diabetes Awareness Month." Edinburg, TX: The County of Hidalgo, TX. Retrieved May 10, 2013, from http://www.co.hidalgo.tx.us/index.aspx?NID=1033.

Himma, Kenneth E. 2005. "A Dualist Analysis of Abortion: Personhood and the Concept of Self Qua Experiential Subject." *Journal of Medical Ethics* 31(1):48–55.

Horton, Sarah. 2004. "Different Subjects: The Health Care System's Participation in the Differential Construction of the Cultural Citizenship of Cuban Refugees." *Medical Anthropology Quarterly* 18(4):472–489.

Horton, Sarah, and Judith C. Barker. 2009. "'Stains' on their Self-Discipline: Public Health, Hygiene, and the Disciplining of Undocumented Immigrant Parents in the Nation's Internal Borderlands." *American Ethnologist* 36(4):784–798.

———. 2010. "Examining the Cumulative Effects of Oral Health Disparities for Mexican American Farmworker Children." *Medical Anthropology Quarterly* 24(2):199–219.

HRSA (Health Resources and Services Administration). 2013. *Find Shortage Areas: MUA/P by State and County*. Washington, DC: US Department of Health and Human Services. Retrieved May 9, 2014, from http://muafind.hrsa.gov/.

Hurley, Laura, Allison Kempe, Lori A. Crane, Arthur Davidson, Katherine Pratte, Stuart Linas, L. Miriam Dickinson, and Tomas Berl. 2009. "Care of Undocumented Individuals with ESRD: A National Survey of US Nephrologists." *American Journal of Kidney Diseases* 53(6):940–949.

Inhorn, Marcia C. 2003. *Local Babies, Global Science: Gender, Religion, and In Vitro Fertilization in Egypt*. New York: Routledge.

International MotherBaby Childbirth Organization. 2008. "Basic Principles of the International MotherBaby Childbirth Initiative." Ponte Vedra Beach, FL: International MotherBaby Childbirth Organization. Retrieved March 20, 2008, from http://www.imbci.org/ShowPage.asp?id=179.

Johnson, Laurie. 2008. "HCHD Opens First Dialysis Center." *Houston Public Media*, July 25. Retrieved May 16, 2014, from http://app1.kuhf.org/articles/1217004009-HCHD-Opens-First-Dialysis-Center.html.

Jordan, Brigitte, and Robbie Davos-Floyd. [1993] 1978. *Birth in Four Cultures: A Cross-Cultural Investigation of Childbirth in Yucatan, Holland, Sweden, and the United States*. Long Grove, IL: Waveland Press.

Kaufman, Sharon R., and Lynn M. Morgan. 2005. "The Anthropology of the Beginnings and Ends of Life." *Annual Review of Anthropology* 34:317–341.

Krueger, Paul M., and Theresa O. Scholl. 2000. "Adequacy of Prenatal Care and Pregnancy Outcome." *The Journal of American Osteopathic Association* 100(8):485–492.

Lazarus, Ellen S. 1994. "What Do Women Want? Issues of Choice, Control, and Class in Pregnancy and Childbirth." *Medical Anthropology Quarterly* 8(1):25–46.

Lu, Michael C., and Jessica Susan Lu. 2008. "Prenatal Care." In *Encyclopedia of Infant and Early Childhood Development*, edited by M. M. Haith and J. B. Benson, 569–604. San Diego, CA: Academic Press: Elsevier.

Martínez, Oscar J. 1994. *Border People: Life and Society in the US-Mexico Borderlands*. Tucson: University of Arizona Press.

Martínez, Oscar J., ed. 1996. *US-Mexico Borderlands: Historical and Contemporary Perspectives*. Wilmington, DE: Scholarly Resources, Inc.

McIntyre, Douglas A. 2014. "America's Thinnest (and Fattest) Cities," *USA Today*, April 7. Retrieved May 16, 2014, from http://www.usatoday.com/story/money/business/2014/04/06/americas-thinnest-city/7306199/.

NIDDKD (National Institute of Diabetes and Digestive and Kidney Diseases). 2006. "Treatment Methods for Kidney Failure: Hemodialysis." Washington, DC: US Department of Health and Human Services. Retrieved October 18, 2013, from http://kidney.niddk.nih.gov/kudiseases/pubs/hemodialysis/.

Noonan, Kelly, Hope Corman, Ofira Schwartz-Soicher, and Nancy E. Reichman. 2013. "Effects of Prenatal Care on Child Health at Age 5." *Maternal and Child Health Journal* 17(2):189–199.

Ong, Aihwa. 1999. *Flexible Citizenship: The Cultural Logics of Transnationality*. Durham, NC: Duke University Press.

Portes, Alejandro, and József Böröcz. 1989. "Contemporary Immigration: Theoretical Perspectives on its Determinants and Modes of Incorporation." *International Migration Review* 23(3):606–630.

Radha Krishna, Lalit Kumar. 2014. "Accounting for Personhood in Palliative Sedation: The Ring Theory of Personhood." *Medical Humanities* 40(1):17–21.

Rapp, Rayna. 2001. "Gender, Body, Biomedicine: How Some Feminist Concerns Dragged Reproduction to the Centre of Social Theory." *Medical Anthropology Quarterly* 15(4):466–478.

Rising, Sharon Schindler, and Rima Jolivet. 2009. "Circles of Community: The CenteringPregnancy Group Prenatal Care Model." In *Birth Models That Work*, edited by R. E. Davis-Floyd, L. Barclay, B. Daviss, and J. Tritten, 365–384. Berkeley: University of California Press.

Rosaldo, Renato. 1994. "Cultural Citizenship in San Jose, California." *PoLAR: Political and Legal Anthropology Review* 17 (2): 57–64.

Rose, Nikolas, and Carlos Novas. 2005. "Biological Citizenship." In *Global Assemblages: Technology, Politics and Ethics as Anthropological Problems*, edited by A. Ong and S. J. Collier, 439–463. Malden, MA: Wiley-Blackwell.

Rosenberg, Deborah, Arden Handler, Kristin M. Rankin, Meagan Zimbeck, and E. Kathleen Adams. 2007. "Prenatal Care Initiation among Very Low-Income Women in the Aftermath of Welfare Reform: Does Pre-Pregnancy Medicaid Coverage Make a Difference?" *Maternal and Child Health Journal* 11(1):11–17.

Sargent, Carolyn F. 2005. "Counseling Contraception for Malian Migrants in Paris: Global, State, and Personal Politics." *Human Organization* 64(2):147–156.

———. 2006. "Reproductive Strategies and Islamic Discourse: Malian Migrants Negotiate Everyday Life in Paris, France." *Medical Anthropology Quarterly Special Issue* 20(1):31–49.

———. 2012. "Special Issue Part I: 'Deservingness' and the Politics of Health Care." *Social Science & Medicine* 74(6):855–857.

Schmitter Heisler, Barbara. 2007. "The Sociology of Immigration: From Assimilation to Segmented Assimilation, from the American Experience to the Global Arena." In *Migration Theory: Talking Across Disciplines*. 2nd ed., edited by C. B. Brettell and J. F. Hollifield, 83–112. New York: Routledge.

Sheik-Hamad, David, Elian Paiuk, Andrew J. Wright, Craig Kleinmann, Uday Khosla, and Wayne X. Shandera. 2007. "Care for Immigrants with End-Stage Renal Disease in Houston: A Comparison of Two Practices." *Texas Medicine* 103(4):53–58.

Starr, Paul. 1984. *The Social Transformation of American Medicine*. New York: Basic Books.

Stein, Ruth E., Michele J. Siegel, and Laurie J. Bauman. 2006. "Are Children of Moderately Low Birth Weight at Increased Risk for Poor Health? A New Look at an Old Question." *Pediatrics: Official Journal of the American Academy of Pediatrics* 118(1):217–223.

Tandon, S. Darius, Fallon Cluston-Keller, Lucinda Colon, Patricia Vega, and Alina Alonso. 2013. "Improved Adequacy of Prenatal Care and Health Care Utilization among Low-Income Latinas Receiving Group Prenatal Care." *Journal of Women's Health* 22(12):1056–1061.

Tandon, S. Darius, Lucinda Colon, Patricia Vega, Jeanne Murphy, and Alina Alonso. 2012. "Birth Outcomes Associated with Receipt of Group Prenatal Care among Low-Income Hispanic Women." *Journal of Midwifery & Women's Health* 57(5):476–481.

TDHHS (Texas Department of Health and Human Services Commission). 2014. "CHIP Perinatal Coverage." Austin: Texas Department of Health and Human Services. Retrieved May 7, 2014, from http://www.hhsc.state.tx.us/chip/perinatal/ClientInformation.htm#WhoMayQualify.

Texas Children's Health Plan. 2012. "CHIP Perinate Program Unborn Schedule of Benefits." Houston, TX: Texas Children's Health Plan. Retrieved May 7, 2014, from http://www.texaschildrenshealthplan.org/uploadedFiles/For_Members/For_Pregnant_Members/CHIP%20Perinatal%20Schedule%20of%20Benefits-Unborn.pdf.

Texas CHIP Coalition. 2005. "Children's Health Insurance Program Perinate Policy (As directed by the 79th Legislature, Regular Session)." Austin: Texas CHIP Coalition. Retrieved May 2, 2014, from http://www.texaschip.org/pdf/CHIPPerinateSummary.pdf.

Texas Health and Human Services Commission. 2009. "Health Facts Profile 2009: Cameron County." Austin: Texas Department of Health and Human Services Commission. Retrieved May 2, 2014, from http://www.dshs.state.tx.us/chs/.

Unnithan-Kumar, Maya. 2004. "Introduction: Reproductive Agency, Medicine and the State." In *Reproductive Agency, Medicine and the State: Cultural Transformations in Childbearing*, edited by M. Unnithan-Kumar, 1–24. New York: Berghan Books.

US Census Bureau. 2013a. "Hidalgo County Quick Facts." Washington, DC: US Census Bureau. Retrieved April 12, 2013, from http://quickfacts.census.gov/qfd/states/48/48215.html.

———. 2013b. "State and County QuickFacts: Cameron County, Texas." Washington, DC: US Census Bureau. Retrieved May 2, 2014, from http://quickfacts.census.gov/qfd/states/48/48061.html.

————. Social, Economic and Housing Statistics Division. 2013c. *Small Area Health Insurance Estimates (SAHIE) 2011 Highlights*. Washington, DC: US Census Bureau. Retrieved May 15, 2014, from http://www.census.gov/did/www/sahie/data/2011/SAHIE_Highlights_2011.pdf.

US Department of Health and Human Services. 2002. "State Children's Health Insurance Program: Eligibility for Prenatal Care and Other Health Services for Unborn Children." *Federal Register* 67 (191): 61956–61974. Retrieved September 29, 2014, from https://www.cms.gov/Regulations-and-Guidance/Regulations-and Policies/QuarterlyProviderUpdates/downloads/cms2127f.pdf.

Van Berckelaer, Anje C., Nandita Mitra, and Susmita Pati. 2011. "Predictors of Well Child Care Adherence Over Time in a Cohort of Urban Medicaid-Eligible Infants." *BMC Pediatrics* 11(1):36.

Vargas, Jose Antonio. 2011. "My Life as an Undocumented Immigrant." *New York Times*, June 22, MM22.

Vila, Pablo. 2000. *Crossing Borders, Reinforcing Borders: Social Categories, Metaphors and Narrative Identities on the US-Mexico Frontier*. Austin: University of Texas Press.

Waggoner, Miranda R. 2013. "Motherhood Preconceived: The Emergence of the Preconception Health and Health Care Initiative." *Journal of Health Politics, Policy and Law* 38(2):345–371.

Wailoo, Keith, Julie Livingston, and Peter Guarnaccia. 2006. *A Death Retold: Jesica Santillan, the Bungled Transplant, and Paradoxes of Medical Citizenship*. Chapel Hill: University of North Carolina Press.

Weir, Sharada, Heather E. Posner, Jianying Zhang, Georgianna Willis, Jeffrey D. Baxter, and Robin E. Clark. 2011. "Predictors of Prenatal and Postpartum Adequacy in a Medicaid Managed Population." *Women's Health Issues* 21(4):277–285.

Will, Jonathan F. 2013. "Beyond Abortion: Why the Personhood Movement Implicates Reproductive Choice." *American Journal of Law & Medicine* 39(4):573–616.

Willen, Sarah S. 2012a. "How is Health-Related 'Deservingness' Reckoned? Perspectives from Unauthorized Immigrants in Tel Aviv." *Social Science & Medicine* 74(6):812–821.

————. 2012b. "Migration, 'Illegality,' and Health: Mapping Embodied Vulnerability and Debating Health-Related Deservingness." *Social Science & Medicine* 74(6):805–811.

CHAPTER 9

The Role of Elite Mexican Women Immigrants in Maintaining Language and Mexican Identity

HARRIETT D. ROMO AND OLIVIA MOGOLLON-LOPEZ

In general, the gender and socioeconomic status of migrants influence the process of migration, the lives of the migrants, and the rate and process of integration into US society. Gender is one of the oldest forces shaping human lives, and although gender has not had a dominant place in the majority of migration studies, gender strongly influences migration and migrants' experiences (Pessar and Mahler 2003; Gordillo 2010; Donato, Piya, and Jacobs 2014). With the increased insecurity in Mexico, a small but increasing number of well-educated Mexican entrepreneurs are coming to the United States and bringing their families with them. These migrants are part of the group of highly skilled workers that, Orrenius and Zavodny (2010) argue, US immigration policy, particularly toward Mexico, should focus on to benefit the US economy. Orrenius and Zavodny (2013) note that although the average education level of Mexican immigrants to the United States has risen over time, only about 5 percent of adult Mexican immigrants are college graduates.

The United States has implemented temporary foreign worker programs and investor visa programs that allow professionals and those with higher levels of education to enter the United States. Programs such as the Trade NAFTA (TN), aimed at Mexicans and Canadians, and a broader H-1B visa program allow higher-skilled immigrants to work in the United States legally. Technology companies and industries that need researchers and other professionals have also voiced support for a more economically based immigration policy that increases the number of visas for high-skilled, well-educated immigrants. Four US senators introduced such a bill in January 2013 with the support of major technology employers such as Microsoft, Oracle, and others (Preston 2013). President Obama's executive order issued in November 2014 offered work visas for high-skilled legal immigrants brought to the United States by US companies and made it slightly easier for those already here to switch jobs without jeopardizing their immigration status (Nagourney, Lovett, and Goel 2014).

The wives of highly educated male immigrants with H-1B visas have been restricted from working in the past, and studies have shown that many experienced loss of independence linked to visa restrictions as a spouse. Pallavi Banerjee (2013) studied the experiences of spouses affected by the Immigration Act of 1990 and the H visa category, 25 percent of whom are from India. She found that spouses and children of any of the H (1, 2, and 3) visa holders can apply for an H-4 dependent visa. The term of the visa aligns with the term of the employed spouse, but under previous regulations the H-4 visa holder was not allowed to work legally in the United States, could not have a Social Security card, and, in some states, could not drive.

Most of the spouses of high-tech workers were proficient in English and had high human capital, some with higher degrees than the professionally "skilled" husband. Banerjee (2013) reported that being restricted from working or blocked from continuing to pursue a professional career often caused women to fall back on internalized gendered understandings of the role of the woman in families as the one responsible for 95 percent of the household work and continuous parenting. Banerjee's (2012) research demonstrated how visas can shape family structures and familial relationships for high-tech workers by reinforcing a patriarchal family form, with the man as the breadwinner and the woman as the homemaker. Some women experienced depression and resentment as they struggled to cope with state-imposed dependence on the worker obtaining the visa. US Citizenship and Immigration Services (2015) changed these regulations effective May 2015 to extend eligibility for employment authorization to certain H-4 dependent spouses of H-1B nonimmigrants who are seeking employment-based lawful permanent-resident status.

Another type of visa, the EB-5 Immigrant Investor Program, which has existed since 1990, encourages the immigration of wealthy families and allows up to ten thousand people each year to obtain legal permanent-resident status for themselves and their immediate family members by investing one million dollars in the United States. Participants in the program can also get a green card by investing $500,000 in an area where the unemployment rate exceeds 150 percent of the US average (US Citizenship and Immigration Services 2012). Beneficiaries of this program receive conditional permanent-resident status for two years upon their admission to the United States as EB-5 investors. After two years, if the investor has satisfied certain eligibility criteria, including having created or preserved at least ten full-time jobs for qualifying US workers, the conditions are removed and the immigrant and his or her family become unconditional lawful permanent residents of the United States (US Citizenship and Immigration Services 2013). Chinese immigrants have dominated the EB-5 visa category, with about 85 percent of the total number of these visas awarded. Mexican nationals represent only a small fraction of the total EB-5 immigrant visas awarded, but their numbers are increasing (US Department of State 2014).

Indeed the United States is receiving a more varied and economically important flow of immigrants than in the past. Americans are inclined to welcome these upper-tier immigrants, believing they contribute to economic growth (Hainmueller and Hiscox 2010), although Peter Elkind with Marty Jones wrote a cover article in the August 11, 2014, *Fortune* magazine titled "Citizenship for Sale" that was highly critical of the growing EB-5 visa program.

This chapter looks at the experiences of a distinct group of Mexican migrants, the "elite," those with high levels of education and ample funds for investments and for initiating businesses in the United States. This group has received little attention because these elite immigrants constitute only a small proportion of the Mexican immigrant population, which is dominated by immigrants with relatively low education levels (Bean et al. 2013). In this study, through interviews with a group of elite Mexican immigrant families, we have explored how these immigrants' spouses incorporate into the United States.

There is a history of the elite fleeing Mexico to the United States, particularly to Texas and California, during difficult economic periods or times of unrest. This was the case during the Mexican Revolution and, more recently, as a result of the increased insecurity generated by the Mexican government's war on drugs. A large number of elites have settled in San Antonio, Texas. The area has a growing number of recent Mexican immigrants from wealthy or highly educated families who have experienced threats of kidnappings or problems with extortion from drug cartels or who simply want to live in a more secure environment. Mexican entrepreneurs, seeing economic opportunities in the United States, have taken advantage of the possibility of obtaining work visas or permanent-resident cards for themselves and their families through investment.

This chapter is based on a qualitative study of Mexican entrepreneurs currently living in San Antonio. Although we do not know how many Mexican entrepreneurs are in the United States, we do know that they are present in many large cities, such as Houston, Los Angeles, San Diego, and New York (Hernández-León 2008). Previous studies have shown that female migrants have very different migration experiences when they migrate with their families compared to females migrating alone (Foner 2005, 2009). In the elite Mexican families interviewed, the men owned businesses, ran restaurants and construction companies, worked as investment advisors and bankers, began franchises of US businesses, or worked as professionals. While this type of immigrant is not characteristic of the majority of Mexican immigrants to the United States, their numbers are increasing. Their socioeconomic status facilitates their interaction with US institutions and social networks, whereas their investment visas allow them to bring their families and to return to Mexico as needed—advantages not accessible to working-class legal or unauthorized immigrants. Lowell (2000), for example, has documented a growing demand for skilled immigrants and support for legislation to increase the number of skilled temporary workers with H-1B visas in the United States, particularly in specialty fields in computer-related occupations. Another major difference between higher-income and working-class immigrants is that investment and professional visas allow those visa holders to bring their families at the same time, as a family unit. This is in contrast to stage migration, in which a worker migrates and later brings other family members, common among working-class migrant families.

In this study we focus on the wives of elite immigrants who enter the United States on investment or professional visas. The spouses of these male entrepreneurs and professionals spoke of the relevance of traditional roles of women as wives and mothers and the importance of the family for both parents and children. Work by Segura (1992) emphasized the responsibility of Mexican women in maintaining cultural traditions as part of their roles as wives and mothers. Overall, studies have shown that the family within Mexican culture is perceived as a value important to preserve (Malkin 1999). Through incorporation processes, gendered practices, and discourses that reinforce gender roles, migrants and those they interact with in the receiving society reproduce or contest hierarchies of gender, power, and privileges (Pessar and Mahler 2003). When migrants and later generations enter into institutionalized social relationships in the United States (such as the labor market, religion, and schools) that interact with ideological factors to condition gender relations and roles and responsibilities, they must work to maintain traditional roles and relationships or adapt to those of the receiving community. When that receiving community is populated with large numbers of members of their same ethnic group, traditional cultural roles may be reinforced strongly through social networks (Bankston 2014). Thus, gender relationships, roles, and ideologies are fluid, not fixed, as migrants incorporate selectively into a receiving society. Women must take on some aspects of the new community to effectively manage their families in their new homes, schools, and neighborhoods. At the same time, they are reinforcing cultural traditions, roles, behaviors, values, and responsibilities brought with them from their home cultures (Parrado and Flippen 2005).

Methodological Approach

Sample and Participant Selection

Participants in this study represent families who had migrated to San Antonio, Texas, on investment or professional visas. Many had to bring significant financial capital in businesses or investments to qualify for these visas. Investment visas, such as the E1 or E2 visas, allow business owners or investors to immigrate with the entire family, permit spouses to apply for a work permit, and allow children to attend US public schools. Professional visas, such as the H-1B or TN, allow immigrants to bring the entire family and authorize children to attend US public schools but, until 2015, did not grant a work permit to the spouse of the main applicant (US Citizenship and Immigration Services 2015).

The researchers identified initial participants in the study through key informants whose children attended private Catholic schools that we knew enrolled a number of elite Mexican children and through an organization formed by Mexican entrepreneurs with over two hundred members in the city. These two distinct initial sources provided a diversified network of participants (Berg 2009). Using a snowball technique, researchers asked initial families interviewed to refer other families meeting the characteristics of the study. The research team interviewed fourteen families, including twenty-five parents and twenty-seven adolescent youth from Mexico living in San Antonio on investment or professional visas. We used participant observation as we attended events where these families interacted, such as school events, religious services, organizational meetings, and community activities. We also visited with them in their homes before and after the interviews.

Research Process

Based on previous research with transnational families (Marquez and Romo 2008), the researchers constructed an extensive structured interview guide in English and Spanish that asked about reasons for moving to the United

States, characteristics of the neighborhoods where the families resided in Mexico and upon arriving in the United States, family background in Mexico, work experiences in Mexico and the United States, educational experiences, language use in the home, work, community involvement, religion, friendship networks, transnational contacts and visits, raising children, and experiences in the United States. All research protocols were approved by the University of Texas at San Antonio institutional review board. The two authors, one of whom is Mexican, and two Mexican-origin sociology graduate students, all bilingual in English and Spanish, conducted the interviews as a team in the families' homes. Interviews lasted one-and-a-half to two hours. Native Spanish speakers transcribed the interviews. Coding was done using ATLAS.ti, a qualitative research software suite, and the research team met regularly to discuss themes and content analyses as they emerged (Bailey 2007). The researchers constructed case studies based on the interviews and observations in the home (Yin 2009). This chapter is based on our observations and interviews with the women in the fourteen families whose spouses received the entrepreneurial or professional visas and lived in the San Antonio community.

Maintaining Mexican Culture

In the following case studies, analyses of responses from interviews with the wives of elite immigrants illustrate some of the ways these families attempted to reinforce Mexican cultural values and traditions, Mexican lifestyles, Mexican identity, and the Spanish language in their homes. The women in these families are well educated, with the majority having completed a bachelor's degree in Mexico or at least some college. Two had completed masters' degrees in Mexico. Although the wives of entrepreneurs holding investment visas were allowed to work in the United States if they chose to do so, only three of the women interviewed were employed outside the home. Four of the families had lived in the United States long enough to have applied for and received permanent-resident status or had an adult family member with US citizenship. The families interviewed had resided in the United States from three to fourteen years. Most certainly, time in the United States influenced the women's ability to maintain many of the Mexican aspects of family life, with families integrating US ways of life and English into their lifestyles the longer they resided in the United States and the longer their children attended US schools. The areas emphasized in these analyses represent aspects of cultural adaptation that have been emphasized in other studies (Alba 1990; Waters 1999; Levitt and Waters 2002; Kasinitz, Mollenkopf, and Waters 2004).

Cultural Aspects of Family Life

Food is one of the aspects of ethnic identity that is perhaps the easiest to maintain. Women pass on traditional recipes, ways of preparing and serving food, and ethnic foods from generation to generation. In the case of these families, women made an effort to preserve ethnic foods because they believed they were an important part of their cultural identities. San Antonio, with its majority Hispanic population, created sufficient demand for products needed in Mexican dishes that big food chains such as Wal-Mart and local supermarkets offered these ingredients and facilitated the families' ability to maintain traditional cuisine. Recent Mexican immigrants distinguished "authentic" Mexican food originating in Mexico City or the interior of Mexico from Tex-Mex adaptations. Three of the families interviewed had brought with them their *nana*, the woman who had cared for their children in Mexico, and these women helped cook traditional Mexican foods. Some compromises might be made as families adapted to the more hectic US schedules, such as store-bought tortillas or canned beans, but the migrants themselves helped generate a number of new restaurants and taco stands in San Antonio that prepared street foods of Mexico and more traditional dishes.

Irene Acosta explained, for example, that food preparation in her household was "exactly the same" as in Mexico and she still cooked as if she were in Mexico. She also noted that in San Antonio many of the non-Mexican residents sought out Mexican food, making this form of cooking profitable for small family restaurants as well as for larger upscale restaurants. Recent Mexican immigrants also shared food styles with their Anglo and Mexican American friends and neighbors. Irene pointed out that her children had "taught their friends to eat Mexican food."

> The form of cooking is exactly the same. I cook as if I were in Mexico, and the best part is, well, here you can find whatever Mexican product that you want. Then, my form of cooking, I don't know any other form of cooking except that of Mexico. Then, in that regard everything is the same as if we were in Mexico, but here [in San Antonio] they also seek out Mexican food, and in that way, my children have taught their friends to eat Mexican food.

The large concentration of recent Mexican immigrants in San Antonio has generated numerous upscale Mexican restaurants, markets that carry specialized *chiles* and spices needed in traditional Mexican foods, and, more recently, with the arrival of Mexican entrepreneurs, restaurants, Mexican food to go, and taco trucks that sell foods from the interior of Mexico and more traditional preparations compared to the Tex-Mex adaptations of Mexican Americans. This makes it easy for families to continue to prepare and eat foods as if they were still in Mexico.

Ofelia Lozano explained how her *nana* had taught her the recipes she had prepared for Ofelia's family growing up in Mexico. Ofelia had recorded the recipes in a little book that she kept with her in the United States. Many of the elite Mexican families had international experiences and traveled widely before coming to the United States, similar to elite migrants in other countries (Ley 2010), so while keeping Mexican traditional cuisine alive in the family, they also incorporated hamburgers, chicken wings, Japanese, and Chinese foods into the family meals. Ofelia described how she had maintained Mexican cuisine with the help of the person who had worked for her family in Mexico and now worked for her in the United States. Her family liked other ethnic foods as well:

> Now it is the same. I only prepare Mexican food. This is because when I came here I asked the person who helped us, the daughter of my *nana*, "I don't know how to cook, what am I going to do?" I wrote all the recipes in a little book, and that is how I began to cook because I had no idea. Until now, she was the one who always cooked for me. So, this is how I learned to cook, but here, the same as in Mexico, we like hamburgers and chicken wings, but we also eat Indian food, Japanese food. We like sushi, Chinese food as well. A little bit of everything.

These women made conscious efforts to maintain traditional Mexican foods, efforts made easier because of the Mexican influences already existing in San Antonio, a city that has a long history of Mexican migration and currently has a Hispanic majority population, primarily of Mexican origin. The ability to bring Mexican household help who could assist in maintaining traditional foods supported the efforts of these women in preserving a traditional Mexican kitchen. The families' international experiences, even before coming to the United States, added to the cosmopolitan experiences of these families, who were open to incorporating different types of foods.

Mexican History

The children in these families, especially those who were young when the families arrived in the United States, have spent a large portion of their lives in the United States attending US schools. Many were too young to have attended school in Mexico or had attended only the early elementary years in Mexican schools before their families came to the United States. US schools do not teach Mexican history, so the majority of the children have not been exposed to important historical events or persons from Mexican history. A few of the families have made efforts to seek out books about Mexican history or plan family vacations to historic places in Mexico, like Ofelia's family. In some cases, the older children's interests in learning more about Mexican history have stimulated parents to pursue books about Mexico so that they themselves will be informed about the important dates and milestones in Mexico to teach their children. When asked about her efforts to transmit Mexican cultural traditions and history to her children, Ofelia explained how her oldest child's interest in Mexican history inspired her to read and learn more about their native country's origins and development.

> Interviewer: Have you tried to learn more about the culture or history of Mexico?
>
> Ofelia: Yes, all the time. And lately it has been my son who has motivated me. His interest in the history of Mexico is impressive. He reads and reads books. He knows much more than I do. Then he asks me a question which I don't know the answer for and I have to read about it, such as what happened during the War of Reform? And I have to do research. I think for my son, one of the things that has strengthened his [Mexican] identity is to know about the history of his country of origin, even though he doesn't live there. He has read so much that it has motivated me and forced me a bit to learn more to keep up with him.

Ofelia explained that learning about the history of Mexico has strengthened her son's identity as Mexican. His avid interest in Mexico has motivated him to seek out books about Mexican history and forced his parents to learn more to keep up with him and be able to respond to his questions about his heritage.

Daniela Ramos, who had studied history in Mexico, felt confident in her own knowledge of Mexican history but realized that her children were the ones who experienced the impact of missing Mexican history lessons in US schools. She perceived that her children were "green" or uninformed about Mexican history. Her father gave the family books about Mexico, but the children hardly ever opened them. She was shocked when her youngest child asked if Benito Juárez was the one who gave the *grito de independencia*. This incident illustrated to her that her child did not have a good understanding of Mexican history and its sequence of events. She realized that she would have to send her child back to Mexico to rediscover her roots, which she arranged to do.

> Interviewer: Have you tried to learn more about the culture or history of Mexico?
> Daniela: Not at present. I say I know about history [of Mexico], but I would like for my children to be more informed about it. Truth is, they are "green." My father gave us history books, but they don't even open them up, never. They get really confused. When my daughter was younger she used to say to me, "Mom, was Benito Juárez the one who gave the *grito de independencia*?" I would say "No, Juárez didn't even hear the *grito*." I told her I had to send her to Mexico, and that's when I sent her for a year [she laughs].

Often the families did not realize that their children were missing out on important cultural knowledge about their home country until a child made some comment that alerted the parents to cultural loss. Daniela arranged to send her daughter to Mexico to reimmerse her in Mexican culture. Other families had sent children back to Mexico for summer camp to help them improve their Spanish. The visas available for investors and entrepreneurs allow family members to go and come from Mexico as they wish, which enables them to maintain family connections, friendships, and cultural ties with their communities of origin. Daniela's was not the only family to send children back to reinforce their Spanish-language skills or cultural knowledge. However, as reports or threats of violence increased, families were less inclined to send children back to Mexico and were more likely to determine to remain in the United States.

Strong Family Orientations

As Segura (1992) noted, Mexican women are seen as responsible for maintaining the traditional culture through their roles as wives and mothers. Almost all the women interviewed conformed to those traditional roles of spouse and mother and chose not to work in jobs that might create demands on their time away from the family. Nine of the fourteen women interviewed did not work at all outside of the family. Three worked in informal ways, such as teaching tennis classes at the country club, teaching art lessons to other Mexican women and to Mexican children, or taking care of a few children in their homes. Two of the women who had completed masters' degrees in Mexico worked in professional staff positions, both of which were related to Mexico. One of them worked part-time with flexible hours so that she could pick up her children from school. These women were all college educated but organized their lives around their families. None of the women had infant children, although several had a child still in elementary school.

Sofía Salinas, who had worked prior to marriage, explained when asked if she continued to work in her career area in the United States that her husband would not allow it: "Now that I'm married I don't work . . . at all, because my husband is a very traditional Mexican man who believes that women should not work."

All but the two professional women concurred with the belief that the woman's main responsibilities were to the family and children. Only one of the working women interviewed was in a financial position that required the woman's contribution to the household income, because she was divorced and had a daughter in college in the United States. All of the other women's earnings were considered supplemental to the family economy and not the major source of income.

Susana Peña, quoted below, noted that "*la familia es la familia*" [family is family] and all members of the family were obligated to support one another. She emphasized to her children that one could have hundreds of friends, but it was family members who would be there in times of need and that brothers and sisters must help one another in all areas, economically and morally, and act as a family unit.

> Interviewer: What things did your parents teach you about Mexican culture? What was most important to them?
> Susana: Family unity. . . . Yes, because I tell them, "Look you can have a hundred friends, but family is family. It makes no difference if you are on the other side of the world, if you need anything, you call me [by telephone], and you know I am going to help you." So this is what we try to teach them, we [the parents] won't be here forever, but between brothers and sisters, you have to help one another in all areas, economically or morally. To be united.

Susana emphasized the importance of family support and family obligations. None of these families were sending remittances to Mexico, although all noted that if someone needed something special from the United States or help once in a while, they, of course, would provide it. The extended family of the majority of these families remained in Mexico, but their parents and relatives were well off and did not depend on the earnings of family members in the United States. All but two of the families had come to the United States for investment or economic mobility reasons because they saw opportunities for improving their families' futures by starting businesses in the United States or extending family businesses in Mexico to the United States. One of the most recently arrived families had received death threats, and the family left Mexico immediately because of fears of violence. The wife talked of the difficulty of leaving her parents and close friends behind. The families all maintained contact through telephone calls, e-mails, social media, and visits from those in Mexico. Those who had not had direct experiences with insecurity returned to Mexico occasionally for family visits. Even though several of the women commented on missing the household help available when living in Mexico, and missing aging parents, siblings, and close friends, they all acknowledged that the move was important for the family.

Religion

Religion frequently becomes more important for migrant families when they leave their community of origin and move to a new country. This was true for many of these families once they decided to live in the United States. The uncertainties of life in a new community and the fears brought about by threats of violence or kidnappings in Mexico that caused some of the families to move to the United States increased the importance of faith in their lives. Susana explained that she attended mass more frequently in the United States than she had in Mexico. When asked about the intensity of her religious beliefs she said: "They are a little more intense here in the United States than in Mexico . . . or a lot more intense, because, I don't know if it is because you live in another country that you feel you need more faith and more of God's support."

Two of the Catholic churches in the area where the families resided in San Antonio offered mass in Spanish. When members of our research team attended the Spanish-language services, it was obvious that members of the parish and large numbers of those attending the Spanish-language mass were Latinos who spoke Spanish with their spouses and children. Susana was especially religious and had conducted catechism classes for the children of other Mexican immigrants in her home.

Paulina Benavídez was also very religious, and when she lived in Mexico City, she participated in the celebrations of the Virgen de Guadalupe. When she arrived in San Antonio she tried to seek out groups of Guadalupanas but found none in the upper-income neighborhood where she lived.

She decided to begin celebrations for the Virgin herself following the traditions in Mexico, such as the traditional *pozolada*. She invited Mexican friends on Facebook, through e-mails, and in person to her home in December, and they organized their own ceremonies for the Virgen de Guadalupe. When we visited her home the day after the ceremony, her large, beautifully furnished living room was filled with numerous vases of red roses from the celebration. In her interview, she proudly told us about the values she was teaching her children and the ceremony in her home on December 12 that had been attended by some fifty or sixty other Mexican women.

> Interviewer: What aspects of the Mexican culture are you maintaining?
>
> Paulina: The food. The values. Especially the Mexican values. I want my children to learn to ask for permission and say excuse me and please, to be well mannered and respectful. The celebrations for the Virgen de Guadalupe, for sure, as true Catholics. To go to mass . . . well, that happens worldwide. . . . In Mexico, in Mexico City, every year there's a big celebration to honor the Virgin of Guadalupe. And here, when I got here [to San Antonio] I asked around to find out if somebody was going to organize a celebration for the Virgin of Guadalupe, or if there was going to be an event so I could attend. But no, I heard nothing about a celebration. No news. And for that reason, I began to celebrate the Virgen de Guadalupe with the traditional *pozolada*, a pork stew that is a very typical Mexican plate which is customary when we celebrate the Virgin.
>
> Interviewer: What do you do? Tell me about the celebration.
>
> Paulina: Well, I invite my friends openly on Facebook, or in e-mails, or through word of mouth. When they arrive, we start by singing the traditional hymns for the Virgin of Guadalupe. Later, we recite a meditation written by a priest who's a friend. We meditate and talk about the example of the Virgin Mary, of the Virgin of Guadalupe, as an example in our lives, as Catholic women and mothers, as wives, sisters, and daughters, of every aspect of womanhood. We set her up as an example to follow. After the meditation, we pray the rosary. After the rosary, the singing begins . . . the classic "Ave María," such a beautiful song. Last year, I brought mariachis to sing "Las Mañanitas." And so it is, each year we change according to what's available, right? And when we finish the event, we sit down together and eat a delicious plate of *pozole*.
>
> Interviewer: More or less how many people?
>
> Paulina: About fifty to sixty. And a security guard came over and asked my chauffeur if there was a wake because there were so many people and it

was so quiet . . . in silence. He said, "No, they are celebrating the Virgin of Guadalupe and praying the rosary." So the guard said, "Here they never do that. . . . How strange" [laughter]. They were surprised.

Paulina lived in a large, expensive, gated community, frequently referred to by other Mexicans as "little Mexico." Homes advertised in the local newspaper for sale in that neighborhood ranged from $250,000 to over $400,000, and a large number of high-income Mexican nationals lived in that community. She explained that it was important for her children to maintain Mexican values and "*que sean educados*," to be polite, respectful of their parents, and respectful to others, attributes highly regarded in Mexican culture. She also stressed the importance of maintaining her Catholic faith. She described in detail the celebration of the Virgin of Guadalupe that she had organized and emphasized the example the Virgin provided for her and her friends as Mexican women—to be Catholic, to be good mothers, wives, sisters, daughters, and to excel in all aspects of womanhood ("todos los aspectos de la mujer"). The women followed the traditions associated with Mexican celebrations of the Virgin, including meditation about what it meant to be a woman, discussing examples the Virgin represented for them to follow, and the traditional rosary and songs celebrating the Virgin. The year before, she had included mariachis, groups of Mexican musicians who play traditional music for a fee. The event ended with a traditional Mexican dinner of *pozole*, a hominy and pork soup.

In the Westside of San Antonio, one of the largest working-class Mexican barrios, there are groups of women who celebrate the Virgin of Guadalupe on December 12, the Virgin's saint's day, but there had been few such celebrations in the high-income gated community where Paulina lived. She even commented that the security guard for the neighborhood had been curious about the crowd because the celebration was quiet and somber and had asked her chauffeur what was happening. The guard expressed surprise when the chauffeur explained about the celebration of the Virgin of Guadalupe because he had never seen these celebrations in that wealthy neighborhood.

This event was interesting because Paulina took it upon herself to bring the traditional Mexican celebration to her upper-income neighborhood in the United States and to her Mexican immigrant friends. The celebration reinforced the traditional roles of women—to be good mothers, good wives, and supportive sisters and daughters—and their meditations reassured them of their value in the roles they played as women in their immigrant families.

Language

The Spanish language is an important part of Hispanic identity, and all of these Mexican families had determined to maintain Spanish in their homes and raise bilingual children. Research has shown that language and identities are "constructed, dynamic and hybrid, and as such, are subject to change in a never ending process of symbolic boundary construction and reconstruction" (Romaine 2011, 13). Identifying with a culture normally implies positive attitudes toward the language used in its associated communities, and this was true for the families interviewed. All families had the rule that only Spanish could be spoken in the home. One father suggested to his two adolescent children that they should speak English at home to help the mother learn the language since she spoke little English, but the children rebelled and insisted that they speak Spanish at home so that they would not lose their Spanish-language skills.

Irene and others emphasized that their family had determined to speak Spanish from their very arrival in San Antonio because the family believed that fluency in Spanish was an important part of the children's education and essential for maintaining contact with family members in Mexico.

Lorena Franco explained that when they first arrived, her children began to speak English among themselves and she had forbidden it, because she recognized that if they did not speak Spanish at home on a daily basis, the children would forget the language. She had to correct them daily because her daughter had begun to translate literally, and Lorena wanted her daughter to speak correct Spanish. We asked the parents whether their children identified as Americans or Mexicans, and Spanish was definitely a strong aspect of their identification. When we asked Lorena how she thought her children identified themselves, she asserted that they definitely identified as Mexicans, but she also described how the children gradually began to use English rather than Spanish if the parents did not emphasize Spanish.

> Interviewer: How do you think your children identify themselves? Do you have any idea how they respond?
> Lorena: I think they respond . . . I don't think, I am sure that they respond that they are Mexicans from Mexico City. Definitively, they identify as Mexicans and I believe in the long term . . . because I say, to date and since we arrived, they have always had to speak Spanish at home. Because at the beginning, especially my daughter, when she began speaking English, they began speaking English among themselves . . . and I didn't let them because if you let them, soon they are going to speak English among

themselves and they are not going to speak Spanish. And to this day I keep correcting them. My daughter at first began translating words literally.

Lorena was firm in her commitment to make sure her children spoke Spanish at home. She realized, when her daughter began learning English and translating literally rather than speaking correct Spanish, that it was important for her to correct her, to keep the children from speaking English among themselves, because she recognized correctly that if Spanish was not reinforced in the home, the children would quickly lose their Spanish skills.

The families struggled with these issues because the children attended schools in which instruction was in English. Research has confirmed that immigrant children quickly learn English, which is dominant even in communities like San Antonio with a majority Hispanic population.

Susana, a Mexican immigrant mother with US-born children, also emphasized Spanish in her home and, although initially it was difficult for her children to participate in their English-speaking schools, the teachers reassured her that her children would learn English. She recognized that if the children did not maintain Spanish in the home, they would quickly lose their Spanish-language skills. Her children were born in the United States and have always lived in the United States, but she stated that the children were completely bilingual. She acknowledged that the Spanish language remained one of the most important cultural aspects to maintain and, thus, the family prohibited the speaking of English in the home, even charging the children ten cents per word if they spoke in English. Her child's kindergarten teacher had encouraged Susana to speak to the children in Spanish at home, recognizing the importance of the home language. Susana was concerned because her son did not speak at all in his classroom, and she was concerned that the child would not make friends or get along in school. The teacher reassured her that the child would learn English quickly. Susana noted the teacher's "excellent" advice and bragged about her children's bilingual skills. When asked what Mexican cultural aspects were most important to maintain in the United States, Susana replied that the Spanish language was absolutely the most important:

The language, absolutely. In my house it is forbidden to speak in English. We only speak Spanish and, as a matter of fact, if the children speak much in English or they begin speaking among themselves in English, I began to charge them ten cents a word . . . so they stopped speaking it. This interests me a lot, and I believe some of the best advice that my son's first teacher in kindergarten gave me was, "Don't allow your children to speak English because they are going to lose their Spanish." At first I was worried because my son, who used to be very outgoing in Spanish, at school would not open his mouth or establish relationships with anyone, he was a different person. We were very worried so I told the teacher, "Should I speak to him in English, teach him words? What should we do to help him make friends?" And she told me, "Don't worry, he is going to learn it, sooner or later he is going to learn English, but [if you don't speak to him in Spanish] he might forget his Spanish . . ." And I think that was excellent advice because, I see it, with many people who have just recently arrived, maybe two or three years here in the United States and the children already don't speak Spanish. And my children, although they were born here and always have lived here, . . . they speak both languages perfectly.

Susana had noticed other Mexican immigrant children who began school in English and quickly lost their Spanish, and she was grateful that her child's kindergarten teacher in the United States had encouraged her to emphasize Spanish in the home. Although her children were born in the United States and were US citizens, she definitely wanted them to be completely bilingual and maintain the Spanish language.

Modo de Vida (Way of Life)

Many of the women interviewed told us that the most important Mexican cultural aspects maintained in the United States were the ways they lived their daily lives. Culture was not something they taught directly; it was the way they interacted in their homes, the foods they prepared, the language they used to communicate with one another, the music they listened to, the books they read, and the ways they organized their lives. Ofelia Lozano explained this well:

Interviewer: What aspects of the Mexican culture do you still maintain?
    Ofelia: I maintain a lot. We continue speaking Spanish in the home, all the time. Our food is Mexican food. I don't prepare anything else. The decoration of the house, the home decoration, is completely Mexican. The hours are Mexican, even though it would be easier to eat at the time everyone eats here. We continue to have a late lunch, at around four p.m., and a late dinner, at around nine. Although we are trying to change that. We read a lot in Spanish. I read a lot in Spanish, and my son, more than anyone else, reads a lot in Spanish. We don't watch television in Spanish. I don't like television. Food, language, hours, ways of relating to people, and we have

talked about that. We still have that way of relating to people that is . . . I don't know how to explain it . . . that way of relating that is not so blunt. It remains very prudent, very friendly. The style of relating to other people. That has been important. The type of books we read, the style of music we listen to. We continue to listen to a lot of music in Spanish.

Ofelia highlighted the important role of the mother in the home in maintaining the Mexican way of life, ways of relating with one another in their home and in their daily lives. In this family, it was important even to maintain the Mexican style of eating meals in the late afternoon and later in the evening, despite the pressures of life in the United States to adapt to US customs. Families made special efforts, often guided by the woman of the house, to maintain traditions: the style of decorating the home, the way family members interacted, the books they read, the music they listened to, and preparation of traditional foods. Many of these families had been in the United States for several years. For example, Ofelia and her family had been in the United States for over ten years and recently had acquired permanent residency status. All of the families we interviewed planned to remain in the United States, but despite these commitments to the United States, they worked hard to maintain Mexican lifestyles and ways of interacting with others, the Spanish language, and Mexican values and traditions. In a similar manner, Maribel Gómez told us that nothing had changed in their home as a result of migration. Although her family now lives in the United States, life goes on just as it had in Mexico: "Well . . . in my home nothing has changed. Everyone continues the same, we speak Spanish here. I want my children to be perfectly bilingual, to speak both languages without accents or anything. The Mexican food, everything's the same, with our traditions and culture."

Sofía Salinas pointed out that her family maintained family meal times with everyone at the table and noted that the interactive dinner conversations were important for her and her husband. She noticed that Americans were often too rushed to have family dinners and did not value after-dinner conversations as much as Mexicans, particularly her family.

Interviewer: What aspects of Mexican culture do you continue maintaining in your home, and what has changed with the passage of time?

Sofía: Well, for example, the traditions. We sit every day for meals together, I set the table every day as if visitors were coming, and we sit together every day like that. I put everything on the table to help ourselves, as if company were coming. This seems like a tradition from there [Mexico]. Over there it is easy to do because you have help, but I try to continue to do it here, even though I don't have help. What other things seem different there than here? . . . Well, that, that is something I've seen different between Americans and Mexicans. To sit at the table, and the dinner conversation as well. We usually have conversations at dinner time; we don't just eat and jump up. We eat and we remain sitting because it is the only time we are all together and we talk together. This is very important for me. Well, and for my husband.

Ways of arranging schedules and family interactions emerged as one of the most noted cultural differences identified by the women participants in this study. All had noticed the ways Americans organized their lives around time. Paulina was particularly upset by the ways Americans entertained within certain time frames. Below, Paulina emphasizes how disconcerted she felt when Americans invited her to parties within a particular time framework. She preferred a Mexican style of entertaining in which she described the guests arriving at various times and staying as long as people continued to enjoy themselves. She disliked invitations that stated a short time for parties or lunches. She felt offended by the ways Americans organized children's parties inviting only selected children. She described Mexican styles of entertaining as more flexible, more open, and more inclusive.

For example, Americans have preset hours. From this time to this time. . . . First they say . . . the family, or the mother . . . the parties are from twelve to two. Two hours. Or one to three or two to four. So you get there, you have a soda, chips, a snack. You come and go in two hours. "Two hours? I'm not going. I'm not going!" By the time I get there with my children, get them in the house to play. To get them out, [they say] "What's your problem? We just got here." Mexicans live for the celebrations. It is very important in our culture . . . the celebration, part of the moment. You say, "What? There isn't going to be a party?" To us, that is not a celebration. The upbringing is completely different. They [Americans] invite five children, when we invite fifty. At home, the same. I imagine that they also have schedules, right? A half-hour for television. Two hours to play. I don't know. And here, no. In Mexico, children run, come in, go out, they come and go.

Paulina was shocked at the orderly, scheduled lives that American families lived and the way they tightly scheduled their children's time and events. She found the rigidity of American social events completely different from the more open and free-flowing Mexican events. The hours of meals and the family togetherness at mealtimes also emerged as a cultural tradition Mexican families tried to maintain. Some families waited until they picked up their children from school at two p.m. or later to have the family meal. Sofía Salinas noted that as her children married or went to the university, their lives became more hectic, with each coming and going at different times. She explained that it was not an adaptation to US culture that altered the family's ways of doing things, because the family would have changed in Mexico as well, as the children grew and became more involved in their own lives. It was the transformation in the family that determined their changed way of life, not living in the United States.

> I cannot have a schedule here, it's like everything shifted. In Mexico we would get up, eat at three . . . we sat at the table and ate together, and here you lose that, but I haven't discovered why. I have talked about it with my friends . . . yes, but it has changed because my children have grown up. When they were little, we would all gather at the table. But maybe in Mexico it would also have changed. One got married, the other is at the university, another leaves at the time the other arrives. So, I don't think it is because we're here [in the United States] that things changed, what has changed is my family, not the place.

Sofía lamented the lost cultural traditions of Mexico associated with family mealtimes when everyone gathered around the table together for the main meal in the afternoons. She regretted that this did not happen any more in the United States and at first could not determine why things had changed. She preferred the Mexican family tradition of having meals together but recognized that things would probably also have changed in Mexico as children grew older and developed independent lives outside the home. She concluded that it was not immigrating to the United States that had altered the ways they ate together but that their family lifestyles had changed as the children grew up and attended the university, got married, and had their own lives. She recognized that family adaptations would have occurred in Mexico as well and it was not just the immigrant experience in the United States that forced family changes.

Daniela Ramos had also thought about the immigrant process and the changes it demanded and concluded that the atmosphere in San Antonio did not require acculturation changes because the city was "pure Mexican," and as a result, she and her family had never felt they had to adapt to US culture. She told her mother that she never felt as if she were a foreigner in the United States because they arrived and lived among other Mexicans. Daniela's experiences emphasize the importance of the concentration of Mexicans in San Antonio and the Mexican influences on the city. Daniela never felt out of place or different as a result of being Mexican. She explained:

> Interviewer: Do you still maintain, for example, the food that you give your family? Do you try to feed them at the same time [as in Mexico]? Do you feel more Mexican?
>
> Daniela: I am going to be honest. I have never questioned myself, never, if I'm Mexican or not. I told my mother that I have never felt like a stranger in this country . . . never. As a matter of fact, ever since we arrived I've lived almost entirely in a Mexican bubble. So I have never felt like a stranger. Do you understand? I am very happy here because my environment is all Mexican.

Family and Work outside the Home

The majority of the women we interviewed were well educated. All had completed high school, several had completed college and held masters' or professional degrees, and several had worked in Mexico before they were married. One had been an architect, but her professional credentials in Mexico were not recognized in the United States. Another had majored in psychology and worked in a large transportation company in Mexico City. Spouses who had lived in the United States for several years and whose husbands had applied for and received permanent-resident status had obtained permission to work in the United States. Only one, a woman who had gotten a divorce from her husband, worked full-time in a professional position, doing so for a Mexican company that had a branch office in San Antonio. The other women chose not to work outside of the home or worked in part-time positions that allowed them to be with their children.

Iris García, who had studied psychology, taught tennis lessons at the country club the family belonged to in their gated community. She noted that it was not work that she particularly liked, because she was trained as a psychologist, but it was a type of work that allowed her to be with her children. She explained: "This work is not the type of work that I would like to have, because I really enjoyed psychology, but it is work that lets me be with my children. I feel that I am leaving behind what I want to do to take care of my children, but I feel that I only have a short time longer to go, so I'm going to finish and then do what I want to do."

Iris realized that in the United States, perhaps more than in Mexico, to achieve a certain social status, women had to work to supplement the household income, but not in all homes. When she lived in Mexico, in her social circles, women's work was seen as a hobby and the husband was the one who went to work. She had begun to see that in the United States, if one wanted to reach certain social levels, women had to work; perhaps this was changing in Mexico as well. Iris had permanent-resident status in the United States but lacked the proper credentials to work as a psychologist. She had no desire to return to school even though she would have liked to do something related to her career. At the time of this study, she spent her spare time playing tennis, visiting with her friends, going on vacations with her family, and taking care of her children, her husband, and her home. She told us that for her, success was to have a functioning family and to be happy with what she had, always wanting more, but being content with what she had. She concluded: "I can feel that I am really successful in my life and someone can say 'Iris? Why? She hasn't done anything.' But I can feel very successful because I have my children. I am happy about the way they are." Iris and several of the other women missed being able to work in their professional careers, but they recognized that being with their children was an important responsibility for the family.

Discussion

Visa changes in 2015 extended eligibility for employment authorization to qualifying spouses of professional immigrants with H-1B visas, the new rules allowing them to work and contribute to the household income. This opens opportunities for the female spouses of elite Mexican immigrants with H-1B visas to pursue careers and professions. Spouses of entrepreneurs with E1 and E2 visas are eligible to apply for work permits. Nevertheless, only one of the women we interviewed chose to work full-time outside the home in a job that was not organized around her family schedule. She was divorced and supported herself and her child. It remains to be seen if changes in women's empowerment, migrant adaptation, and evolving expectations for gender relations for highly skilled workers and their families will affect parenting and gender relationships in these entrepreneurial Mexican migrant families.

Parrado and Flippen (2005) emphasized that US residency, women's human-capital endowments, household characteristics, and social support all influence the reconstruction of gender relations in the receiving country. The concepts of familism and gendered roles of the woman as mother and caretaker of the home and family remain strong in Mexican culture and were strongly verbalized in the interviews conducted with these families. One respondent, an architect in Mexico, could not pursue her career in the United States because her professional license in Mexico is not recognized in the United States. While she regretted not being able to continue her profession, she felt strongly that her role as mother to their three young children was most important for the family at this time. Another spouse, who had a master's degree and worked part-time because her husband had gotten green cards for her and their three children, did not wish to work full-time because she felt it was important for her to spend time with her children before they left for college.

Immigration policy that allows these women and their families to choose whether the spouse will work will prevent women from being completely dependent on the male visa holder. The 2015 extension of eligibility for employment announced by the US Department of Homeland Security allows spouses of certain H-1B visa holders to work in the United States. The initiative might affect 97,000 people the first year and 30,000 each year after that (US Department of Homeland Security 2014). Proponents say these changes will attract more foreign talent and open up opportunities for their highly educated spouses.

Zhou and Bankston (1998) have argued that a dense ethnic community can provide a bulwark against assimilation to US culture, while others have argued that assimilation is an avenue to upward mobility (Alba and Nee 1999) and is likely to happen with Mexican immigrants over time as they acknowledge the need for English-language skills and social networks beyond their ethnic group. As wives of elite Mexican immigrants and dependent children enter the US labor market, they are exposed to more pressures to take on aspects of US culture in order to incorporate into the US community. These elite Mexican immigrants have high levels of education, economic resources, and other characteristics that residents admire and desire in immigrant populations. These characteristics also promote assimilation. Empirical research and the cases presented in this chapter suggest that there is a more nuanced approach to incorporation based on the conditions of migration, the class origin of immigrants, and the contexts of reception (Portes and Boroez 1989; Bankston 2014).

The US Southwest, given its increasing Hispanic population, and San Antonio, as a majority Hispanic city, are examples of the social channels created that open ways for the entry and settlement of elite Mexican immigrants and for the maintenance of their Spanish language and Mexican heritage. Hirschman and Massey (2010, 6) note that while the largest destination states for immigrants, such as New York, California, Illinois, Texas, and Florida, still attracted the most immigrants in the late 1990s, the proportion of Mexican immigrants settling in those areas has dropped to 60 percent as migrants move to new destinations in the South and throughout the United States. Incorporation in these new destinations that have not had a history of Mexican migration may take quite different patterns. US cities along the US-Mexico border and throughout the southwestern states with high concentrations of Mexican population continue to attract Mexican immigrants, especially those with high levels of education and resources.

San Antonio, Texas, has a long history of Mexican working-class and elite migration and settlement. The city and state were once a part of Mexico. Thus, in communities such as San Antonio, it is unclear what "assimilation" means. Assimilation can mean cultural loss, but it can also mean cultural gain (Kasinitz, Mollenkopf, and Waters 2004). The recent influx of well-educated Mexican immigrants who speak Spanish fluently and espouse Mexican cultural values has replenished the Mexican cultural influence in San Antonio (Jiménez 2010). The women in the families interviewed in this study maintained the values and aspects of their Mexican culture by continuing the traditional roles of wife, homemaker, and mother while their husbands worked successfully in the United States and their children attended US schools. Social class and gender influenced patterns of acculturation, but so did visa status. As with the group of elite Mexican women interviewed for this project, having the resources and visas permitting them to return to Mexico to visit friends and relatives allowed these women opportunities to maintain strong ties to their communities of origin. High levels of education and financial resources also opened doors to social and formal institutions and relationships in the receiving community.

These upper-income migrants clustered together, buying expensive homes in particular gated neighborhoods that have become a new kind of elite "ethnic enclaves." All of the families interviewed consciously tried to maintain the most important aspects of their Mexican culture—traditional foods and customs, the Catholic religion, the Spanish language, and lifestyles and interpersonal relationships that characterized their Mexican heritage. The pride these families bring to their Mexican culture and their strong Mexican identities replenish Mexican American ethnicity, and as Jiménez (2010, 251) argues, this relationship to their heritage culture and identity "alter[s] the relationship between structural and cultural forms of assimilation that scholars have taken for granted."

A city like San Antonio, with its majority Hispanic population and many venues where Spanish is spoken daily, facilitates continuity of Mexican culture. These elite families have the socioeconomic resources and levels of education to adapt well to the United States, but some of the primary roles of the wives of these entrepreneurs are enforcing the use of Spanish in the home, bringing Mexican Catholic traditions to their communities, and reinforcing Mexican values and ways of interacting with their families and children. The women themselves, their husbands, and their children all value this role and respect the mother of the family as mainly responsible for cultural maintenance.

The husbands and children, in their interviews, emphasized the important role of these women in nurturing the family, being a good mother, and keeping the Mexican culture vibrant within their families. The families chose to live in close proximity to other Mexican families of similar socioeconomic status, and they reported that most of their social interactions were also with Mexican families of similar backgrounds. There are sufficient numbers of elite Mexican families in San Antonio to form a social network that helps support Mexican culture and a lifestyle similar to the one they experienced in Mexico. Several respondents also mentioned that it was important for persons of their socioeconomic status to speak Spanish and maintain Mexican culture because this enhanced the image of Mexicans in the United States. During a formal meeting of an organization formed by mostly male Mexican business owners to help other Mexican investors, members of the organization discussed the importance of the golf tournaments, social magazine, and galas they sponsored in changing the image of the Mexican immigrant in the United States. The women interviewed in this study felt valued and supported for the important role they played in their families and within the US Mexican community.

We argue that, although this group of elite Mexican immigrants is not representative of the majority of Mexican migrants in the United States, the elite are playing an important part in elevating and maintaining the status of Spanish and of Mexican traditions in the United States. They do not believe that they have to assimilate completely to the American way of life or to speak only English to do well in the United States. They accommodate to be successful in their businesses and in US schools, but they do not substitute American ways of life for Mexican styles of life or give up the Mexican customs and Mexican identity they value. They are firm in their commitments to maintaining Mexican culture and traditions, and they hold highly the role of the wives and mothers in their families. This group, like the Mexican-origin population studied by Jiménez (2010, 253) in Garden City and Santa Maria, California, is not "an aggrieved minority that has confronted obstacles to mobility."

The elite Mexican immigrant experience is exemplary of the complexity of the Mexican immigrant experience in the United States and the importance of context. The duration of Mexican immigration in the United States and the precedent of elite Mexicans coming to cities in the US Southwest in times of difficulty and for economic opportunities continue. The concentration of Mexican population and strong Mexican cultural traditions in the US Southwest and in cities like San Antonio are central factors shaping the processes of Mexican immigrant acculturation and Mexican ethnic identity. Marriage and family responsibilities are also strong factors affecting immigrant women's labor force participation. Immigration regulations that allow spouses of professional and investor visa holders to work and to pursue professional careers give women the option to decide whether or not to work outside the home, allowing them to make choices that are best for themselves and their families. However, strong cultural values and expectations of women's roles in the family may continue to influence these decisions.

References

Alba, Richard D. 1990. *Ethnic Identity: The Transformation of White America*. New Haven, CT: Yale University Press.

Alba, Richard D., and Victor Nee. 1999. "Rethinking Assimilation Theory for a New Era of Immigration." In *The Handbook of International Migration: The American Experience*, edited by C. Hirschman, P. Kasinitz, and J. DeWind, 135–160. New York: Russell Sage Foundation.

Bailey, Carol A. 2007. *A Guide to Qualitative Field Research*. 2nd ed. Thousand Oaks, CA: Pine Forge Press.

Banerjee, Pallavi. 2012. "Constructing Dependence: Visa Regimes and Gendered Migration in Families of Indian Professional Workers." PhD dissertation. University of Illinois at Chicago. Retrieved April 30, 2015, from http://hdl.handle.net/10027/9771.

———. 2013. "'I Call it the Vegetable Visa:' A Gender Structure Analysis of Family Lives of Dependent Visa Holders." Presented at the Council on Contemporary Families, 16th Annual Conference, Immigrant Families As They Are, Miami, FL.

Bankston III, Carl L. 2014. *Immigrant Networks and Social Capital*. Malden, MA: Polity Press.

Bean, Frank D., Susan K. Brown, Mark A. Leach, James D. Bachmeier, and Jennifer Van Hook. 2013. "Unauthorized Mexican Migration and the Socioeconomic Integration of Mexican Americans." In *Changing Times: America in a New Century*, edited by J. R. Logan, 1–34. New York: Russell Sage Foundation.

Berg, Bruce L. 2009. *Qualitative Research Methods for the Social Sciences*. Boston, MA: Allyn & Bacon.

Donato, Katharine M., Bhumika Piya, and Anna Jacobs. 2014. "The Double Disadvantage Reconsidered: Gender, Immigration, Marital Status, and Global Labor Force Participation in the 21st Century." *International Migration Review* 48(S1):S335–S376.

Elkind, Peter, and Marty Jones. 2014. "Citizenship for Sale: The Dark, Disturbing—and Rapidly Growing—World of the EB-5 Visa Program." *Fortune*, August 11, 51–62.

Foner, Nancy. 2005. *In a New Land: A Comparative View of Immigration*. New York: University Press.

Foner, Nancy, ed. 2009. *Across Generations: Immigrant Families in America*. New York: University Press.

Gordillo, Luz María. 2010. *Mexican Women and the Other Side of Immigration: Engendering Transnational Ties*. Austin: University of Texas Press.

Hainmueller, Jens, and Michael J. Hiscox. 2010. "Attitudes toward Highly Skilled and Low-Skilled Immigration: Evidence from a Survey Experiment." *American Political Science Review* 104(1):61–84.

Hernández-León, Ruben. 2008. *Metropolitan Migrants: The Migration of Urban Mexicans to the United States*. Berkeley: University of California Press.

Hirschman, Charles, and Douglas S. Massey. 2010. "Places and Peoples: The New American Mosaic." In *New Faces in New Places: The Changing Geography of American Immigration*, edited by D. S. Massey, 1–21. New York: Russell Sage Foundation.

Jiménez, Tomás R. 2010. *Replenished Ethnicity: Mexican Americans, Immigration, and Identity*. Berkeley: University of California Press.

Kasinitz, Philip, John H. Mollenkopf, and Mary C. Waters. 2004. *Becoming New Yorkers: Ethnographies of the New Second Generation*. New York: Russell Sage Foundation.

Levitt, Peggy, and Mary C. Waters. 2002. *The Changing Face of Home: The Transnational Lives of the Second Generation*. New York: Russell Sage Foundation.

Ley, David. 2010. *Millionaire Migrants: Trans-Pacific Life Lines*. West Sussex, UK: Wiley-Blackwell Publishing.

Lowell, Lindsay B. 2000. "The Demand and New Legislation for Skilled Temporary Workers (H-1B) in the United States." *People and Place* 8(4):29–35.

Malkin, Victoria. 1999. "La reproducción de las relaciones de género en la comunidad de migrantes: Mexicanos en New Rochelle, Nueva York." In *Fronteras fragmentadas*, edited by G. Mummert, 475–98. Michoacán, Mexico: El Colegio de Michoacán.

Marquez, Raquel, and Harriett D. Romo. 2008. *Transformations of La Familia on the US-Mexico Border*. Notre Dame, IN: University of Notre Dame Press.

Nagourney, Adam, Ian Lovett, and Vindu Goel. 2014. "Immigration's Turmoil? California Has Lived It For Decades." *New York Times*, November 23, A1, A23.

Orrenius, Pia M., and Madeline Zavodny. 2010. *Beside the Golden Door: US Immigration Reform in a New Era of Globalization*. Washington, DC: The American Enterprise Institute for Public Policy Research.

————. 2013. *Immigrants in the US Labor Market.* Working Paper 1306. Dallas, TX: Federal Reserve Bank of Dallas.

Parrado, Emilio A., and Chenoa A. Flippen. 2005. "Migration and Gender among Mexican Women." *American Sociological Review* 70(4):606–632. doi: 10.1177/000312240507000404.

Pessar, Patricia R., and Sarah J. Mahler. 2003. "Transnational Migration: Bringing Gender In." *International Migration Review* 37(3):812–846.

Portes, Alejandro, and Jozef Boroez. 1989. "Contemporary Immigration: Theoretical Perspectives on Its Determinants and Modes of Incorporation." *International Migration Review* 23(3):606–630.

Preston, Julia. 2013. "Skilled Science Workers at Focus of Second Senate Proposal on Immigration." *New York Times,* January 29, A15.

Romaine, Suzanne. 2011. "Identity and Multilingualism." In *Bilingual Youth: Spanish in English-Speaking Societies,* edited by K. Potowski and J. Rothman, 7–30. Philadelphia, PA: John Benjamin Publishing Company.

Segura, Denise A. 1992. "Chicanas in White-Collar Jobs: You Have to Prove Yourself More." *Sociological Perspectives* 35:163–182.

US Citizenship and Immigration Services. 2012. "EB-5 Immigrant Investor." Washington, DC: US Department of Homeland Security. Retrieved November 24, 2014, from http://www.uscis.gov/working-united-states/permanent -workers/employment-based-immigration-fifth-preference-eb-5/eb-5-immi grant-investor.

US Citizenship and Immigration Services. 2013. *EB-5 Adjudications Policy* [Memorandum]. Washington, DC: US Department of Homeland Security. Retrieved April 30, 2015, from http://www.uscis.gov/sites/default/files/USCIS /Laws/Memoranda/2013/May/EB-5%20Adjudications%20PM%20%28 Approved%20as%20final%205-30-13%29.pdf.

————. 2015. "DHS Extends Eligibility for Employment Authorization to Certain H-4 Dependent Spouses of H-1B Nonimmigrants Seeking Employment-Based Lawful Permanent Residence." Washington, DC: US Department of Homeland Security. Retrieved April 30, 2015, from http://www.uscis.gov/news/dhs -extends-eligibility-employment-authorization-certain-h-4-dependent-spouses -h-1b-nonimmigrants-seeking-employment-based-lawful-permanent-residence.

US Department of State. 2014. "FY2014 EB-5 Visa Statistics by Immigrant Origin, Report of the Visa Office 2014, Table V (Part 3)." Retrieved April 30, 2015, from http://travel.state.gov/content/dam/visas/Statistics/AnnualReports/FY2014 AnnualReport/FY14AnnualReport-TableV.pdf.

Waters, Mary C. 1999. *Black Identities: West Indian Immigrant Dreams and American Realities.* Cambridge, MA: Harvard University Press.

Yin, Robert K. 2009. *Case Study Research: Design and Methods.* 4th ed. Los Angeles: SAGE Publications.

Zhou, Min, and Carl L. Bankston III. 1998. *Growing Up American: The Adaptation of Vietnamese Adolescents in the United States.* New York: Russell Sage Foundation.

PART 3

RETURN MIGRATION
AND REINCORPORATION

The final section of the book includes chapters by Agustín Escobar Latapí and by Víctor Zúñiga, Edmund Hamann, and Juan Sánchez García that illuminate important reincorporation issues when Mexican migrants return to Mexico. President Obama has the onerous record of presiding over the greatest number of deportations of unauthorized immigrants of any US president. According to the nonprofit Immigration Policy Center (2014), the US federal government has for the past two decades been pursuing "an enforcement-first approach to immigration control." The Immigration Policy Center reported in 2014 that the Obama administration alone is responsible for over two million deportations. The same account noted that since the mid-1990s the number of "removals" (deportations) has tended upward, and since 2005 voluntary return has been available to even fewer apprehended migrants. Deportation with criminal consequences for reentry to the United States has become the preference of US immigration authorities.

The increased risk of returning to Mexico and not being able to cross back has prompted an increment in the number of Mexican families settling more permanently in the United States. This also means that there are an unprecedented number of young people who are likely to be affected by US enforcement policies and deportation tactics that target their parents, neighbors, or other relatives (Dreby 2014). On December 16, 2014, US Secretary of Homeland Security Jeh C. Johnson opened the country's largest immigration detention facility in Dilley, Texas, about eight-five miles northeast of the border city of Laredo, Texas (Preston 2014). The facility can hold up to twenty-four hundred migrants who have illegally crossed the border. The fifty-acre center is especially designed to hold women and their children while their deportation cases move through the courts. The center has drawn angry criticism from advocates, lawyers, and faith leaders who represent the immigrants. They argue that prolonged confinement is inappropriate for young children and mothers who pose no security risks. The center is run by the Corrections Corporation of America, a private prison company that estimates a cost of $296 a day for each detainee (Preston 2014). Officials refurbished a camp that had been used by workers in the oil and gas exploration boom in the area. Each cabin, which can accommodate up to eight people in bunk beds, has a small kitchen, couches, a television, a bathroom, and beds for infants. They have set up a preschool in a trailer and a classroom for older children to attend classes five hours a day, five days a week. The center depends on volunteer lawyers, and judges hear cases by video conference. Mr. Johnson told the reporter covering the opening of the center that the United States wants "to send a message that our border is not open to illegal immigration" (Preston 2014).

Many of the adults returning to Mexico confront serious barriers to reentering the Mexican labor market or qualifying for Mexican social services. Additionally, they face the serious psychological implications of families divided by deportation, loss of social and economic status, and lack of resources. The *New York Times* (Archibold 2014) featured the plight of Mexican migrants deported from the United States to Tijuana, Mexico, and the incapacity of the city to incorporate the large numbers of deportees who arrive on a daily basis.

Upon their return to Mexico, US-born children of Mexican parents as well as Mexican children who attended early years of schooling in the United States in English face numerous barriers in Mexican schools taught in Spanish, a language they may not speak or understand. Children also face prejudices among peers because they do not fit in and may experience psychological trauma because of friends or family members left behind.

Agustín Escobar explores the level of access of "return migrants" to social programs in Mexico. Return migrants may have voluntarily decided to go back to Mexico after living and working in the United States or may have been "removed" or "deported" by the United States government. Escobar's chapter identifies policy issues that affect the reintegration of Mexican migrants into Mexican communities. While Mexico may have prepared pamphlets and advertisements about the dangers migrants might encounter in the United States, Escobar argues that in practice the Mexican government largely discouraged migrant returns for many years because the country heavily depended on remittances migrants sent back to Mexico. Due to increasing vulnerabilities of migrants in the United States and greater probability of being caught and incarcerated, the situation has changed.

The author presents a brief history of deportations, or "repatriations," of

Mexicans from the United States beginning in the late 1920s during the Great Depression. He also discusses the Bracero Program implemented during the 1960s and the *maquiladora* industry in the 1970s as ways the United States and Mexico attempted to regularize the demand for Mexican labor. Changes occurred in Mexican policy in the 1990s, when Mexico began to recognize the Mexican diaspora by creating the Programa para las Comunidades Mexicanas en el Exterior and the Instituto de los Mexicanos en el Exterior. As US policies begin to criminalize undocumented migrants and increase deportations, Escobar raises questions of how Mexico should receive these return migrants.

Interviews that Escobar conducted with deportees have documented injustices in the handling of deportations, including denial of food and proper clothes, separation of families, and inadequate processing on both sides of the border. In conclusion, Escobar brings attention to the current situation of repatriated migrants, who in many cases do not return to their communities of origin but instead concentrate in the most dynamic urban areas of Mexico, facing challenges of unemployment, lack of access to social security, and poverty.

The second chapter in the section, by Víctor Zúñiga, Edmund Hamann, and Juan Sánchez García, illustrates the dilemmas faced by Mexican schools receiving students who are returning from the United States. These scholars explore the binational schooling trajectories of students who have had school experiences in Mexico and the United States. They analyze the experiences of students attending schools in the Mexican states of Nuevo León and Zacatecas, states with long histories of migration to the United States, and Puebla, a Mexican state with a relatively small number of transnational students but with a high percentage of students who had at least one member of their extended family residing in the United States at the time of their surveys.

The authors present the variety of transnational experiences that students may have had, such as living with their parents and siblings in the United States and Mexico, living in families divided by borders, or separated through deportation or other migration-related events. Their work also explores the ways students who have never migrated perceive their transnational peers. They take into account the number of years and the percentage of school years children spent in the United States, how the transnational students felt they were treated in US schools, language transitions and discontinuities, curricular gaps, and the ways migrant children are classified and categorized in US schools.

Four typologies of students illustrate the students' varied experiences.

The most common category represents children born in Mexico who accompanied their parents to the United States, attended school there, and returned to Mexico. A second group of students, born in the United States, experienced schooling in both the United States and Mexico. They are legally binational, with American citizenship because of birthplace and Mexican citizenship because of parents' nationality. A small, third group spent part of their school year in Mexico and part in the United States every year. Students in the final group were born in the United States but returned to Mexico at an early age and attended only Mexican schools. Children born in the United States and those with US citizen parents have the possibility of returning to the United States in later years because they are US citizens. The researchers emphasize the huge dissimilarities among these students. Populations of such students differ in each state and region in terms of migration experiences. For example, the number and proportion of transnational students with divided families are much more characteristic in some regions than in others. There are also higher concentrations of families with migration experiences in some areas than others and a diversity of indigenous identities. These students are not "all over Mexico" but are concentrated in specific regions and locales and, the authors emphasize, "they are students we share."

Circumstances surrounding immigration are complex and changing rapidly as Mexico and the United States attempt to regulate their border and take positions on immigration policy. An epilogue by Janeth Martinez is included in this section to capture the most recent developments in legislation, court decisions, presidential actions, and strategies related to the issues discussed in this book.

In conclusion, Harriett Romo argues that Mexican migration to the United States is different from other migrations because of the historical relations of the two countries, the extended legal border that artificially separates a socially and economically integrated geographic area, and the economic interdependence of Mexico and the United States. The history of discrimination and prejudice against Mexicans in the United States and the role of Mexican Americans in the American civil rights movement have been unprecedented in experiences of other ethnic immigrant groups. Moreover, the large number of unauthorized Mexicans crossing the Mexico-US border and the concentration of Mexican-origin adults and children residing in the United States make the Mexican-origin population one of the largest and most significant immigrant groups in the country.

Given the unique relationship between Mexico and the United States, it is essential that both countries work together to protect the rights of migrants, resolve complex social ramifications of migration, and propose long-term solutions to current inequities in immigration policies. Doing this will not be easy. Republicans have assailed President Obama's immigration measures, saying he overstepped his constitutional authority with his sweeping program of deportation reprieves for youth meeting Deferred Action for Childhood Arrival criteria and for undocumented parents of US-born children and legal permanent residents.

Mexico struggles with continued drug-related violence and mistrust of police and local officials and has not spoken out about US immigration policies or detention centers. Demonstrations in Mexico have raged throughout the country protesting the federal government's inability to resolve the mysterious disappearance of forty-three students preparing to become teachers who were confronting governmental corruption (Agren 2014). Youth in both countries have mobilized for immigrant rights, comprehensive immigration policies, a halt to corruption, and greater participation in government. Yet by making themselves visible, undocumented youth in the United States risk being identified by authorities and anti-immigrant groups, which leaves them vulnerable to deportation and retaliation (Gonzales 2008).

Both the United States and Mexico face serious problems as they attempt to define policies to protect their national borders and economies and manage the incorporation and reincorporation of migrants. Mexico and the United States struggle to control immigration in an increasingly global environment in which lack of economic opportunities in home communities, violence and insecurity, complex human rights debates, and citizenship and national sovereignty issues confront nations throughout the world.

References

Agren, David. 2014. "Mexico: 'A Feeling of Being Fed Up.'" *USA Today*. November 20, 7A.

Archibold, Randal C. 2014. "A Border Limbo for the Displaced, at Home in Mexico No More." *New York Times*, November 28, A12.

Dreby, Joanna. 2014. "The Modern Deportation Regime and Mexican Families: The Indirect Consequences for Children in New Destination Communities." In *Constructing Immigrant "Illegality": Critiques, Experiences, and Responses*, edited by C. Menjívar and D. Kanstroom, 181–222. New York: Cambridge University Press.

Gonzales, Roberto G. 2008. "Left Out but Not Shut Down: Political Activism and the Undocumented Student Movement." *Northwestern Journal of Law and Social Policy* 3:1–22.

Immigration Policy Center. 2014. "The Growth of the U.S. Deportation Machine." Washington, DC: American Immigration Council. Retrieved April 3, 2014, from http://www.immigrationpolicy.org/just-facts/growth-us-deportation-machine.

Preston, Julia. 2014. "Detention Center Presented as Deterrent to Border Crossings." *New York Times*, December 16, A17.

CHAPTER 10

Mexican Social Policy and Return Migration

AGUSTÍN ESCOBAR LATAPÍ

The fight against organized crime in Mexico and the equally arduous, although less lethal, struggle against chronic recession in the United States have relegated issues of vital importance to the future of both countries to a secondary position. In fact, the economic cycles and course of events since 1994 have negatively affected the outlook for Mexico and the United States and shifted both countries' priorities. Lack of congruency in objectives has prevented the United States from implementing effective policies to curtail drug use and arms trafficking. Similarly, lack of consistency in priorities has precluded Mexico from carrying out meaningful policies to improve the state of its economy. Both the United States and Mexico are dealing with issues that affect their survival and permeate political life. Not surprisingly, when compared with the challenges of confronting organized crime in Mexico and economic recession in the United States, all other issues, including migration, are relegated to a distant second. Overall, the US recession and the Mexican war on drugs deeply impacted public policy and institutions in both countries.

An important group of Mexicans has been forgotten as a result of the war against organized crime in Mexico and the US struggle with recession: people returning from the United States to Mexico. A significant proportion of Mexican migrants eventually choose to return to Mexico to live or work. Over time, these returning migrants have been received in Mexico in different ways. In recent years, return migration from the United States has accelerated due to numerous factors, including an expansion of the US Border Patrol, heightened border-security operations that began in the United States in 1993, increased deportations as an immigration-control strategy initiated by President George W. Bush and implemented by President

Barack Obama, the collapse of the US construction sector, and the deep economic crisis in the United States.

This chapter analyzes the profile of return migrants in order to determine administrative and political actions required to address their needs and their capacity to enroll in existing Mexican social programs. Migrants returning to Mexico in recent years are particularly vulnerable. People who entered the United States as unauthorized migrants are often forbidden to return to the United States under penalty of incarceration. In this context, social and economic reintegration of returning migrants should be a priority of Mexican public policy. Although it is difficult to expect cooperation from the government of the United States, it is important to demand compliance with international and US laws and with existing repatriation agreements. It is also critical to substantially increase the amount of information and assistance that deportees receive upon arrival in Mexico. As Mexican citizens, return migrants must have access to public services and social programs. Additionally, given the harsh circumstances many migrants face in the United States, it is necessary to implement measures that encourage those considering migration to remain in Mexico.

"Laissez Partir": Let Them Leave

A pressing transformation of Mexico's broad approach toward undocumented migration should include a change in the attitudes and public policies that confront migrants upon their return to Mexico. The children of those migrants, who are Mexican citizens but might not have the documents to prove their citizenship, are particularly vulnerable.

The main goal of Mexican policy on migration should be to generate conditions that discourage undocumented migration (Escobar Latapí 2009). The problem of unauthorized Mexican migration to the United States might not have required urgent attention in the past, but intervention was clearly the correct approach even then. As a result of earlier policies of nonintervention, today Mexico faces an annual return of hundreds of thousands of migrants removed and deported from the United States. Passel and Cohn (2014) estimate that in 2012, 52 percent of the 11.2 million unauthorized immigrants in the United States were Mexican. The Mexican government's nonintervention stance in regard to undocumented migration has been a public policy in itself, although one manifested by default.

The governments of Mexican presidents Ernesto Zedillo (1994–2000) and Vicente Fox (2000–2006) sought a closer relation with Mexicans in the United States and with the US government to improve existing legal and procedural policies regarding undocumented Mexican immigrants in the United States. However, the implementation of measures aimed at curtailing population flows has never been considered seriously. This policy by default, which can be labeled *laissez partir*—let them leave—has meant that in practice the Mexican government is aware that hundreds of thousands of its citizens leave the country every year without proper documents but does nothing substantial to prevent or decrease the intensity of migration besides distributing posters, leaflets, and media warnings about the dangers undocumented migrants face.

The Mexican government's policy of nonintervention has been mainly shaped by two factors, one internal and one external. Internally, since 1982 the Mexican economy has confronted a series of financial crises that migrants helped lessen with remittances (*remesas*) sent from the United States to relatives in Mexico. It has been easier for the Mexican government to force people to tackle financial problems through emigration rather than creating stable, well-paying jobs in Mexico. In addition, until 1996 the US and Mexican economies behaved in a countercyclical pattern: booming economies in the United States ameliorated Mexican financial crises and vice versa.

The external factor is related to an inconsistent US migration policy. Until 2007, US border protection agencies would make some effort to stop undocumented immigrants at the border, but once successfully across, as long as they kept a low profile these migrants had great freedom to live and work in the United States. Employers virtually never faced fines or incarceration for hiring unauthorized workers, and the number of people deported was low. The Mexican government's approach toward undocumented migration was based on the perception that the United States did not have a coherent policy regarding irregular migrants. Unauthorized immigrants were vulnerable, and their working and living conditions were inferior to conditions faced by authorized residents, but irregular migrants were tolerated and their offense, from a legal point of view, was considered an administrative violation, not a crime. Being apprehended or repatriated had few consequences.

There were intentional discrepancies in undocumented migration management: for example, state-of-the-art border surveillance, but considerable technological lags in employment eligibility verification tools in the workplace; repatriation or deportation of undocumented immigrants, but no real punishment for employers. In practice, these contradictions resulted in policy that sustained the flow of undocumented workers while appearing tough on irregular migration and border control.

The US government's inconsistent attitude toward irregular migration changed gradually, sometimes with highly publicized announcements and at times in total silence. The end result was a radical change in the environment and prospects for undocumented migrants in the United States. The risks associated with undocumented migration increased substantially as work opportunities declined. There is now a high probability that irregular migrants will be taken advantage of, abused, arrested, imprisoned, and, months later, repatriated with a threat of incarceration if they ever try to enter the United States again without proper documentation. Under these circumstances, Mexican migrants are no longer solving subsistence problems by migrating to the United States, but rather, they are putting their lives and the livelihood of their families at risk and hindering the future possibility of finding a well-paying job because of a criminal record. A Mexican government that plays down these issues and does not acknowledge the costs of undocumented migration is not taking care of its citizens' welfare.

The gradual change in the de facto US immigration policy has also resulted in a new scenario of criminalization of irregular immigration. Although the number of audits and amounts of penalties for employers who violate immigration laws have increased, US immigration policy continues to favor employers. The system in place allows business owners to avoid responsibility if they follow certain verification procedures when hiring workers. Nevertheless, it is no longer accurate to say that US immigration authorities simply detain immigrants or prevent them from living in the United States. Today, US federal, state, and local legislations consider irregular immigrants criminal offenders and treat them as such. The new immigration policy of the United States is consistent: for unauthorized immigrants who still choose to live there, the risk of deportation or imprisonment has increased significantly and does not decrease over time.

Doing nothing to prevent undocumented migration and the violation by Mexican citizens of the laws of its northern neighbor and main commercial partner places the government of Mexico in a strange position of indifference. This is especially evident when the criminalization of irregular migrants has become widespread in the United States. The lack of a well-defined Mexican migration policy has fostered the growth of a hostage undocumented population in the United States that weakens the market position of new migrants as well as Mexico's relations with the United States.

Mexico's Precedents in the Face of Deportation

For decades, tense relations prevailed between the Mexican government and people of Mexican origin in the United States. This situation had several causes, including the fact that at times the Mexican diaspora consisted of people who experienced Mexico's internal wars or repressive government and fled the country. Another cause, more relevant to this chapter, is the ambiguous and sometimes contradictory position of the Mexican government in relation to the "repatriation" of Mexican citizens from the United States (Ayón 2006). Some of those repatriations included the removal of persons born in the United States who had no home or family in Mexico.

After 1929, rising unemployment in the United States motivated an increase of repatriations to Mexico (Alanís Enciso 2007). It is estimated that during the ten years following the US Great Depression, approximately four hundred thousand Mexicans and Mexican Americans were "repatriated" (Kanstroom 2007, 214–224). Repatriations were carried out in many ways, and the Mexican government actively participated in some of them. The Mexican government established agricultural settlements in northern Mexico that were effectively colonized by returning migrants. Furthermore, despite the fact that many of the repatriations were forced and that some of the people affected were citizens or legal residents of the United States, the Mexican government collaborated with the United States to facilitate the procedure. Policies were specifically formulated to invite Mexicans residing in the United States to voluntarily return to Mexico. However, these policies were contradictory (Alanís Enciso 2007). The guidelines established that only unemployed people or those with abilities, trades, or professions valuable to Mexico's development would be repatriated, but it is not clear that this is what happened in practice. The guidelines also stated that return migrants would receive help to incorporate productively in Mexico.

In practice, except for the aforementioned agricultural settlements in northern Mexico, returnees received little help from the Mexican government. Local Mexican governments and newspapers in northern Mexico did not view the repatriations positively. The Mexican economy had been impacted by the economic depression in the United States and, as a result, repatriated Mexicans had a difficult time finding jobs. At first, the media and local governments in Mexico opposed repatriations, but later they pointed out that if Mexico was going to receive returnees from the United States, those returning should receive at least as much help as the Spanish refugees who were arriving in Mexico at the same time (Guerin-González 1985).

Repatriations from the United States continued well beyond the end of the Great Depression (1939–1940), until the Mexican government negotiated a decrease in repatriations with California and Texas. Alanís Enciso (2007) considers that the Mexican government's real stance, at the time, favored Mexicans' staying in the United States. Nevertheless, Mexico had to take action to avoid criticism that it was not doing enough for its own citizens when Spanish refugees were being received with great hospitality. The role of the Mexican government in the 1930s US deportations and Mexico's inability to provide work opportunities for returnees led to a tense and distant relationship between the diaspora and the Mexican government until at least the 1970s.

Different US policies regarding immigration have prompted varying responses from the Mexican government. With the end of the Bracero Program in 1964, the *maquila* industry emerged in Mexico (Menchaca 2011). One objective of the *maquila* initiative was to employ hundreds of thousands of Mexicans who would no longer travel to the United States for temporary jobs. It is questionable whether the maquiladora initiative fulfilled its initial purpose. For the first fifteen to twenty years of its implementation, maquiladoras employed semiskilled women for sewing and lightweight assembly industries, a substantially different worker profile from the typical bracero. Nevertheless, the program succeeded in providing abundant manufacturing employment in a region along the US border with very limited development.

From the late 1980s, and formally in 1990 with the creation of the Program for Mexican Communities Abroad (Programa para las Comunidades Mexicanas en el Exterior), the Mexican government sought to establish closer relations with Mexican immigrants in the United States. This represented a substantial change in attitude. In 2001, the rapprochement was strengthened with the creation of a presidential office for Mexicans living abroad, which became more institutionalized and democratic in 2003 with the creation of the Institute for Mexicans Abroad (Instituto de los Mexicanos en el Exterior) and the election of its first advisory board, made up exclusively of Mexicans living abroad (González Gutiérrez 2006).

Concurrent with the effort to strengthen relations with Mexicans living overseas, the Mexican government sought to establish dialogue with the US government regarding the large population of undocumented Mexican immigrants living in the United States. The discussions reached a high note when US president George W. Bush hosted a dinner for Mexican president Vicente Fox a week before the attacks of September 11, 2001. After the attacks, with attention diverted to preventing terrorism, the United States abandoned talks about immigration. Despite the break in negotiations, the Mexican government continued advocating for the rights of migrants regardless of their immigration status.

The criminalization of undocumented immigrants in the United States, however, represents a serious dilemma for the Mexican government. Is it reasonable for the Mexican government to continue claiming that undocumented migrants are not criminals but honorable, hard-working people looking for opportunities abroad when US laws now consider them felons? Does this position of the Mexican government encourage a behavior—unauthorized migration—that is now considered a crime in the United States? In this light, would it not make more sense to encourage the return and reintegration of undocumented migrants to Mexico and to discourage their departure? And, if they return, what kind of Mexican citizens will returning migrants be, and how will they be received in their country?

The Return Process: *How Many Are There?*

Both Mexican and US demographers detected significant changes in population flows between Mexico and the United States in 2008 (Passel and Cohn 2009; Berumen Sandoval 2011). This was the second time that the use of official statistics from both countries made it possible to detect short-term changes in migration patterns. The first occurred during the US economic recession in the early 2000s.

Mexico has two different reliable databases to analyze migration flows: the National Survey of Occupation and Employment (Encuesta Nacional de Ocupación y Empleo [ENOE is its acronym in Spanish]) and the Migration Survey in Mexico's Northern Border (Encuesta Sobre Migración en la Frontera Norte de México [EMIF Norte is its acronym in Spanish]). ENOE is a survey in which approximately sixty thousand households across the country are visited every three months for a total of five times. Migration information is obtained by taking note of family members who are present on one visit and not during another and by collecting information about which family members come back or leave, where they are going or where they came from, and why. In the second survey (EMIF), people arriving at numerous points along Mexico's northern border, both from the south (Mexico) and the north (the United States), are interviewed. Information about their origin, their destination, reasons for their move, and their socioeconomic profile is obtained.

ENOE collects data on Mexican employment trends. Because of its design, ENOE underestimates two kinds of movements: the return to Mexico of entire families (since new households have a low probability of being included in the sample)[1] and households leaving the country from one observation to the next (because they are categorized simply as missing, not as having emigrated).

EMIF was specifically designed as an international migration survey along the border. It captures movements occurring at land border crossings and at air and land terminals along Mexico's northern border. EMIF underestimates documented flows of people traveling to the United States on tourist visas from areas in Mexico not included in the survey as part of the northern border. It also overestimates the traditional crossing strategy of poor, undocumented migrants, who arrive by land and typically take some time to arrange a crossing once they get to the Mexican side of the border, thus increasing the probability of being interviewed. Repeat crossings, including failed crossings, also tend to be overestimated because of the increased probability of being interviewed while waiting to arrange a crossing. Data from the two surveys are analyzed here to examine changes in migration trends.

Data from US surveys, such as the American Community Survey (ACS) and the Current Population Survey (CPS), have their own biases. Mexican demographers have pointed out that the questions included in the ACS and CPS overestimate Mexican immigration to the United States. If this is correct, the overall change in the migration balance could be more significant than indicated here.

Data from ENOE (figure 10.1) and EMIF (figure 10.2) show a substantial decrease in migration flows. Both departures from and returns to Mexico declined from 2005 to 2010 (figure 10.1). However, emigration to the United States decreased more substantially than return migration, from over a million leaving in 2005 to 368,000 migrants leaving in 2010. ENOE data indicate a considerable decrease in net population loss in Mexico in this period, from 680,000 in 2005 to 106,000 in 2010.

EMIF data show the same trends as ENOE in outgoing and return migration, although total numbers differ (figure 10.2). In terms of net population changes, according to EMIF, Mexico had a net population gain in 2001, which represents an important difference in assessment from other Mexican and American data sources. The positive balance shown here is probably derived from a larger-than-usual number of returns through land crossings in 2001. As stated earlier, EMIF focuses mainly on land crossings at the border, which results in an overestimation of the flow of undocumented migrants, of residents of the border area, and of low-income individuals. Air travel from and to nonborder terminals by people with any type

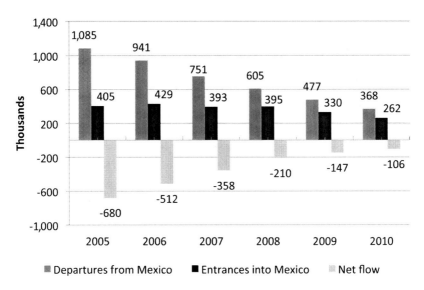

Figure 10.1. Mexican migration to the United States: outgoing, incoming, and net population gain or loss in Mexico according to ENOE (2005–2010). *Source*: Berumen Sandoval (2011). © Salvador Berumen Sandoval. Courtesy of Salvador Berumen Sandoval.

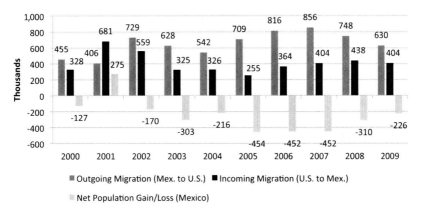

Figure 10.2. Mexican migration to the United States: outgoing, incoming, and net population gain or loss according to EMIF (2000–2009). *Source*: Berumen Sandoval (2011). © Salvador Berumen Sandoval. Courtesy of Salvador Berumen Sandoval.

of visa is not recorded by EMIF, and neither are the returns of undocumented Mexicans to Mexico by air. In summary, however, according to data from ENOE and EMIF, between 255,000 and 438,000 people returned to Mexico every year from 2005 to 2010.

Estimates from the US CPS and ACS do not differ substantially from ENOE and EMIF calculations, although net balances differ. Nonetheless, US sources provide total numbers of undocumented people of any national origin living in the United States, not just from Mexico. The estimated number of undocumented people living in the United States has declined from its peak of 12.2 million in 2007, to 11.7 million in 2008, 11.3 million in 2009, 11.4 million in 2010, 11.5 million in 2011 (Passel, Cohn, and Gonzalez-Barrera 2013), 11.2 million in 2012, and 11.3 million in 2013 (Passel et al. 2014). The decline could be partially attributed to a segment of the Mexican undocumented population in the United States either receiving permanent-resident status or being replaced by new authorized immigrants and newly arriving US citizens from Mexico. A net population loss for Mexico can be consistent with the stabilization (zero net growth) in the number of undocumented Mexican migrants residing in the United States and can be explained by a gradual legalization of a portion of the undocumented Mexican population in the United States.

Deportations

The proportion of Mexican citizens within the total irregular population in the United States has remained fairly stable. Although Mexicans constitute approximately 52 percent of the undocumented population, they represent around 70 percent of unauthorized migrants in removal proceedings (Passel and Cohn 2011; Passel, Cohn, and Gonzalez-Barrera 2013). This may illustrate a bias in the implementation of US immigration laws against undocumented migrants from Mexico, who are more likely to be deported than irregular immigrants from other countries. According to personal communication with the author from a member of the High-Level Working Group on Migration and Consular Affairs, a group within the Binational Commission, this bias was discussed during the 1990s with United States immigration authorities. One explanation for the high percentage of Mexican migrants among individuals in deportation proceedings might be that undocumented Mexicans are at a higher risk of being apprehended and deported because of general characteristics, such as age (younger migrants are at more risk because they openly engage in activities such as work, which makes them more vulnerable to deportation); another possibility is that their physical appearance makes them targets of discriminatory practices.

Table 10.1. Mexicans deported and repatriated from the United States

| | Number of deportations (removals) | | | |
Year	With a criminal background	Without a criminal background	Total	Repatriations (returns)[a]
2005	70,779	98,252	169,031	928,908
2006	73,171	113,555	186,726	914,435
2007	76,967	132,029	208,996	792,584
2008	77,531	169,732	247,263	710,849
2009	99,616	177,569	277,185	468,722
2010	128,396	145,519	273,915	353,892
2011[b]	145,133	142,945	288,078	205,158
2012	151,444	152,301	303,745	131,983
2013	146,298	168,606	314,904	88,042

Source: Berumen Sandoval, Ramos Martínez, and Ureta Hernández 2011; USDHS (2011a, 2011b, 2013); Simanski 2014.
Note: This table excludes apprehensions and returns carried out by the Border Patrol.
[a]Berumen Sandoval, Ramos Martínez, and Ureta Hernández (2011) estimated the number of Mexicans repatriated (returned) for the years 2005 through 2008 by calculating the share of Mexicans apprehended as a portion of the total number of apprehensions and applying that ratio to the total number of returns.
[b]For number of removals and returns from 2011 to 2013 (Simanski 2014).

Listed above (table 10.1) are data for deportations (removals) and repatriations (returns) of Mexicans. The number of repatriations has been clearly declining since 2005 (also see Rodríguez Chávez 2011). Nonetheless, the total number of deportations has been increasing steadily. The figures for removals are the most worrisome because they represent individuals whose deportation has been ordered by a judge and who are forbidden to return to the United States. People who have gone through deportation proceedings are imprisoned if they are apprehended trying to return in defiance of the ban. The first column in table 10.1, "with a criminal background," denotes deportations with a conviction. However, a large number of these offenses would not be considered criminal violations for legal residents. Researchers (Escobar Latapí, Lowell, and Martin 2013; Rosenblum and McCabe 2014; Rosenblum and Meissner 2014) have pointed out that such offenses are often used as an excuse to include undocumented migrants in programs aimed at the removal of foreign criminals. The author's fieldwork has provided evidence that some Mexicans are included in the group "with a criminal background" without having a criminal record.

How Are Mexicans being Deported and Repatriated?

Since the end of the Bracero Program, the scant political importance given to return migrants by the Mexican government has meant that for decades migrants went back to Mexico without any support from the government. Consequently, migrants' expulsion or repatriation conditions were largely determined by US authorities. Moreover, due to the lack of support from the Mexican government, return migrants were vulnerable to extortion and abuse by all kinds of authorities, companies, and criminals during the journey back to their communities. In 1990, the Mexican government's attitude seemed to change when officials began to view migrants as valuable economic and political actors whose rights did not expire because they crossed the US-Mexico border. To cultivate the relationship with Mexicans in the United States, the Mexican government established the Program for Mexican Communities Abroad (Programa para las Comunidades Mexicanas en el Exterior), the General Directorate for Consular Protection (Dirección General de Protección Consular), and more recently, the Institute for Mexicans Abroad (Instituto de los Mexicanos en el Exterior). A program to support returning migrants (Programa Paisano) was also implemented to battle the problem of extortion of migrants returning to Mexico on a permanent or temporary basis.

This trend of increased attention by the Mexican government to the repatriation process of its citizens is illustrated in the government's resolve to establish binational agreements with the United States. Although the North American Free Trade Agreement included a chapter devoted to migration, its scope was limited. At the time of the negotiation of the agreement, the Mexican government decided in favor of a gradualist strategy, which it trusted would slowly result in broad and satisfactory migration agreements for both countries (US Commission on Immigration Reform 1997). Other elements of the gradualist approach included agreements on consular notification, help for Mexicans under arrest, repatriation of dead bodies, and binational persecution of human smugglers.

In 1996, a memorandum of understanding (MOU) on consular protection for Mexican and US citizens was signed by both countries. Following this first MOU, today there are more than thirty repatriation agreements between local authorities along the border. There are also agreements with nonborder states and local governments, basically related to consular communication. The original 1996 memorandum was modified and expanded in 1998 and again in 2004. Mexican authorities consider the 2004 MOU, titled "On Safe, Orderly, Dignified and Humane Repatriation," the most comprehensive agreement and the one that offers, on paper, the most protection to migrants. The memorandum includes the following main topics:

1. unconditional respect for the human rights of Mexican citizens;
2. preservation of family units;
3. special treatment for disabled people, older adults, unaccompanied minors, and other vulnerable individuals;
4. help in reporting cases of human rights violations and assurances that any reported cases will be investigated;
5. creation of mechanisms to identify incidents of abuse or violation of these rights; and
6. guarantee of consular notification and access to consular assistance.

In the late 1990s and early 2000 the Mexican government publicized that these MOUs, despite their limited binding power, were achieving a significant improvement in the way in which repatriated Mexicans were being treated. As a result, similar instruments were put in place between Mexico and some Central American countries.

However, after 2000 the situation deteriorated dramatically. At the 2005 bilateral meeting of Mexican border authorities, the Ministry of Foreign Affairs (Secretaría de Relaciones Exteriores [SRE, Spanish acronym]) presented an assessment of the repatriation process. The ministry's reports were clearly negative. The Ministry of Foreign Affairs stated that there was a "continued lack of notification from the North American authorities in regard to the repatriation of people from vulnerable groups such as older adults, minors, pregnant women, and the infirm and disabled." The ministry also pointed out that there was hardly any coordination between US authorities and Mexico's National Migration Institute (Instituto Nacional de Migración [INM, Spanish acronym]) and border consulates for the return of unaccompanied minors; that there was an increase in the number of citizens from other countries "repatriated" to Mexico; and that large numbers of vulnerable people were being repatriated outside the established schedules. Furthermore, the report stated that there was a "lack of interest and willingness, in some instances, on the part of North American authorities, to detect and punish abuses committed by some federal immigration agents against migrants," and that "it was necessary to improve communications with Mexican authorities when ex-convicts were repatriated" (SRE and Subsecretaría para América del Norte 2005).

In 2008, the author accompanied officers from Mexico's INM on a tour of a border bridge in Ciudad Juárez. From visits to the bridge it was evident that Mexican authorities were not always notified as to who was being repatriated or when. The lack of coordination hindered Mexican authorities' efforts to interview deportees regarding their situation, record their complaints, and offer them assistance. On the US side of the border, the officer in charge of deportations stated that he was not aware of any bilateral agreement that required US authorities to give notice to Mexican officials regarding deportation proceedings or treatment of deportees.

In September of 2011, the author interviewed several people in charge of "migrant houses" in Tijuana and Ciudad Juárez, as well as some municipal officials in charge of migrant reception programs. The interviews focused on the condition of Mexicans being repatriated and the social programs available to them upon their return to Mexico. The interviews had three main objectives: to verify whether US authorities were adhering to existing repatriation agreements, to learn about the conditions in which migrants were repatriated, and to probe whether the administrative measures ordered by the government of President Obama in July 2011 were actually being implemented.[2]

President Obama's orders were issued through an administrative memorandum in which the US Department of Homeland Security (DHS) instructed Immigration and Customs Enforcement to exercise discretionary authority to stop deportations of noncriminal undocumented immigrants who did not pose a threat to the United States. This was specifically intended to include young people who were brought to the United States by their parents, who had committed no crime, and who were enrolled in school or enlisted in the military. It also included mothers of US citizens and, in general, those who had committed no crime and paid taxes. The memorandum did not grant legal permanent status to undocumented migrants. It just established that nonpriority undocumented immigrants who had committed no crime other than their immigration offense were not to be persecuted or deported. Interviews conducted by this author sought to explore whether migrant houses along the Mexican northern border detected a change in the number of migrants with and without criminal records being deported after July 2011.

The Reception System for Deported and Returned Migrants

Today, as in the past, some migrants freely choose to return to Mexico. However, in recent years the number of migrants deported and returned has increased as a proportion of the total number of people returning to Mexico (USDHS 2010). The reception process of returnees should include more than access to shelter. It requires binational coordination at the different levels of government and public-private collaboration. Both types of repatriations—"returns" without a warrant from a judge due to apprehension in the immediate vicinity of the border, and especially "removals," which are more complex deportation processes with longer-term consequences—place returning migrants in precarious and vulnerable situations. The return process, beginning with the apprehension and processing in the United States until the potential reunification with the family, includes multiple stages that can take months and ideally requires the assistance of different agencies. The "return system" includes agents from the Mexican INM and several other government agencies, as well as personnel from various national and international nongovernmental organizations. These organizations may or may not have the backing or be in coordination with the Mexican government. Nonetheless, the manner in which the return system operates and its extent vary greatly in different cities along the border.

In Tijuana, the Coalition for Human Rights incorporates the key agencies in charge of receiving returning migrants in specialized houses and shelters. Mother Asunta's Institute (El Instituto de la Madre Asunta) receives women; the Young Men's Christian Association (YMCA) receives youth; the Migrant House (Casa del Migrante) receives adult men; and the Mexican National System for the Comprehensive Development of the Family (Desarrollo Integral de la Familia [DIF, Spanish acronym]) receives children. According to coalition members,[3] management of the flow of returning migrants has greatly improved since the coalition was created. The coalition has permission from the Mexican authorities to receive returned or deported migrants at the international bridge and give them advice regarding specially trained people or institutions that may assist them. Coalition organizations receive public funding through the state government, but the vast majority of their income (85%) comes from other sources.

As a result of the coordination of the various agencies in one coalition, returning migrants are channeled to the different institutions in the city in an orderly manner, and a single person can collect and manage all relevant information. The coalition has a presence at the international bridge from 10 a.m. to midnight and has the support of the state government to refer people in need of medical attention to hospitals in Baja California. Coalition staff give returning migrants advice on family reunification and recovery of belongings. If migrants have the proper documentation with them, staff can also explain the implications of their deportation proceedings.

There is no similar coalition in the border city of Ciudad Juárez, Mexico. The agencies in Juárez have not been assigned a space at the international bridge where they can privately interview deportees. Personnel from the various agencies are allowed to greet migrants on the Mexican side of one of the border bridges in the city but are required to meet with returnees at the office of the INM, which, in their opinion, discourages migrants from talking openly.

Since 2008 deportation and return migration flows have changed substantially. At present, the YMCA in Tijuana receives approximately twenty-five hundred young people per year, while before 2008 the number was twice as high. However, Tijuana YMCA staff have not perceived meaningful changes in the procedures followed by American authorities in charge of deportations since July of 2011, when the aforementioned DHS memo was issued. Staff members mentioned cases in which, according to memo guidelines, the migrant should have clearly received a stay of deportation, and yet the person had recently been sent back to Mexico. Staff in the various agencies assisting returning migrants pointed out in interviews with the author that the MOU, referred to in Mexico as the Program for Humane Repatriation, has not been implemented by US authorities according to stipulations. For example, consider the following:

1. According to the Program for Humane Repatriation, before a deportation there must be consular notification. However, the number of deportations carried out by the Obama administration has been very high, and the consular resources of the Mexican Ministry of Foreign Affairs are limited. As a consequence, Mexican consular officials frequently have excessive workloads resulting in deficient certifications that the deportee is in good health and has not been mistreated by agents from the US DHS or other agencies (such as local police officers). Often the certification is done not in person but rather via telephone or videoconference, making it impossible for the Mexican consul to determine if the migrant is being intimidated or if he or she shows signs of physical abuse.

2. In some cases US authorities use crossing points and schedules that have not been agreed upon for repatriations, even to return members of vulnerable populations. The bridges in Tamaulipas, for example, were never registered as part of the Program for Humane Repatriation. Nonetheless, the return of migrants through the state of Tamaulipas has increased as a result of the US "lateral deportation" policy, that is, the practice of sending migrants back to Mexico far away from where they originally crossed

the border in order to reduce the probability that they may try to use established networks to return to the United States. Repatriations through Tamaulipas have continued regardless of serious problems of violence and insecurity in that state.

3. US officials in charge of the legal process of deportation, including agents responsible for transporting deportees to the border, sometimes misinform them. A migrant shelter lawyer who was interviewed by the author in Tijuana, Mexico, reported that US officials do not always follow the requirement of translating the judge's rulings to the person being deported. Furthermore, the lawyer said, in some cases agents intentionally mistranslate a judge's rulings to prevent resistance on the part of deportees and demands for trials that immigrants might win. Some returned migrants are misled to think that by crossing the bridge back to Mexico, they will have a chance to obtain a visa or to soon return to the United States. The same lawyer noted that some deportees are under the impression that US authorities are "doing them a favor by returning them to Mexico by voluntary repatriation," when in reality their papers indicate that they were expelled for life or for a very long time without the option of applying for a visa. In many cases, once in Mexico, returning migrants discard the legal paperwork they were given in the United States, making it very difficult to assess their true legal status.[4]

4. Deportees commonly arrive in Mexico without their belongings and with no clear understanding of the processes they need to follow to recover them. Each US DHS agency has its own policy for recovery of personal belongings, making the process quite complicated. The US Customs and Border Protection Agency, which is responsible for those arrested at crossing points, will return a migrant's belongings in twenty-four to forty-eight hours if the person makes the request immediately. Unfortunately, if there is no official from the Mexican INM or a representative from one of the civil-society organizations at the bridge at the time of deportation, returning migrants may not be made aware of the possibility of requesting their belongings. Interviewees mentioned that although officers in charge of deportations have the obligation to inform the person being deported about the process for the recovery of his or her possessions, they do not always do so, or they do it speaking very quickly in English. (The author interviewed a large number of deportees in Jalisco who reported that all their belongings were taken from them and never recovered.)

5. The vast majority of returnees are repatriated without identification documents, which makes them even more vulnerable. Because of security con-

cerns, for example, returning migrants are not allowed to board buses to travel back home without proper identification. In some cases, when returnees sought shelter at a migrant house or were received back in Mexico by staff of the INM, they were given an identification document. However, issuing identification cards is not a common practice.

6. Some respondents reported that DHS and other US officials punished returning migrants and made people suffer. Interviewees in Tijuana mentioned that about 20 percent of return migrants had not received food in twenty-four hours. Respondents in Juárez did not experience the same situation but agreed that the food they received in the previous twenty-four hours was limited to biscuits and water. In winter, some migrants apprehended in the river were returned wearing wet clothes instead of being provided with an extra set of clothing, according to regulations. Several of the return migrants interviewed stated that while being held in immigration detention facilities in the United States, they were moved up to five times from one detention center to another. A representative of the Mexican Ministry of Foreign Affairs claimed to have talked to people who had been moved from a cage-like punishment cell, where detainees are not supposed to be held for more than twelve hours, to another of equal characteristics so as to not exceed the maximum time in any one punishment cell. The end result, however, was that migrants were held in punishment cells for more than the allowed time.

7. The problem of separated families is especially difficult. Some respondents stated that they were not informed of where or when their family members would be returned. The US lateral repatriation policy makes family reunification even more complicated. When children are separated from their parents and handed over to the DHS unaccompanied minors program, DHS requires documentation from the Mexican agency in charge of supervising children's welfare (DIF) to certify the good condition of the home where minors are to be returned to. In many cases, because of the poverty of the parents, DHS requirements are hard to meet, thus making it difficult for parents to recover their children.

There is evidence that suggests that the US government is not implementing agreements and repatriation programs according to stipulations. It is also clear that agencies in charge of giving support to returning migrants need better coordination, and that insecurity is a serious problem confronting migrants on their return to Mexico. The fact that security forces in Mexico do not recognize provisional identification cards provided by official Mexican government agencies is particularly disturbing.

The Profile of Return Migrants

The profile of return migrants is based on interviews carried out in 2010 with returnees received by the Mexican INM and a random sample of migrants claiming to have been expelled from the United States drawn from the Migration Survey in Mexico's Northern Border (Encuesta Sobre Migración en la Frontera Norte de México, known as EMIF Norte).

The proportion of returning adult men has increased, with a corresponding decrease in women and minors. However, the number of unaccompanied returning minors stands out: 72 percent of youngsters are repatriated alone, and 24 percent of those are under the age of twelve (Rodríguez Chávez 2011). The duration of stay in the United States of repatriated migrants is increasing. The percentage of those who state that they were apprehended after more than a year of stay has surged. When asked what country they consider to be their country of residence, in 1999 three percent said that they resided in the United States; in 2010 this figure rose to thirty percent (Consejo Nacional de Población, Instituto Nacional de Migración, and Colegio de la Frontera Norte 2012, based on EMIF 2010).

It is important to point out that not all migrants returning to Mexico have been expelled from the United States and that not all of them travel back to Mexico by land. Consequently, a large number of return migrants are not counted by the EMIF. It is realistic to assume, however, that the uncounted return migrants are less vulnerable. These are people returning to Mexico voluntarily who in general have the necessary documents to return to the United States legally. In spite of the EMIF's limitations, data collected by this survey is reliable and should be taken into consideration in the design of Mexican public policy aimed at the reincorporation of returning migrants.[5]

Access to Social Programs

A comprehensive analysis of migrant return by Masferrer and Roberts (2009) shows that a large number of migrants of rural origin return to larger and more dynamic cities in Mexico rather than their communities of origin. This is an old trend, already noticeable in the first studies done on the subject of return migration in Jalisco (Arroyo, Winnie, and Velázquez 1986) and in studies carried out in the first decade of this century in numerous mid-size cities of western Mexico (Papail and Arroyo 2009).

According to the 2005 Mexican census, destinations with a positive balance were Quintana Roo, Baja California Norte, and Baja California Sur (Masferrer and Roberts 2009). By population size, mid-size cities show a higher rate of return. By region type, more people return to the northern border and southeastern states, where there is a more dynamic economy. There are, however, a number of migrants who still return to poor and marginalized communities in Veracruz, Oaxaca, Chiapas, and Puebla. The 2005 population count reports that households with return migrants have better housing, have more household appliances (stove, refrigerator, etc.), and are less dependent on social security, even when controlled by locality size.

In order to direct social policy, each year the Ministry of Social Development (Secretaría de Desarrollo Social [Spanish acronym SEDESOL]) identifies areas within the country as Priority Attention Zones (Zonas de Atención Prioritaria, [Spanish acronym ZAP]) based on criteria issued by the National Council for Evaluation of Social Policy (Consejo Nacional de Evaluación de la Política de Desarrollo Social [Spanish acronym CONEVAL]). Priority attention areas are primarily characterized by high levels of marginalization, lack of development, and poverty. In 2009, 1,251 municipalities, preponderantly but not exclusively rural, were classified as ZAPs. These municipalities include 16 percent of the total population of Mexico.[6]

CONEVAL applies a survey in these areas to determine socioeconomic conditions and to plan the implementation of diverse social programs. In 2009, CONEVAL, in collaboration with the Center for Research and Advanced Studies in Social Anthropology (Centro de Investigaciones y Estudios Superiores en Antropología Social [Spanish acronym CIESAS]), applied a survey that included basic information about migration to ninety-three hundred households.[7] The survey helped estimate the access to social programs in households with and without domestic or international migrants. The level of access of returning migrants to public social programs in ZAPs is of particular interest because, by comparison, if returnees have access to programs in these poorer and more isolated parts of the country, it would be expected that migrants returning to areas with higher socioeconomic indicators will be better off.

In the 2009 CONEVAL survey, 7.2 percent of households indicated that at least one family member had migrated during the last two years (Banegas González 2012). Domestic migration represented 4.6 percent of households, and the rest were international migrants. When calculated per person, the emigration rate is 4 per every 1,000 inhabitants per year, a number not significantly different from the percentage determined by a household survey in poor, rural, and marginalized areas in 1998 (the Home Evaluation Survey [Encuesta de Evaluación de los Hogares, Spanish acronym ENCEL]). It is likely that the emigration rate increased from 2000 to 2005, and that the 4 per 1,000 rate reflects the decline in emigration in recent years already documented (see also work by Lowell, Pederzini, and Passel 2008).

Results from the 2009 CONEVAL survey suggest that the emigration rate in the poorest and most marginalized municipalities in Mexico exceeds the national average. Banegas González (2012) points out that there is evidence in this survey to suggest that the relation between poverty and emigration has intensified. Banegas González (2012) also presents EMIF numbers reporting that 3,445 people from Chiapas left for the United States in 2000, while in 2008 this figure rose to 83,000. In the case of Veracruz, the number of people who migrated from this state to the United States increased from 9,044 in 2000 to 35,000 in 2008. Veracruz and Chiapas are two of the poorest states in Mexico. These numbers indicate a significant change in the social and geographical makeup of outgoing migration to the United States. The demographic characteristics of people migrating to the United States from ZAPs are no surprise: 76 percent are men with a low average level of schooling (8.9 percent illiterate). The majority of migrants (66 percent) are not heads of households, but dependents (sons). This last number is interesting because 42.8 percent of households with migration are headed by women, in comparison with 16.9 percent of households without migration. Consequently, the high proportion of dependent sons migrating to the United States is an indication that male heads of households had migrated earlier. Families with migrants have 0.3 percent fewer members than the average for ZAPs, meaning that households with migrants were slightly above the average before the migration of one or more family members.

Consistent with other government statistics, the 2009 CONEVAL survey indicates that, in comparison with families with no migration, households with family members who have migrated tend to have lower percentages of children attending school and less access to social security. However, families with migrants have a smaller proportion of homes with dirt floors and a greater number of household appliances.

The CONEVAL survey does not allow for a comparison of income levels between households with and without migration. In order to assess this, food security—which is strongly related to income—was evaluated. Households with international migration show a significantly lower level of food insecurity. In general, 47.6 percent of households with international migration have food security. If only households with international migration in the areas of traditional emigration are analyzed, the percentage of families with food security rises to 62.3 percent.

In ZAPs, the percentage of households that received remittances (*remesas*) in 2009 (3.6%) is lower than the national average for 2006 (5.8%). The decline in remittances may be a consequence of the economic recession in the United States. However, it is important to point out that by the time of the 2009 CONEVAL survey, 75.5 percent of households in ZAPs had a family member who had migrated within the previous two years. Remittances are associated with lower levels of poverty and greater food security. In traditional migration regions, the percentage of households with international migration that receive remittances is slightly higher than in ZAPs.

The CONEVAL survey seeks to determine whether households with international migration have access to social programs on par with households with no international migrants. In general, CONEVAL survey data show no significant difference in access to social programs between households with and without international migration. In the case of the Opportunities Program (Oportunidades), there is no significant difference in access between the two groups. With regard to the Popular Insurance (Seguro Popular[8]), Pension Program for Older Adults (Pensión para Adultos Mayores[9]), and Program for Direct Support for Rural Areas (Programa de Apoyos Directos al Campo [Spanish acronym PROCAMPO[10]]), households with migration have slightly better access.

Data collected from the survey shows a positive correlation between food security and international migration. The causality of the correlation, however, is unclear. That is, it is not clear whether better food security promotes international migration or whether higher rates of international migration improve food security. It is possible that the poorest households in ZAPs have lower migration rates. It is also likely that international migration improves total household income and therefore decreases poverty (and food insecurity). When taking access to social programs in consideration, data points to higher food security among households with international migration that participate in social programs.

CONEVAL data suggests there is no systematic exclusion of migrants or households with migrants from social programs. Nevertheless, our team did anthropological fieldwork in twelve communities in four states (Chiapas, Oaxaca, Michoacán, and Jalisco) in order to research the issue further. We deliberately selected at least one community from each state with a high rate of migration. We analyzed access to social programs with the Attention and Management Trajectory technique (Trayectoria de Atención y Gestión [Spanish acronym TAG]). This method allows the researcher to analyze in detail what happens from the moment a person learns of the existence of a program or service until he or she gains access to it or not. It is not possible to address all the ethnographic findings of the research in this paper; therefore, the discussion will focus on two particularly relevant cases in the state of Oaxaca.

Municipalities from the Cañada and Costa Chica regions of Oaxaca have been challenging areas for a long time. SEDESOL tried different strategies to help people replace dirt floors in their homes (Firm Floor Program [Programa Piso Firme]) before finding one that worked. On a first attempt, SEDESOL hired a construction company from Oaxaca with no experience in the region. When company employees had to deal with regional political actors who wanted to intervene in different aspects of the process, they opted to do the least possible. The company decided to leave construction materials at a central location in the village and inform people that they could pick up the materials and lay their own floors. Households without men or with migrant men almost without exception could not carry out the work because women and children could not pick up the materials and did not have money to pay laborers. Social unrest erupted in the communities because many potential beneficiaries were not notified or were unable to pick up the materials. Taking advantage of the antagonism that surfaced in the communities against SEDESOL, some leaders organized mass protests to promote their own agendas.

After a failed second attempt, SEDESOL decided to establish a regional office in the area to monitor the progress of its programs and manage them. This office took over the work that SEDESOL usually leaves in the hands of local governments. SEDESOL's regional office was in a better position to implement the programs efficiently because it was able to coordinate the work directly. On the downside, however, it meant that municipal governments' contributions toward the programs were minimal.[11]

At the time of the study, the regional office was monitoring at least once a month the advances in programs to replace dirt floors and increase access to electricity and drinking water in the region. Progress in the programs occurred due to better monitoring and management but also because the population and community leaders had agreed to the projects.

This experience illustrates that assuming that all households in a locality have access to certain resources (labor force, in this particular case) is a mistake. It is also erroneous to take for granted that local governments will be able to coordinate and collaborate efficiently with contractors, communities, local leaders, and even other levels of government.

The second case discussed in this chapter is the Opportunities Program.

The program was originally established in 1997 as Progresa and renamed Oportunidades in 2002. This incentive-based subsidy program was designed to help poor families living in rural and urban areas in Mexico invest in human capital for their children focusing on the improvement of education, health, and nutrition outcomes (Sosa-Rubi, Galarraga, and Harris 2007). The program had been in place for more than ten years when we did our research. A good number of people in the communities we analyzed had adequate understanding of how Oportunidades worked. Beneficiaries of the program were aware, through their networks of contacts, of when funds would be available and how to manage required medical appointments and meetings with social workers. A significant number of women had been able to drop their migrant spouses from the program to avoid being denied benefits. Even though the husbands remained part of the family, because of their prolonged absences and consequent inability to fulfill program requirements, the whole family would have been out of compliance.

Despite the ability to navigate the program, Oportunidades beneficiaries still faced a myriad of challenges. For example, when forced to move in search of work, as is common among poor people, Oportunidades users were at risk of not keeping up with requirements and consequently being dropped from the program. In general, notwithstanding the efficiency of Oportunidades as a targeted social program, the organizational structure of some of the poorest families is incompatible with program requirements.

An additional factor that hinders the access of households with migrants to social programs in Mexico is the reluctance of local government officials to grant family members the required documentation to apply for benefits. Municipal authorities and agencies often do not issue birth certificates or proof of residence to returning migrants. They may deny a "senior citizen certificate" to a return migrant who obtained a pension in the United States because, in their opinion, the person does not need a Mexican pension. They may not issue birth certificates to the children of migrant couples because they question the need for Mexican documentation when the children already have American documents. It is also common practice among local governments to increase the cost of government-issued documents during registration periods for social programs. Higher costs make the documents unaffordable for many people. Finally, people who have to flee conflict areas, particularly due to violence, have a hard time obtaining official identification documents. In many cases, the same people who expelled them are in charge of processing their documents. The end result is the emergence of a group of "undocumented people in their own homeland," without access to social programs or political rights.

Final Reflections

In this paper the author confirms findings and policy recommendations from previous studies (Escobar Latapí 2008, 2009). The nature and volume of Mexico-US migration, as well as the goals of the migrants themselves, are mainly defined by the sizable difference in the economies of Mexico and the United States and the ambivalence of US immigration laws that allow migrants to enter the country during growth periods and severely punish them during periods of economic crises and recession. There are signs that indicate that the latest US economic crisis and the implementation of repressive policies have resulted in a considerable decrease in Mexican migration to the United States. This suggests that, to a certain extent, when economic growth returns to the United States, markets will operate in the opposite direction and the number of Mexican migrants will again increase. However, the Mexican government's policy of "letting migrants go," coupled with the appeal of the US job market, generated a large and vulnerable group of migrants already residing in the United States who are in a better position than potential new migrants to access newly created jobs.

Other factors that affect migration flows are not cyclical and will probably not be impacted by economic growth. The legal framework that regulates migration to the United States, for example, will most likely not return to the lax immigration policies of the 1970s and 1980s. Since the terrorist attacks of September 11, 2001, the agencies in charge of security in the United States have acquired considerable power and must justify the significant resources allocated to them through programs aimed at securing the border and curbing irregular immigration.

The combination of perverse policies in Mexico and the United States has resulted in the emergence of a large group of Mexican job seekers who find themselves in the United States in precarious situations. Access to undocumented migrant workers has allowed employers in the United States to lower wages and working conditions. With no real expectations of support from the US government, the Mexican government must assume the responsibility of implementing policies to discourage migration and prevent further surges of vulnerable Mexican migrants in the United States.

The Mexican government must develop effective social programs to protect low- and middle-income Mexicans, thus reducing incentives to migrate to the United States as unauthorized workers. Strengthening social-security programs would free remittances to be invested in improving living standards instead of having to be allocated to contingencies and emergencies. Furthermore, an efficient social-security system accessible to all, including returning migrants, would serve as an incentive for undocumented immigrants to return to Mexico when they are being increasingly excluded from social-security programs in the United States.

Notes

We are very grateful for the support of the Assistant Secretary for Population, Migration and Religious Affairs at the Mexican Ministry of the Interior for helping coordinate interviews in several cities in Mexico's northern border. Laura Pedraza was responsible for a considerable amount of research for this chapter.

1. ENOE collects data from five observation groups or panels per collection cycle, with only one new group added to the sample per cycle.

2. People interviewed were Uriel González and Esmeralda Flores from the Coalition for Human Rights (Tijuana), Gabriela Morales Navarrete from the Center for Migrants' Human Rights, and Gabriela Garcia, former program (municipal) officer for migrants' services. Morales Navarrete, and García were interviewed in Ciudad Juárez.

3. The author interviewed staff in charge of various migrant shelters in Ciudad Juárez and Tijuana during July 2011 and then again in May 2012.

4. The author was able to verify the accuracy of this statement during the course of an interview with a person deported by airplane. The deportee thought the officer in charge of the process had been very generous. The official told the migrant he had confirmed that, with DHS authorization, the migrant would be granted a visa to return to the United States if he applied in Mexico. However, the deportation documents did not mention this concession, and on the contrary, stated that the migrant was being expelled without any mitigations.

5. The discrepancy between the number of people deported during a five-year period and the number of people who report having come back from the United States during the same five years is very large. From 1996 to 2000 the number of deportations was twice as large as the number of people who were reported in the Mexican census to have lived in the United States during those years before coming back to Mexico. More recently the discrepancy in the numbers has increased. In the five years from 2000 to 2005 it grew to 3 to 1. Of course, deportations are events, and the census counts people reported as residents in a Mexican home, but the disparity is worthy of analysis. It is likely that migrants who have arrived back in Mexico are being underestimated, but it may also mean that some deported migrants in a specific five-year period have gone back to the United States.

6. The first definitions of ZAPs only included municipalities. The most recent definition, however, also includes communities that are outside ZAP municipalities but have high levels of poverty and low socioeconomic development.

7. The author directed a four-state field-based study (The Quality of Accountability) to analyze effective access to social programs in Mexico's ZAPs. As part of this study, we selected a number of high-emigration communities in which we specifically targeted migrant families in order to compare their ability to access social programs to that of nonmigrant families. All unreferenced verbatim statements in this section are derived from this study.

8. Seguro Popular was initiated in 2001 by the Mexican government as an effort to fund and improve access to health care for the poor living in rural and urban areas (Sosa-Rubi, Galarraga, and Harris 2007).

9. Pensión para Adultos Mayores is a pension program for adults age 65 and older and offers coverage at the national level. Eligible adults and their beneficiaries receive economic support, health information, access to services, and access to institutions that offer productive activities and occupations (http://www.sedesol.gob .mx/en/SEDESOL/Pension_para_adultos_mayores).

10. PROCAMPO emerged as a result of NAFTA's implementation in 1994. It offers an "income transfer payment to Mexican farmers that compensates them for subsidies received by foreign competitors" (Garcia-Salazar, Skaggs, and Crawford 2011).

11. In one of the municipalities included in the study, the contribution was 7 percent. In another from the same region, it was 35 percent (Sánchez López 2012).

References

Alanís Enciso, Fernando Saúl. 2007. *Que se queden allá: El gobierno de México y la repatriación de mexicanos de Estados Unidos (1934–1940)*. Tijuana, Baja California, Mexico: El Colegio de la Frontera Norte/El Colegio de San Luis.

Arroyo, Jesús, William Winnie, and Luis Arturo Velázquez. 1986. *Migración a centros urbanos en una región de fuerte emigración: El caso del Occidente de México*. Guadalajara, Jalisco, Mexico: Centro de Investigaciones Sociales y Económicas de la Facultad de Economía de la Universidad de Guadalajara.

Ayón, David R. 2006. "La política mexicana y la movilización de los migrantes mexicanos en Estados Unidos." Paper presented at the Annual Meeting of the Latin American Studies Association, March 15–18, San Juan, Puerto Rico.

Banegas González, Israel. 2012. *Migración, pobreza y políticas públicas: Reporte de investigación, encuesta en zonas de atención prioritaria*. Guadalajara, Jalisco, Mexico: CIESAS Occidente.

Berumen Sandoval, Salvador. 2011. "Migración neta y flujos de la emigración mexicana a partir de la ENOE y la EMIF NORTE." Paper presented at the first meeting of the Binational Group: El bienestar de los migrantes mexicanos en Estados Unidos y México, May 23, Mexico City.

Berumen Sandoval, Salvador, Luis Felipe Ramos Martínez, and Isabel Ureta Hernández. 2011. "Migrantes mexicanos aprehendidos y devueltos por Estados Unidos: Estimaciones y características generales." Mexico City: Instituto Nacional de Migración.

Consejo Nacional de Población, Instituto Nacional de Migración, and Colegio de la Frontera Norte. 2012. *Encuesta sobre migración en la frontera norte de México, 2010: Serie anualizada 2003–2010*. Mexico: Secretaría de Gobernación.

Escobar Latapí, Agustín. 2008. "Mexican Policy and Mexico U.S. Migration." In *Mexico-U.S. Migration Management: A Binational Approach*, edited by A. Escobar and S. Martin, 179–216. Lanham, MD: Lexington Books.

———. 2009. "Can Migration Foster Development in Mexico? The Case of Poverty and Inequality." *International Migration* 47(5):75–113.

Escobar Latapí, Agustín, Lindsay Lowell, and Susan Martin. 2013. *Binational Dialogue on Mexican Migrants in the U.S. and in Mexico: Final Report.* Washington, DC: Woodrow Wilson Center. Retrieved December 5, 2014, from http://www.wilsoncenter.org/event/integrating-mexican-immigrants.

Garcia-Salazar, Jose Alberto, Rhonda Skaggs, and Terry L. Crawford. 2011. "PROCAMPO, the Mexican Corn Market, and Mexican Food Security." *Food Security* 3(3):383–394. doi:10.1007/s12571-011-0138-z.

González Gutiérrez, Carlos. 2006. "Del acercamiento a la inclusión institucional: La experiencia del instituto de los mexicanos en el exterior." In *Relaciones estado—diáspora: Perspectivas de América Latina y el Caribe*, edited by C. González, 181–220. Mexico City: Miguel Ángel Porrúa.

Guerin-González, Camille. 1985. "Repatriación de familias inmigrantes mexicanas durante la gran depresión." *Historia Mexicana* 35(2):241–274.

Kanstroom, Daniel. 2007. *Deportation Nation: Outsiders in American History.* Cambridge, MA: Harvard University Press.

Lowell, Lindsay B., Carla Pederzini, and Jeffrey Passel. 2008. "The Demography of Mexico-U.S. Migration" In *Mexico-U.S. Migration Management: A Binational Approach*, edited by A. Escobar and S. F. Martin, 1–32. Lanham, MD: Lexington Books.

Masferrer, Claudia, and Bryan R. Roberts. 2009. "Características y alcances de la migración mexicana de retorno, 2000–2005." Paper presented at the Seminario Permanente de Migración del Occidente de México, December 16, Tlalpan, Distrito Federal, Mexico.

Menchaca, Martha. 2011. *Naturalizing Mexican Immigrants.* Austin: University of Texas Press.

Papail, Jean, and Jesús Arroyo. 2009. *Migración a Estados Unidos y autoempleo: Doce ciudades pequeñas de la región centro occidente de México.* Guadalajara, Jalisco, Mexico: Universidad de Guadalajara.

Passel, Jeffrey S., and D'Vera Cohn. 2009. *A Portrait of Unauthorized Immigrants in the United States.* Washington, DC: Pew Hispanic Center. Retrieved October 16, 2014, from http://www.pewhispanic.org /2009/04/14/a-portrait-of-unauthorized-immigrants-in-the-united-states/.

———. 2011. *Unauthorized Immigrant Population: National and State Trends, 2010.* Washington, DC: Pew Hispanic Center. Retrieved October 16, 2014, from http://www.pewhispanic.org/2011/02/01/unauthorized-immigrant-population-binational-and-state-trends-2010/.

———. 2014. *Unauthorized Immigrant Totals Rise in 7 States, Fall in 14: Decline in Those from Mexico Fuels Most State Decreases.* Washington, DC: Pew Research Center. Retrieved July 7, 2015 from, http://www.pewhispanic.org/2014/11/18/unauthorized-immigrant-totals-rise-in-7-states-fall-in-14/.

Passel, Jeffrey S., D'Vera Cohn, and Ana Gonzalez-Barrera. 2013. *Population Decline of Unauthorized Immigrants Stalls, May Have Reversed.* Washington, DC: Pew Hispanic Center. Retrieved October 20, 2014, from http://www.pewhispanic.org/2013/09/23/population-decline-of-unauthorized-immigrants-stalls-may-have-reversed/.

Passel, Jeffrey S., D'Vera Cohn, Jens Manuel Krogstad, and Ana Gonzalez-Barrera. 2014. *As Growth Stalls, Unauthorized Immigration Population Becomes More Settled.* Washington, DC: Pew Research Center. Retrieved July 15, 2015, from http://www.pewhispanic.org/2014/09/03/as-growth-stalls-unauthorized-immigrant-population-becomes-more-settled/.

Rodríguez Chávez, Ernesto. 2011. "Volumen y características de los mexicanos repatriados con base en registros del INM y de la EMIF de la Frontera Norte." Paper presented at the First Meeting of the Binational Group: El bienestar de los migrantes mexicanos en Estados Unidos y México, May 23, Mexico City.

Rosenblum, Marc R., and Kristen McCabe. 2014. *Deportation and Discretion Reviewing the Record and Options for Change*. Washington, DC: Migration Policy Institute. Retrieved December 4, 2014, from http://www.migrationpolicy.org/research/deportation-and-discretion-reviewing-record-and-options-change.

Rosenblum, Marc R., and Doris Meissner. 2014. *The Deportation Dilemma: Reconciling Tough and Humane Enforcement*. Washington, DC: Migration Policy Institute. Retrieved December 5, 2014, from http://www.migrationpolicy.org/research/deportation-dilemma-reconciling-tough-humane-enforcement.

Sánchez López, Gabriela. 2012. *Acceso a la información, servicios y apoyos en zonas de atención prioritaria, Oaxaca*. Guadalajara, Jalisco, Mexico: CIESAS Occidente.

Simanski, John F. 2014. *Immigration Enforcement Actions: 2013*. Washington, DC: US Department of Homeland Security.

Sosa-Rubi, Sandra, Omar Galarraga, and Jeffrey E. Harris. 2007. "Heterogeneous Impact of the 'Seguro Popular' Program on the Utilization of Obstetrical Services in Mexico, 2001–2006: A Multinomial Probit Model with a Discrete Endogenous Variable." NBER Working Paper Series. Working Paper 13498. Cambridge, MA: National Bureau of Economic Research. Retrieved November 20, 2014, from http://www.nber.org/papers/w13498.pdf.

SRE (Secretaría de Relaciones Exteriores) and Subsecretaría para América del Norte. 2005. "Mecanismos de repatriación entre agencias federales de EE.UU. y México." Paper presented at the Twelfth Border Legislative Conference, December 9–10, El Paso, TX.

US Commission on Immigration Reform. 1997. *Mexico-United States Binational Migration Study: Migration between Mexico and the United States*. Washington, DC: US Commission on Immigration Reform.

USDHS (Department of Homeland Security). 2010. "Table 38: Aliens Removed by Criminal Status and Region and Country of Nationality: Fiscal Years 2001 to 2010 (*XLS, 78 KB*)." *Yearbook of Immigration Statistics: 2010*. Washington, DC: US Department of Homeland Security. Retrieved October 20, 2014, from http://www.dhs.gov/yearbook-immigration-statistics-2010.

———. 2011a. "Table 40: Aliens Returned by Country of Nationality: Fiscal Years 2009 to 2011 (*XLS, 45 KB*)." *Yearbook of Immigration Statistics: 2011*. Washington, DC: U.S. Department of Homeland Security. Retrieved October 20, 2014, from http://www.dhs.gov/yearbook-immigration-statistics-2011-3.

———. 2011b. "Table 41: Aliens Removed by Criminal Status and Region and Country of Nationality: Fiscal Years 2002 to 2011 (*XLS, 80 KB*)." *Yearbook of Immigration Statistics: 2011*. Washington, DC: US Department of Homeland Security. Retrieved October 20, 2014, from http://www.dhs.gov/yearbook-immigration-statistics-2011-3.

———. 2013. *2012 Yearbook of Immigration Statistics*. Washington, DC: U.S. Department of Homeland Security, Office of Immigration Statistics.

CHAPTER 11

Students We Share Are Also in Puebla, Mexico: Preliminary Findings from a 2009–2010 Survey

VÍCTOR ZÚÑIGA, EDMUND T. HAMANN,
AND JUAN SÁNCHEZ GARCÍA

Most accounts of American immigrants have tended to describe newcomers as emigrating from particular countries like Italy, Germany, or Poland. Yet, tremendous variations existed within national boundaries with some regions and districts experiencing intense bursts of emigration and others almost none at all.
JOHN BODNAR, *THE TRANSPLANTED: A HISTORY OF IMMIGRANTS IN URBAN AMERICA*

Increasingly, emigrants from Mexico to the United States are taking their children with them when they migrate. Additionally, children born to Mexican parents living in the United States may have dual US and Mexican citizenship. Later their parents may return to Mexico with their children who have now learned English and adapted to the US way of life. The US Supreme Court decision *Plyler v. Doe* allows undocumented children living in the United States to attend US public schools through grade twelve, which means that when their immigrant parents return to Mexico or send their children back to Mexico to live with relatives, the children may have spent several years in US schools and may be unfamiliar with Mexican educational programs. Depending on their age and time in the United States, they may have been taught entirely in English and may be lacking in academic Spanish-language skills. Their return to Mexico creates demands in Mexican schools to identify those students and determine how to incorporate them into the Mexican educational system. This includes providing Spanish-language instruction and a national curriculum that varies significantly from the US instructional program. This chapter explores the effects on the Mexican educational system of the increasing numbers of these transnational students who have experienced schooling in both the United States and Mexico and presents data showing where they are concentrated in Mexico.

Findings from Mexican Schools in the States of
Nuevo León, Zacatecas, and Puebla

In 2004 our research team began to observe, explore, and analyze the binational schooling trajectories of students attending public and private schools in Nuevo León and Zacatecas. Both states are characterized by a long history of international migration from Mexico to the United States and, perhaps a less-recognized phenomenon, from the United States to Mexico. Inhabitants of Nuevo León, Mexico, have been moving between Texas and Northeast Mexico since the second half of the nineteenth century. Historian González Quiroga (1993) has chronicled kin networks linking cities, counties, and regions from that time. Based on family ties, migrants profited from trade opportunities in an emerging capitalist order. However, workers and families that participated in those migratory circuits constituted only a small proportion of the total population of Nuevo León.

Indeed, Monterrey, Nuevo León's capital, has been better known for *pulling* international and internal immigrants to its metropolitan area than for *pushing* emigrants to the United States (Zúñiga 1993; Zúñiga and Sánchez 2010). The 2010 Mexican Population Census shows that 76,153 individuals left metropolitan Monterrey between 2005 and 2010 to go to other regions of Mexico. During those years the Mexican census counted 133,647 individuals who came to metropolitan Monterrey from other regions of Mexico. Thus, the demographic gain for Monterrey was more than 50,000 people in that period. Between 2005 and 2010, 16,448 individuals left metropolitan Monterrey to migrate legally to the United States (0.4 percent of the population).

Zacatecas, Mexico, is another story. This Mexican state shares with Nuevo León an international migratory tradition dating from the nineteenth century. Zacatecas, however, is different in terms of the much higher proportion of its people who have lived and worked in the United States. Following the typology proposed by Durand and Massey (2003), Zacatecas is part of Mexico's central western region, known as the historical heart of Mexican migration to the United States. Today, half of the Mexican-born population in the United States was born in that part of Mexico (Durand and Massey 2003).

Based on our estimates, the basic school system in Nuevo León (mandatory from first to ninth grade) enrolled 10,500 transnational students in November 2004. This figure represented 1.6 percent of total enrollment. In turn, the Zacatecas school system registered 7,500 transnational students in November 2005, representing almost 2.4 percent of that state's total enrollment.

The transnational students we interviewed in Nuevo León mainly had US school experiences in Texas, although many other states were also represented. Most transnational students in Zacatecas named California as the US state in which they attended school. Other US states in which transnational students from Zacatecas attended school were Nebraska, Georgia, Massachusetts, Maryland, Wisconsin, and Oregon. The preponderance of Texas as destination or origin for Nuevo León transnational students is notable; more than 66 percent of them had lived in Texas and only in Texas. Very few had lived in California (6 percent), and a small proportion had attended schools in new destinations of Mexican immigration (Zúñiga and Hernández-León 2005), such as Georgia, Alabama, or North Carolina. In contrast, 40 percent of transnational children and adolescents from Zacatecas had been enrolled in schools in "new Latino diaspora" states (Hamann and Harklau 2010) with very few in Texas schools (16 percent). In sum, both Nuevo León and Zacatecas school systems have been receiving students from American schools recently, but the population clearly differed in terms of the geographic distribution of students' prior US school experiences.

Transnational students in Nuevo León typically had lived with their parents and siblings in both the United States and Mexico, while in Zacatecas we found much more geographically dispersed families, families "divided by borders" (Dreby 2010), and families with more complex stories of separation and deportation. Some of those stories had tragic endings that impacted the students' life courses (C. Suárez-Orozco and M. Suárez-Orozco 2001; Zúñiga and Hamann 2008; C. Suárez-Orozco, M. Suárez-Orozco, and Todorova 2010).

Transnational students in Zacatecas also had longer US school experiences than those from Nuevo León. We employed two indicators for measuring the length of children's school experiences in the United States: the number of school years spent in the United States and the percentage of school years in the United States as a proportion of the student's total years of schooling. The first indicator can be misleading because the number of school years spent in US schools is a function of the age of the student, while the second better conveys the impact of the schooling on each side of the border. Thus, utilizing the second indicator, we found that half of the transnational students in Zacatecas had completed more than 30 percent of their school trajectory in the United States, compared with a third of students in Nuevo León. In other words, 66 percent of transnational students in Nuevo León had studied mainly in Mexico, but only half of transnational students in Zacatecas had completed most of their studies in Mexico.

With a clear understanding of the Nuevo León and Zacatecas cases, not just from our 2004 and 2005 school visits but also from subsequent years of scrutinizing data collected from these states, as 2010 approached we were aware that important pieces of the US-Mexico migration story were missing. Puebla, for example, was representative of the kind of Mexican state that our collected data did not describe well. Puebla and other states in the southern region of Mexico, such as Oaxaca and Guerrero, did not participate substantially in international migration during most of the twentieth century. Moreover, unlike Zacatecas and Nuevo León, Puebla has a considerable indigenous population and a much more complex and heterogeneous school system. We were aware of studies by Binford (2003), Cortina and Gendreau (2003), and Smith (2003, 2006) that focused on Puebla. Their research, however, concentrated on a specific subregion of the state or offered limited quantitative information.

To expand on what we had learned in Nuevo León and Zacatecas, in November 2009 we began collecting data on transnational students in a third Mexican state, Puebla. Funded by the Programa de Educación Básica sin Fronteras (Subsecretaría de Educación Básica, Secretaría de Educación Pública), the research team surveyed a representative sample of 18,829 students enrolled in 214 schools in Puebla and found 110 students with transnational school experiences. Additionally, in the spring of 2010 we returned to several Puebla schools and conducted in-depth interviews with transnational students and their teachers. The interviews yielded valuable information regarding students' education experiences, comparisons between Mexican and American schools, and migration dynamics. From these interviews we compiled more than five hundred pages of stories and descriptions illustrating the complex and rich trajectories of transnational students.

International Migration and the School System in Puebla: A Quick Picture

The public school system in Puebla, Mexico, has 2,925 elementary schools (*primarias*, first to sixth grade) and 1,726 junior high schools (*secundarias*, seventh to ninth grade) that enrolled almost one million students during the 2009–2010 school year. In this section we present data from a subsample of students in the fourth to ninth grades ($n = 11,998$). Younger children (grades first to third) were usually unable to respond to even basic questions included in the survey, such as where they had lived in the United States. Although the number of transnational students in Puebla proved relatively small, we were surprised when almost half of the 18,000 students we sur-

Table 11.1. International family dispersion of students in elementary and junior high schools in Nuevo León (2004), Zacatecas (2005), and Puebla (2009)

Family members living in the United States at the times of the survey	Puebla	Nuevo León	Zacatecas
Father	8.2%	4.5%	15.9%
Mother	2.1%	0.6%	1.6%
Siblings	9.6%	2.9%	16.7%
Any nuclear family members	19.9%	8.0%	34.2%
Other family members: uncles, aunts, cousins, nephews, etc.	48.0%	39.6%	61.8%
None	33.4%	53.3%	29.2%

Source: Subsample of students 4th–9th UDEM-CONACYT survey 2004, Nuevo León = 10,063 students; UDEM-CONACYT survey 2005, Zacatecas = 7,619 students, and UDEM-Programa de Educación Básica sin Fronteras survey 2009, Puebla = 11,998.
Note: Totals exceed 100% because some categories are not mutually exclusive.

veyed reported that they had at least one member of their extended family (uncles, cousins, nephews, etc.) residing in the United States at the time of our survey. This meant that the United States was a part of a huge number of students' everyday lives because they often received news, gifts, or phone calls from across the border, or *el otro lado*. When we focused more narrowly on nuclear families, 20 percent of our survey respondents reported at least one core figure living, studying, or working in the United States. The percentage of internationally divided families in Puebla (almost 20 percent) was greater than in Nuevo León (8 percent), but below that of families in Zacatecas (34 percent) (see table 11.1). These figures might overestimate the number of divided families because some of the students may belong to the same family.

About 25 percent of students matriculated in schools in Puebla reported having had contact with transnational students or peers who had school experiences in the United States. Unlike what we observed in Zacatecas, the nontransnational (mononational) students in Puebla seemed to be building borders, dividing themselves from their transnational peers. Many mononational children stated: "They [students with school experience in the United States] are different from me." They grounded this claim on a variety of arguments: differences in the manner of speaking, access to technologies or goods, wealth, money, and even skin color. One student who had never left Mexico wrote, "They speak a strange language, they are blond, that is why one calls them 'gringos,' and they have more money than us." In the same line, another mononational student said, "They act differently from us, they have a different accent, a different Spanish." One more mononational child insisted that transnational students were arrogant and carried themselves as if they were superior to mononationals, "When they arrive here [in Puebla] from abroad they feel superior, and when someone wants to talk with them, they ignore us."

As might be expected, language barriers and differences in experiences are the most important dividing characteristics between transnational students and their mononational peers. Often, Puebla students with no school experiences in the United States considered that transnational students did not speak Spanish well. They had ample reasons for concluding that their transnational peers were not sufficiently proficient in Spanish. Some pointed to accents, others to the fact that transnational students mixed English and Spanish. Language as a dividing factor in elementary and junior high schools in Puebla is probably related to the reality that transnational students returning to Puebla have had longer school trajectories in the United States than students returning to Nuevo León and Zacatecas, a finding we discuss further below.

Language was not the only issue that divided transnational and mononational students. Mononational students in Puebla conceptualized American schools as institutions where Mexican children were not welcome. They imagined that Mexican children were mistreated, discriminated against, or abused there. The word choices that some Puebla mononational students used to describe American schooling were surprising, such as "racism," "discrimination," "hate," "illegal," and other similar notions. Their discourse in interviews reflected negative perceptions about American schools without particular references or evidence. In contrast, transnational students in Puebla described their experiences in American schools as stories of success, learning, good relations with peers and teachers, and fruitful activities. In Zacatecas, we did not detect the negative perceptions regarding the treatment of Mexican children in the United States prevalent among mononational students in Puebla (see table 11.2).

The legal status of transnational children and their parents may have influenced the children's perceptions of school. We did not ask the children if they resided in the United States as authorized migrants or not. However, it seems likely that a few of the students we met in Puebla were unau-

Table 11.2. Perceptions of treatment accorded to Mexican students in US schools (respondents with no US school experiences)

Treatment	Students in Puebla	Students in Zacatecas
Bad	49%	28%
The same as here (Puebla/Zacatecas)	32%	43%
Good	19%	29%
Total	100%	100%

Source: Subsample of nontransnational students 4th–9th UDEM-CONACYT survey 2005, Zacatecas = 7,396; and UDEM-Programa de Educación Básica sin Fronteras survey 2009, Puebla = 11,913.

thorized when they were in the United States and/or in mixed-status families. Therefore, their US experience (or their parents' experiences) might have been haunted by the prospect of deportation. Because we did not ask about immigration status, we have little information about students in that cohort or about their family members who might have experienced deportation. What we do know is that US schools tend to be remembered fondly by students in the study.

Where Are the Transnational Students in Puebla?

Children and adolescents ages six to fifteen who have completed part of their schooling in Mexico and part in the United States make up the majority of transnational students in Mexico. In our samples we found a few students older than fifteen (sixteen to nineteen), but they represented just a small proportion of the total (1.5 percent). Previous research has shown that transnational educational experiences are not simple. They are accompanied by language transitions and discontinuities (Panait 2011), curricular gaps and ruptures (Hamann and Zúñiga 2011), multiple literacies (Guerra 1998), family geographical dispersions (Zúñiga and Hamann 2011), teaching mismatches, and hyphenated or transnational ethnic identities (Vandeyar 2011). All these experiences are increasingly emergent phenomena that are evident in Mexican and American schools.

During their stay in the United States, transnational students are usually classified according to their English proficiency and racial or ethnic identities. US schools identify immigrant children as beginner, intermediate, or advanced English-language learners (ELLs), and, for purposes of measuring achievement and identifying achievement gaps, they are also classified as Hispanic or Latino students. They are rarely characterized as migrants or sons and daughters of migrants. The definition of *migrant* is most frequently used in US public schools to identify children who move from one place to another following parents who are engaged in agricultural activities throughout the United States. The US federal government provides funding to boost educational and support services for these migrant children and to ensure that school records are transferred among the US schools they attend.

The US Elementary and Secondary Education Act of 1965, as amended by the No Child Left Behind Act of 2001, contains major statutory provisions that apply to the Migrant Education Program.[1] Although originally targeting children whose parents were migratory agricultural workers, the category was expanded to include children whose families have relocated for other types of work, such as meatpacking. In any case, the US school system rarely considers migrant children as transnational students. For the most part, according to American educational desegregation requirements and Title VII bilingual education policies, language acquisition and racial and ethnic taxonomies rather than transnational experiences often dictate categories for student programs. Thus, as a result of the US school system's guidelines to classify students as migrants, those who might have experienced schooling in both Mexico and the United States might not be identified as such.

Although a more elaborate taxonomy of transnational students is described in Zúñiga and Hamann (2009), from our surveys for this study we identified four types of transnational students. A first group includes students who were born in Mexico, accompanied their parents or others to the United States, attended American schools, and then returned to Mexico and enrolled in the Mexican schools where we found them. This group constitutes the most common category (60 percent). Generally, the students started their schooling in Mexico and then went to the United States before returning to Mexico. In some cases, however, children arrived in the United States when they were very young, so that they began their schooling in American schools even if they were born in Mexico.

A second group of students were born in the United States, began their schooling there, and some years later came to Mexico for the first time in their lives. These two types of students represented about 30 percent of the total transnational school population in Zacatecas and Nuevo León. Those born in the United States are legally binational, with American citizenship because of their birthplace and Mexican citizenship conferred from their parents' nationality. A third type of transnational student included children who spent part of the school year in the United States and part in Mexican schools every year. These students were exceptional and represented a very small fraction of our samples.

Finally, we need to consider the children who are transnational, but not transnational students. In this case we are referring to children who were born in the United States but did not attend American schools because they returned with their parents to Mexico at an early age. Due to their dual nationality and transnational history, they have a high probability of returning to the United States and enrolling in American schools (according to their own expectations as recorded in our surveys). They are candidates for becoming transnational students at a later stage in their lives. Moreover, their perception of the school system in Mexico may differ from that of their classmates, as these students can more tangibly consider how or whether what they are learning in their Mexican classrooms would affect their potential future in the United States (Zúñiga and Hamann 2013).

We found students from all four of these categories in Puebla. According to our estimates, there were about six thousand transnational students in Puebla attending elementary and junior high schools in 2009–2010. Students with previous schooling experiences in the United States represented a mere 0.6 percent of the total Puebla elementary and junior high student population of 966,000 students. The proportion of transnational students in Puebla is significantly smaller than the proportion of such students in Nuevo León and Zacatecas but consistent with the information we have about regional variations in international migration intensity in different Mexican regions. In fact, Puebla is considered a region of low international migration intensity compared with Zacatecas, Guanajuato, Michoacán, or Jalisco. At the same time, Puebla has a short Mexico-US migration history, even if Smith (2003) found residents from Puebla or Poblanos who arrived in New York during the 1940s. Those individuals and families were exceptions and pioneers and did not represent a regular and mature migration network from Puebla to New York.

The migratory flow from Puebla to the United States is young compared with the migrations from Zacatecas and Nuevo León. The latter two states represent Mexican regions with more than a century of history of international migration. The intensity and length of their respective migratory histories explain much of the difference in the proportion of transnational students in the schools in these three states.

Especially in the case of Puebla, we must also pay attention to huge in-

Table 11.3. Geographical concentration and dispersion of transnational students in the state of Puebla

Region	Number of students surveyed	Number and proportion of transnational students	Municipalities included in the region
Sierra Norte Huauchinango	2,745	4 (0.1%)	Zihuateutla, Cuautempan, Xicotepec, Chignahuapan
Sierra Nororiental	2,553	2 (0.08%)	Zapotitlán de Méndez
Valles de Serdán	2,218	11 (0.5%)	Cañada Morelos, Tecamachalco, Quecholac, Guadalupe Victoria
Region of Puebla City	5,683	21 (0.4%)	Domingo Arenas, Puebla, Tepeaca, San Pedro Cholula, Cuautlancingo, Juan C. Bonilla
Atlixco-Izúcar	1,974	28 (1.4%)	Izúcar de Matamoros, Chietla, Atzala, Atlixco, Tlapanalá, Tepexco, Tulcingo, Tepeojuma, Tilapa
Mixteca	1,339	32 (2.4%)	Huehuetlán el Chico, Tepexi de Rodríguez, San Jerónimo Yayacatlán, Jolalpan, Xayacatlán de Bravo, Acatlán, Axutla
Tehuacan-Sierra Negra	2,317	12 (0.5%)	Tlacotepec, Tepanco, Ajalpan, Zinacatepec
Total	18,829	110 (0.6%)	

Source: UDEM-Programa de Educación Básica sin Fronteras Survey 2009, Puebla = 18,829.

ternal variations. Indeed, if we focused on some portions of the state, it would seem that Puebla had practically no transnational students at all, while if focusing on other regions, the profiles would be closer to those of Nuevo León and Zacatecas. The percentage of transnational students in Puebla as a whole does not reflect the reality of the different regions in the state. Puebla has 217 municipalities. In our representative sample of schools and students, we collected information from 98 of those municipalities and were able to identify regional differences and confirm the findings of other scholars (D'Aubeterre 2000; Marroni 2000; Binford 2003; Smith 2003; Marroni 2006; Cordero Díaz 2007; Cota-Cabrera et al. 2009; Mancillas and Rodríguez 2009) who report that international migration from Puebla and Oaxaca to the United States has its roots primarily in a micro-region referred to as the Mixteca. Our conclusion is corroborated by research in New York and California that identified the origins of Mexican newcomers (Velasco Ortiz 2002; Smith 2003, 2006; Cornelius et al. 2009).

Among the ninety-eight Puebla municipalities included in our sample, we found transnational students in only thirty-five. Moreover, 50 percent of these transnational students were enrolled in schools located in municipalities in two specific regions: Izúcar/Atlixco and the Mixteca Poblana (see table 11.3). It is worth noting that the proportion of transnational students in the Mixteca Poblana is very similar to the proportion found in Zacatecas. In turn, the region of Atlixco/Izúcar, which is slightly northwest of the Mixteca, has a percentage of students with previous school experience in the United States comparable to that of the Nuevo León school system.

Transnational Students in Puebla

In this final section we analyze and discuss four preliminary findings that constitute unique traits of Puebla transnational students. First, students in Puebla, unlike those in Zacatecas, were enrolled primarily in schools in California (28 percent) and New York (22 percent). The remainder went to schools in Arizona, Colorado, Georgia, Minnesota, North Carolina, Texas, Washington, and Florida, but in very small proportions. The limited number of destinations illustrates how the Puebla migratory network is less mature and not as strong as networks connecting other parts of Mexico with the United States. Thus, Poblano migrants, comparatively, lack the contacts, knowledge, and resources that Zacatecanos have accumulated through several generations of migration.

Second, we found that transnational students in Puebla spent relatively more time in American schools than students in Nuevo León and Zacatecas. For most of them, the years of schooling in the United States were proportionally more extensive than the years enrolled in Mexican schools. For example, only 25 percent of students in Nuevo León studied half or more than half of their school years in the United States. In Zacatecas, 32 percent of the students studied half or more than half of their school years in the United States. In Puebla, we found that more than 50 percent of transnational students had spent a greater amount of time in US schools than in Mexican schools. Indeed, Poblano transnational students were more Americanized than those we met in Zacatecas. The relative importance of American schooling as a proportion of total schooling for transnational students in Puebla might help explain why they were considered "different from us," a reaction from students who had not experienced life in the United States, which we discussed earlier in the chapter. The proportion of years in American schools without doubt also influenced Puebla transnational students' self-declared language proficiencies: 57 percent of them claimed to be bilingual in Spanish and English, and none of them indicated that they spoke another language besides Spanish or English. In contrast, mononational students in Puebla mirrored the multilinguistic landscape of the state's school system: 13 percent of fourth-through-ninth-grade students reported speaking an indigenous language at home different from the dominant Spanish language. They spoke Nahuatl, Mixteco, Totonaco, Popoloca, Otomí, and other languages.

Third, we learned that a high percentage of transnational students in Puebla belong to internationally divided families. Half of the students had lived separated from their fathers, and 25 percent of them had lived separated from their mothers. As Dreby (2010) has pointed out, the issue of families divided by borders is clearly linked to fragmentation, school failures, and complex kin networks. As a consequence, grandparents, particularly grandmothers who become caretakers of children left behind when parents migrate, play new roles associated with the globalization of working-class people in regions of Mexico such as Puebla and Oaxaca.

At this preliminary stage in the analysis of the Puebla data, we can say, first, that our findings confirm quantitatively the issue of divided families that Dreby (2010) has observed ethnographically. Second, results show that divided families are much more characteristic of certain regions and locales than others. Data collected in Nuevo León and Zacatecas indicated deep regional differences, but not the pattern of family division. Thus, high-frequency separation of nuclear family members is a trait associated not with international migration in general but rather with some strategies or conditions that were more common in Puebla (Zúñiga 2015).

Finally, we found that a large number of transnational students in Puebla identified themselves as Mixteco, not as Mexican, not as American, and not as Mexican American. Although ostensibly an indigenous identity, Mixteco was a cultural or ethnic identity privileged by those who were born in the United States, in comparison to transnational children born in Mexico, particularly in the state of Puebla. In contrast to our observations in Nuevo León and Zacatecas, very few Poblano transnational students identified with the label Mexican American and none identified themselves as American. We recognize that the meaning of these patterns of identification cannot be explained by our surveys. It is necessary to analyze the interviews in more detail to explore why students in Puebla preferred a local/regional/ethnic/cultural Mixteco identity instead of national identities such as American or Mexican or dual identities such as Mexican American.

Conclusion

Our research demonstrates that some of the students that the United States and Mexico *share* are also in Puebla. These transnational students are mostly from very specific areas of the state of Puebla, and, furthermore, the locations of their US experiences also seem to be particular to California and New York City. Most of these transnational students are bilingual and have acquired a number of "American" traits as a result of their length of stay in American schools. We estimate there are six thousand transnational students in Puebla, and although they represent a small fraction of the state's total enrollment, an important proportion of them are Americans by birthplace. Due to their dual nationality, they can imagine their adult lives in both countries.

The strongest finding of this preliminary analysis is not that we found the students we share in Mexico, but that they are geographically dispersed and concentrated in certain Mexican schools and regions across the country. Thus, if we want to have effective educational policies to welcome transnational children and improve their schooling conditions in Mexico, we need to develop maps showing the concentration patterns. Furthermore, addressing the needs of transnational students requires attention to their experiences as migrants. As noted by Zúñiga and Hamann (2014, 11), children negotiate and experience their transition from one country to another in "different and complex ways." Making sense of transnational students' needs requires further attention to the reasons behind their return or migration to Mexico and children's perceptions of the changes in their lives and their futures (Zúñiga and Hamann 2014). Policies aimed at reintegrating or incorporating transnational children should consider how children experience, make sense of, and negotiate migration at the macro (legal status, economic conditions, job availability), meso (regional and community), and micro (family and individual) levels (Zúñiga and Hamann 2014, 3).

Transnational students are not simply "all over" Mexico; they are in specific regions and locales. This conclusion suggests a useful parallel with what Valdés, Capitelli, and Alvarez (2011, 6) noted about the United States in their book *Latino Children Learning English*: "Across the country [in the

United States], 70 percent of young English language learners are being educated in 10 percent of all elementary schools." Valdés, Capitelli, and Alvarez (2011) concluded that these figures demonstrate the extent of segregation that children of immigrants experience in American schools. Valdés (2001) also found that segregation often meant that Spanish-speaking students did not learn English because they had few interactions with English-speaking students. Our research adds that nothing different is happening in Mexico. In Mexico there are also high concentrations of transnational children in specific regions. In the United States, language differences may highlight the hypersegregation faced by children of immigrants in American schools. In Mexico, language differences also influence transnational children's incorporation experiences. Irrespective of the terminology we use, the consequences are similar. *They are the students we share.*

Notes

This paper was originally presented at the Bilateral Perspectives on Mexican Migration Conference organized by the University of Texas at San Antonio Mexico Center, March 3 and 4, 2011, San Antonio, Texas. Anabela Sánchez, an associate professor of sociology at the Universidad de Monterrey (UDEM), was in charge of the survey coordination in Puebla. The team of researchers is especially thankful for her valuable and professional assistance, as well as for the support offered by Lizbeth Hernández Sierra and Letycia Herrera Fuentes in Puebla and Blanca Cruz in Monterrey.

1. Also known as Education of Migratory Children, Title I, Part C. (US Department of Education 2004). For text of the act, see http://www.ed.gov/esea.

References

Binford, Leigh. 2003. "Migración 'acelerada' entre Puebla y Estados Unidos." In *Etnografía del Estado de Puebla Centro*, edited by E. Masferrer Kan, E. Díaz Brenis, and J. Mondragón-Melo, 58–67. Puebla, Mexico: Secretaría de Cultura del Estado de Puebla.

Bodnar, John. 1987. *The Transplanted: A History of Immigrants in Urban America.* Bloomington: Indiana University Press.

Cordero Díaz, Blanca L. 2007. *Ser trabajador transnacional: Clase, hegemonía y cultura en un circuito migratorio internacional.* Puebla, Mexico: Consejo Nacional de Ciencia y Tecnología (CONACYT), Benemérita Universidad Autónoma de Puebla.

Cornelius, Wayne A., David FitzGerald, Jorge Hernández-Díaz, and Scott Borger, eds. 2009. *Migration from the Mexican Mixteca: A Transnational Community in Oaxaca and California.* San Diego: Center for Comparative Immigration Studies, University of California San Diego.

Cortina, Regina, and Mónica Gendreau, eds. 2003. *Immigrants and Schooling: Mexicans in New York*. New York: Center for Migration Studies.

Cota-Cabrera, Bribrilia, Emily Hildreth, Andrea Rodríguez, and Viridiana C. Zárate. 2009. "San Miguel Tlacotepec as Community of Emigration." In *Migration from the Mexican Mixteca: A Transnational Community in Oaxaca and California*, edited by W. A. Cornelius, D. FitzGerald, J. Hernández-Díaz, and S. Borger, 1–30. San Diego: Center for Comparative Immigration Studies, University of California San Diego.

D'Aubeterre, María E. 2000. *El pago de la novia: Matrimonio, vida conyugal y prácticas transnacionales en San Miguel Acuexcomac Puebla*. Puebla, Mexico: El Colegio Michoacán/Benemérita Universidad Autónoma de Puebla.

Dreby, Joanna. 2010. *Divided By Borders: Mexican Migrants and Their Children*. Berkeley: University of California Press.

Durand, Jorge, and Douglas S. Massey. 2003. *Clandestinos: Migración México–Estados Unidos en los albores del siglo XXI*. Zacatecas, Mexico: Universidad Autónoma de Zacatecas and Editorial Porrúa.

González Quiroga, Miguel Á. 1993. "La puerta de México: Los comerciantes texanos y el noreste mexicano, 1850–1880." *Estudios sociológicos de El Colegio de México* 11(31):209–236.

Guerra, Juan C. 1998. *Close to Home: Oral and Literate Practices in a Transnational Mexicano Community*. New York: Teachers College Press.

Hamann, Edmund T., and Linda Harklau. 2010. "Education in the New Latino Diaspora." In *Handbook of Latinos and Education: Theory, Research and Practice*, edited by E. G. Murillo Jr., S. Villanes, R. T. Galvan, J. S. Muñoz, C. Martinez, and M. Machado-Casas, 157–169. New York: Routledge.

Hamann, Edmund T., and Víctor Zúñiga. 2011. "Schooling and the Everyday Ruptures Transnational Children Encounter in the United States and Mexico." In *Everyday Ruptures: Children, Youth and Migration in Global Perspective*, edited by C. Coe, R. R. Reynolds, D. A. Boehm, J. M. Hess, and H. Rae-Espinoza, 141–160. Nashville, TN: Vanderbilt University Press.

Mancillas, Bazán, and Daniel Rodríguez. 2009. "Muy cerca pero a la distancia: Transiciones familiares en una comunidad poblana de migrantes." *Migraciones internacionales* 5(1):35–64.

Marroni, María. 2000. "Él siempre me ha dejado con los chiquitos y se ha llevado a los grandes…. Ajustes y desbarajustes familiares en la migración." In *Migración y relaciones de género en México*, edited by D. Barrera and C. Oehmichen, 102–122. Mexico City: Grupo Interdisciplinario Sobre Mujer, Trabajo y Pobreza, Instituto de Investigaciones Antropológicas de la Universidad Nacional Autónoma de México.

———. 2006. "Migrantes mexicanas en los escenarios familiares de las comunidades de origen: Amor, desamor y dolor." *Estudios Sociológicos de El Colegio de México* 24(72):667–699.

Panait, Catalina. 2011. "Cuentos de mis escuelitas: La princesa y el hombre de hojalata: Transiciones, rupturas e identidades lingüísticas en alumnos con escolaridad circular." MA dissertation, Universidad de Monterrey, Monterrey, Mexico.

Smith, Robert C. 2003. "Imagining Mexican Educational Futures in New York."

In *Immigrants and Schooling: Mexicans in New York*, edited by R. Cortina and M. Gendreau, 93–123. New York: Center for Migration Studies.

———. 2006. *Mexican New York: Transnational Lives of New Immigrants*. Berkeley: University of California Press.

Suárez-Orozco, Carola, and Marcelo Suárez-Orozco. 2001. *Children of Immigration*. Cambridge, MA: Harvard University Press.

Suárez-Orozco, Carola, Marcelo Suárez-Orozco, and Irina Todorova. 2010. *Learning a Newland: Immigrant Students in America Society*. Cambridge, MA: Harvard University Press.

US Department of Education. 2004. "Part C: Education of Migratory Children." Washington, DC: US Department of Education. Retrieved November 4, 2014, from http://www2.ed.gov/programs/mep/index.html.

Valdés, Guadalupe. 2001. *Learning and Not Learning English: Latino Students in American Schools*. New York: Teachers College Press.

Valdés, Guadalupe, Sarah Capitelli, and Laura Alvarez. 2011. *Latino Children Learning English: Steps in the Journey*. New York: Teachers College Press.

Vandeyar, Saloshna, ed. 2011. *Hyphenated Selves: Construction, Negotiation and Mediation of Immigrant Identity within Schools—Transnational Dialogues*. Amsterdam, Pretoria: Rozenberg Publishers.

Velasco Ortiz, Laura. 2002. *El regreso de la comunidad: Migración indígena y agentes étnicos. Los mixtecos en la frontera México–Estados Unidos*. Mexico City: El Colegio de México/El Colegio de la Frontera Norte.

Zúñiga, Víctor. 1993. "Evolución de la migración internacional en un municipio de la zona metropolitana de Monterrey: El caso de Ciudad Guadalupe, Nuevo León," In *TLC: Impactos en la frontera norte*, edited by A. D. Flores, 195–206. Mexico City: Universidad Nacional Autónoma de México.

———. 2015. "Niños y adolescentes separados de sus familias por la migración internacional: El caso de cuatro estados de México." *Estudios Sociológicos de El Colegio de México* 33(97):145–168.

Zúñiga, Víctor, and Edmund T. Hamann. 2008. "Dispersión de las familias transnacionales." In *Alumnos transnacionales: Las escuelas mexicanas frente a la globalización*, 179–189. Mexico City: Secretaría de Educación Pública.

———. 2009. "Sojourners in Mexico with U.S. School Experience: A New Taxonomy for Transnational Students." *Comparative Education Review* 53(3):329–353.

———. 2011. "Volviendo a visitar la noción de transnacionalidad: Comunicación transfronteriza y redes diaspóricas en alumnos migrantes internacionales en las escuelas de México." In *Procesos comunicativos en la migración: De la escuela a la feria popular*, edited by J. J. Olvera and B. Vázquez, 29–59. Tijuana, Mexico: El Colegio de la Frontera Norte.

———. 2013. "Understanding American-Mexican Children." In *Regarding Educación: Mexican-American Schooling, Immigration, and Bi-national Improvement*, edited by B. Jensen and A. Sawyer, 172–188. New York: Teachers College Press.

———. 2014. "Going To a Home You Have Never Been To: The Return Migration of Mexican and American-Mexican Children." *Children's Geographies* 1–13. doi: 10.1080/14733285.2014.936364.

Zúñiga, Víctor, and Rubén Hernández-León, eds. 2005. *New Destinations*. New York: Russell Sage Books.

Zúñiga, Víctor, and Anabela Sánchez. 2010. "Familia y migración internacional en la zona metropolitana de Monterrey: Constantes y variables en los últimos 40 años." In *Cuando México enfrenta la globalización: Permanencias y cambios en el área metropolitana de Monterrey*, edited by L. Palacios, C. Contreras, V. Zúñiga, T. Blöss, D. Mercier, V. Baby-Collin, and C. Sheridan, 249–269. Monterrey, Mexico: Universidad Autónoma de Nuevo León.

Continuing Immigration Developments

JANETH MARTINEZ

Immigration continues to be a dramatically unfolding debate in the United States and around the world as national economies decline and violence and insecurity send refugees and migrants to other countries. Europe's leaders have grappled with curbs on immigration (Cowell and Bilefsky 2014); refugee camps of thousands of displaced people have become informal cities (Kimmelman 2014); families and young children flee besieged countries (Kramer 2014); and large numbers of migrants severely tax the resources and add to debates over fears of immigration and economic competition in communities where they arrive (Povoledo 2014). Many migrants have died after paying smugglers to transport them in small boats from North Africa to Europe. Human traffickers charged approximately 450 people on board one freighter up to $6,000 each for a chance to secure new lives in Europe (Povoledo and Cowell 2015). Another freighter carrying an estimated 850 migrants capsized off the coast of Libya in April 2015, leaving most of the passengers unaccounted for (Yardley and Bilefsky 2015).

In the summer of 2014, the United States and Mexico experienced a similar humanitarian crisis when a surge of unaccompanied children passed through Mexico and crossed the South Texas border illegally (Preston 2014a). Mexican cartels were reported to be charging up to $7,500 to bring an unaccompanied minor or a mother with children from Central America through Mexico to the United States (Preston 2014b). Deepening poverty, an increase in sustained violence—particularly in El Salvador, Guatemala, and Honduras—and a desire to reunite with family members in the United States seemed to be the greatest factors driving the increased migration of unaccompanied children to the US-Mexico border in the summer of 2014.

The deputy secretary of the US Department of Homeland Security reported that immigration enforcement agents were working with the governments in Mexico and Central America to discourage migrants, warning of the dangers of the journey to the United States (Preston 2014c). President Obama ordered the US Federal Emergency Management Agency to coordinate the efforts of federal agencies and state and local governments to shelter the children. One shelter, at Lackland Air Force Base in San Antonio, Texas, set up by the US Department of Health and Human Services, received over twelve hundred minors (Preston 2014c). Other shelters were established in South Texas, California, and New Mexico. Archibold (2014) estimated that during 2014, about fifty-seven thousand unaccompanied children were apprehended at various points across the US southwest border, with the Border Patrol station in the Rio Grande Valley of Texas reporting that some days they apprehended two hundred youth a day. The White House called for additional funding for aggressive border enforcement and opened a twenty-four-hundred-bed detention center in Dilley, Texas, in December 2014.

Jonas and Rodriguez (2014) argue that the dominant paradigm in US migration literature has been based on Mexican migration, which is overwhelmingly labor migration. They argue that US migration policies should be expanded to account for the dynamics of insurgencies and civil wars, environmental disasters, and social violence occurring in the North American region. Central American migration passing through Mexico to reach the United States challenges Mexican migration policies as well as US-Mexico relations and allows powerful nonstate actors and corrupt officials to prey upon transit migrants in Mexico and at the US-Mexico border (Jonas and Rodriguez 2014, 203).

President Obama's Executive Actions on Immigration

In lieu of a legislative solution to the broken US immigration system, the US House of Representatives voted on piecemeal measures that failed to address pressing immigration problems. For example, House Republicans approved a bill that allocated only a fraction of the money needed to address the challenges posed by the unprecedented migration of unaccompanied children from Central America. On November 20, 2014, President Obama addressed the nation announcing a number of executive actions in response to the inability of Congress to pass comprehensive immigration reform legislation (Immigration Policy Center 2014). With opposing views on the subject, Republicans and Democrats have been unable to reach a consensus regarding immigration policy.

As has been mentioned in previous chapters, over 11 million undocumented immigrants reside in the United States (Migration Policy Institute 2014; Passel et al. 2014). Many have lived in the United States for years, are established members of their community, have children who are US-born citizens, and live in constant fear of deportation. In 1986, President Ronald Reagan signed the Immigration Reform and Control Act, granting nearly 2.7 million immigrants permanent-resident status (Cohn 2014). Although both Democratic and Republican presidents have used their executive authority to act on immigration in the past, only President Reagan was able to grant millions of undocumented immigrants a path to citizenship through legislation (Office of the Press Secretary 2014). The most recent attempt to pass an immigration reform bill dwindled after the US House of Representatives, dominated by Republicans, failed to pass a bipartisan bill approved by the Senate in June 2013 (Dinan and Sherfinski 2013).

In response to political pressure to address immigration, President Obama announced in November 2014 his Immigration Accountability Executive Actions (Immigration Policy Center 2014). Although the proposed actions do not grant undocumented immigrants legal permanent status or a path to citizenship, they provide eligible individuals with temporary relief from deportation and allow them to apply for work authorization. The executive actions also focus on improving the efficiency of the US immigration system to expedite the processing of immigration benefits and to encourage business innovations, while at the same time enforcing legal action against individuals considered threats to national security and public safety (Immigration Policy Center 2014). According to the Migration Policy Institute, an estimated 5.2 million people could benefit from the president's newest deferred action plan—Deferred Action for Parents of Americans and Lawful Permanent Residents, or DAPA—and the revised Deferred Action for Childhood Arrivals (DACA) program (Migration Policy Institute 2014).

Republican leaders opposed President Obama's executive actions on immigration (Shear, Preston, and Parker 2014). Former Speaker of the House John A. Boehner (R-Ohio) stated that "House Republicans would fight the president tooth and nail" (Shear, Preston, and Parker 2014). Many disapproved of the president's decision to implement immigration reform through executive action (Parlapiano 2014), while many others endorsed giving undocumented immigrants relief from deportation and allowing them to work legally. The president and immigration reform supporters considered these actions a necessary "first step towards common-sense reforms to an outdated immigration system" (Immigration Policy Center 2014).

President Obama's executive actions aimed at improving the current US immigration system by effectively enforcing immigration laws, facilitating the legal immigration process, promoting economic prosperity through new business innovations, helping immigrants incorporate into their new communities, and encouraging eligible legal permanent residents to apply for citizenship (Immigration Policy Center 2014). A series of memorandums were issued to offer guidelines for the implementation of the proposed initiatives and to direct agencies to develop policies and recommendations to improve the current system (Immigration Policy Center 2014).

Deferred Action

The focal point of President Obama's 2014 executive actions is the expansion of protection from removal, or deferred action, for a large number of undocumented migrants currently in the United States. The president authorized the Department of Homeland Security (DHS) to expand the 2012 DACA to increase the pool of eligible youth. He also approved the creation of the DAPA program, which allows deferral of deportation for the parents of children who are US citizens or legal permanent residents. These programs offered temporary protection against deportation and enabled eligible undocumented immigrants to apply for work permits. Estimates suggest that nearly 5.2 million unauthorized immigrants may benefit from DAPA and the expanded DACA program (Migration Policy Institute 2014).

The DAPA initiative could benefit nearly 3.5 million unauthorized immigrant parents of US citizens or legal permanent residents (Krogstad and Passel 2014). Individuals who have US citizen or legal permanent-resident children born on or before November 20, 2014, have continuously resided in the United States since January 1, 2010, and are not an enforcement priority are eligible for deportation relief and work authorization for three years (Johnson 2014a). US Citizenship and Immigration Services (USCIS) will consider requests for deferment on a case-by-case basis to determine eligibility under the guidelines set by the memorandum issued November 20, 2014. Applicants must pay a fee of $465 to cover the costs of implementing the program (Johnson 2014a). According to the Pew Research Center, approximately 44 percent of those eligible for DAPA are from Mexico, the largest percentage of any nationality (Krogstad and Passel 2014).

Although President Obama offered millions of unauthorized immigrants temporary protection from deportation through DACA and DAPA, these programs do not lead to legal permanent residency or to a path to citizenship and can be revoked at any time. Only Congress holds the authority to grant unauthorized immigrants a path to permanent legal status (Krogstad and Passel 2014).

Streamlining the Legal Immigration System

A second component of President Obama's executive actions aimed at streamlining and modernizing the US legal immigration system. The president called on immigration agencies to improve the current visa-issuing system and to ensure that all available immigrant visa numbers (green cards) are used according to demand. DHS Secretary Jeh Johnson directed the USCIS to take steps to reduce wait times for employment-based immigrant visas and to ensure that all immigrant visas authorized by Congress are issued. Additionally, immigrants waiting for work-sponsored legal-permanent-resident cards will have more flexibility to change jobs or employers without losing their place in line (Immigration Policy Center 2014; Johnson 2014c). On February 24, 2015, DHS announced the approval of new rules authorizing work permits for spouses of H-1B visa holders who have been approved for legal permanent residency but are waiting for a visa number to become available (USCIS 2015).

In an effort to boost the US economy and support job creation, the 2014 executive actions included measures to streamline the process of awarding visas to highly skilled foreign workers and investors. President Obama's executive actions amended the Optional Practical Training (OPT) Program, which allows foreign students educated in US universities to gain experience through work in their fields of study. The proposal expanded the number of degrees eligible for OPT and allowed students in the STEM (science, technology, engineering, and math) fields to work in the United States for longer periods of time (Immigration Policy Center 2014; Johnson 2014c).

Enforcement and Border Security

Enforcement and border security is the third component in President Obama's executive actions. Securing the southern border and reducing the number of illegal entries into the United States remains a top priority. During the Obama administration the number of deportations has been at a record high (Alba 2013). Analysts have attributed the large number of deportations to the president's efforts, thus far unsuccessful, to pressure Congress to pass a bill fixing the broken immigration system (Preston 2014d). In response to Congress's failure to pass immigration reform, President Obama's executive actions included measures to prioritize the removal of criminals and individuals who pose a threat to national security and turn attention away from people with deep ties to their communities in the United States who have no criminal record (Preston 2014a). According to the president's 2014 executive orders, the DHS should give precedence to the removal of undocumented immigrants involved in or suspected of criminal activity, those convicted of a serious crime or felony, and recent illegal border crossers (Johnson 2014b).

Several initiatives seek to ensure that immigration agencies and officers are effectively using resources and implementing new enforcement priorities (Johnson 2014b). Measures include the creation of three joint task forces charged with enforcing security at the US-Mexico border by stopping the illegal flow of goods and individuals, reducing criminal and terrorist activity, and deterring and preventing undocumented immigration, while simultaneously allowing the legal flow of people and goods into the United States (Johnson 2014e). Additional personnel will collaborate with the Department of Justice to restructure court procedures to expedite the removal of high-priority individuals and close cases of people who are low priority (Office of the Press Secretary 2014). DHS also discontinued Secure Communities, a highly contentious program in which state and local enforcement agencies collaborated in the identification and removal of criminal aliens under their custody (Johnson 2014d). Secure Communities was replaced with the new Priority Enforcement Program, which will, according to the newly established enforcement priorities, focus on apprehending individuals actually convicted of specific crimes (Immigration Policy Center 2014; USDHS 2014).

These presidential executive actions have the potential to significantly impact the lives of millions of undocumented immigrants living in the United States. Although the proposed deferred action represents only temporary relief from deportation, it could improve the living and working conditions of millions of people who are eligible for the DACA and DAPA programs. Changes to the visa system will benefit foreign students graduating from US colleges and universities and a number of highly skilled workers and their spouses. However, under the new executive actions, undocumented parents of eligible DACA recipients do not receive protection.

There are reasons to suspect that many eligible applicants for DACA and DAPA may be hesitant to apply due to significant barriers, such as high application fees, fear of identification, and lack of certainty related to the nature of the programs (Migration Policy Institute 2014). Although the president has proposed temporary protection to millions of undocumented immigrants living in the United States, these actions do not lead to legal permanent residency or citizenship.

In November 2014, Texas filed a lawsuit to stop the implementation of President Obama's new executive orders (*State of Texas, et al., v. United States of America, et al.*, B-14-254 [2015]) and was joined by twenty-five other states. On February 16, 2015, one day before thousands of undocumented immigrants could begin applying for legal protection and work permits under the expanded DACA program, Federal Judge Andrew S. Hanen ruled in favor of Texas, and the coalition of states it is spearheading, blocking implementation of DAPA and the DACA expansion (Preston 2015; Shear and Preston 2015). In response, more than 150 civil rights, labor, and immigration advocacy groups filed briefs with the US Fifth Circuit Court of Appeals defending the deferred action initiative (American Immigration Council 2015). On April 7, 2015, Judge Hanen denied the Obama administration's request to lift the injunction placed on the president's deferred action programs (Shear 2015). On May 26, 2015, the Fifth Circuit Court of Appeals denied the request to stay the injunction blocking the implementation of DAPA and the expanded DACA. Polarized views have intensified the liminal status of eligible DAPA and DACA individuals.

Mexico-US Migration: A Global Perspective

Immigration from Mexico should be considered in the larger global context. The US Council on Foreign Relations, an independent, nonpartisan research group founded in 1921, sponsored an independent task force to assess issues of current and critical importance to US foreign policy. As a result, in 2014 the council released the report *North America: Time for a New Focus*, which addresses US foreign policies. The report urges the United States, Canada, and Mexico to work together to develop and act on a common vision for North America. The document includes numerous important recommendations on energy infrastructure, environmental protection, economic competitiveness, innovative border programs, improvement of physical infrastructure, and strengthening of security. The task force report urges the United States, in conjunction with Canada, to build upon the Mérida Initiative to support Mexican efforts to strengthen the democratic rule of law, dismantle criminal networks, reduce smuggling and drug consumption, and contribute to the development of resilient and cohesive communities.

In urging the three countries to build a North American community, the report recognizes the important role that immigrants and their descendants have played in shaping the United States. The council concludes that most Americans recognize that current immigration policies are not serving US national interests and that changes are needed (Petraeus, Zoellick, and O'Neil 2014, 77). The task force report strongly recommends passage of comprehensive US federal immigration reform and identifies issues of importance, such as secure US borders, visas based on economic need, recruitment of more talented and skilled people to settle in the United States, and a pathway to legalization for undocumented immigrants now in the United States.

Finding some way to incorporate the large population of undocumented immigrants remains a public policy imperative. A report by Passel and Cohn (2014) at the Pew Research Center found that although Mexicans are the majority of unauthorized immigrants in the United States (52 percent in 2012), both their numbers and their share have declined in recent years. However, as the number of unauthorized Mexicans dropped, undocumented immigrants from South America, European countries, and Canada held steady (Passel and Cohn 2014, 9), and unauthorized immigrants from Asia, the Caribbean, Central America, and other regions grew slightly.

One of the task force members, Maria Otero, stressed the importance of addressing social and economic inequality among and within Canada, the United States, and Mexico by promoting resilience of the poorest, supporting women's economic empowerment, and improving educational quality and access (Petraeus, Zoellick, and O'Neil 2014, 85). The task force report suggests that Mexico and the United States can take the lead in deepening the integration and cooperation among the three sovereign democratic states of North America and that this should be a central priority for US policy. The chapters in this book offer insights and recommendations that can help make this happen.

References

Alba, Francisco. 2013. "Mexico: The New Migration Narrative." *Migration Information Source.* Washington, DC: Migration Policy Institute. Retrieved December 12, 2014, from http://www.migrationpolicy.org/article/mexico-new-migration-narrative.

American Immigration Council. 2015. "Unprecedented Coalition Ask Court to Reverse Texas Ruling Blocking Immigration Initiatives." Washington, DC: American Immigration Council. Retrieved April 7, 2015, from http://www.americanimmigrationcouncil.org/newsroom/release/unprecedented-coalition-ask-court-reverse-texas-ruling-blocking-immigration-initiate.

Archibold, Randal C. 2014. "Trying to Slow the Illegal Flow of Young Migrants." *New York Times International.* July 21, A4.

Cohn, D'Vera. 2014. "How the 1986 Immigration Law Compares with Obama's Program." Washington, DC: Pew Research Center. Retrieved December 15, 2014, from http://www.pewresearch.org/fact-tank/2014/12/09/how-the-1986-immigration-law-compares-with-obamas-program/.

Cowell, Alan, and Dan Bilefsky. 2014. "European Agency Reports Surge in Illegal Migration, Fueling a Debate." *New York Times International,* May 31, A10.

Dinan, Stephen, and David Sherfinksi. 2013. "Boehner Puts Brakes on Immigration Reform: Issue may Linger Past Midterm Elections." *Washington Times,* November 13. Retrieved December 29, 2014, from http://www

.washingtontimes.com/news/2013/nov/13/boehner-house-wont-negotiate-senate-immigration/?page=all.

Immigration Policy Center. 2014. "A Guide to the Immigration Accountability Executive Action." Washington, DC: American Immigration Council. Retrieved November 26, 2014, from http://www.immigrationpolicy.org/special-reports/guide-immigration-accountability-executive-action.

Johnson, Jeh Charles. 2014a. *Exercising Prosecutorial Discretion with Respect to Individuals Who Came to the United States as Children and with Respect to Certain Individuals Who Are the Parents of U.S. Citizens or Permanent Residents* [Memorandum]. Washington, DC: US Department of Homeland Security.

———. 2014b. *Policies for the Apprehension, Detention and Removal of Undocumented Immigrants* [Memorandum]. Washington, DC: US Department of Homeland Security.

———. 2014c. *Policies Supporting U.S. High-Skilled Businesses and Workers* [Memorandum]. Washington, DC: US Department of Homeland Security.

———. 2014d. *Secure Communities* [Memorandum]. Washington, DC: US Department of Homeland Security.

———. 2014e. *Southern Border and Approaches Campaign* [Memorandum]. Washington, DC: US Department of Homeland Security.

Jonas, Susanne, and Nestor Rodriguez. 2014. *Guatemala-US Migration: Transforming Regions.* Austin: University of Texas Press.

Kimmelman, Michael. 2014. "Refugee Camp Evolves as a Do-It-Yourself City." *New York Times,* July 5, A1.

Kramer, Andrew E. 2014. "Evacuating Children along a Dangerous Ukraine Route." *New York Times International,* June 16, A4.

Krogstad, Jens Manuel, and Jeffrey S. Passel. 2014. "Those from Mexico Will Benefit Most from Obama's Executive Action." Washington, DC: Pew Research Center. Retrieved December 15, 2014, from http://www.pewresearch.org/fact-tank/2014/11/20/those-from-mexico-will-benefit-most-from-obamas-executive-action/.

Migration Policy Institute. 2014. "MPI: As Many as 3.7 Million Unauthorized Immigrants Could Get Relief from Deportation under Anticipated New Deferred Action Program." Washington, DC: Migration Policy Institute. Retrieved November 26, 2014, from http://www.migrationpolicy.org/news/mpi-many-37-million-unauthorized-immigrants-could-get-relief-deportation-under-anticipated-new.

Office of the Press Secretary. 2014. "Fact Sheet: Immigration Accountability Executive Action." Washington, DC: The White House. Retrieved November 24, 2014, from http://www.whitehouse.gov/the-press-office/2014/11/20/fact-sheet-immigration-accountability-executive-action.

Parlapiano, Alicia. 2014. "What is President Obama's Immigration Plan?" *New York Times,* November 20. Retrieved November 24, 2014, from http://www.nytimes.com/interactive/2014/11/20/us/2014-11-20-immigration.html.

Passel, Jeffrey S., and D'Vera Cohn. 2014. *Unauthorized Immigrant Totals Rise in 7 States, Fall in 14: Decline in Those From Mexico Fuels Most State Decreases.* Washington, DC: Pew Research Center's Hispanic Trends Project. Retrieved July 17, 2015, from http://www.pewhispanic.org/2014/11/18/unauthorized-immigrant-totals-rise-in-7-states-fall-in-14/.

Passel, Jeffrey S., D'Vera Cohn, Jens Manuel Krogstad, and Ana Gonzalez-Barrera. 2014. *As Growth Stalls, Unauthorized Immigrant Population Becomes More Settled.* Washington, DC: Pew Research Center. Retrieved July 16, 2015 from, http://www.pewhispanic.org/2014/09/03/as-growth-stalls-unauthorized-immigrant-population-becomes-more-settled/.

Petraeus, David H., Robert B. Zoellick, and Shannon K. O'Neil. 2014. *North America: Time for a New Focus.* Independent Task Force Report No. 71. New York: Council on Foreign Relations.

Povoledo, Elisabetta. 2014. "Palace of Squatters Is a Symbol of Refugee Crisis." *New York Times International.* June 15, A6.

Povoledo, Elisabetta, and Alan Cowell. 2015. "Traffickers Set Freighters on a Course for Italy and Flee, Leaving Migrants Aboard." *New York Times International.* January 3, A6.

Preston, Julia. 2014a. "New U.S. Effort to Aid Unaccompanied Child Migrants." *New York Times,* June 3, 2014, A14.

———. 2014b. "New U.S. Effort to Aid Unaccompanied Child Migrants." *New York Times,* June 6, A14.

———. 2014c. "Snakes and Thorny Brush, and Children at the Border Alone." *New York Times,* June 26, A14.

———. 2014d. "Obama's Immigration Plan Could Grant Papers to Millions, at Least for Now." *New York Times,* November 15. Retrieved November 19, 2014, from http://www.nytimes.com/2014/11/16/us/obamas-immigration-plan-could-grant-papers-to-millions-at-least-for-now.html.

———. 2015. "States Are Divided by the Lines They Draw on Immigration." *New York Times,* March 30, A10.

Shear, Michael D. 2015. "Judge Refuses to Let Obama's Executive Actions on Immigration Proceed." *New York Times,* April 9, A14.

Shear, Michael D., and Julia Preston. 2015. "Dealt Setback, Obama Puts Off Immigration Plan." *New York Times,* February 18, A1.

Shear, Michael D., Julia Preston, and Ashley Parker. 2014. "Obama Plan May Allow Millions of Immigrants to Stay and Work in U.S." *New York Times,* November 13. Retrieved November 19, 2014, from http://www.nytimes.com/2014/11/14/us/obama-immigration.html.

State of Texas, et al. v. United States of America, et al., B-14–254 (2015).

USCIS (US Citizenship and Immigration Services). 2015. "DHS Extends Eligibility for Employment Authorization to Certain H-4 Dependent Spouses of H-1B Nonimmigrants Seeking Employment-Based Lawful Permanent Residence." Washington, DC: US Department of Homeland Security. Retrieved April 22, 2015, from http://www.uscis.gov/news/dhs-extends-eligibility-employment-authorization-certain-h-4-dependent-spouses-h-1b-nonimmigrants-seeking-employment-based-lawful-permanent-residence.

USDHS (US Department of Homeland Security). 2014. "Fixing Our Broken Immigration System through Executive Action—Key Facts." Washington, DC: US Department of Homeland Security. Retrieved November 24, 2014, from http://www.dhs.gov/immigration-action.

Yardley, Jim, and Dan Bilefsky. 2015. "Captain of Migrant Boat Hit Rescue Ship, Prosecutors Say." *New York Times,* April 21. Retrieved April 22, 2015, from http://www.nytimes.com/2015/04/22/world/europe/italy-libya-migrant-boat-capsize.html.

Is Mexican Migration to the United States Different from Other Migrations?

HARRIETT D. ROMO

There has been much discussion in the sociology literature about the nature of migrations and the incorporation of newcomers into the United States, from the early work by Robert E. Park (1964) and Milton Gordon (1964) to more recent discussions of differences in European-based groups' experiences and those from Latin America, Asia, and the Middle East (Alba 1990; Portes and Rumbaut 1990; Alba and Nee 2003; Kasinitz et al. 2008). What is recognized by more recent scholarship is the diversity of immigrants' origins, the circumstances of their exit from their home countries, and the contexts of contemporary US cities and rural areas where newcomers settle. This chapter proposes that Mexican migration is different from other migrations for a number of reasons.

The ways migrants enter the United States and whether the migrants can become US citizens have played an important role in the experiences of Mexicans in the United States. Large-scale immigration from Mexico is reshaping American society and culture. Debates about what sort of Americans the children of immigrants will be—or whether some groups of immigrants should be allowed a route to citizenship at all—have been prominent concerns expressed in US media, proposed immigration legislation, and immigration policy. US policy decisions have profound implications for Mexico in terms of loss of human talent and financial capital, the ways Mexican citizens are received in the United States as migrants, and the reincorporation of undocumented migrants who may be deported or return home voluntarily after long stays in the United States.

Scholars have documented a "culture of migration" to the United States that encourages young Mexicans to see the journey north as a rite of passage (Kandel and Massey 2002). Sojourns to the United States for residents of many Mexican states with long histories of migration have provided a way of supporting one's family and a path to socioeconomic improvement and upward mobility that reinforces the migration cycle despite difficult economic times and tightened border security in the United States (Kandel and Massey 2002; Hawkins et al. 2010). This long history of migration has created a transmission of values among family members, friends and coworkers, community institutions (such as schools, churches, and the government), the media, and the community at large that influences perceptions and beliefs about the cultural acceptance of migration (Kandel and Massey 2002). It is common in many Mexican communities to find a large number of families who currently have a family member working in the United States or have had family members who have worked there. In some rural sending communities the majority of the males of working age migrate to the United States for work, leaving women, children, and the elderly to tend small farms or family businesses.

As some of the chapters in this collection have noted in their reviews of the history of Mexican migration, before 1965 immigrants to the United States were overwhelmingly European, but after 1965, Hispanic (mostly Mexican) and Asian migrants have dominated. The chapters in this book, by both Mexican and American scholars, focus on Mexican migration to the United States. In this final chapter, I use topics raised by the authors included in this volume to make the case that Mexican immigration to the United States is distinct. To do so I rely heavily on the following characteristics: (1) the history of Mexico–United States relations; (2) US proximity to Mexico and the extensive two-thousand-mile shared land border; (3) the treatment of Mexicans in the US Southwest during Jim Crow and the influence of the Mexican American civil rights movement; (4) the interconnectedness of the United States and Mexico in a regional North American economy; and (5) demographic patterns, including the continuity of Mexican migration, the concentration of Mexican-origin population in the US Southwest, and the presence of large numbers of unauthorized Mexican migrants who reside in the United States and have done so for many years.

The History of Mexico-US Relations

Prominent historians have written about the extensive and complex history of Mexico-US relations (Gamio 1930; Wilkie [1967] 1970; Womack 1970; Acuña 1981; Weber 1982, 1988; Coatsworth 2003). It is not the intent of this narrative to review these excellent works; rather, my intent is to highlight some of the key historical events that have shaped the unique character of Mexican migration to the United States. No other ethnic group in the United States has had the same relationship with its native country as people of Mexican origin.

After Mexico gained independence from Spain, the Mexican government continued colonization patterns, sending soldiers, missionaries, and settlers to establish missions and presidios in the northern Mexican frontier. At the same time, particularly in the territory now called Texas, settlers from the United States moved into the area seeking land grants. The Anglo settlers initially expressed loyalty to Mexico, despite the fact that they did not become Mexican citizens or Roman Catholic. Suspicious of these intruders, Mexico hastened to settle the area to secure Mexican claim over the land. Around 1835, revolutionary movements on the part of the Anglo settlers concerned the Mexican government, and Mexican general Antonio López de Santa Anna and his army marched to Texas to put down the uprisings.

The United States, with its policy of Manifest Destiny, saw an opportunity to acquire more land along its southern border. After a brief period of independence, in 1845 Texas was incorporated into the United States, once again provoking armed conflict with Mexico. The US war against Mexico (1846–1848) and the annexation of nearly half of Mexico's territory, including the present-day US states of Arizona, California, New Mexico, Nevada, Utah, and parts of Colorado, profoundly impacted relations with Mexico as well as with individuals of Mexican descent in the United States. The US appropriation of nearly half of Mexican territory in 1848 shaped subsequent relations between the two countries and the social and economic position of Mexicans and Mexican Americans. Massey (2007, 118), in his book *Categorically Unequal*, explored the origins and development of the American stratification system and argued that with the end of the war and the signing of the Treaty of Guadalupe Hidalgo in 1848, some fifty thousand Mexicans became US citizens and went from being a majority in their own country to a minority in an alien land.

Following incorporation into the United States, Mexicans experienced subjugation and racial and ethnic prejudice despite guarantees in the Treaty of Guadalupe Hidalgo allowing them to maintain their Spanish language and Mexican culture. By the end of the nineteenth century, Mexicans in the United States had been transformed socially and economically into a subordinate people who experienced widespread discrimination and exclusion (Grebler, Moore, and Guzman 1970). Rodolfo Alvarez (1985, 38) has argued that this "psycho-historical experience of a rapid and clear break with the culture of their parent country, and subsequent subjugation against their will and on what the indigenous population considered to be its 'own land' makes the experience of the Mexican Americans different from other immigrant populations that migrated to the United States in the nineteenth and twentieth centuries."

As a result of continuous migration, Mexicans have, along with other Hispanics, become the largest minority group in the United States. Kitty Clavita (1994) provides a well-documented overview of US policies regarding Mexican immigration that will be briefly summarized here, with notations from other researchers who support her arguments. Mexican immigration gained momentum in the pre–World War I period because of the high costs of European immigrant labor and the labor activism of these European immigrant workers. US senators debating immigration policy in 1911 argued that Mexicans were "not easily assimilated" and "less desired as a citizen than as a laborer" (Clavita 1994, 58). Policy makers argued that because of Mexico's proximity to the United States, Mexicans provided a low-cost, flexible workforce, and that most Mexican workers would return to Mexico. Mexican migrant labor was also exempted from the literacy test requirement and the payment of an eight-dollar head tax imposed by the Immigration Act of 1917 because southwest growers depended on a plentiful supply of Mexican labor (Tichenor 2002).

Mexican workers were again actively recruited when European immigration temporarily halted during World War I, and approximately five hundred thousand Mexicans crossed into the United States during the 1920s (López 1981, 660). In an example of labor flexibility promoted by employers, thousands of Mexicans living in the United States were deported during the US economic depression in the 1930s when Mexican labor was no longer needed (Clavita 1994, 59).

The Bracero Program, initiated with an agreement between the United States and Mexico in 1942, institutionalized the flexible and temporary nature of Mexican labor migration, with the US Immigration and Naturalization Service exercising "benign neglect with regard to undocumented labor," especially toward Mexican laborers needed to harvest US crops (Clavita 1994, 60; Levario 2012). By the time the Bracero Program ended in 1964, almost five million Mexican workers had been brought to the United States as temporary workers (Clavita 1994, 61). Also, when the number of bracero visas was insufficient to meet the agricultural demand, employers increasingly recruited undocumented migrants directly (Massey 2007, 126). Many have argued that the employer-worker relationships established by the Bracero Program laid the foundation for the increased undocumented immigration that followed. The majority of those unauthorized migrants were Mexican.

The Proximity of Mexico

The history of the US-Mexico border region is fraught with struggles over boundaries, property rights, and, at times, violence (Levario 2012), but for a long time this border remained relatively open. The Border Patrol was not established until 1924 (Massey 2007, 121). Today, with modern transportation, people can easily commute by airplane or by automobile from the United States to Mexico to do business, live, visit, or spend time with extended families. All along the border, people live in contiguous twin cities, such as Laredo, Texas, and Nuevo Laredo, Mexico; El Paso, Texas, and Ciudad Juárez, Mexico; Tucson, Arizona, and Nogales, Mexico; and San Diego, California, and Tijuana, Mexico, where workers, tourists, and schoolchildren cross the border frequently and sometimes daily. Efforts to reform US immigration policies, such as the McCarran-Walter Act in 1952, which set annual quotas of immigrants based on the proportion of people from the country present in the United States in 1920, set no limit for Western Hemisphere countries, including Mexico. Later modifications in 1965 and in 1978 eliminated separate hemispheric limits and established a uniform limit of twenty thousand immigrant visas per country per year, including Mexico.

In response to the end of the Bracero Program in 1964 and the return of nationals who tended to remain in the border area (Dear 2013), Mexico launched a program to promote industrial development, boost tourism, and upgrade living standards in towns along the US-Mexico border. This initiative primarily benefited Tijuana and Nuevo Laredo. Mexico also introduced the Border Industrialization Program, which led to the Mexican maquiladora (assembly plant) industry. Maquiladoras allowed imported raw materials and components from the United States to be assembled in Mexico and returned to the United States as finished products, further reinforcing the international integration of the two countries' economies (Dear 2013).

Despite the economic connections and Mexico's efforts to improve the border area, stereotypes and discrimination against Mexican immigrants persisted. Clavita (1994, 63) argues that although the reaction against Mexican immigrants is similar to racist and protectionist reactions against other immigrant groups, it is different because of the proximity of Mexico and the undocumented status of many Mexican immigrants. Clavita and others have suggested that the "fear that in the 1980s the United States had lost control of its borders" has largely been focused on the Mexican border and Mexican immigrants, not the Canadian border.

Later immigration reforms, such as the Immigration Reform and Control Act of 1986 (IRCA), largely benefited Mexicans, with the majority of legalized immigrants under IRCA provisions coming from Mexico (Bean, Vernez, and Keely 1989, 69). In spite of employer sanctions included in IRCA, most scholars of immigration have concluded that in the long run, IRCA did not decrease immigration, either documented or undocumented. Undocumented migration has remained high since the 1950s, with Mexican workers constituting the majority of this population in low-wage sectors of the economy, such as agriculture, construction, in-home childcare and housecleaning, hotels, and restaurants. Once again, the Immigration Act of 1990 gave special attention to Mexican immigration by attempting to reduce the backlogs for visas for Mexican nationals (Clavita 1994, 75).

In its focus on economic imperatives, the 1990 Immigration Act added employment-based preferences for workers with needed job skills, professionals, and investors. Employment-based preferences included visas for spouses and children (Lee 2013). This may have fostered the more recent increases in Mexican immigrants with higher levels of education and capital. Increased insecurity in Mexico has also encouraged migration of high-income Mexican families. Martin (1994, 84) characterizes US immigration policy as "benign neglect" and notes that politicians "struck a responsive chord" when in the 1980s they called for securing the US-Mexico border and denying social services to unauthorized immigrants in California, the US state with the highest Mexican immigrant population. Several states receiving recent immigrants from Mexico, such as Arizona, Georgia, Alabama, South Carolina, and Utah, passed restrictions in 2011–2012 to deny social services, education, and access to drivers' licenses to unauthorized immigrants. Many of these actions primarily focused on Mexicans, and some agents enforcing those laws have been accused of racial profiling and discriminating against Mexican American citizens.

The Mexican American Civil Rights Movement

The Mexican-origin population in the United States has played a major role, along with African Americans, in the struggle for civil rights for minority groups, more so than any other immigrant group. Mexicans have also experienced extensive discrimination because of color and language differences.

Early US census counts did not distinguish Mexican-origin populations because the major concern was to distinguish between "black" and "white." As Jim Crow laws emerged during the 1930s–1960s, concern focused on who was "nonwhite." During the Jim Crow era, especially in the US Southwest, Mexicans and Mexican Americans experienced segregated schools, discrimination, violence, intimidation, and racial exclusion similar to that experienced by blacks (Montejano 1987; Gutiérrez 1995; Massey 2007; Telles and Ortiz 2008). Instructions for the 1930 census provided detailed definitions of those considered nonwhite, including Mexicans.

Nobles (2000, 72) found this definition for Mexicans in instructions for census takers in 1930: "Practically all Mexican laborers are of a racial mixture difficult to classify, though usually well recognized in the localities where they are found. In order to obtain separate figures for this racial group, it has been decided that all persons born in Mexico, or having parents born in Mexico, who are definitely not white, Negro, Indian, Chinese, or Japanese, should be returned as Mexican." Nobles (2000) reported that in earlier censuses, Mexicans had been classified as white, but the category "Mexican" was added because of the increase in the number of Mexicans who entered the southwestern United States during and after the Mexican Revolution between 1910 and 1928.

In the 1960s, as part of the Chicano Movement, Mexican Americans walked out of schools in Los Angeles and protested inferior educational opportunities and racial discrimination in workplaces and voting. Mexican Americans also initiated the early legal school desegregation cases, such as the Westminster, California, case in which Gonzalo Méndez filed a suit in the federal courts in 1945 on behalf of some five thousand Mexican residents of the district against school officials of Orange County, California (McWilliams 1968, 280–283), laying the groundwork for the US Supreme Court decision in *Brown v. Board of Education* that desegregated US public schools.

After 1965, Mexicans experienced new discrimination because of the rise of undocumented immigration. They were seen as threats to the nation's security, displacing US workers and infringing on American culture, the English language, and the US way of life (Chavez 2001). While the Irish and Jewish immigrants to the United States also experienced discrimination and were stereotyped as threats to what was perceived by white Protestant immigrant groups as "American culture," these groups did not actively participate in an ethnic civil rights movement such as the Chicano Movement. African Americans and Native Americans were activist civil rights leaders, but those groups did not experience the anti-immigration sentiment that Mexicans experienced.

Many Mexican American leaders who testified before the Rodino subcommittee to investigate illegal immigration in the early 1970s were tied to groups that opposed unauthorized immigration, such as Cesar Chavez's United Farm Workers, the AFL-CIO labor union, and the League of

United Latin American Citizens. These groups saw undocumented Mexican immigration as an obstacle to Mexican American integration. However, new civil rights groups arose, such as the Mexican American Legal Defense and Education Fund and National Council of La Raza, which mobilized to influence immigration policy making and addressed the legal rights of Mexican immigrants (Tichenor 2002). Eventually some of the earlier groups recognized that the rights of Mexican immigrants were tied closely to the civil rights of Mexican Americans in issues of job discrimination and other civil rights infringements.

There are many examples throughout US history and policymaking regarding undocumented Mexican immigrants. In the 1950s, despite growing public anger toward undocumented immigration, many members of Congress who had defended national-origins quotas supported both legal and illegal Mexican immigration because of pressures from growers, ranchers, and other employers (Tichenor 2002). US national borders have remained porous and inadequately regulated, and unauthorized immigration, the majority of which is of Mexican origin, has remained the focus of considerable media attention and public alarm. Although the United States has been successful in creating an image of border security through such efforts as Operation Gatekeeper (Nevins 2002), Mexican subjugation continues because at least one-fifth of Mexican-origin residents lack any legal claim on American society when they are present without authorization (Massey 2007, 157). Lee and Bean (2010, 12) argue that "whereas European immigrants of America's past have come to symbolize the search for opportunity and hope, today's non-European immigrants seem to generate anxiety. . . ." Lee and Bean (2010) point out that some native-born white Americans assume that Mexicans are unwilling to assimilate and adopt mainstream cultural values. Bankston (2014) argues that this lack of incorporation may be due to the communities in which the new immigrants live and the segregated schools their children attend. The growth and dispersion of the Mexican population in the United States to new destinations has not decreased their residential isolation because of intensifying segregation of Mexican-origin communities (Lichter 2010).

Economic Ties

The economy of the United States in general and the economies of many US southwestern states in particular are closely tied to Mexico. The North American Free Trade Agreement (NAFTA 2012) entered into force in 1994 and opened up the US market to increased Mexican imports and the Mexican market to the United States and Canada, creating one of the largest single markets in the world (Villarreal and Fergusson 2015). Bilateral trade issues have required the two countries to work collaboratively to resolve trade disputes involving sugar, tomatoes, tuna, and trucking, among others (M. Villarreal 2014). Despite these issues, a number of studies have found that NAFTA has promoted even stronger economic ties between Mexico and the United States. Most scholars have found that NAFTA brought economic and social benefits to the Mexican economy as a whole, but that the benefits have not been evenly distributed throughout the country (Villarreal and Fergusson 2015).

According to the US Congressional Research Service (M. Villarreal 2014), as of July 2014, Mexico was ranked third among top trading partners of the United States, only slightly behind number two, China. Canada, which is also a partner in NAFTA, was number one. That same report identified the United States as, by far, Mexico's leading partner in merchandise trade. Fitzgerald (2009) noted that the creation of a Mexican lobby in the United States has become one of Mexico's serious foreign policy goals. In 2012, the United States imported over $277 billion in goods from Mexico and exported $215 billion to Mexico (US Census Bureau 2012b). These numbers increased to $294 billion in imports from Mexico and $240 billion in US exports to Mexico in 2014 (Villarreal and Fergusson 2015). Mexico is the number-one trading partner with Texas, with an increase of 20 percent in millions of dollars of exports to Mexico from 2010 to 2011 (US Census Bureau 2012a). According to economic reports about the impact of NAFTA, the United States is the largest source of foreign direct investment in Mexico. Mexican foreign investment in the United States was $17.6 billion in 2013, an increase of over 1,000 percent from 1993 (Villarreal and Fergusson 2015, 20).

Mexico's exports have diversified from primarily oil to an array of manufactured products, making Mexico one of the largest exporters in the world. The maquiladora industry, mentioned previously, is an important component of Mexico's manufacturing sector and has helped attract investment from the United States. Maquiladoras allow US companies to locate their labor-intensive operations in Mexico and lower their labor costs in the overall production process (M. Villarreal 2014). Economists have pointed to the interconnections of the Mexican and US economies, with some arguing that the loss of jobs in the United States is directly related to US companies outsourcing and shipping jobs to Mexico and other countries as a result of the trade agreements encompassed in NAFTA. However, as noted above, Mexican firms now export large quantities of goods to Canada and the United States, which is creating jobs and incentives for certain groups of Mexicans to stay at home (Kapenda 2009). Others have argued that NAFTA has been especially harsh for Mexico's rural and indigenous people and has contributed to the economic deterioration of living standards in rural and southern Mexico, political activism, and increased migration (Rivera-Salgado 2000). Nonetheless, no one disputes the important ongoing economic relationship between the United States and Mexico.

Another important distinction regarding Mexican immigration is the economic importance of the remittances migrants send back to their communities of origin. In Mexico, there are thousands of households receiving remittances from migrants working in US agricultural fields and urban areas. While individual transfers may not be large—a few hundred dollars here and there—the total sum of remittances sent back to Mexican families from the United States can reach enormous dimensions and plays an important role in the Mexican economy. According to the US Congressional Research Service report on US-Mexico relations, remittances are one of the three highest sources of foreign currency for Mexico, along with oil and tourism (M. Villarreal 2014). A significant portion of the remittance money received by Mexican households from workers living in the United States is spent on food, clothing, health care, and other household expenses, with women the primary recipients (Federal Reserve Bank of Dallas 2004; Inter-American Development Bank 2010). Massey and Parrado (1994) found that earnings from work in the United States provided an important source of startup capital in 21 percent of new business formations in Mexico. Woodruff and Zenteno (2007) estimated that remittances are responsible for almost 20 percent of the capital invested in microenterprises in urban Mexico. Although transnational economic ties between the United States and Mexico are extremely beneficial to both economies, researchers have emphasized the transborder fragmentation of families—citing sacrifices, difficulties of assuming caregiving by elderly grandparents or other relatives in the country of origin, the emotional costs of divided families, and the stress of survival strategies across borders (Dreby 2010; Abrego 2014).

Because of these interconnections, some economists have argued that the US Southwest and the northern states of Mexico should be considered one economic region (Reynolds 1970), even more so than the Canadian-US border area. Some policy experts emphasize the importance of US-Mexico trade and argue that the two governments can improve cooperation in cross-border commerce and can invest more in improving border infrastructure. Heightened security measures along the US-Mexico border often result in costly disruptions in production chains because of extended and unpredictable wait times at the border (M. Villarreal 2014; Villarreal and Fergusson 2015). Also, an increasing number of wealthy Mexican families are taking advantage of investor visa opportunities in the United States to flee insecurity in Mexico (Hennessy-Fiske 2013).

As Mexican president Peña Nieto and the Mexican Congress implement economic reforms in the energy sector, particularly in the Gulf of Mexico shared with the United States, the two countries will continue to negotiate important economic relations. Cooperation between the United States and Mexico continues in areas of bilateral trade, environmental and labor issues, transportation, economic growth, immigration, and security enhancement. Policy initiatives in both countries play a strong role in determining whether the broader North American economic integration will run smoothly (Massey, Durand, and Malone 2002). Despite some policy shortcomings, the economies of Mexico and the United States are closely intertwined. The economic conditions in both countries play an important role in migration patterns, return migrations, and immigrant well-being.

The Large Mexican-Origin Population in the United States

The shared two-thousand-mile-long border, which for many years was relatively open; the history of conquest that immediately incorporated Mexican citizens into the United States; continuous years of circular labor migration; the largest number of undocumented immigrants in the United States; and a large and growing Mexican American population of multigenerational presence make the experiences of Mexican migrants different from the migrations of any other ethnic group in the United States. Telles and Ortiz (2008, 11) argue that "the century-long immigration, preceded by conquest and an additional sixty years of low intensity circular immigration, is unlike that of any other ethnic group in the United States."

Along with other Hispanic groups, Mexicans are having an impact on every region of the United States: on politics, on culture, on the economy, and on social interactions. Jiménez (2010) argues that the Mexican-origin population in the United States is exceptional in many respects, but particularly in regard to the duration and extent of immigration. He proposes that continuous Mexican migration to the United States has resulted in "replenished ethnicity" among the Mexican-origin population already in the United States. Telles and Ortiz (2008) also point out that the ethnic dominance of a single group in the US Southwest is quite unlike the immigration patterns of other areas in the United States, which are more diverse. The high concentration of Mexican-origin population in major cities throughout the US Southwest means that Mexican immigrants have a relatively easy process of incorporation. They find housing in Mexican-dominant neighborhoods, speak Spanish in commercial areas and major institutions, enroll their children in English-as-a-second-language or bilingual education programs, and easily find ingredients in local supermarkets for cooking Mexican foods. They are likely to have coworkers who are Mexican or at least speak Spanish. While their growing numbers continue to generate anti-immigrant legislation in states like Arizona, Georgia, and even California and Texas, Mexican immigrants can easily identify with the Latino culture and communities in the United States, as well as in new destination sites such as small towns and large cities in the interior or on the coasts (Massey 2008).

The ethnic dominance of the Mexican group in the US Southwest is quite different from the immigration experience on the East Coast or in the Midwest, which was and still is characterized by multiple national groups, primarily of European background. It also contrasts with Asian immigration patterns, which were halted for the Japanese and Chinese during periods of intense nativism in the United States (McLemore and Romo 2005).

Telles and Ortiz (2008, 12) note that the historical depth and demographic size of the Mexican-origin population in the United States is unlike that of any other ethnic group. Although there are distinct differences in the experiences of Mexican Americans and Mexican immigrants, as documented by Gutiérrez (1995), and between Mexicans and other Latinos, public recognition, media treatment, and anti-immigrant sentiment often seem to be the same. Telles and Ortiz (2008) argue that other Latinos are often perceived, labeled, and treated as Mexicans, and collectively racialized as such.

Increased attention to homeland security, expansion of the US Border Patrol, and attempts to fence off the US-Mexico border have not deterred Mexican immigration to the United States. US Homeland Security border control efforts have redirected undocumented immigration to entry points in more hazardous areas, which has resulted in increased deaths of migrants and has deterred some migrants from attempting to cross the border, but migration has not stopped (Nevins 2002; Dear 2013). Patterns do seem to be changing, however. According to Andres Villarreal (2014), Mexican migration to the United States has dramatically decreased due to worsening employment opportunities and severe contractions in key sectors of the US economy that employ migrants, increases in border enforcement, improvements in the Mexican economy, and a decline in Mexican fertility. The largest drop in migration occurred among economically active young men with low levels of educational attainment.

As a result, recent trends suggest a zero net migration from Mexico in which there were approximately equal numbers of return Mexican migrants and new migrants in the United States (Passel, Cohn, and Gonzalez-Barrera 2012). Border violence and insecurity in parts of Mexico have motivated upper-income Mexicans to consider permanently relocating to the United States and have caused many Mexican workers already in the United States to stay rather than return, reducing the circularity of Mexican migration (Passel, Cohn, and Gonzalez-Barrera 2012). Mexico's policy of allowing dual nationality encouraged many immigrants reluctant to give up Mexican citizenship to begin the process toward US permanent residence and citizenship (Romo and Rodriguez 2006).

Many unauthorized Mexicans brought children to the United States, and others have had children born as US citizens (Yoshikawa 2011; Passel et al. 2014). As undocumented migrant children attended US schools and matured, they faced the dilemma of feeling American, even if they lacked official citizenship (Gonzales 2011). With the increased emphasis on criminalizing undocumented immigration in the United States, the rise in the number of deportations, and the number of families with both citizen and undocumented family members (Menjívar and Kanstroom 2014), Mexico and the United States face difficult policy debates about how to regulate migration (Dear 2013).

Figures from the US Department of Homeland Security (DHS) Office of Immigration Statistics (2013) show that Mexican citizens accounted for 70 percent of the foreign nationals apprehended in 2012. Ninety-eight percent of Border Patrol apprehensions occurred along the southwest border, with Mexican nationals accounting for 64 percent of total detainees and 73 percent of all aliens removed in 2012. According to the 2011 USDHS report, Mexican nationals accounted for 83 percent of the unauthorized population apprehended by US immigration authorities, 73 percent of those forcibly removed, and 77 percent of those who departed without an immigration hearing in 2010. Because Mexicans are the immigrant group most affected by the increased deportations, Dreby (2014) found that in many local contexts in the United States, Mexican families feel targeted by the individual whims of police officers, experience the threat of emphasis on immigration enforcement, fear that deportation will separate their families, and live with the stigma associated with criminalized immigration.

Again, while there are many similarities among the Mexican immigrant experience and the experiences of other immigrant groups, these factors combine to make Mexican immigration distinct. Thus far, policy makers have acknowledged the history of US-Mexico relations, taken advantage of the flexibility and circularity of Mexican migration, allowed different immigrant quotas for the Western Hemisphere, and negotiated important trade agreements with Mexico, such as NAFTA. The United States has also treated Mexican immigrants differently by increasing security on the Mexican border to decrease undocumented entries to a greater degree than on the Canadian border.

Other processes of handling immigration are distinct for Mexican immigrants as well. In July 2014, President Obama sent a letter to the US Congress seeking more than $3.7 billion in emergency appropriations for rapidly expanding border enforcement actions and humanitarian assistance programs to cope with unrivaled numbers of unaccompanied minors and adults bringing children from El Salvador, Honduras, and Guatemala across the US-Mexico border. Fast-track US immigration procedures are already in place to deport young migrants from Mexico (USDHS 2013). The majority of unaccompanied minors arriving in 2014 came through Mexico from Central American countries plagued by violence, gangs, and poverty. Mexico is unique as a nation that receives immigrants from other countries, particularly Central America; it is a country of transit for migrants from Central America and other countries to the United States; and it is also sending a large number of its own citizens to the United States as migrants, both documented and undocumented. Thus, Mexico must play an important role in helping to control undocumented border crossings at the US-Mexico border.

President Obama recognized the liminal legal status, a term emphasized by Menjívar (2008), of the youth brought to the United States as children by their undocumented parents when he authorized Deferred Action for Childhood Arrivals (DACA) in June 2012. The initiation of DACA changed the Obama administration's immigration enforcement policy to temporarily defer deportations for eligible undocumented youth and young adults, the majority of whom are from Mexico (Gonzales and Bautista-Chavez 2014). In the 2014 executive order extending DACA, President Obama also recognized the growing number of US-born children whose parents are undocumented and subject to deportation by including in the 2014 order the Deferred Action for Parents of Americans and Lawful Permanent Residents, or DAPA.

Not all responses to President Obama's efforts to aid immigrants have been positive. The magnitude of the November 2014 actions raised serious legal and constitutional questions and fueled Republicans' charges of "imperial overreach" (Hirschfield Davis 2014). Governors of twenty-six states, led by the newly elected governor of Texas, filed a federal lawsuit in Brownsville, Texas, to halt the president's actions. They warned that the president's initiative would encourage a new wave of illegal crossings at the southwest border, forcing Texas and other states to spend additional funds on law enforcement, health care, and education for immigrants. The case argued that the president violated his constitutional duty to enforce the laws and illegally placed new burdens on state budgets (Montgomery and Preston 2014). In February 2015 the federal district court in the Southern District of Texas blocked the implementation of the immigration actions announced by President Obama in November 2014, forcing the federal government to appeal the decision. These legal actions have temporarily halted the implementation of the 2014 DAPA and DACA initiatives.

While President Obama's actions have the potential to defer deportation for large numbers of young unauthorized immigrants and the unauthorized immigrant parents of American-born children and legal permanent residents, many undocumented immigrants do not qualify for deferred action. The United States must still find ways to address the large number of unauthorized immigrants who continue to reside and work in the United States, the majority of whom are from Mexico. Mexico also must find ways to reincorporate the large number of persons the United States has deported or who have decided to return voluntarily.

Debates regarding immigration reforms continue in the United States. At the same time, the Mexican government attempts to fight pervasive insecurity and violence and to address extensive poverty and corruption in Mexico. The complex and unique relationship between Mexico and the United States, as demonstrated in this chapter, demands that both nations work together, recognizing that Mexican immigration is different from that of other groups. The policies the United States enacts regarding immigration have crucial impacts in Mexico and vice versa. Scholars in this volume acknowledge the interconnectedness of these neighboring countries and address the shared history and economic ties that continue to impact migration patterns, the immigration policies that affect both nations, the incorporation of immigrants and return migrants, the importance of regional and national economies, and the effects of migration on human lives on both sides of the border.

References

Abrego, Leisy J. 2014. *Sacrificing Families: Navigating Laws, Labor, and Love across Borders*. Stanford, CA: Stanford University Press.
Acuña, Rodolfo. 1981. *Occupied America: A History of Chicanos*. New York: Harper and Row.

Alba, Richard D. 1990. *Ethnic Identity: The Transformation of White America*. New Haven, CT: Yale University Press.

Alba, Richard D., and Victor Nee. 2003. *Remaking the American Mainstream: Assimilation and Contemporary Immigration*. Cambridge, MA: Harvard University Press.

Alvarez, Rodolfo. 1985. "The Psycho-Historical and Socioeconomic Development of the Chicano Community in the United States." In *The Mexican American Experience: An Interdisciplinary Anthology*, edited by R. O. de la Garza, F. D. Bean, C. M. Bonjean, R. Romo, and R. Alvarez, 33–56. Austin: University of Texas Press.

Bankston, Carl L. III. 2014. *Immigrant Networks and Social Capital*. Malden, MA: Polity Press.

Bean, Frank D., Georges Vernez, and Charles B. Keely. 1989. *Opening and Closing the Doors: Evaluating Immigration Reform and Control*. Lanham, MD: University Press of America.

Chavez, Leo. 2001. *Covering Immigration: Population Images and the Politics of the Nation*. Berkeley: University of California Press.

Clavita, Kitty. 1994. "U.S. Immigration and Policy Responses: The Limits of Legislation." In *Controlling Immigration: A Global Perspective*, edited by W. A. Cornelius, P. L. Martin, and J. F. Hollifield, 55–81. Stanford, CA: Stanford University Press.

Coatsworth, John H. 2003. "Mexico." In *The Oxford Encyclopedia of Economic History*, edited by J. Mokyr, 501–509. New York: Oxford University Press.

Dear, Michael. 2013. *Why Walls Won't Work: Repairing the US-Mexico Divide*. New York: Oxford University Press.

Dreby, Joanna. 2010. *Divided by Borders: Mexican Migrants and Their Children*. Berkeley: University of California Press.

———. 2014. "The Modern Deportation Regime and Mexican Families: The Indirect Consequences for Children in New Destination Communities." In *Constructing Immigrant "Illegality:" Critiques, Experiences, and Responses*, edited by Cecilia Menjívar and Daniel Kanstroom, 181–204. New York: Cambridge University Press.

Federal Reserve Bank of Dallas. 2004. "Workers' Remittances to Mexico." *El Paso Business Frontier*. Retrieved December 18, 2014, from http://www.dallasfed.org/assets/documents/research/busfront/bus0401.pdf.

Fitzgerald, David. 2009. *A Nation of Emigrants: How Mexico Manages Its Migration*. Berkeley: University of California Press.

Gamio, Manuel. 1930. *Mexican Immigration to the United States*. Chicago: University of Chicago Press.

Gonzales, Roberto G. 2011. "Learning to Be Illegal." *American Sociological Review* 76:602–19.

Gonzales, Roberto G., and Angie M. Bautista-Chavez. 2014. "Two Years and Counting: Assessing the Growing Power of DACA." Washington, DC: American Immigration Council. Retrieved July 14, 2014, from http://www.immigrationpolicy.org/special-reports/two-years-and-counting-assessing-growing-power-daca.

Gordon, Milton M. 1964. *Assimilation in American Life*. New York: Oxford University Press.

Grebler, Leo, Joan Moore, and Ralph Guzman. 1970. *The Mexican-American People: The Nation's Second Largest Minority*. New York: Free Press.

Gutiérrez, David G. 1995. *Walls and Mirrors: Mexican Americans, Mexican Immigrants, and the Politics of Ethnicity*. Berkeley: University of California Press.

Hawkins, Brian, Yedid Minjares, Lauren Harris, and Juan Rodriguez de la Gala. 2010. "Values in Conflict: Youth in a Culture of Migration." In *Mexican Migration and the U.S. Economic Crisis: A Transnational Perspective*, edited by Wayne A. Cornelius, David Fitzgerald, Pedro Lewin Fischer, and Leah Muse-Orlinoff, 161–184. San Diego: University of California, San Diego, Center for Comparative Immigration Studies.

Hennessy-Fiske, Molly. 2013. "Wealthy, Business-Savvy Mexican Immigrants Transform Texas City." *Los Angeles Times*, March 24. Retrieved March 25, 2013, from http://www.latimes.com/news/nationworld/nation/la-na-sonterrey -20130324.

Hirschfield Davis, Julie. 2014. "Obama Takes an Action That Has Its Precedents but May Set a New One." *New York Times*, November 21, A19.

Inter-American Development Bank. 2010. "Mexico and Remittances." Washington, DC: Inter-American Development Bank. Retrieved July 14, 2014, from http://www.iaadb.org/mif.

Jiménez, Tomás R. 2010. *Replenished Ethnicity: Mexican Americans, Immigration, and Identity*. Berkeley: University of California Press.

Kandel, William, and Douglas S. Massey. 2002. "The Culture of Mexican Migration: A Theoretical and Empirical Analysis." *Social Forces* 80(3):981–1004.

Kapenda, Simon. 2009. "NAFTA: The Good, the Best, and the Ugly for the Americas." *Ezine Articles*. Retrieved December 1, 2014, from http://ezine articles.com/?NAFTA,-The-Good,-The-Best,-and-The-Ugly-For-the-Americas &id=1965563.

Kasinitz, Philip, John H. Mollenkiopf, Mary Waters, and Jennifer Holdaway. 2008. *Inheriting the City*. New York: Russell Sage Foundation.

Lee, Catherine. 2013. *Fictive Kinship: Family Reunification and the Meaning of Race and Nation in American Immigration*. New York: Russell Sage Foundation.

Lee, Jennifer, and Frank D. Bean. 2010. *The Diversity Paradox: Immigration and the Color Line in Twenty-First Century America*. New York: Russell Sage Foundation.

Levario, Miguel Antonio. 2012. *Militarizing the Border: When Mexicans Became the Enemy*. College Station: Texas A&M Press.

Lichter, Daniel. 2010. "Residential Segregation in New Hispanic Destinations: Cities, Suburbs, and Rural Communities Compared." *Social Science Research* 39:215–230.

López, Gerald P. 1981. "Undocumented Mexican Migration: In Search of a Just Immigration Law and Policy." *UCLA Law Review* 28:615–714.

Martin, Phillip L. 1994. "The United States: Benign Neglect toward Immigration." In *Controlling Immigration: A Global Perspective*, edited by W. A. Cornelius, P. L. Martin, and J. F. Hollifield, 83–99. Stanford, CA: Stanford University Press.

Massey, Douglas S. 2007. *Categorically Unequal: The American Stratification System*. New York: Russell Sage Foundation.

Massey, Douglas S., ed. 2008. *New Faces in New Places: The Changing Geography of American Immigration*. New York: Russell Sage Foundation.

Massey, Douglas S., Jorge Durand, and Nolan J. Malone. 2002. *Beyond Smoke and Mirrors: Mexican Immigration in an Era of Economic Integration*. New York: Russell Sage Foundation.

Massey, Douglas S., and Emilio A. Parrado. 1994. "Migradollars: The Remittances and Savings of Mexican Migrants to the USA." *Population Research and Policy Review* 13:3–30.

McLemore, S. Dale, and Harriett D. Romo. 2005. *Racial and Ethnic Relations in America*. Boston, MA: Pearson and Allyn and Bacon.

McWilliams, Carey. 1968. *North from Mexico: The Spanish-Speaking People of the United States*. Westport, CT: Greenwood.

Menjívar, Cecilia. 2008. "Educational Hopes, Documented Dreams: Guatemalan and Salvadoran Immigrants' Legality and Educational Prospects." *Annals of the American Academy of Political and Social Science* 620:177–193.

Menjívar, Cecilia, and Daniel Kanstroom. 2014. *Constructing Immigrant "Illegality": Critiques, Experiences, and Responses*. New York: Cambridge University Press.

Montejano, David. 1987. *Anglos and Mexicans in the Making of Texas, 1836–1986*. Austin: University of Texas Press.

Montgomery, David, and Julia Preston. 2014. "17 States Suing on Immigration." *The New York Times*, December 4, A1.

NAFTA (North American Free Trade Agreement). 2012. "NAFTA." Retrieved April 26, 2015, from NAFTANow.org.

Nevins, Joseph. 2002. *Operation Gatekeeper: The Rise of the "Illegal Alien" and the Making of the U.S.-Mexico Boundary*. New York: Routledge.

Nobles, Melissa. 2000. *Shades of Citizenship: Race and the Census in Modern Politics*. Stanford, CA: Stanford University Press.

Park, Robert E., ed. 1964. *Race and Culture*. Glencoe, IL: Free Press.

Passel, Jeffrey, D'Vera Cohn, and Ana Gonzalez-Barrera. 2012. *Net Migration from Mexico Falls to Zero—and Perhaps Less*. Washington, DC: Pew Hispanic Center. Retrieved November 26, 2014, from http://www.pewhispanic.org/2012/04/23 /net-migration-from-mexico-falls-to-zero-and-perhaps-less/.

Passel, Jeffrey S., D'Vera Cohn, Jens Manuel Krogstad, and Ana Gonzalez-Barrera. 2014. *As Growth Stalls, Unauthorized Immigrant Population Becomes More Settled*. Washington, DC: Pew Research Center's Hispanic Trends Project. Retrieved November 26, 2014, from http://www.pewhispanic.org/2014/09/03/as -growth-stalls-unauthorized-immigrant-population-becomes-more-settled/.

Portes, Alejandro, and Rubén G. Rumbaut. 1990. *Immigrant America: A Portrait*. Berkeley: University of California Press.

Reynolds, Clark W. 1970. *The Mexican Economy: Twentieth Century, Structure and Growth*. New Haven, CT: Yale University Press.

Rivera-Salgado, Gaspar. 2000. "Transnational Political Strategies: The Case of Mexican Indigenous Migrants." In *Immigration Research for a New Century: Multidisciplinary Perspectives*, edited by N. Foner, R. G. Rumbaut, and S. Gold, 134–156. New York: Russell Sage Foundation.

Romo, Harriett, and Maria Rodriguez. 2006. "Dual Nationalities: Mexican Americans and Mexican Immigrants Explore Issues of Citizenship." In *Migración a los Estados Unidos: Más allá de los números*, edited by M. Melgar Adalid, 151–188. San Antonio: UNAM, Escuela Permanente de Extensión en San Antonio, Texas.

Telles, Edward E., and Vilma Ortiz. 2008. *Generations of Exclusion: Mexican Americans, Assimilation and Race*. New York: Russell Sage Foundation.

Tichenor, Daniel J. 2002. *Dividing Lines: The Politics of Immigration Control in America*. Princeton, NJ: Princeton University Press.

US Census Bureau. 2012a. "State Exports for Texas: Total U.S. Exports (Origin of Movement) via Texas." Washington, DC: US Census Bureau. Retrieved December 1, 2014, from http://www.census.gov/foreigntrade/statistics/state/data/tx.html.

———. 2012b. "Foreign Trade: 2012 US Trade in Goods with Mexico." Washington, DC: US Census Bureau. Retrieved December 1, 2014, from http://www.census.gov/foreign-trade/balance/c2010.html.

USDHS (US Department of Homeland Security). 2011. *Immigration Enforcement Actions: 2010*. Washington, DC: Office of Immigration Statistics. Retrieved December 1, 2014, from http://www.dhs.gov/xlibrary/assets/statistics/publications/enforcement-ar-2010.pdf.

———. 2013. *Yearbook of Immigration Statistics: 2012*. Washington, DC: US Department of Homeland Security, Office of Immigration Statistics. Retrieved December 1, 2014, from http://www.dhs.gov/yearbook-immigration-statistics-2012-enforcement-actions.

Villarreal, Andres. 2014. "Explaining the Decline in Mexico-U.S. Migration: The Effect of the Great Recession." *Demography* 51:2203–2228. doi:10.1007/s13524-014-0351-4.

Villarreal, M. Angeles. 2014. *U.S.-Mexico Economic Relations: Trends, Issues, and Implications*. Washington, DC: Congressional Research Service. Retrieved December 1, 2014, from http://fas.org/sgp/crs/row/RL32934.pdf.

Villarreal, M. Angeles, and Ian F. Fergusson. 2015. *The North American Free Trade Agreement (NAFTA)*. Washington, DC: Congressional Research Service. Retrieved April 26, 2015, from www.crs.gov R42965.

Weber, David J. 1982. *The Mexican Frontier, 1821–1846: The American Southwest under Mexico*. Albuquerque: University of New Mexico Press.

———. 1988. *Myth and the History of the Hispanic Southwest*. Albuquerque: University of New Mexico Press.

Wilkie, James H. [1967] 1970. *The Mexican Revolution (1910–1963): Federal Expenditure and Social Change*. Berkeley: University of California Press.

Womack, John. 1970. *Zapata and the Mexican Revolution*. 6th ed. New York: Alfred A. Knopf.

Woodruff, Christopher, and René Zenteno. 2007. "Migration Networks and Microenterprises in Mexico." *Journal of Development Economics* 82:509–529.

Yoshikawa, Hirokazu. 2011. *Immigrants Raising Citizens: Undocumented Parents and Their Young Children*. New York: Russell Sage Foundation.

Contributors

Francisco Alba is a professor and researcher at El Colegio de México. He is an economist and demographer and a specialist in the development implications of demographic change and on international migration. He has published on Mexican migration and migratory policy, population and development, regional integration, Mexico-US relations, and related topics. Professor Alba is member of the Advisory Council of Mexico's Migration Policy Unit and a former member of the Advisory Board of Mexico's Migration Institute. He was a member of both the United Nations Committee for the Protection of Migrants' Rights and the Global Commission on International Migration.

Professor Alba is also a former member of the Mexico–United States Binational Study on Migration, the Board of Trustees of the Population Reference Bureau, and the Committee on Population at the US National Academy of Sciences' National Research Council. He was trained as a demographer at El Colegio de México and has done graduate work in the social sciences at the Institute of Political Studies, Paris, and the University of Texas at Austin.

James D. Bachmeier is an assistant professor in the Department of Sociology at Temple University. His research examines the integration of immigrants in the United States and focuses specifically on the Mexican-origin population. He is also engaged in research that evaluates the measurement of immigrants' legal status in national surveys and the role that legal status plays in the integration of Mexican immigrants and their children. His research articles have appeared in *Demography*, *Social Forces*, *Social Science Research*, and *International Migration Review*. He is also the author (with Frank D. Bean and Susan K. Brown) of the book *Parents without Papers*, published by the Russell Sage Foundation.

Frank D. Bean is a Distinguished Professor of Sociology and director of the Center for Research on Immigration, Population and Public Policy at the University of California, Irvine. His research focuses on demographic change and international migration and immigrant integration. A member of the Council on Foreign Relations, he has been a Guggenheim fellow and a visiting scholar at the Russell Sage Foundation; the Transatlantic Academy in Washington, DC; the American Academy in Berlin; the Research School of Social Sciences at the Australian National University; and the Center for US-Mexico Studies at the University of California, San Diego.

His book (with Jennifer Lee) *The Diversity Paradox: Immigration and the Color Line in 21st Century America* received the Otis Dudley Duncan (Best Book) Award for Distinguished Scholarship in Social Demography from the American Sociological Association's Population Section in 2011. His new book (with Susan K. Brown and James D. Bachmeier) is *Parents without Papers* (Russell Sage Foundation 2015).

Susan K. Brown is an associate professor of sociology at the University of California, Irvine. Her research examines the integration of immigrants across multiple generations, residential mobility, and inequality of access to higher education. She is the author of *Beyond the Immigrant Enclave: Network Change and Assimilation* (2004).

Jorge Durand is a professor at the University of Guadalajara and associate professor at Centro de Investigación y Docencia Económica (CIDE). He is codirector, with Douglas S. Massey, of the Mexican Migration Project (since 1987) and the Latin American Migration Project (since 1996) sponsored by Princeton University and Universidad de Guadalajara. He is a member of Mexico's National System of Researchers (Level III), the Mexican Academy of Sciences, and the National Academy of Sciences of the United States.

In the last thirty years he has studied the migration between Mexico and the United States. Among his publications as author and coauthor are *Return to Aztlán* (1987), *Más allá de la línea* (1994), *Miracles on the Border* (1995), *Migrations mexicaines aux Etats-Unis* (1995), *Beyond Smoke and Mirrors* (2002), and *Clandestinos* (2003).

He has been a visiting professor at the Universities of California, Los Angeles; Chicago; Pennsylvania; and Warsaw as well as at Bielefeld University and the French Centre National de la Recherche Scientifique. Currently he is an opinion columnist for the newspaper *La Jornada* in Mexico.

Agustín Escobar Latapí is the general director at the Centro de Investigación y Estudios Superiores en Antropología Social (known as CIESAS) in Mexico. He works mostly on social policy and Mexican emigration to the United States. He was elected and reelected to the board of the National Policy Evaluation Council (CONEVAL) in 2006 and 2010. He is also a top-level member of the Mexican National Researcher System and of the Mexican Academy of Sciences. He is or has been a member of a number of academic, advisory, and editorial boards for institutions and organizations, such as the International Organization for Migration, the Institute for the Study of International Migration, the French Institute for Development Research, the Mexican National Science Council, and the Mexican Migration Institute.

Escobar Latapí's most recent projects include a binational dialogue on the well-being of Mexican migrants in the United States and in Mexico and a project to create a rigorous qualitative evaluation system for the use of public officials and researchers in Mexico (2012–2014). Between 2010 and 2011 his main research projects included the study of effective access to social services and programs by the poor in general and by the migrant poor and their families in low-income, isolated Mexican regions. From 2004 to 2007, Dr. Escobar codirected a binational study of Mexico-US migration with Susan Martin of ISIM-Georgetown. His most recent books deal with migration management, poverty and migration, social mobility, qualitative evaluation design, and the interaction between cash-transfer programs and their social, political, and epistemological contexts.

Michael Feil received his bachelor's degree and officer commission in the US Army from the US Military Academy in West Point, New York. He subsequently earned separate master's degrees in operations research and national security. Through twenty-eight years of military service, his involvement with national security and vulnerable populations spanned assignments in the United States, Europe, Asia, and the Western Hemisphere. As deputy commander for the US Army element supporting activities in the Caribbean and Latin America, he directed security and disaster–relief efforts in support of several nations and in cooperation with many nongovernmental agencies.

Upon retirement from military service, Feil served as the director of binational security and small business initiatives for a US-Mexico nongovernmental organization with offices in Mexico City and San Antonio, Texas. His consulting clients include the Panama Canal Authority and several government entities, both within the United States and overseas.

Today, Feil resides in the Washington, DC, area and supports the US Department of Veterans Affairs.

K. Jill Fleuriet is an associate professor of anthropology at the University of Texas at San Antonio (UTSA). Dr. Fleuriet is a cultural and medical anthropologist specializing in health, gender, and inequality in the US-Mexico borderlands. Two theoretical questions guide her research in medical anthropology: How are bodily experience and well-being shaped by access to different forms of social, economic, and political capital? How can these different forms of capital produce health inequalities? Dr. Fleuriet's current research revolves around unexplained differences in birth outcomes among low-income Mexican immigrant and Mexican American women living in South Texas.

Her recent writing weaves together borderlands, health inequalities, and motherhood literatures to suggest that different pregnancy-related social statuses due to immigration experience and Mexican and American discourses of motherhood can influence birth weight. Dr. Fleuriet has been a visiting scholar at the UTSA Mexico Center, the UTSA Child and Adolescent Policy Research Institute, the UTSA Institute of Texan Cultures, and the Shared Research Core at the School of Nursing at the University of Texas Health Sciences Center at San Antonio. She is currently a fellow in the Society for Applied Anthropology. Dr. Fleuriet received her BA (Harvard College), MAs (San Diego State University, Stanford University), and PhD (Stanford University) in anthropology.

Roberto G. Gonzales is an assistant professor at the Harvard University Graduate School of Education. Professor Gonzales is a leading authority on the experiences of undocumented immigrant youth and young adults. Since 2003 he has been engaged in what is arguably the most comprehensive study of undocumented immigrant young adults in the United States. In his book, *Lives in Limbo: Undocumented and Coming of Age in America*, published by University of California Press, professor Gonzales followed 150 undocumented young adults for twelve years as they made critical transitions to adulthood. In addition, his National UnDACAmented Research Project, which has surveyed nearly 2,700 undocumented young people, is the largest data-collection effort on this population to date.

Edmund T. Hamann is a professor in the University of Nebraska–Lincoln's Department of Teaching, Learning, and Teacher Education. An anthropologist of education interested in the interfaces between education policy and practice, particularly as these fields relate to transnationally mobile students and families, he has a PhD in education from the University of Pennsylvania and an MA in anthropology from the University of Kansas. He is editor (with Stanton Wortham and Enrique G. Murillo Jr.) of *Revisiting Education in the New Latino Diaspora* (Information Age Press, 2015).

Janeth Martinez was a graduate student in sociology at UTSA. Her research interests focus on Latino immigrant families in the United States and the educational achievement of children of immigrants. Janeth's thesis, "Messages about Higher Education: Mexican Immigrant Parents' Impact on Their Children's Educational Expectations," examines the role of Mexican immigrant parents in their daughters' pursuit of higher education and how daughters perceive and interpret messages about higher education. Martinez is a member of the Alpha Kappa Delta Sociology Honor Society, Phi Kappa Phi, and the UTSA Golden Key International Honor Society.

She received first place in the research paper category at the UTSA 2014 College of Liberal and Fine Arts Fourteenth Annual Spring Research Conference for a qualitative research study paper titled "The Importance of Social Support at a Four Year College." She also received first place in the student paper category at the UTSA 2015 Sociology Spring Colloquium for a paper titled "Mi Título: Latinas' Negotiation of Messages of Higher Education and their Educational Expectations." She worked as a graduate research assistant at the UTSA Child and Adolescent Policy Research Institute and the UTSA Mexico Center. Janeth is pursuing a doctoral degree in culture, literacy, and language at UTSA.

Milena Andrea Melo is a doctoral candidate in the Department of Anthropology at UTSA. Her dissertation research is funded by the National Science Foundation, the UTSA Mexico Center, UTSA Graduate School, and UTSA Department of Anthropology. Her dissertation research is entitled "Enacting Life: Dialysis among Undocumented Latin American Immigrants in the US-Mexico Borderlands." Melo received an MA in anthropology from UTSA in 2015 and an MA in interdisciplinary studies from the University of Texas–Pan American (UTPA) in spring 2011.

She also holds a graduate certificate in Mexican American studies from UTPA. Melo's research interests include the intersections of policy, healthcare, health disparities, citizenship, lived experiences of chronic illness, immigrant health, poverty, access to health care in public and private institutions, transnational youth experiences, DACA/Dreamers, and the US-Mexico borderlands.

Liliana Meza González is a senior researcher at the Ministry of Labor and Social Welfare in the Mexican federal government. She earned her bachelor's and master's degrees in economics from the Instituto Tecnológico Autónomo de México and her MA and PhD in labor economics from the University of Houston. She was a full-time professor and researcher at the economics department in the Universidad Anáhuac and Universidad Iberoamericana, both in Mexico City, and was the technical secretary of the social cabinet during President Calderón's administration. She has served as invited professor at American University and invited researcher in the Institute for the Study of International Migration at Georgetown University. Dr. Meza González has been a consultant for the Inter-American Development Bank and for the World Bank. She was also coordinator of the migration office in the Jesuit Universities System in Mexico.

She has published more than twenty-five articles in journals and books, especially on migration and labor issues, and has edited five books on migration and social-policy issues. She is currently working on a book regarding the social responsibility of Jesuit universities toward migrant groups in Mexico, and she is part of the North America–Central America Migration Dialogue. Liliana Meza currently lives in Mexico City.

Kandy Mink Salas is an assistant professor in the Department of Higher Education at Azusa Pacific University (CA) and program director of the College Counseling and Student Development Program. Dr. Mink Salas's research centers on college student women leaders and the undocumented and DACAmented student experience. Prior to her time as a faculty member, she spent twenty-eight years as a student affairs professional at the University of San Diego and at California State University, Fullerton, where she served as dean of students and associate vice president for student affairs.

Olivia Mogollon-Lopez joined UTSA as program coordinator of the UTSA Mexico Center in October 2006. As program coordinator, she oversees partnerships with other universities, organizations, and institutions in Mexico and the United States. She has helped draft memorandums of understanding with Mexican universities and research centers for the implementation of joint projects. In addition, she helps organize and coordinate ad hoc multidisciplinary Mexico-related research groups.

She also organizes the application process and recipient selection for the Mexico Center Educational Research Fellowship, which funds UTSA faculty and students to do Mexico-related research in any discipline.

Since joining the Mexico Center, Ms. Mogollon-Lopez has participated in research projects on Mexico-US migration, transnationalism, the civic activism of undocumented immigrants, and elite Mexican migration to the United States. She has been the coeditor of immigration articles in *A Bilateral Perspective on Mexico-U.S. Migration* and a managing editor for a special issue on Mexico and Latin America of the *International Journal of Qualitative Studies in Education*. Ms. Mogollon-Lopez holds an MS in Public Policy and a BA in Political Science from the Instituto Tecnológico Autónomo de México.

Pia M. Orrenius is a vice president and senior economist at the Federal Reserve Bank of Dallas and an adjunct professor at the Hankamer School of Business, Baylor University. At the Federal Reserve Bank of Dallas, Orrenius is a regional economist working on economic growth and demographic change. Her academic research focuses on the labor-market impacts of immigration, unauthorized immigration, and US immigration policy, and her work has been published in the *Journal of Development Economics, Labour Economics, Industrial and Labor Relations Review*, and *American Economic Review Papers and Proceedings*, among others. She is coauthor of the book *Beside the Golden Door: U.S. Immigration Reform in a New Era of Globalization* (2010, AEI Press).

Dr. Orrenius is a research fellow at the Tower Center for Political Studies at Southern Methodist University and at the Institute for the Study of Labor in Bonn, as well as a visiting scholar at the American Enterprise Institute. She was senior economist on the Council of Economic Advisers in the Executive Office of the President, Washington, DC, in 2004–2005. She received her PhD in economics from the University of California at Los Angeles and BA degrees in economics and Spanish from the University of Illinois at Urbana-Champaign.

Joanna B. Perez is the daughter of Guatemalan immigrants and grew up in a predominantly Latino immigrant community in Los Angeles, California. In 2009, Joanna earned a bachelor of arts degree in sociology with a double minor in labor and workplace studies and civic engagement from the University of California, Los Angeles. In 2011 Joanna earned a master of arts degree in sociology with a minor in Latina/Latino studies from the University of Illinois at Urbana-Champaign. Currently, Joanna is a PhD candidate in sociology at the University of Illinois. Her research focuses on how systems of power and inequality as well as the intersectionality between race, class, gender, sexuality, and immigration status impact marginalized communities. Joanna's dissertation research focuses on activism among undocumented Latino young adults in the United States. She has received numerous awards and recognitions for her work, including recently being selected as a fellow of the American Sociological Association Minority Fellowship Program.

Henoc Preciado is the coordinator of the Titan Dreamers Resource Center at California State University, Fullerton, the first of its kind in the twenty-three-campus California State University system designed primarily to serve the needs of undocumented students. Henoc provides leadership and strategic planning for the center, assists students with academic and emotional support, provides referrals to financial assistance, provides information on programs and services designed to improve retention and graduation rates, and encourages students to connect with one another. As a scholar-practitioner, Henoc is active in publishing and presenting research related to the undocumented student experience. He has presented at a number of regional and national organization conferences and most recently wrote for the National Forum on Higher Education for the Public Good. He received his master's degree in higher education from Syracuse University in New York and his bachelor of arts degree in English from California State University, Fullerton. Henoc was born in Jalisco, Mexico, and was raised in Anaheim, California.

Harriett D. Romo earned a PhD in sociology from the University of California, San Diego, and master's degrees from the University of California, Los Angeles, and the University of California, San Diego. At UTSA she is the director of the UTSA Child and Adolescent Policy Research Institute and the director of the UTSA Mexico Center. Her book *Latino High School Graduation* (with Toni Falbo) was a finalist for the C. Wright Mills Prize for research of value to the community. She has published articles on language acquisition, Latino foster youth, immigrant children, and Mexican immigrant families.

Her sociology textbook *Race and Ethnic Relations in America* (with S. Dale McLemore) is used widely in college sociology classes. Other publications include an edited book (with Raquel Marquez), *Transformations of La Familia on the U.S.-Mexico Border* (University of Notre Dame Press, 2008), and an edited collection of research on Mexico published by the

University of Veracruz in 2012. She has been the principal investigator on grants from the US Department of Health and Human Services, the US Department of Housing and Urban Development, the US Small Business Administration, the US Department of Education, the Ford Foundation, and the Rockefeller Foundation.

Ariel G. Ruiz earned an MA degree from the School of Social Service Administration at the University of Chicago in 2014. His research interests focus on undocumented immigrants' experiences of incorporation in the United States. He has conducted research on the barriers and experiences that hinder undocumented students' academic success and life outcomes in the state of Washington. More recently, his research projects analyze demographic trends and methodological approaches to estimate the number of undocumented immigrant populations and their service needs in the United States. In 2011 he earned a bachelor of arts degree in sociology from Whitman College, where his research interest in immigration originated.

Juan Sánchez García holds a doctorate in social sciences, focusing on sustainable development. He has two master's degrees: one in "middle school with specialty in pedagogy" and the other in educational technology. A *profesor normalista*, he also holds degrees in communication sciences and pedagogy.

Sánchez García has participated in research groups and academic teams working in two lines of research: the return of transnational students in Mexican schools and social and educational changes in teacher professional development.

Sánchez García has taught in elementary, middle, and high schools and graduate education for thirty-four years. Currently, he is director of the Research and Innovation to Improve the Quality of Education Program at the Institute of Research, Innovation and Graduate Studies in Education in Monterrey, Mexico.

Jason Saving is a senior research economist and adviser at the Federal Reserve Bank of Dallas. In this position, he conducts research on public policy issues. Saving joined the Federal Reserve Bank of Dallas in 1996, following a one-year postdoctoral fellowship at George Mason University's Center for Study of Public Choice. He holds a bachelor of arts in mathematical economic analysis from Rice University and a master of arts and PhD in economics from the California Institute of Technology. Saving is the author of articles on income taxation, inequality, American welfare policy, European economic integration, and other policy issues. His articles have appeared in such journals as *Economic Inquiry*, the *Southern Economic Journal*, and the *National Tax Journal*.

Raquel Torres is a graduate student at UTSA. She received her BA in English from UTSA in 2012 and is working toward her master's in English. Her research areas include Latina/o and Chicana/o literature; postcolonial and transnational literature; diaspora and border studies; gender, race, and class; feminism; and queer studies. Previously, Torres was an undergraduate and graduate research assistant for the UTSA Mexico Center. Her current title is program coordinator for the UTSA Women's Studies Institute. Torres served as a cochair for the 2015 UTSA Women's History Month, one of the largest women's history celebrations in the nation.

Madeline Zavodny is a professor of economics at Agnes Scott College in Decatur, Georgia. She is also a research fellow of the Institute for the Study of Labor in Bonn, Germany. Her research areas are labor and health economics and economic demography. Much of her research focuses on economic issues related to immigration, including *Beside the Golden Door: U.S. Immigration Reform in a New Era of Globalization* (AEI Press, 2010), co-authored with Pia Orrenius. She received a BA in economics from Claremont McKenna College and a PhD in economics from the Massachusetts Institute of Technology.

Víctor Zúñiga is a professor of sociology at the Tecnologica de Monterrey, Mexico, and a tier 3 (highest level) member of Mexico's Sistema Nacional de Investigadores. He holds a PhD in sociology from the Université de Paris VIII–Vincennes. Dr. Zúñiga was a dean of Research and Extension at the Universidad de Monterrey from 2012 to 2015. His research focuses on international migrant children and migrant integration in the United States. He coedited *New Destinations: Mexican Immigration in the United States* (2005, Russell Sage Books).

Index